D0405868

NOBODY KNOWS THE TRUFFLES I'VE SEEN

Also by George Lang

The Cuisine of Hungary
The Café des Artistes Cookbook
Lang's Compendium of Culinary Nonsense and Trivia
Gundel 1894–1994 (with Zoltán Halász)

Nobody Knows the Truffles I've Seen

GEORGE LANG

ALFRED A. KNOPF · NEW YORK 1999

THIS IS A BORZOI BOOK
PUBLISHED BY ALFRED A. KNOPF, INC.

Copyright © 1998 by George Lang
All rights reserved under International and Pan-American Copyright Conven-
tions. Published in the United States by Alfred A. Knopf, Inc., New York, and
simultaneously in Canada by Random House of Canada Limited, Toronto.
Distributed by Random House, Inc., New York.

www.randomhouse.com

Library of Congress Cataloging-in-Publication Data
Lang, George.
Nobody knows the truffles I've seen / George Lang.
p. cm.
Includes index.
ISBN 0 679-45094-7
1. Lang, George, 1924–   . 2. Restaurateurs—United States—
Biography. I. Title.
TX910.5.L36L36   1998
647.95´092—dc21
[B]   97-42598
CIP

Manufactured in the United States of America
Published March 23, 1998
Reprinted Once
Third Printing, March 1999

My parents' wedding picture, 1921

There were no statues erected
for members of my family.
These words carved out of
admiration, affection and
sorrow should serve as such.

The Time to Write Your Memoirs is...

- *When you discover that autobiography is an unrivaled vehicle for telling the truth about other people;*

- *When you realize that confession is good for the soul, even if it's bad for the reputation;*

- *When you realize that you may not be around to tell your children about your childhood, about their ancestors in a strange little country, and about the years when God refused to get involved;*

- *When you begin to wonder if you dreamt all of your past or if someone is dreaming it for you.*

CONTENTS

I am sorry that I am not able to find adequate words to express my gratitude to Judith Jones, my editor, for her great skill, talent, and dedication in shaping this book.

Living my life was arduous at times. Writing about it was almost as difficult. But my hardest task is trying to express my love and appreciation to my wife, Jenifer, whose genuine enthusiasm, guidance, and forbearance made this book possible.

I also regret that I can't thank enough the friends and associates who helped me along the way with my memoir. I am especially beholden to:

Robert Caro, for his overview of the manuscript and for his invaluable counsel;

Zoltan Hálász, who has supplied vital information throughout the years;

Doe Lang, for suggesting the title of this book (in 1967!);

John Lukács, for his historical perspective, wise observations, and improvements to the manuscript;

William Safire, for his encouragement;

Cullen Stanley, my indispensable and delightful agent; and

Barbara Stenstrom, my assistant, for her tireless help.

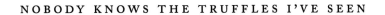

NOBODY KNOWS THE TRUFFLES I'VE SEEN

Rendezvous with My Past

To me, everything begins with a question.

I wrote this book because over the last half century I have often wondered whether I dreamt my past or if someone has been dreaming it for me.

The answer came to me during a trip to Hungary, to show my wife the town where I was born and educated. During the seemingly interminable flight, I fell into the kind of receptive haze that can be produced by a solitary prison cell or long hours of jet vibrations—both experiences with which I am painfully familiar.

In my flight-trance, I was walking along Palotai Street, near our family home in the ancient town of Székesfehérvár, and suddenly I was stopped by a bright-looking young man who mumbled something about wanting to talk to me. Without waiting for an answer, he adjusted his steps to mine with great ease.

I didn't feel like talking to anyone and I tried, politely, to get rid of him, but he just kept walking with me. Suddenly he looked at me intently with his slanted blue eyes and said, "Do you remember when you were my age? You were determined to play the Bach G-Minor Unaccompanied Sonata the way it should be played. What happened?"

I was too shocked to say anything.

He continued, "During sleepless nights, you hoped to emulate Alberti, the archetypal Renaissance man whose life encompassed a half-dozen disciplines, including music, writing, philosophy, and painting and who, at the same time, indulged in the more earthy pleasures of life."

I finally found my voice and said defiantly, "I did learn and practice six different disciplines, and like him I tried to re-create myself through the power of my mind."

Whereupon he looked bemused, just as I do when confronted with sophistry. "You resolved not to care about what the world is concerned with, and to focus on things the world disregards."

"But don't you see," I answered with growing confidence, "those who live by this theory will remain professional adolescents for life."

He turned left at the end of Vár Boulevard without waiting for my reply.

By this time, I was trying to get away from the odd, mesmerizing stranger, yet I followed him because I was stunned at how much he knew about me. He turned to me and said, "In your thirties you were obsessive; in your forties you spent too much time on making it; in your fifties you didn't believe in anything with the possible exception of yourself, and now, in your sixties, you are like a ship without sail or rudder, on the vast ocean, whose captain has forgotten where he came from and where he is going."

"What can I do at this late date?" I stammered. "And who are you, anyway, and how do you know me, turning my insides out like my father used to do with an old jacket in his tailor shop?"

There was silence as we arrived at the street where I was born. He made a funny kind of gesture, the kind I used to make when I said good-bye to my friends many decades ago, and said with a faint smile as he disappeared toward the park, "George, don't you remember me? I am you at eighteen. Don't you recognize yourself and your dreams?"

My trance was interrupted by the instruction to fasten our seat belts for the descent to Ferihegy Airport in Budapest.

I felt with undeniable force that I must respond to my alter ego's accusations, and when I returned to my hometown in Hungary, I wondered if I could base my recollections on the music in my life that has sustained me for as long as I can remember, or on survival, an art form at which I became so inventive that for a while I had a false feeling of immortality. Or perhaps I could organize the fragments of my life around my sweet and steady friends. Yet another approach might be to recall childhood flavors and aromas, vivid and unaltered by later experiences, unalloyed sensations of the palate. I wasn't sure at the time how I would go about it, but I knew that all these would play a part.

In writing about my early life, I am taking a serious chance, because while confession is good for the soul, it can be bad for the reputation. So, my beloved wife, Jenifer, and my dear children, Brian, Simon, and Georgina, and everyone else reading these words, fasten your seat belts for a trip back to the summer of 1924, to the town of Székesfehérvár, where, in a cramped little bedroom, a baby emerges from his mother's womb and is greeted by the customary slap of a midwife.

The only thing of which my hometown of (at the time) 42,000 people could be proud was its unpronounceable name and the fact that in the eleventh century King Stephen made it the capital of Hungary and built there a magnificent basilica surrounded with walls, parts of which exist to this day. More recently (before World War II), Székesfehérvár's mayor mortgaged the city to try to turn it into a spa by digging for hot mineral waters. What he did find was delicious, naturally carbonated water close to our house. Unfortunately, it took another half-century to reach the era of *mise-en-bouteille* waters. Székesfehérvár's history is otherwise not so amusing. Its inner city was destroyed by assorted invaders on a regular basis. During the winter of 1944 it changed hands between Russian and German forces three times.

My father married my mother in 1921, and the newlyweds moved from their nearby villages to the "big town," where my father started his custom tailor shop, using their single-room apartment as a workshop. A few years later he moved his business to a store in the center of town, which was created by splitting the wide entrance hallway of a baroque building in half and enclosing it with walls.

The front of the tiny shop was filled with yard goods and a tall standing mirror. The workshop in the rear was populated by a foreman, a couple of junior assistants, an apprentice, and my father, of course. In between was the cutting table, the sole domain of Father. He always kept a couple of canaries in the workshop, and whenever he worked on the sewing machine it inspired them so much that they sang like two coloratura sopranos auditioning for the mad scene from *Lucia di Lammermoor.*

Until I was six years old, my parents and I lived in an apartment on Main Street, in a building that faced the town's only theater. I do not want to give the false idea of a sumptuous flat—the single small room served as a bedroom, a workshop, and even as a playroom for me, flanked by a kitchen. In one corner of the kitchen my father made a collapsible board that functioned as a chopping block; when extended, it served as a work surface for my mother to pull strudel dough with the backs of her hands (if you stretch it with your hands in palm-down position, it tears) and also as a dining table for the three of us. Miraculously (or so it seemed to me at the time), it could even be lowered and turned into a play table for me when it was not otherwise engaged. But to me its primary function was as a surface upon which my mother made so many variations on the basic sponge cake recipe that Grandma Gizella had given her that she was able to serve us a different version for months on end.

Carelessly, no one recorded my first words, but according to my mother, I began to eat the same foods as my parents at a very early age, and two people had to feed me with speedily alternating spoons because I screamed impatiently between bites. Clearly I was precocious; I already knew what foods were worth consuming. And I was just as impatient then as I have been for the rest of my life—my daily prayer being "Please, God, give it to me, and *now!*"

One of my first memories is of a long-ago evening, and of a family sitting at a round table close to a large cream-colored ceramic stove. It is the little boy's job to bring a basketful of chestnuts from the larder so that the father can cut a deep cross into each before putting them into the smoldering coals. The child, consisting mostly of a **pair** of almond-shaped eyes and prominent cheekbones, and dressed in short pants, sits on the edge of a big chair, eager to wolf down a dozen chestnuts; he tries to convince his father, not an easy man to sway, that the chestnuts are cooked.

The big world doesn't seem to exist for this family; the three of them are insulated by their affection for each other, by the pleasure of the crackling fire, and by the taste of the improbably vivid tangerines in the center of the table, combined with the comforting texture of the roasted chestnuts.

I remember some of these fragments firsthand, but my recollections were augmented over the years by stories about my childhood told by my

Me at age four

mother, for whom my father was only second to me, closely followed by her parents and God, in that order.

Long-buried memories don't emerge in order of importance. Our bathroom and, of all things, the outdoor toilet appeared on my inner screen when I began writing this chapter. It was located in a cobblestone-paved yard and was supplied with yesterday's newspaper cut to pieces of convenient size which made it impossible to put together any story. As for the bath part, a portable enamel tub was brought in from the outside when my mother was able to wear down my resistance. An early form of

Jacuzzi was approximated by a revolving paddle my father made for me from pinewood. We collected rainwater for the weekly washday, and my mother and our maid scrubbed with the hard, brown, homemade soap in the *teknő*, a large wooden tub in the shape of a topless coffin, then put the huge sheets through a wringer.

Although the firewood was delivered already cut to about a foot in length, by the time I was about twelve it was mostly my job to split the logs with a hatchet to different degrees of thickness, depending on their intended use.

Milk was delivered every morning, except Sunday, by a horse-drawn wagon, from which the milkman would fill a large tin container we had left on the street. A tinker came every now and then to patch and reline our aging pots and vessels as needed.

When my father had a toothache, to save the expense of going to a dentist he would put on his tooth a small lump of the blue crystalline copper oxide he used to spray on the plants—highly poisonous, but apparently effective. When one of my baby teeth refused to come out and the new tooth was already pushing underneath, my father's foreman would tie the tottering tooth to the window sash with a strong thread and close the window lightning fast, pulling the tooth with spectacular success.

My mother was proud of our white wooden icebox. Icemen came every morning to put a huge ice block into its metal-lined compartment. The crystal radio in my parents' bedroom could, on rare occasions, even bring in a station broadcasting from Bratislava, at least a hundred miles away. I felt privileged to have all these modern devices.

A sobering lesson that served me well throughout my life occurred when I was four years old in the aforementioned cobblestoned yard used by the several tenants of our one-story building. Mother made *vizes uborka*, water-pickled cucumbers topped with sprigs of dill and a slice of bread (as opposed to the vinegar-pickled ones that are put up to last through the winter), in one-gallon jars, and these she kept in a sunny spot in the yard. Finding one of these imposing jars absorbing the ripening rays of the sun, I turned it sideways with some difficulty and began to roll it on the cobblestones with as much speed as my little legs allowed. It didn't take long before disaster struck and the broken shards of glass mixed with the pickles while the pickle juice soaked into the dirt between the glistening stones. My father, who was home for his customary lunch at exactly noon (always followed by a thirty-minute nap and a prompt return to his shop at one-thirty), heard the crash and came out to survey the disaster; he then gave me one of the most memorable beatings I ever received.

My parents worked *látástól vakulásig* (from predawn until dark), and when I was six years old they were finally able to buy a splendid house. It had enough space for a huge rosewood case filled with books, a dining room decorated with gilt-framed still-life paintings of food, a large garden flanked by a yard for me, a real indoor bathroom, and, most important, a great kitchen where I could watch my mother turn ordinary things like flour, eggs from the few chickens we kept, and vegetables from our garden into dizzyingly delicious luncheons, the main meal of our day.

When, many decades later, my friend Jacques Français, one of the foremost stringed-instrument dealers of our time, opened his huge steel-lined vault to show me a mind-boggling collection of seventeenth- and eighteenth-century violins and cellos, what came to my mind was my mother's pantry jammed with edible treasures, the pride of my family and the subject of envy of my friends. I am sure Jenifer was puzzled by my improbable parallel until I told her about the Great Pear Incident.

My search for the perfect ripe pear began over a half-century ago, long enough to warrant public confession. It happened during one of the summers when it was my cousin Évi Kellner's turn to stay with us. My parents and hers (our mothers were sisters) had an alternating exchange program that made our respective parents ecstatic every second year. I must have been about twelve years old when Évi arrived at the beginning of July, and I proudly showed her the new trees in the garden, the big rose garden in full bloom, my dog Tiger performing his latest tricks, and my precious books, which included a volume of letters written by Mozart's father to his son. The guided tour also passed by the very same pantry filled with huge enamel vessels of goose fat, bins of different types of flour, crates of beans, rows of pickled vegetables, jams, sauerkraut, and especially jars of compotes made from the fruits in our garden, which stood in rows like fat-bellied soldiers. Unfortunately, permission to open a jar of those precious desserts was not an everyday occurrence.

The very first day of my cousin's arrival, I sneaked into the pantry during the night and made a tiny hole with one of my mother's sewing needles in the cellophane covering one of the jars. This let air into the jar, causing a slight spoilage, and, miracle of miracles, as soon as my mother noticed it, we were served pear compote. I glanced triumphantly toward my cousin, but she hardly had time to be impressed, as she was swallowing half a pear almost without chewing.

Several times during the summer we ate pear compote, thanks to my nefarious scheme. One day, upon returning from an especially satisfying soccer match in the neighborhood and entering my favorite room, the kitchen, I could feel an ominous silence. My mother had grown suspicious about the ongoing compote epidemic, and that morning she had discovered that the jars were spoiling in a very orderly fashion, one after another on the shelf. Then came the final clue for Mother Sherlock: the entire row was at precisely the height I could reach! Fortunately the grownups were so amused by my resourcefulness that my mother told me to pick any compote I wanted for a snack, with or without holes.

I had already acquired the knack of not waiting for things to happen, but of making them happen.

During one of the summer vacations we spent in Évi's hometown, Tamási, there was a day when we just couldn't leave the local swimming pool to get back to her house in time for the noon luncheon. We sneaked in about a half hour late, wearing our most innocent expressions.

"How could you be so late?" asked Annuska, Évi's mother. "Your father is furious with both of you!"

I'm not sure which of us came up with the outrageous answer: "We kept looking at the church clock, and we left when it said ten minutes to noon. Only at the last minute did we notice that a big black bird was perched on the big hand of the clock, stopping it from moving."

The funny thing is that, during a recent visit to Tamási, Évi and I saw the same church clock with a black bird sitting on the big hand, and we both wondered aloud if this was a descendant of the bird that had helped us in our hour of need.

Fond as we were of each other, Évi and I had a running argument over who could eat the hottest cherry peppers—no mean task in Hungary. On market days we would separately scout the farmers' stands for the hottest peppers in every shape and color, and then confront each other with our finds. It wasn't easy to buy a single pepper, but often we were given just a sample. When Évi chose one, hoping that it was smoking-hot, I had to bite and swallow a piece, and then it was her turn to survive my choice. There was no clear winner in this decade-long fiery contest, but it hooked me for life on this particular form of masochism.

Even as a child, I would ask myself, Why do I eat it, why does it give me pleasure? When the poet Pablo Neruda visited Hungary in the 1960s, he wrote:

The feaster offers his tongue
As a sacrifice to the gods;
Cries,
Sweats,
and writhes
When swallowing a flaming morsel.

A family is made up of a cast of characters with more than one casting director. Ours was fortunate to have two leading players who were well balanced to produce a good show. My father's uncompromising approach to life and duty was balanced by my mother's love, which provided me with a warm feeling of trust and safety. There were probably few hours of the day in her brief life when I was not part of her thoughts. Today I often tell my children vignettes about my mother, hoping that the little stories will become part of our continuing family lore.

My mother did everything fast: writing, walking, working, even speaking; there was so much to tell, especially when the subject was me. To the amusement of her friends and my father's employees, she used to talk about me, piling on superlatives, intoning a kind of a nonstop exaltation. The foreman in my father's shop, István Halvax, bless his memory, had a great sense of humor, and one day he hired a court stenographer to record secretly the stream of adjectives and stories my mother told about me.

Naturally, I had to be the best-dressed kid in town. My father was proud of his ability to lay out a suit pattern on the fabric in such a way that he needed less fabric than any other tailor in Székesfehérvár. My mother would then snatch away the leftover pieces and make little outfits for me whenever she had the time. One evening when my parents' friends the Stauszes were having dinner with us, my father, half boasting, half complaining, said, "I'm willing to bet you that Gyuri has probably a dozen pair of shorts, and I can prove it." My mother naturally wouldn't admit it, and protested. So my father started collecting the little pants from different armoires, drawers, and shelves, and found forty-two pairs. It became a standing joke in our family; whenever anybody said "forty-two," everyone would burst out laughing while my mother blushed proudly.

When I was four, my mother took me to a local photographer to have my picture taken as a birthday present to my father. When I refused to change into a dark-blue velvet outfit she had made especially for the occasion, the exasperated photographer took a picture of me standing on top of a bench in his studio, wearing one of the aforementioned forty-two outfits (the picture is now on the dust jacket of this book).

I have no doubt that both my father and mother did engrave their behavior on me, as well as transmitting many of their personal traits, and I have passed those on to my children. I was an only child, born during an era of economic recession in a society where *egyke,* "the single little one," was the vogue, so that he or she could be given the best of everything. I believe this influenced my entire life.

Although I can't remember my father ever praising me—it was just not his style—one of his remarks, which I treasure, made me feel praiseworthy, at least for an afternoon. I recalled this event a couple of years ago when our six-year-old son, Simon, ran a race. He came in perhaps sixth in a field of a dozen kids, but I praised him, telling him that for his age he did extremely well.

When I was six years old, in the first grade, I won first prize in a similar race, and received a silver medal with the Roman numeral I engraved on one side. Panting hard, I ran to my father, who had been watching, to receive his praise. With a faint smile on his face, carefully measuring his words, he told me, "I *expect* my son to be the first."

The only physical difference among the men in my family in the last three generations on my father's side is that Grandfather Ármin had a huge handlebar mustache, which shrank to quite modest dimensions on my father's face, and got lost altogether when my turn came (although once I grew a mustache in an attempt to look like a cook). My father was a short, stocky man of uncommon physical strength, a hot temper, and a disposition that was eminently fair toward anyone who was willing to do a little more than was necessary. He was a multitalented craftsman, yet he had completed only six years of elementary school because he had had to go to work full-time at thirteen to help his father, who was a tailor and a descendant of tailors for many generations. He was proud of being a superb craftsman and once, during an argument with his friends about their respective professions, he ended the discussion by saying, "Let's not forget that after God, the tailor creates the shape of a human being! And also remember," he added, "that before Adam became a gardener, he and Eve, as it is described in Genesis, sewed fig leaves together to make nifty aprons for themselves."

Recruited in 1912, my father had already served two years in the Austro-Hungarian army when the big war broke out in 1914, and he was shipped immediately to the Russian front. Within the first few months he was seriously wounded, was captured, and spent two years as a prisoner of war in Siberia. He escaped, with several of his cronies, by swimming across the Amur River to China; he was among the few who made it to relative freedom. The Chinese authorities, in order to show the world that they were more civilized than the warring Occidental barbarians, treated these escaped prisoners quite decently, and Father was interned in a small remote town near Tientsin (now Tianjin), where he worked mostly as a tailor. At one point he made a deal with the mayor (after providing him with an entire wardrobe) that he would teach his four sons to speak English if the mayor would get him to a ship sailing for Europe. The lessons continued for about a year, just after the war ended, when Father caught the SS *President Grant* in Port Arthur to return home. Father managed to bring back all sorts of precious gifts, Chinese silks and such, some of which he presented to my mother when they were married in 1921.

Whenever he was depressed (which was quite often during the last few years of his life), my father would try to imagine what had happened the first time the mayor's sons had a chance to try out their English on a native speaker. You see, my father didn't speak a word of English, so he had taught the boys Hungarian. A couple of decades later I would have to emulate his resourcefulness in order to survive.

I grew up with the comforting feeling that my father could do anything. With the help of one of his friends he built an addition to our house, doing everything himself down to the last detail—he even installed the locks and sewed the drapes. He also cultivated implausibly dark blue roses in his beloved garden. In his playfulness, he grafted apple branches to one of our pear trees, and within a couple of years it was the only tree in the county that grew two kinds of fruit—neither of them very good, by the way. He even taught himself to play the piano after a fashion, and I remember when my parents' friends would stay too long after a dinner party at our house, my father would sit down at our upright Pleyel to play the "Rákóczi March," which in Hungary instantly reminded everybody what the function of a march is.

Many of my fellow members in snobbish food and wine societies could learn something of a true appreciation of dining from the time my father instructed me about the proper way to order and eat boiled beef, a dish that is not popular in our current culinary flea market (except, of course, at our Café des Artistes in New York). This important rite of passage happened on a Sunday during the summer. Since my mother was away visiting her parents (which always put my father in a dark mood), he took me for lunch to a nearby garden restaurant and there initiated me into the joys of *húsleves fött marhahússal* (the Austro-Hungarian pot-au-feu). My entire childhood comes back to me with the arresting aroma of this dish, and lingers in my memory like a sparkling ribbon amid the thousands of smells I have accumulated since.

After ordering the meal, a process that amounted to a protracted negotiation with the waiter, my father unfolded the enormous starched napkin and tied it around his neck. Then he set the salt and paprika cellars and the mustard pot within reach, and the waiter brought out a large soup tureen full of fragrant broth. My father ladled into his soup plate enough broth to reach the line running around the top, though at the second helping he failed to respect this line, since the soup lived up to its promise of greatness.

Next came a large platter filled with steaming marrow bones, surrounded by sliced and toasted kaiser rolls. He spread the marrow on a piece of toast, sprinkling it with salt and paprika.

At this point the waiter's assistant brought a large carafe of local white wine and poured it into thick-walled tumblers. When we had our fill of marrow toast and a little wine (mine having been watered), a steaming mountain of boiled beef appeared, each cut reclining lazily on the platter, flanked by a bowl of grated horseradish in vinegar, and a dish of currant sauce. Soon it became clear to me that my father had a game plan. He began with a rather insignificant piece of meat and worked himself up to the finest chunk, which squirted juice when he pierced it with his fork, meanwhile giving intermittent attention to the little potatoes, carrots, knob celery, parsnip, and Savoy cabbage that came from the same pot. I copied him eagerly, following his every move, though I had no mustache to wipe afterwards.

This was my indoctrination. And ever since, I have been trying to duplicate this experience. All week I used to anticipate the Sunday mornings when I could keep company with my father. It always began with the ritual of removing his precious gold I.W.C. Schaffhausen watch from one of the walnut armoires in our bedroom (my parents and I slept in the same room), polishing it with a soft chamois, and then opening up its hunter's case with an affection that went beyond the appreciation of a beautiful objet d'art. Then, with slow, measured motions I would wind it up, adjusting the time before putting it back in its protected hiding place.

This family tradition is carried on by my son Simon, who is named after my father (and my wife's paternal grandfather), and who performs the weekly ritual of winding my Schaffhausen watch.

In 1961, when I opened the spectacular Tower Suite restaurant in New York, on top of the Time-Life building, one evening a guest, whose table I had just passed, took out his watch to check the time—always a disturbing sign during pre-theater seatings. The watch looked familiar to me, and when I expressed an interest, he removed it from its chain and showed it to me. It was the same type of I.W.C. Schaffhausen watch my father had owned. I told the owner that holding a watch that was exactly like my father's had a profound effect on me.

The next day the guest phoned me and said he had a large watch collection and since this watch seemed so important to me, he would be willing to sell it to me at the price he had paid for it at a London auction years earlier. Buying this watch did induce me to become an avid collector of fine repeaters, early chronometers, and skeleton watches, mostly because I felt that watches are perhaps the only objects in which artists, scientists, and craftsmen collaborate with spectacular results. This particular watch is still my prize possession.

My father also owned a silver Omega for everyday use, which he wore attached to a chain affixed to his lapel buttonhole. He had bought it in a pawnshop, and had asked a jeweler friend to cover up the initials of the previous owner with a little gold oval plaque, but to leave the plaque blank. Today I realize that not having his initials engraved there was consistent with the mentality of those who had experienced diaspora throughout history, to be ready at any time to sell their belongings and run.

I was an alien even in my own hometown, in the country that passed the first so-called *zsidótörvény,* or "Jewish law," when I was fourteen years old. Before that, anti-Semitism was not institutionalized, though, like other Hungarian national sports, it enjoyed great popularity.

By the time I was fifteen, in 1939, the world outside my family and friends was becoming more and more a hostile camp, and I learned—together with my other Jewish friends—that we had no place in that society. In my hometown, anti-Semitism was not something one talked about, it was just there, permeating the air like noxious gas, and one learned to live with it. For instance, the man who owned the grocery on the corner of the street where I lived was Mr. Krausz, who, when introducing himself, invariably clicked his heels while sticking out his right hand and said, "Krausz—but not Jewish."

Each year more and more poison entered the bloodstream of the Hungarian nation, and it eventually had a tragic effect on my entire family. In retrospect, one of my most heartrending memories of my father is from 1942. He was sitting at the round table at the foot of the bed, writing in a long leather- and linen-bound book, the official ledger of the local tailors' guild. His handwriting was overly careful, like that of most men who are self-taught. He was the secretary of the guild, and he took the job very seriously.

After signing the entry, he pushed the book toward me so I could read it. On the page were the words of a man who was proud, defiant, yet broken to the world he lived in, addressed to his fellow tailors. The sentences were an attempt to understand and to explain and live with the fact that he had to resign because of the latest of a series of "Jewish laws" that would prevent him from continuing in this unpaid, honorary position. He told me that many of his erstwhile colleagues remained neutral fence-sitters at best. If he had been able to read the Greek philosophers, he would have learned that those who stand on the sidelines are just as guilty as the active malefactors.

The last paragraph of his entry is etched in my mind: "Since I was thirteen years old, there has not been a day when I did not toil in one or another tailor's workshop, and I am proud of being a tailor. I received one of the highest military awards during World War I, the Silver Medal for Valor, and I consider myself as patriotic as anyone who is now wrapping the red, white, and green flag around their stomachs."

Then he went to a sideboard where he kept a bottle of *törköly pálinka*, the rough-edged Hungarian brandy, downed a full shot, and quietly said to me, not really believing it, "Maybe, *Gyurikám*, you'll grow up in a world that is more just."

Bless his memory, his words were prophetic.

I must have been about fourteen years old when my parents were called into the principal's office in the Ybl Miklós Real Gymnasium, the school I attended, because of a prank I had organized which had one of our teachers as its target.

Nobody liked our history teacher, and one day when he gave us a particularly time-consuming homework assignment, I suggested to my classmates during recess that we should all submit identical papers reading, "Sorry, but I didn't understand the homework assignment. Which of the four King Béla's were we supposed to write about—Béla I, II, III, or IV?"

It didn't take too much detective work to discover the originator of the prank, and my parents were sternly informed of the incident by the principal.

When I returned home, my father asked me ominously if the story was true, and even before I could answer, he started hitting me very hard while my mother cried and begged him to stop. At one point in this one-sided confrontation, I did the unthinkable: with all my strength, I got hold of his hands, trying to end the humiliation and the pain.

My declaration of independence against my father had to end as a classic paradox: If I couldn't stop him, I would lose, but in asserting my independence, I would find out that he was not all-powerful. Turning on my father went against all fundamental Jewish teachings, and looking at his face made me realize that, for that moment, he regarded me like a son who had died. Eventually we both felt (I certainly did) the need to be forgiven and to start all over again. It helped me to see that my temper came from my father, and he probably at last understood that brutality, even when based on good intentions, is not an effective tool to use in raising one's offspring. It was especially difficult for him, because my father was never good at expressing intimate feelings, although now I know that he loved me unconditionally. He invested everything in my mother and me, and I like to think that I inherited his unlimited energy, his total commitment to his profession, and his constant affection toward his family, but that I was spared his rigidity.

During that winter my father was sick in bed, from an infection that set in after he cut himself with his straight razor while shaving. He lay in bed with bandaged face, knocked out by strong painkillers. Hovering around his bed, I showed such concern and affection that it surprised him almost as much as it overwhelmed me, after what had happened between us.

He pulled me to his chest and whispered hoarsely, "My son, my son, I do have a son who loves me!"

Lamentably, not too many years were left to us to prove him right.

My two grandfathers and their families lived in villages next to each other. They shared the same religion, age, and other decisive statistics, yet it would be hard to imagine two people who were more different. My paternal grandfather, Ármin, had never gone to an opera in his life, and I am sure he never heard of the composer Kodály or his masterpiece *Háry János,* which is about a retired mercenary who returns to his village and tells tall stories about his exploits. Nevertheless, my grandfather did a pretty good approximation of the fictional soldier. I remember him sitting in front of his home in the village of Mezőkomárom with a *csibuk* (the long-stemmed pipe that Hungarians inherited from the occupying Turkish forces in the sixteenth century) in his mouth. He was telling me how he could have married the royal princess as a reward for his bravery in Bosnia-Herzegovina, where he was an infantryman in the *Kaiserliche und Königliche* Austro-Hungarian army, but for the machinations of the evil Archduke somebody-or-other. This was one of the more believable stories from his vast repertoire.

Ármin used to go to Budapest twice a year to buy yard goods for his tailor shop, and a canny merchant there, knowing his penchant for carp heads poached in paprika-flavored fish broth, would take him to the same restaurant time after time, plying him with this delicacy. At the end of the lunch he would casually put a piece of paper in front of my grandfather, saying, "Just sign this, Uncle Ármin, and everything will be taken care of." IOUs were nothing to kid around with in Hungary—not paying them was a felony, and my father and his sister and three brothers had to chip in regularly to get him out of trouble. So at one point, when Grandfather was probably barely middle-aged, they persuaded him to retire and live happily in his village, avoiding fish heads and *váltók,* as the IOUs were called, knowing that it would cost them much less in the long run.

Ignácz Láng (whose name I took after the war), my maternal grandfather, on the other hand, was a sage, a person of biblical presence, who served as the rabbi and cantor for the entire congregation consisting of about one hundred families in the small town of Tolna-Tamási. There is a story about him that illustrates how a rabbi-scholar could deal with a problem in a very unorthodox manner, matching the solution to the problem.

My cousin Évi was the only Jew in her class. Not having a place to go during the classes in religion, she would sit quietly at the back of the classroom. At the end of many of these classes, however, the priest-teacher would point at her and roar, "*Your* people killed Jesus Christ!" Naturally, when the class let out, the other kids taunted and pushed her around, yelling ugly epithets, until the next class began.

After one such incident she ran to Grandfather Ignácz, crying and asking for help. First he set about consoling her, and then he instructed her what to do if this happened again.

A week later the same scene was repeated, with the priest again shouting at her, "Your people killed Jesus Christ!" Whereupon twelve-year-old Évi rose to her full height and said cheerfully, "Sorry, Father, you're mistaken. It was the Jews from the *next village* who did it." The laughter of the kids, who suddenly realized the absurdity of the priest's statement, reestablished peace in the class, and the priest never brought up the subject again.

Once I asked my grandfather one of my typically adolescent questions, convinced that finally I had come up with the kind of conundrum to which even he, a wise rabbi, had no answer. "Grandfather, one of my friends walked out of a used-book store with a book hidden under his jacket without paying for it, and no one noticed it. According to the Bible, every sinner pays for his sins. But it doesn't quite work that way all the time. Does it?"

Grandfather looked at me with his gentle yet penetrating blue eyes, stroked his goatee, and replied, "*Gyurikám* [Hungarian for "my little George"], your friend *is* punished for what he did. The punishment is that the next time he will do it he will have less fear, and each time he commits the crime it will seem more and more trivial to him, *and that is his punishment*. Most likely, the final consequence will be much more serious than the penalty for stealing a used book."

For me, intellectual sparring in my early adolescence became not only a pleasure but a necessity. I had almost unlimited energy when it came to irreverence toward representatives of assorted gods, but with the chief rabbi of our temple, Dr. Pál Hirschler, I had little chance of winning a round. His commentaries on the books of Esther and Nahum are still taught in theological seminars around the world, but his translation of the book of Ezekiel, which he completed in the Székesfehérvár ghetto in 1944, was never published. A wispy, gentle person, he died in Auschwitz.

After a sermon that he had based on Genesis, I mentioned to Rabbi Hirschler that God must have rigged up some temporary expedient when he said on the very first day of creation, "Let there be light," since it was only on the fourth day that He came up with the bright idea of setting the sun and the moon in the firmament, throwing in the stars for good measure. If he had an answer to this riddle, he kept it to himself.

Dr. Hirschler must have seen something in me, unless he considered me one of the ways God was testing him, and he often talked to me after Saturday morning services. At one point, when I had just read a book about the origins of the universe, I asked him his opinion about the scientific explanation of the creation of the earth. He invited me into his study, where his mother offered me hot chocolate. There he told me the story of a scientist whose best friend was a pious rabbi. The two argued endlessly about how the universe began. Using scientific theory, the professor tried to convince the rabbi that the story in Genesis should be considered fiction. A few days later, upon entering the rabbi's study, the scientist noted an overturned inkwell on top of the rabbi's desk, defacing the blotter. On further examining the mishap, he noticed the following words apparently trailing away from the ink blot: ". . . and God created heaven and earth, and on the seventh day God finished his work which he made . . ."

"Who wrote this sentence?" asked the scientist.

"According to you," said the rabbi, "the world was created accidentally, over a very long time. You see, my dear friend," he continued, with a little smile, "when I accidentally knocked over the inkwell, part of the blotch became this sentence as one of the unlimited variations the ink could form. Isn't this just about as reasonable as your hypothesis, and as logical?"

The moral of this and many other stories of Dr. Hirschler's is that when your rabbi is an inventive thinker and raconteur, religion often is able to explain the unexplainable.

After I completed the fourth year of the *Real Gymnasium* (the equivalent of the U.S. eighth grade), my father insisted that I quit school for a year and work in his shop to learn his trade. "Gyuri," he said, "no one knows what's going to happen, but as a tailor you will always be able to make a living."

It was a difficult year for me, even humiliating to some degree, wearing a worker's cap instead of the school uniform with the silver-braided cap, and being left out of the world of students. But I did take the tailor's exam at the end of the year, and then returned to school. Four years later, when I was in a forced-labor camp, my father's plan would indeed save my life.

In the new school I entered after my year of tailoring, I was the only Jew in my class. Being a reasonably good athlete made me almost acceptable to my gentile classmates, but Hungarian national pride, which was inseparable from prevailing ethnic and religious prejudices, poisoned many parts of my world. It was commonly believed, before the state of Israel was born, of course, that Jews were weak, made lousy soldiers, and were unable or unwilling to do heavy physical work. After a few frustrating arguments with some of my loudmouthed schoolmates, I decided to show them a thing or two. During the next summer vacation, because one of the job captains knew my father, I got a job in the stone quarry on the outskirts of town, a kind of work that was unheard of for a high school student. My job was to throw the sharp-edged, often huge rock pieces into a metal wagon that ran on rails, and then to push the wagon to an area for processing.

The labor was extremely strenuous for a fifteen-year-old student, and parts of my body hurt that I hadn't even known existed. My mother would fill a huge bag of food for me to take with me to the quarry. After a few days she half-jokingly observed that the amount of food I consumed cost more than what I was earning. I kept the job for three weeks, making sure that a few of my classmates came out to see me working side by side with day laborers twice my size.

Did it make any difference?

As far as my worthy schoolmates in the overwhelmingly non-Jewish school were concerned, it changed their attitude not one iota. To paraphrase Samuel Johnson's line about patriotism, anti-Semitism is the first (and certainly not the last) refuge of scoundrels.

At the predictable age I developed a crush on a pretty girl named Marika, and I asked her one day to come with me to the Árpád movie house, where one had to buy a ticket for assigned seats—the closer to the screen, the cheaper the ticket. I saved pennies for a week to be able to invite her to sit with me in the seats in the first or second row, and it was a staggering blow to my budding machismo when she declined.

"If you don't come with me to the movies, I'll hang myself in front of your window," I declared in an appropriately grave tone.

And then came the real blow—she replied sweetly, with a crushing one-liner: "Oh, please don't do it, you know Daddy doesn't like for you to hang around the house."

She did come once to the local athletic field to watch me run the hundred-meter dash, an event I was quite passionate about. My physique was far from ideal for this competition, since I have rather short legs, a thin but overly muscular upper body, and, of all things, rather flat feet. From the first grade on, however, I won most races by developing a carefully worked-out starting technique, which gave me an advantage in the critical beginning of the race. Also, I had almost boundless energy combined with a will to win and a loathing for losing.

I did become a loser, however, during a race in the city of Szolnok when I was about sixteen years old. To my surprise and delight, the local chapter of Máv Előre, the sport club of the state railroads, invited me to be a member, and I participated in the hundred-meter regional championship, coming in third, with a time of 11.6 seconds. Later, in the four-hundred-meter relay, one of the four participants from our club became indisposed, and I was asked to take his place. Never having run this race, which was just around the soccer field where the events were held, I started running exactly the way I did in my usual hundred-meter event, and the entire stadium stood up cheering, thinking that they were witnessing the birth of a new world sensation. Unfortunately, when I got to about the middle of the race, my lungs didn't quite seem to fit their usual location and I felt ready to explode. By the time I was able to pass the baton to the next teammate, he had to start with a fifteen-meter handicap.

This event had a decisive influence on my future life. I realized that the old adage that there are things that look impossible until you do them is an attractive theory, but to learn one's limitations *before* embarking on a project is the first step in life's feasibility studies.

An anthropologist must gather material in all sorts of ways before he is able to reconstruct the past. One of the ways I was hoping to collect and reconstruct the first two decades of my past was to listen to the friends I grew up with. So in 1961, after a fifteen-year hiatus, I decided to return to Hungary and my hometown. Considering how few of Székesfehérvár's Jews survived the war, it was a miracle that four of the seven members of my old crowd were still around to sit with me at a table at the Alba Regia Restaurant (so called after the original Latin name of the town). Well into the night we recalled with glee the outlandish games we played, which, in some ways, seasoned us for times to come.

The world we grew up in had no telephones, certainly not in our homes or our fathers' businesses; mothers rarely had full-time jobs, and I didn't know anyone who was divorced or had changed professions; school discipline was so strict that I literally had to salute anyone who was in a grade higher than I was; and the tax collector had to depend on my father's mood in order to enter his shop to meekly request payment.

There were no hot dog carts on the street, no ice cream vendors, but we did have the pumpkin lady. Always a clear signal of the arrival of fall was the appearance of an elderly woman in fingerless gloves who presided over a rusty black iron grill in the same way that a Caribbean street player cajoles music out of his steel drum. She would keep re-arranging pumpkin pieces on the grill until each one was cooked to a creamy texture with a slight charcoal edge. As my friends and I passed by the corner where she'd had her cart, we recalled the great day when one of our fathers asked us who could eat the largest number of pumpkin slices, and stood by while we consumed world-record quantities. Watching his idea turn into a major expenditure, the father grew more and more anxious, and at last he told us that unfortunately he had an appointment on the other side of town, calling an abrupt end to our pumpkin-olympiad.

School in our town, just as in the rest of Hungary, was highly competitive, but our gang made sure that nothing interfered with our favorite diversions. A typical after-school activity at the age of twelve went something like this: The five of us who made up the core of the gang—Jancsi, Laci, Gyuri, Pista, and I—would roam the little streets of our medieval town, throwing challenges at each other, such as to enter a store that we had no business to be in. When my turn came to choose, I dared Laci to go into a lady's corset shop. Of course he had to improvise a reason that was good enough to avoid either being thrown out bodily or having his father notified, which would result in certain punishment. He entered the shop, filled with rotund ladies, and asked innocently, "Excuse me, but I have to find my mother, and I was told that she may be here." Although the story was implausible at best—since a youngster of our age would never have been asked to go to a corset shop—he got away with it. And then it was my turn to meet the challenge.

We passed by a pastry shop where our mothers got together to add sweet calories to the—presumably—piquant stories they exchanged. As

*At the local pool with the gang (1937). I'm at far left; János
Stelczer ("Satyú") is standing second from right*

it happened, in the window display of luscious desserts there was a
golden-yellow, fully packed *krémes,* a sort of Napoleon pastry, with a desperate fly caught in its cream filling. While we watched the fly's hopeless
attempt to escape, my friends came up with a devilish plan: I was to go in
and order a *krémes,* and I had to request the one in the window, complete
with the fly.

I sat down at one of the shop's marble-topped tables, and, when the
pretty waitress in her bone-hard, starched headdress reluctantly served
me the pastry, everybody in the room watched, appalled, as I devoured
the confection, fly and all, thus evening the score in the game. Decades
later I would recall this incident when a host in Mexico offered me a
glass of pulque, the Mexican spirit made from the agave plant, and
served with it the customary special treat of thick, white, crisp-fried
maggots.

Children getting an allowance must be part of the American Bill of
Rights, but in Hungary we had to do all sorts of odd jobs to be able to
buy that *krémes,* with or without a fly. One of the more colorful sources of

income appeared twice a year, when the circus came to town. Instead of a 50-horsepower motor, the carousel was powered by eight money-hungry kids, each pushing one spoke, way above the revolving figures, making it turn in a rather erratic manner.

As I spent time with my childhood friends, I was pleased to find that some of the old spark was still there, even after all they had been through. At the end of the evening they convinced me that we should visit the house I'd been born in, if for no other reason than to see the impressive plaque at the entrance. True to the irreverent spirit of our childhood, it turned out to be a For Rent sign my cronies had put up for the occasion.

I was pleased that every one of my friends remembered when, at the age of sixteen, wanting to surprise a girl with whom I was infatuated, I had dug up a couple of chrysanthemum bushes from our garden and planted them in front of her courtyard window. I didn't sleep all night, waiting for her reaction in the morning. Unfortunately, during the night it snowed, making the white chrysanthemums invisible. I was so embarrassed that I never told her the story.

The day after our evening at the Alba Regia, we ambled along Palotai Street, where our family house was located, and passed by the Nyuli Bakery, which released a basketful of memories. Bread was not only a staple, but was also almost sacred in our home, almost godlike, as rice is for the Balinese. From ancient times, the bread a person ate was emblematic of his rank, and based on this criterion, we were the blue-bloods of Fejér County. I had to do many of the little jobs around the house, the easiest of which was each week writing little labels with our name on them, sticking them on top of the bread dough my mother had prepared, and then taking the two huge risen loaves in woven straw baskets to the nearby bakery to be baked. At Friday's lunch my father would take one of the fresh loaves, which seemed like the work of a master potter, bless it, and, ritualistically, holding the loaf tight against his chest, cut a little piece for all of us, using our special white bone-handled bread knife. Then he broke off a small chunk for himself and invariably told my mother, after thoughtfully tasting it, "This time it is the best ever." My maternal grandfather, during the bread ceremony in their home, always put a little salt on his first taste and, as a little affectation (and a sign of affection), for many years I imitated him.

Bread was almost as important to us as air, water, or life itself, and when we dropped a piece of bread on the floor we had to kiss it and then, unless it was hopelessly dirty, eat it. Sometimes my mother made fancy loaves of challah with bread-dough birds perched on the top, with peppercorns for piercingly realistic eyes. We were convinced that if bread were the medium, Michelangelo would have been outclassed by her in a competition.

Most every small-town household in Hungary had its steady procession of beggars during the Depression years of the early 1930s, and my mother's favorite, if that's the right word, was an old ragpicker who assumed the casual air of a gentleman beggar, one who begged only as a hobby. He came every Friday, knowing that it was bread-baking day, to collect a few slices of fresh bread from us, as well as from our neighbors. One particular day he showed up before lunch, and my mother apologized that the bread was still uncut, so she was unable to give him any. He cheerfully countered, pointing to his bulging canvas bag, "It's all right, ma'am, I can give you change!" My mother, who loved good repartee, promised him an entire loaf the next week. Knowing her, I am sure he received it.

When a girl married in central Europe, she got a piece of starter dough from her mother, as did mine in 1921, when she married my father, just as her mother did when she married my grandfather Ignácz in 1890. There was more continuity in the weekly bread-baking than in the ever-changing governments and elastic borders of our part of the world.

Another constant in my life that turned out to be fundamental was a passion for cooking.

Watching my maternal grandmother's tiny figure leaning over the blue-and-white enameled pots, continually adjusting and stirring like a possessed alchemist, was, and still is, an inspiration to me. She infused old formulas with new energy, and taught my mother the importance of skill, flavor, and appropriateness for an occasion. My friends would usually avoid kitchens as alien territory, but I headed for the kitchen when I came home from school, to watch my mother kneading dough for bread or dumplings. By the age of ten I cooked simple dishes fairly well, though my mother was uneasy with the way I would make slight alterations in the traditional recipes, which had not changed in her family for generations.

In addition to different tastes, I was also seeking different worlds, and one of the great gifts I received for my bar mitzvah was a red bicycle that probably meant more to me than a car to an American youngster who comes of age, because I had not been allowed to ride my father's precious bicycle since the day I had almost crashed it.

The very first trip I took on it was to the nearby village of Csór, perhaps eight kilometers from our house. Approaching the village on the two-lane road, I felt like a great explorer nearing his goal after months of arduous trekking. The little village had a general store on its main (and only) street. Parking my new bike, I walked into the store, not quite sure what language the natives spoke, and in a delicious euphoria I bought a pencil, expecting to find a strange foreign imprint on it. To my disappointment, it was the same kind of pencil I used in school. This incident stays with me to this day, as I still yearn to find and experience different worlds.

I was fortunate to have my own world before I even entered grammar school. From the time I started making music, the violin was my refuge, and it carried me through difficult times. It wasn't a hobby but a necessity for me, a private language that said everything to me. I had been surrounded by music from the day I was born. Sunday-afternoon radio concerts from Budapest were almost like a sacred ritual. My parents told me years later that as a baby I used to giggle with pleasure when a violin solo was played during the broadcast, even more than when they took me to see a puppet show.

Never having smoked, I have little affinity for cigars, even though they triggered my life as a violinist. One of my father's closest friends was a serious cigar smoker. One day, according to my clearly prejudiced parents' tale, when I was almost four years old I attempted to make a violin out of one of his discarded cigar boxes, fashioning strings of thick silk buttonhole thread from my father's shop. Shortly afterwards, I began taking violin lessons from Professor Horváth, who taught me in exchange for suits my father made for him.

My first, somewhat less than formal debut recital took place in the first grade, when I played the transcript of a simple Hungarian song, "Magasan repül a darú," "The Crane Flies High in the Air," with great success. Years of study with two of the great violin teachers of Hungary, Professors Rados and Waldbauer, followed before I escaped from Hungary in 1946.

Both sides of my family had produced fine violinists and musicians. My paternal grandmother's brother Aladár was a talented violinist who had graduated from the famed Franz Liszt Music Academy in Budapest. He fell in love with, and married, a gypsy girl in around 1870, which was almost the same as a white man in Mobile, Alabama, marrying a black girl during the same period. The newly married violinist with an artist's

27

degree changed his name from Sommer to its Hungarian equivalent, Nyári. Being a good fiddler, complete with a gypsy wife and soon thereafter lots of kids, he shocked the entire family by becoming a *primás*, the leading violinist in a gypsy band. As one of the best, using the name Aladár Nyári, he played in some of the glittering cafés of Budapest. My mother's first cousin Ernő Neufeld was a noted prodigy on the violin, and eventually became one of the first musical directors of Universal Studios in Hollywood. Another of her cousins, Ernő Rapée (né Rappaport), was the first conductor of the legendary Roxy movie-theater orchestra in New York. I had enough of the right kind of musical genes to become a second Heifetz.

In 1940, at sixteen, I received a coveted scholarship to study with Professor Rados, and even before I had graduated from high school I would take the train to Budapest twice a week for my lesson. The next year I moved to Budapest to live in a furnished room on the Buda side of the Danube.

Ever since my cigar-box violin, I had been dreaming about making my own violin and playing it at my future concerts. I thought this would be a profound musical experience, and a first in the world of performers. Also, I always had the urge to learn new skills, and I thought that being able to create the instrument I was playing on would help me comprehend the mystery of sound and acoustics on a different level. So I befriended a fine violin-maker, Mr. Kovács, near the Franz Liszt Music Academy, and in addition to my daily practice, anywhere from zero hours to eight, I apprenticed in his workshop a couple of hours every day to learn how to make a violin. It took me almost a year to complete one instrument, though I should hasten to add that it was with his considerable help.

A few years ago, when my partner, Ronald S. Lauder, and I purchased two of the finest vineyards in Hungary, I made it my business to learn as much as possible about the technique of winemaking, from the planting of the vineyard all the way to the details of making the wine itself. Yet I found that knowing as much about—let us say—the aging potential of wines as did our *maître de chai* did not increase the sensitivity of my palate, just as learning how to cut a perfect purfling on the tender pine of the belly of a violin did not make me better able to hear the subtleties of the fiddle.

And what about the sound of the violin I made? Well, to paraphrase a critic's line about an unfortunate singer, if the G string had had the

High school graduation, 1943.
I'm standing in the center of the third row

quality that the E string was missing, the middle strings would have been very pleasant to listen to.

Although my father generously supported me with a small monthly stipend, I still had continuing problems with my budget.

Take, for instance, the crucial matter of eating. I was not allowed to have a hot plate in my rented room, though the Kőrössy family, my landlords, kindly invited me to their family table every now and then, so I had to be creative to be able to fill my belly between times. An egg, it is said by unemployed philosophers, is a whole day's work for a chicken; I had to work as a page-turner for at least two concerts to be able to obtain one, scrambled, at a neighborhood basement joint.

One day a friend of mine who was a great poker player and a lousy artist (painting away during the day the money he made at night at the poker table) took me to lunch. He was a tall fellow whose legs barely fit under the table. At one point he jumped up and yelled to the waiter to bring over the owner of the restaurant that instant. Apparently a nail, sticking out under the table, had ripped his pants, and he demanded satisfaction. The apologetic owner told us that the lunch was on the house, which barely placated my friend.

It is written that all great men are gifted with the ability to recognize opportunities, and at that very moment I rose to unsuspected greatness.

The very next day I invited a young woman in my class to a modest tavern-type eatery. Lo and behold, when the time came to pay the check, it turned out that my pants had been torn by a nail strategically located under the table. Profuse apologies and "please don't pay for this dinner" followed.

The custom of "going Dutch" was unheard of in the early 1940s in Budapest, and if I went to the theater or the opera, I usually did so unaccompanied. Opera was my real passion, and a performance at the magnificent Budapest Opera House was a red-letter day for me. I never had the money to buy a ticket for a decent seat, so I was always relegated to the standing-room space at the very top of the opera house. After one performance I decided that I would cut down on all my expenses so that each month I could buy a ticket for a seat one level lower than the last; then one day, as I recall the strategy, in eleven months I would arrive at an orchestra seat, if possible in the first row center (a location I don't advise for anyone seeking a perfect opera experience). Yet I never made it to the ground floor of the opera house, because just when I was ready to make my move on the ticket office, fate, in the guise of the Hungarian government, arranged for me another kind of performance.

In the meantime I continued my violin studies in Budapest, playing chamber music and performing here and there, and whenever I returned to my hometown I played sonatas with a comely, dark-haired girl who lived in the nearby village of Seregélyes. Among my deeply etched memories is an evening when we sat under the leafy horse chestnut trees with a carafe of wine glittering in the moon's generous light. The wind held back its breath that evening; the chambermaid sang in the kitchen about a fickle lover, and my friend Ágnes was waiting for the end of the song so she could play my favorite Bach piece for me. At the sound of the first chord, I thought the entire world was well-tempered, and I lived in paradise.

A few years later my friend, her family, the house, and the Bösendorfer piano were gone. Only Bach's music has remained, along with aromas and flavors that my brain and nerves have preserved throughout these years.

It took me many decades to understand the fairy tale in which the wish of the wise person was to be ignorant about his future. I was fortunate to have no idea what the next four years would bring.

CHAPTER 2

The Tenth Circle of Hell

IPPING INTO MY tattered copy of the *Divine Comedy* a couple of months ago, I accompanied Dante and Virgil on their walk through the nine descending circles of hell. Thinking about it later, I felt that my life during the period between February 6, 1944, and July 15, 1946, constituted a tenth circle.

Writing about my family's fate is perhaps the most difficult task I could undertake, but keeping silent about them would be equally difficult. After so many years I still cannot pinpoint the nadir of those days, but I am finally ready to tell of the horrors I lived through. While admittedly I am not a completely impartial witness, I will try to give both sides even if there is only one side.

I should start with the golden age of Hungarian Jewry, which began in the nineteenth century. At that time, a number of powerful politicians and writers realized that Hungary was far behind other central European nations (Hungary never considered itself part of eastern Europe), and saw that if it was to catch up with its neighbors, it needed a strong middle class. To achieve this goal, toward the end of the century laws were passed to emancipate the Jewish population, but before they could be enacted, a depression had spread from western Europe to Hungary, and the country was in a disastrous state economically, which throughout its history had always led to anti-Semitism. In addition to economic factors, the intolerance of a government that reflected the nature of the society eventually produced tragic results. The only way that Hungary could possibly have qualified as an industrial nation was in its ability to manufacture and package its anti-Semitic poison throughout the centuries. The venomous flavor changed frequently, depending on market demand, and on occasion it even imported the raw ingredients from elsewhere.

One of the continuous sources for the hatred was the Roman Catholic Church, the state religion of Hungary established by King Stephen (who was later made a saint), the founder of the country in A.D. 1000. To justify one of the anti-Jewish laws of the early 1940s, a Hungarian government official quoted the mid-sixteenth-century pope Paul IV, who stated in his *Cum Nimis Absurdum* that "the Jews even by their physiques are slaves and one should treat them accordingly."

It is too bad that only a handful of non-Catholic theologians have studied the lives of the five thousand or so Jews who lived in the ghettos of Rome from 1555 into the nineteenth century, squeezed into a dark and filthy few blocks and forced to wear distinctive headgear. Until 1870 the Pope prohibited the Jews from acquiring higher education or from holding office or becoming professionals; they were also proscribed from working outside the ghetto, just to mention a few of the draconian—or papal—restrictions. In addition to a number of special assessments, large sums had to be paid by the Jews annually to the Casa Pia for missionary work *among* Jews.

As far as the Lutheran religion is concerned, in 1543 the aging Martin Luther, following his failure to proselytize the Jews, wrote, "First, their synagogues should be burned; second, their homes should be smashed; third, they should be robbed of their prayer books and their Talmuds. . . ."

It would surprise even many Hungarians to learn that the 1919 Hungarian anti-Bolshevist action and its associated violent anti-Semitism—wrapped in a patriotic movement to regain territories lost after World War I—antedated both the German and Italian fascist movements. I remember hearing my maternal grandfather's stories about the roads lined with Jews hanging from trees following Béla Kún's Bolshevik Revolution in 1919. The combination of anti-Semitism, anticommunism, and supernationalism (which was always present in Hungary) resulted in a wave of terror and a kind of *l'art pour l'art* brutality, and the victims included factory workers, poor peasants, and left-leaning intellectuals by the thousands who would not support their tactics.

The country was ready for almost any kind of counter-movement after World War I. Hungary had lost two-thirds of its historical territory to the newly formed Yugoslavia and Czechoslovakia, as well as to Romania and even Austria; this, combined with the loss of one-third of its Hungarian population and three-fifths of its total population, amounted to a national catastrophe, with many unforeseen results. Finally, the national agenda was distilled down to two principal goals: the restoration of Hungary's original borders, and the solution to the so-called Jewish problem.

Because the ethnic minorities of pre–World War I Hungary were absorbed by its neighboring countries, Hungary became an ethnically homogeneous land, with only the Jews and gypsies left as identifiable groups to be used as scapegoats, especially political and economic ones. Cynical observers would add that perhaps it was the only way that the country's citizens could maintain a feeling of superiority, without which life is not possible in Hungary.

In 1920 the government introduced a *numerus clausus* law, which limited the enrollment of Hungarian Jews in the universities to six percent, and as a result many of the most talented people were forced to emigrate.

How could this have happened in an advanced society? Or, was it an advanced society?

Deplorably, the government's enactment of one law or regulation after another curtailing the lives and rights of Jews did not go against the popular sentiment of the people. As a matter of fact, modern anti-Semitism was formulated in a devilishly clever way in order to appeal to every stratum of the gentile population. Between the two wars there were so many social problems that instead of dealing with them, the society focused on the "Jewish problem."

A key word that was used by Hungarian politicians, historians, and leading citizens trying to rationalize their anti-Jewish attitudes and actions was *otherness*. Generally speaking, the majority of Hungarians are intolerant of anything or anybody different from what they're used to, ranging from traditions and foods to ways of life and, of course, nationality and religion. Because Hungary—as opposed to the Czechoslovak Republic, for instance—had no democratic tradition, a law forbidding intermarriage or any sort of sexual contact between Jews and non-Jews, in order to protect the "purity" of the Aryan race (to which Hungarians did not even belong), did not seem unnatural to the Hungarian populace.

Why the Jews did not revolt against this injustice is a question that has nagged at me throughout my life. One of the reasons was expressed by my father, who once tried to calm me down when I came home after a humiliating experience at school, by telling me that if we accepted the newly passed Jewish laws that were, according to him, just a tactical move to neutralize the extreme right wing, and remained loyal to Hungary, and if we kept supporting the ultraconservative, landed aristocrat-gentry regime, they would protect the 725,000 Jews then living in the country. The tens of thousands of converts, who were suddenly declared Jews under the 1941 racially based law (in spite of the fact that most of them were born and educated as Christians), also needed protection, as it turned out later.

There is a danger in believing that you understand the behavior and feelings of large groups of people within a geographically extensive area just because you are one of them. But I can firmly state that no Jew who lived in our town could imagine that the "final solution" would also happen to our community. After all, we were as aggressively chauvinistic as everyone else around us; our language was the same as theirs, and we were just as vocal and enthusiastic about the Hungarian All-Star soccer team as were our neighbors who crossed themselves a few dozen times a day.

Jewish leaders, and I am referring to the Hungarian variety, still remained proudly patriotic to the end. They advised cooperation with the regime, hoping that this would result in the least damage and injury, following an old Jewish tendency not to run from anti-Jewish regimes but to try to survive under them. Thus the Jewish community leadership became pawns in German hands.

Another reason for this passive acceptance was the brilliant propaganda of the Germans, who were able to fool most Jews into believing the forcefully and continually stated reason for deportation: that its sole purpose was to transport a large number of Jews to other parts of the country, or to Germany, as a workforce. And when it occurred to many of the Jews to question why they were taking children, the elderly, and even cripples, the Germans' well-rehearsed answer was that they were aware of the strong Jewish familial ties and thus did not want to separate family members.

The series of anti-Jewish laws acted as artificial but effective diversions from the serious social, commercial, and agrarian problems of the nation. Between 1938 and 1941, three additional sets of laws were enacted, the last of which, removing all rights of Jews as citizens, was based on the Nuremberg laws of Nazi Germany, and included labor camps for Jews of military age.

By the beginning of 1944, the *Numerus Clausus* had become *Numerus Nullus* in every walk of life. If the government could have restricted the percentage of oxygen that the Jews could breathe, they would have done that, too.

That Adolf Eichmann, accompanying the two German divisions entering Hungary on March 19, 1944, with a small two-hundred-member *Gestapo Sonderkommando,* was able to "solve the Jewish question" could only have been possible with the active or passive support of the majority of the Hungarian people, especially those outside of Budapest, as well as of the Hungarian police and officials. According to the now-available records, within a few weeks the Gestapo received more than 35,000 letters and other pieces of information against Jews, liberals, and Communists in hiding, or about Jews with "mixed blood" who tried to pass as Christians. I must also point out, however, that there were many Hungarian individuals and families who hid Jewish friends, taking enormous chances, knowing that if they were found out they would be treated like the Jews they were protecting.

The remaining few Jewish shops were taken over. Jews could only travel with special permits (which, by the way, were not available). The tickets for the already minimal food allotments were further reduced for Jews. They could not own a car, horse, bicycle, radio, telephone, typewriter, or jewelry. They could not step into a restaurant or bar, or travel on buses or trams, and they were forbidden to enter theaters, museums, hotels, spas, or even public parks. By that time, however, no Jew could work as a professional or in an office, so that part of the Eichmann directive was mostly academic.

Many Jews went into hiding, but tragically most of the leaders of Jewish organizations and rabbis advised waiting; they simply could not believe what they were hearing about what had already happened to Jews in neighboring countries. Thus the Germans would eventually kill three out of every four Hungarian Jews by 1945.

Still, nothing can possibly explain the unexplainable.

Theodore (Tivadar) Herzl, whose dream of a Jewish state became a reality, was right when he presaged the future in a letter he wrote on March 10, 1903, to his friend Ernő Mezei, a Hungarian congressman, during the golden age of Hungarian Jewry. He said, "The faith in assimilation will crush Hungarian Jewry as well. The later this will happen, and the stronger the Hungarian Jewish community will get, the more monstrous and extreme will be the blow, and the more wickedly powerful it will be. There is no escape."

With our advanced technology, by now the hottest day in hell is perhaps measurable. This horror-gauge in my personal hell would explode on the cursed day of June 14, 1944, when nineteen members of my immediate family were deported to Auschwitz from the brick factory in our hometown.

During my high school days, our respected Rabbi Hirschler once made forgiveness the theme of his Saturday sermon, and during the next religion class I politely but gleefully confronted him with my discovery in Deuteronomy, where God declared, "To me belongeth vengeance and recompense."

Regrettably, I don't recall our rabbi's answer, but since 1945, when I learned the fate of my family, I have fervently hoped that this was not just one of those theatrical, inflated promises emanating from above.

Not only can no one ever explain this crucifixion, carried out on an unprecedented scale, but this time the whole world heard the hammering of the nails, yet remained silent.

I often think of creating a memorial for my parents, perhaps a kite that could soar all the way to heaven, and on it I would write the following:

> The only person who dies is the one who does not leave behind something worthwhile.

> The only person who dies is someone who was born truthful and died without being true to his or her ideals.

> The only person who dies is the one who is not going to be missed by his loved ones, talked about with fondness, every now and then toasted with a good glass of wine.

By now it should be obvious to anyone reading this book that my parents have never died.

CHAPTER 3

Welcome to Our Camp

I WAS NINETEEN YEARS OLD when I was ordered to report to a forced-labor camp. Remembering the many horrendous stories I had heard, my first thought was that this would surely end my future as a violinist.

The labor camps were first established in 1940–1941 for Jews "to serve without arms." They were a cross between reform schools where inmates are condemned to chain-gang-type labor, and penal institutions, where they shoot you as a form of warning. The range, however, varied from almost humane treatment to the inhuman massacres in the Ukraine and the mines of Bor in Serbia. Many thousands of wretched labor campers were brought to the Soviet front and used, instead of pigs, to explode hidden mines buried in the fields between the Hungarian and Soviet armies.

From 1943 on, thousands of Hungarian Jews between the ages of sixteen and sixty worked for the Germans and for the Hungarian army as a slave labor force; many of them never returned.

My childhood friend János Stelczer (or Satyú, as we called him) and I luckily had to report to the same labor camp division in the city of Komárom (Komarno), which was divided by the peace treaty after World War I: the area of the city south of the Danube remained Hungarian and the other side became part of Czechoslovakia. In not being sent to the

37

Ukraine, I felt like the lucky man who was hanged, but the rope around his neck broke his fall.

We had about a month to get ready. During this time, my father made me black breeches of the most durable material, with indestructible pockets, all hand-stitched for extra strength, as well as a short leather coat, and a nearby cobbler made me a pair of laced boots. I asked my father to sew a hidden pocket into the pants, but, being experienced in such matters, he rejected the idea and told me that if I was going to take chances, they should be the kind that might save my life. In spite of his advice, I took all the money I had saved and, making pockets by sealing two pages together in one of my books, I did increase my chances of survival. Then my father taught me how, instead of wearing socks, I could wrap my feet in strips of flannel cloth. The many layers of flannel keep one's feet much warmer than even wool stockings, and this saved my feet from frostbite during the following winter.

I chose three books to take with me, neatly fitting them into the outside pocket of my oilcloth backpack. My choices were *The Selected Writings of Epictetus,* the stoic philosopher who thought that the only things always within one's power are one's own self and will, Árpád Tóth's *Morning Serenade,* a bouquet of wistful poems about the longing to find refuge in an imaginary world, and Epicurus's *Ethics,* which extolled the negative aspects of pleasure, meaning freedom from pain and trouble and an independent and peaceful state of body and mind. These books turned out to be eminently satisfying choices; each served me well in a different way.

The teachings of Epicurus became a kind of mantra for me. *Ataraxia,* the state he described as the quietude of our soul, depends on three things: the lack of physical pain, and not fearing death or the gods. At any rate—as he said—gods do not concern themselves with human affairs, and what was happening to me and around me powerfully proved his point.

But the philosophical vitamins I received from good old Epicurus came in a small package: death does not concern us; everything good and bad is contained in our feelings; and thus, if these feelings cease to exist (i.e., after death), we will not be able to perceive the change, and therefore our souls should clearly be free of the fear of death. And just to make sure I'd get it a couple of thousand years after he wrote of it, he added that this awareness should give us the assurance that nothing frightening will last forever, and that within the boundary of life and its tragedies the most perfect safety is within friendship. This idea has remained a leitmotif throughout my life.

Philosophy affects us differently at different periods in our lives, and at a time when everything was getting ready to wither in my garden, the two eminent Greeks' words made me accept natural and unnatural disasters as a matter of course, and allowed me to concentrate on more immediate problems.

Almost as important a part of the backpack inventory as my books was a well-wrapped slab of paprika-coated "bacon," my mother's rendition of the real thing, a kosher version made out of the sides of a well-fed goose.

The last Sunday before I left for labor camp, my father and I took the local train to Mezőkomárom, the village he grew up in, which was about eighty kilometers from our town, to visit a childhood friend of his, a gentile working farmer of comfortable means. I didn't know why he had asked me to take my two violins along, and I had learned not to ask twice if he didn't want to answer the first time. We walked from the train station to the house of his friend, who lived in one of the whitewashed, thatch-roofed houses along Main Street, which, as I recall, was the only real street of the village. After a plate of sausages, hot pepper, and bread, washed down with a glass of wine from his little vineyard, he led us to the rear section of the yard, which was filled with chickens, and we walked up the steps to the top of a silo that held what seemed to me to be many tons of wheat. My father solemnly gave his friend a package sewn into a linen stiffener of the kind that he used underneath the linings of the jackets he made in his shop, and told me to give his friend the double violin case that held my violins.

Then my father embraced his friend and said quietly to him, "I would like you to put this package away just as if it were yours; it contains my wife Ilonka's jewelry. Also this violin case. Bury them in the wheat in this silo, nobody will ever find them. I don't know what's going to happen to me, but at least when George returns, he will have his violins and my wife will have a few pieces of her favorite jewelry." He opened the violin case—I guess just to make sure the instruments were inside—then he opened the small, flat wooden box wrapped in linen that contained the jewelry. I vaguely recall that it contained a few bracelets, a small diamond ring, and the necklace that my mother's eldest brother, Lajos, had bought her, along with a few other objects. It certainly wasn't a dazzling array of precious stones, but every one of those pieces had a special meaning and formed a connection with someone my mother loved.

When we got home, it struck me that I could no longer play on my golden-yellow, sweet-toned violin made by the contemporary Hungarian luthier Orbán, or my fine, nineteenth-century Johann Gottlob Heberlein, and when I sat down to write in my diary, I commented that Shelley's line, "Pleasure that is in sorrow is sweeter than the pleasure of pleasure itself," was nothing but sophistry. Even if my diary had survived, I wouldn't be able to read this page—tears and ink don't mix well. When I told mother about our day, she just sat motionless, braver than I, crying tearlessly, knowing that tears would have to be saved for later.

She did keep one piece of jewelry, a cloisonné medallion of an angel, which she wore most of the time, almost like an amulet. Forty years after this incident, my wife and I were walking on a small side street in Vienna when we passed a small antique shop, and for some reason I turned back to take a look in its window. Jenifer always walks fast and—I still don't know how—I caught a glimpse of the display and noticed my mother's medallion—or perhaps one that was identical to it. We went in to buy it, and when I completed the transaction, the elderly shopkeeper said, "This has been waiting for you for years." Whether this was just a line or part of a supernatural scenario, I will never know—I was too disturbed to continue the conversation, and when I returned a few years later, the store was not there. There are incidents one shouldn't probe too deeply; if it's the same necklace, how it got from Auschwitz to a Viennese antique shop is a question I didn't want to know the answer to. Still, I like to think that it was another of my mother's loving gestures, offering the medallion to my wife, whom she never had a chance to meet.

Ever since I was taken to a hospital in Budapest at the age of six for an operation on a double hernia, whenever I leave my home for an extended period, I look at it as if it were the last time, and try to preserve the moment. On Sunday, February 6, 1944, in the middle of a snowstorm, carrying my crammed backpack, I shut the heavy wooden doorway behind me, and looked back at the façade of our house as I started walking, between my mother and father, toward the railroad station.

When the train arrived, hissing steam, we kissed good-bye—my mother clinging to me, my father trying, as always, to control his emotions. It was the last time I saw them. After a train ride of several hours, we arrived in Komárom and my friend and I walked to the labor camp, lodged in old, dilapidated army barracks. About 1,500 of us were crammed into huge dorms built for about 500 soldiers, with triple-decker beds, a couple of indoor toilets, and a group of vile outdoor latrines.

From the beginning we were treated like prisoners, and though we were not flogged or branded, we had to put on yellow armbands immediately after going through the delousing and haircutting process and relinquishing everything except a few permitted books, photographs, and ten *pengős,* which had then perhaps the equivalent purchasing power of two dollars American. A number of books and essays I have read over the past decades have described forced-labor camp as a kind of prison. For me it is an uneasy comparison, because some prisons are correctional and others try to prevent criminals from committing further violence, but the forced-labor camp, as formulated by the Hungarian state, existed mostly to separate Jewish men from gentiles, and to inflict systematic humiliation. The first time I visited the Roosevelt home in Hyde Park, I was moved by something Eleanor Roosevelt had said: "No one can make you feel inferior without your consent."

It is always incomprehensible to me how even the most inhuman regimentation can become part of a routine life, and the chain-gang-style existence seemed almost normal after a while. It was also unexpected and gratifying that the "I" became "we" for such large numbers of people, and not the other way around. The command structure of the labor camp was strange. Reserve officers—Christians, usually of middle age with the rank of lieutenant or captain—were called in to head the various camps, and the power they exercised was far beyond that of the chief officer of an army battalion. For instance, under certain circumstances they could order the execution of a labor camper or even of an entire group, without checking with anyone. In civilian life most of them were middle-class professionals or businessmen of some sort, and our lives and deaths, and every stage in between, hinged on the personality of the commandant. Some campers were fortunate enough to get a decent person as camp commandant, but others had to live with the erratic—or even maniacal—disposition of someone compensating for an otherwise disappointing life.

Then there were the squalid *keret-legények,* a strange name coined for the job—I could perhaps approximate the nearly impossible translation, but the result would be awkward, so I'll just say that they functioned as our guards. Three or four of these were attached to a group of one hundred or so labor campers, and they were just chosen at random from the army—most of them from the lowest ranks. Soldiers in the Hungarian army were sharply divided according to education. Those with high-school diplomas, designated by a special strip sewn on their sleeves, were eligible to attend officers' school, while the overwhelming number of uneducated recruits came mostly from peasants' or workers' families. Our labor-camp guards, as a rule, were from the latter group.

On the first day we were told that anyone not in his bunk by ten minutes to nine at night would be sent to solitary—which was simply a deep hole in the ground with a rusty metal cover. A few minutes after the lights were turned off, the guards burst into the dorms screaming, "In two minutes everyone must line up in the yard—and we mean two minutes!"

We had no time to get dressed or even put on shoes, although I was able to drag on my leather jacket while trying to squeeze myself through the narrow door, with everyone else trying to do the same. When we got out to the huge open yard, the brutality of that February cold hit us, and in an attempt to prevent our limbs from freezing, we all tried to move our feet and hands, which had started to ache unbearably.

The camp commandant, wearing a well-pressed uniform and with every hair in place, surrounded by his uniformed henchmen, greeted us in a civilized tone, as if the circumstances were quite normal:

"Welcome to our camp. You are here to assist the victorious Hungarian army in its war effort, and if you do as you are told, you won't have any problems. For instance, you were told to stand at attention, yet many of you are making a commotion and just won't stand still."

Then he pointed at a pale, red-haired boy shivering in his long underwear. Almost as if it were a well-rehearsed scene, one of the guards grabbed the boy's head and, with a practiced motion, twisted it halfway around. To make sure we got the full effect, they left him screaming on the icy snow for a while before they took him away. We never saw him again.

During the next few minutes, which seemed like a whole night to us, we were told the rules. I can't say that they were fashioned after the penal code, because they were not nearly as consistent. For example, we were allowed to write and receive letters after the censor had checked the correspondence, and we could receive packages of food, while being otherwise treated as slaves.

Then we were told to return to our bunks, and we were reminded that one of the rules was total silence. Each night a number of soldiers would pass by once or twice, and at that time we could get permission to go to the latrine. Some of the older labor campers, not being able to control their bladders, wet their bunks. This compounded the dizzying fragrance of the dorm, already scented with fumes emanating from our breaths, our pores, and our stomachs.

If ever there was a bug paradise, this was it. Our bodies and the straw-filled mattresses provided the little bastards with hunting grounds, but I got less severely attacked than most of my neighbors. Béla, the bunkmate I befriended, was a middle-aged pharmacist who told me that my blood must have a high salt content, and that was why they attacked me less.

We were lucky in that of the four guards we had to live with, two were very decent to us and the other two didn't go beyond the expected behavior of a prison warden under the circumstances. One of the lenient ones was a pint-sized, part-gypsy soldier who, as compensation for his height, sported a fancy mustache and behaved like the bold warrior. The first time he collapsed in front of us in an epileptic convulsion, one of the labor campers who was a doctor tried to help him, but there was little anybody could do for the pitiful man. When he came to, he acted as if nothing had happened, and we sensed that we, too, were supposed to act the same way.

The other soldier was a tall, reserved sergeant named Lengyel who overheard a conversation in which someone asked me about my musical background, and little by little he became a trusted friend. One day during a lunch break, he told me that painting was his whole life, and he showed me a few photographs of his work, which had a nodding relation to some of the French Post-Impressionists.

In the meantime, nonstop work was enforced, even if it had to be invented. The tasks ranged from assisting in roadbuilding to loading and unloading railroad shipments, and there were days when we had to labor even after a meager dinner, which most of the time featured potatoes or beans. The cooks must have been reading up on Escoffier, whose tenet was that each food should remain true to itself, because neither the beans nor the potatoes were confused with any other ingredient or flavor, except for salt on occasion. Luckily I did receive two packages of food from my mother within the first couple of months, including my favorite *pogácsa* and *mákos beigli*, a butter biscuit and a poppyseed roulade, both of which had the vital characteristic that they could last for weeks without spoiling, especially in wintertime.

My mother was very religious and kept a strictly kosher house, which my father gracefully accepted when they got married. However, he was a typical three-days-a-year Jew, and everything else about the Jewish religion was as irrelevant to him as a Buddhist monk's way of life. My mother, closing one eye, allowed him to hang ham and smoked bacon in a remote section of our attic, and every now and then he would take me up there, bringing along a piece of bread and two *bugyli bicska*, the carven-handled peasant knives he kept with him at all times, and we had a feast. Love can be defined in more ways than perhaps any other word, but her allowing my father to add a side of double-smoked, meaty bacon to the package sent to me may have been a mother's devotion in its purest form. For a young body, hunger is a prime enemy, and a daily slice of this provision reduced the bitter complaint of my stomach for a few weeks.

During this period my parents were still in our hometown. I received my last letter from them on March 17, 1944, two days before the German occupation of Hungary. I would give anything to have that letter today. However, I do remember the last line, written by my mother, the correspondent of the family: "We can't hold your hands, but we will always hold your heart."

We tried to disconnect ourselves from our past so we talked about war, sports, books, women and girls (two entirely different categories in those days), other people, and the miseries around us—but rarely about our families and the lives we left behind. I never discussed with anyone except my friend Satyú my plan to escape whenever I could find the chance. My genes were simply not programmed to accept the cards fate had dealt me.

Then the Allied bombings began. Since I have never been in a sizable tornado, or an earthquake, or in the path of an erupting volcano, I can't compare these with the petrifying experience of lying on the floor and being thrown into the air when a bomb exploded nearby. At one point, some bombs hit the huge tanks of the oil refinery at the nearby Almásfüzitő, and a couple of hundred of us were transported there during the night and ordered to form a bucket brigade to put the fire out. It was so hot close to the burning flames that perhaps it was the only area in the vicinity of the labor camp that even the devil avoided. The idea of trying to put out the blazing oil fire with water was moronic and didn't work at all, which made our keepers more and more furious. When the sun came up and the flames were still burning ten stories high, they forced those of us who were near the fire to get closer and closer, and quite a few of our group eventually died of third-degree burns.

Not following the fire, but *during* it, a master sergeant came from headquarters requesting tailors to report to him. Instantly I ran to him, dragging my friend Satyú with me, and offered our services as the best tailors of Transdanubia, the part of the country we came from. With two other labor campers, we were taken to the officers' quarters located in the center of the city, where we were shown an abandoned tailor shop in the basement. In my haste on my way there, I stepped into a huge pile of manure—and desperately tried to clean off my boots for the interview, with limited success. I kept hoping that everybody had a cold.

Later I learned that our beloved commander felt that his officers looked sloppy, and when he was told about a tailor shop that had closed after the army moved on, he made his decision—maybe just to prove my father's conviction that learning to be a tailor might save my life one day.

Two double bunk beds were put into a small basement room near the shop, and the next day we started work. A slight problem was that although my friend was quite an accomplished furrier (his father had one of the finest fur salons in Hungary), Satyú had never worked as a tailor. As far as my tailoring skills went, I could make a fairly decent vest, hem almost anything that was hemmable, sew in a lining, or produce an acceptable buttonhole (although my father had once said that a truck could turn over it), but that wasn't our assignment. We were supposed to take apart the officers' jackets and recut them to the shape of the wearer. Fortunately, the other two members of our team were terrific at it.

My friend and I took care instead of the worn-out uniforms intended for the lower ranks, and a couple of weeks later, when we began to run out of work, I decided to take action. In order to stay in this cushy place—on rare occasions we even received the same food from the cooks as the officers did—I borrowed the shoemakers' file (they were working next door to us), and, first making sure that no one was going to come in to check on us, I simulated the usual holes that developed mostly around the seats and the knees of the pants. Then we proceeded to fix them. Every day I would apply this treatment to a few pairs of pants in perfectly good condition, so that there was plenty of work for us. At one point I was so overconfident that, to entertain my colleagues, I performed a sketch called "Haute Couture for Worthy Hungarian Officers," making so many holes in a pair of pants during the course of the performance that they could have been used as a sieve.

I tried to enjoy our little dungeon room. My ever-present homing instinct remained intact even at a time when a professional gambler wouldn't have given ten-to-one odds for my future. One night before going to sleep, I found rolls of paper that we were supposed to use for cutting out patterns, and I nailed pieces to the wall alongside my bed, covering them with stanzas from my favorite poets and making little designs in between.

I don't know how, but most of the time we knew what was happening around the world, on the Russian front, or about the Hungarian regent's visit to Hitler. But no one, in or out of the labor camp, could have predicted that on March 19, 1944, the Germans would invade Hungary. What I also didn't know at the time was that my cousin Évi Kellner had been caught in a Budapest bus station on the same day, while she was trying to get back to her family a couple of hours away from the city. She was among the first taken to the notorious Kistarcsa internment camp, then to Auschwitz, yet miraculously she was also among the few who survived.

In my youth, I considered mysterious only such phenomena as why the gut D string on my violin broke five minutes before I had to perform at a student recital, or why the prettiest girl in town fell for the *primus nerdus* of our school instead of for yours truly, but it was never a mystery to me that timing is the key to success, which in 1944 also meant survival. I realized that if I resigned myself to fate my resignation would be promptly accepted, and that to survive I must escape from the labor camp and somehow get to Budapest.

One day Sergeant Lengyel took me aside and, in a conspiratorial whisper, told me that he and the captain of the camp were buddies from way back—I think he said something about coming from the same town. The captain had called him into his quarters the previous night and after they had finished a good part of a bottle of *törköly-pálinka* (the Hungarian version of marc), he, the captain, had confessed that his wife was part Jewish and he had to get false papers for her before it was too late. He had mumbled something about some of the *musz* (the abbreviation of the Hungarian word for the labor campers) who must have contacts with such sources.

By then I was obsessed with going to Budapest, and I blurted out that if I could get there for a few days, I could probably get in touch with the Jewish underground I had heard about, and try to get false papers for her. Lengyel, however, never heard from the captain again. If possible, my anxiety had even increased after Satyú and I, from the relative protection of the sewing machine, heard that the brutality at the camp had increased to the point where guards invented deadly games with the labor campers. One of their popular pastimes was exchanging for food whatever the miserable inmates had left among their possessions, such as fountain pens, sewing kits, or medicine, and then, before the labor campers could eat it, the guards would hang them from a tree by tying strong ropes around their wrists. This form of punishment was standard at all labor camps—only the toes could barely touch the ground, and the pain after a few minutes was unbearable. Fortunately, as I found out the second week of my stay at Chateau Liquidation, after a while you fainted. The justification for using this torture on me, which the brave soldiers recorded in the official ledger (just in case of a Red Cross visit), was that I had stolen bread from my fellow labor campers and had to be taught a lesson. The real reason was that I refused to give one of them my mechanical pencil.

Toward the end of October, Sergeant Lengyel told me he had read about a directive according to which the Hungarian government had agreed to send immediately seventy labor-camp units to Germany to dig ditches for the German army in an attempt to hold off the Russian army on half a dozen fronts. The Germans had an aptitude for coining phrases, and as I read in documents after the war, they called this order *Leihjude*—"borrowed Jew." Since Sergeant Lengyel felt that our group would be part of this *Fussmarsch*, it made it even more urgent that we disappear right away.

Another thing that galvanized me into action was a desperate note I had received at the beginning of November from my girlfriend, the talented pianist Ágnes Weisz, from Budapest. (I seem to have had a penchant for dark-haired pianists with that first name.) On stylish dusty blue stationery she wrote that her father was in labor camp and that her mother and two-year-old sister, together with her, had been forced into a tiny room in one of the Swedish protected houses—arranged by Raoul Wallenberg. She added: "We don't know what's going to happen tomorrow."

We were all taught that doing good was our primary function on earth (although my mother used about ninety percent of her good deeds exclusively for her extended family), but to me, trying to help Ágnes was simply an automatic reaction—and it combined the heady risk of Russian roulette with the drive for self-preservation.

I approached the task of escape systematically, putting together two lists for Mission (nearly) Impossible, dividing the jobs to be done into "musts" and "if possibles," just as I would do with multimillion-dollar projects only fifteen improbably diverse years later.

Personal ID cards in Hungary prominently featured one's religion. If, on the line indicating religion, you had three little letters, *Izr.*—an abbreviation of *Izraelita*—your luck was running out fast. It turned out that my friend and personal Schindler, Sergeant Lengyel, was not only good at the brush technique on canvas, he had access to blank ID cards and was able to make those essential documents look so impressive that we could probably have commandeered a Gestapo vehicle. Another paper cost us Satyú's gold pen and most of my money—an official army order we got from a guard who worked in the office, ordering us to report to another unit in Budapest. I chose the name Hegedüs for the false paper, a common name in Hungary meaning "violinist," reasoning that even if I was awakened in the middle of the night, I would respond to it. Just in case, I also took a few blank ID cards with me, already stamped with a seal as part of the deal with our supplier. Collecting things that have no immediate use or purpose is a habit I inherited from my father. Fortunately, we still had some money left, which we knew would be necessary to get some food along the way when we disappeared.

The Allies kept up their bombing, which had started months earlier, at the beginning of April, and we were waiting for a propitious post-bombing period so that we could get away without being detected. Our plan had to be changed abruptly when we received news through the underground tom-tom that a private who worked in the office from which the transfer order and false papers were stolen was talking about reporting us. Within two minutes we had burned our yellow armbands, and in another half hour we were walking on the highway, trying to hitch a ride to Budapest with a passing military vehicle. Thanks to our assignment in the tailor shop, we were able to get away undetected, with revolvers in our pockets that we had appropriated from the arsenal near our workshop.

I also had a secret weapon hidden in the deepest recess of my backpack. A few times during the first couple of months at the camp some of us had to carry pontoons from the Danube to the shipyard. These were so unbearably heavy that they crushed our shoulders to a bloody pulp, and a couple of times I replaced my friend Béla, the pharmacist, when his turn came. One of these times, in gratitude, he gave me a small, folded wax-paper packet, whispering to me that if I swallowed its contents it would kill me within sixty seconds. Knowing that now I was the master of the time of my departure, and having the means to end my life, gave me the courage to take chances that perhaps I wouldn't have otherwise dared to.

After the liberation I had the powder analyzed in a Budapest laboratory, and it turned out to be powdered aspirin. Still, I bless Béla's memory because in possessing it I became a living example of Machiavelli's theory that an enemy convinced he has nothing to lose is the worst kind of foe.

Luckily we were able to hitch a ride on a number of military wagons and trucks, and in between we stopped at a small farm outside of a village somewhere between Komárom and Budapest. The elderly farmer and his wife were frightened at first when we knocked on their door, but we acted like tired soldiers between battles, and they let us sleep in the kitchen, which was still warm from the woodburning oven. They offered us a glass of wine, but obviously had a very meager supply of food themselves. We were as hungry as two healthy twenty-year-old boys can be after not having had enough to eat for months. After the oil lamps were put out, we feverishly began to search for food. Nothing anywhere, only beans and potatoes in wooden bins in a corner, and salt and flour, none of which could appease our loudly complaining stomachs.

And then we discovered, on top of the cupboard that held the dishes, glass jars filled with something dark brown and tempting. I should add that anything that didn't move would have seemed to us worth sampling. Satyú climbed on top of my shoulder and tore off the parchment paper on the top. He put his finger into the heavy, syrupy contents and said dejectedly, "Yucch, it's molasses!" (The original Hungarian was actually somewhat more expressive.)

It didn't take more time than to say to each other, "You know, it's really like caramel sauce . . ." before we drank a full jar, burying the empty jar in the bottom of the wood bin.

The next morning we sneaked out quietly, just before the sun came up. We did leave a short thank-you note, but what bothers me still after so many years is not only that I stole from those poor farmers, but that I couldn't later make it up to them because I didn't remember their name or the name of their village.

The last truck we hitched a ride on took us close to the Southern Railway Station on the Buda side of Budapest, which was close to our destination. I planned all along to stay with my good friend George Schneller's mother, who lived in this area. I used to visit them often, and on occasion I would be invited to dinner and to stay overnight. She was Christian, but her husband was Jewish, so George was taken to a Ukrainian labor camp. He was a remarkably talented pianist, a student at the Franz Liszt Music Academy, both intellectually and physically well rounded, with a vague but witty mien. As a matter of fact, when I met Peter Ustinov years later, I was quite startled by his resemblance to George Schneller, which was more than just physical. I was told after the war by one of his fellow labor campers that the guards had taken a particular dislike to the awkward, totally passive George, who towered over them with his six-foot height. One day, before the sun came up, they roused him up from sleep and ordered him out into the freezing yard, wearing only the underwear he slept in. They ordered him at gunpoint to climb a tree, which, of course, he couldn't manage, and at the same time to crow like a rooster. The frightened boy tried to scream "Cock-a-doodle-doo," while begging to be let go, but a fusillade finished him off. If the official daily logbook were to be found, I am sure it would contain a brief description of the incident, indicating that a labor-camp inmate by the name of George Schneller went berserk and had to be shot according to the rules.

Getting off the truck and walking to get to Alkotmány Street was an illustrated chapter of hell. There were so many corpses lying on the sidewalks that they lost their identity as bodies and became mere twisted objects. The entire city was a bleeding, pustulous, vermin-infested wound, and Budapest even today still bears some of the marks of the second longest siege of World War II after the battle of Stalingrad.

Yet the horrors of Budapest weren't etched into the minds of the world the way the recent monstrosities of Bosnia have been—the latter are much more real to us because we could see it all on television. Only a handful of photographs and the words of the witnesses remain of the macabre Christmas of 1944 in Budapest.

There are perhaps a half-dozen dates in the twentieth century that have altered the fate of Hungary. The most monstrous was October 15, 1944, when, at twelve noon, Regent Horthy made a dramatic announcement on the radio, declaring to the nation that he had asked for a cease-fire from the Russians. Shortly afterwards, he and his family were taken into custody by the Gestapo, and by nine-thirty that same evening, Ferenc Szálasi, a former army major, a fanatic psychopath with a more rabid hatred of Jews than Hitler, declared a coup. Tens of thousands of Szálasi Arrowcross Militia didn't wait even until morning; within minutes after the proclamation, the militia began shooting fusillades into houses marked with the yellow Star of David. This was followed by a period of horror that lasted almost four months, until the Russian occupation of Pest on January 18 and the takeover of Buda, which was completed on February 13, 1945.

Just as in nightmares, where the ending is usually the most horrific part, Szálasi, the crazed monster who led a very large, well-armed group, many of them fourteen- to sixteen-year-olds, officially took over the country with the title "Leader of the Nation." He was sworn into office in front of the Holy Crown, the symbol of Hungarian authority since the year 1000. Shortly afterwards, the parliament (whatever was left of it) officially named him the ruling regent of Hungary and prime minister, as well as giving him total martial-law power. For the first time in the country's modern history, the positions of head of state and head of government in Hungary were combined in a single person.

Even though the Russian army was fast tightening its steel pincers just a few kilometers away, the Arrowcross Militia acted like the devil's bride planning a wedding and already looking forward to the golden anniversary. At this critical time, when the Hungarian army needed ammunition, the wounded were screaming for ambulances, and the people were starving, one of the first official decrees of Szálasi was to order the new symbols of the Hungarist Nation (as they called themselves) and stage a competition for changing the national crest and military decorations to include the Arrowcross insignia. A greeting that copycatted "Heil

Hitler"—"*Kitartás! Éljen Szálasi!*" ("Prevail! Long live Szálasi!")— together with an apeing of the Nazi salute, the right hand extended forward at an angle, was enforced as national law. A few weeks later, the interior minister ordered that all streets named after someone of Jewish origin were to have their names changed immediately.

Of course I only put together these fragments after the war, when I looked at the records, personal accounts, and stories of this period. At the time I knew only what I saw on the streets of Budapest while we were running for our lives.

The Russian army, which was ready to close its deadly tentacles around Budapest, tried to avoid the total destruction of the city so that it could be used as a strategically located headquarters for the advance toward Vienna. Instead of the carpet bombing that was the modus operandi of the Allied forces, the Russians used their artillery effectively while their planes sprinkled death by throwing small bombs around the clock on the entire city, and their low-flying pilots machine-gunned anything that moved on the streets. As a result, the houses displayed their wounds shamefully, showing their wire and iron innards, and as we entered Mrs. Schneller's apartment house, a shower of bombs made it shake like a cheap canvas stage set when an actor accidentally bumps into it.

The house seemed totally abandoned until we discovered that everybody had moved to the cellar weeks before, as had the rest of the entire city.

We found Mrs. Schneller in a corner of the basement furnished with a mattress, a little table with a chair, a small chest of drawers, and a hanging blanket to provide a semblance of privacy. Even as we embraced, she was furtively looking around, and when I mentioned to her that we hoped we could stay there, sleeping anywhere on the floor of the basement, she whispered to me that a few meters away there was a family whose son was in the Arrowcross Militia and was always looking for Jews in hiding.

We fled a few minutes later, but first she gave us an amazing gift: two pairs of gorgeous wool stockings, which warmed our hearts as well as our feet. I kissed her, and we left feeling like orphans who had just been kicked out of a prospective home.

Walking the streets, we felt lost, desperate for any place to stay for the night.

CHAPTER 4

Naked Among the Cannibals

W E WERE CROUCHING in doorways, trying to make ourselves invisible, when a bunch of Arrowcross hooligans passed by, herding a handful of Jews wearing yellow stars. Other goons were shooting at the low-flying Russian planes with their submachine guns, and the general cacophony was almost unendurable.

Most of the time, people are afraid of the unknown. But standing on the street, with the dark of the evening fast approaching, I was more frightened of the known.

We kept walking toward the Pest side of the city, and after crossing the Elizabeth Bridge, we ran into a building when the air-raid sirens began to howl. Instead of going down to the cellar, we ran upstairs—a good part of the stairway was still negotiable—and broke into the first apartment we found on the second floor. Only one wall had bomb damage, and some of the furniture was still there. We made two beds out of a few upholstered chairs and slept through the night like pampered guests in a five-star hotel, barely noticing the occasional explosions.

The next morning we began our search for some way to continue our lives. Before our escape, a fellow labor-camper had spoken to me about his friend, Jenő Kális, who was in a Zionist underground cell, and he had given us an address in Budapest that was supposedly a meeting place for a handful of its members.

It took us a long time to find the apartment house, which was pock-marked with the usual bullet holes. We walked up to the third-floor apartment whose number Kális had given, where we knocked and knocked and knocked some more. It was five very long and tense minutes before a bearded, ancient-looking man slid the inner lock open but left the chain on, which allowed us to blurt out that we had just escaped from labor camp and were looking for Jenő Kális. With feverish urgency in his voice, he told us that Kális had gone, and begged us to leave at once. Distressed, we walked down the stairs slowly so as not to call attention to ourselves.

Next on our list of possibilities was a printing shop owned by a gentile war widow, Mrs. Felsenfeld, whose name I'd received from another labor-camper. He told me that this woman hated the fascist regime passionately, that she might help us in getting false papers for Ágnes. Her shop was not too far away, although on our way there, as we passed by the unburied bodies of people killed by the Arrowcross, the numbing fear that I thought I had conquered returned.

But we got there safely, and entered the front room of the shop, filled with huge stacks of Jew-hating leaflets printed in bold letters, which Mrs. Felsenfeld was forced to produce for the Arrowcross party on her ancient-looking press. First we asked casually for directions to a street nearby, and I dropped the name of the person in our labor camp who had sent us. Clearly, Mrs. Felsenfeld did not like to deal in mysteries, because her reaction was direct. Without missing a beat, she turned on the radio and continued her work.

"What do you need?" she asked in a flat voice.

"Papers for a family of three in a Swedish safe house, so we can get them out of there," I replied while looking behind me, expecting to feel a gun barrel pressing into my back. I wrote down the vital statistics for Ágnes, her mother, and Mari, her baby sister, guessing at much of it, and in less than half an hour she handed us the papers. I mumbled something about paying her after it was all over, but she just raised her head, indicating the door to the street. Finally I had what I came for, a chance to save my girlfriend and her family, and we were on our way to Légrády Károly Street to one of the Swedish protected houses.

All Hungarian Jews not in labor camps had been deported during the summer of 1944 from every Hungarian community, but those who lived in Budapest had been left for last. Deportation had been stopped in July by Regent Horthy, and the estimated 100,000 Jews still living in the capital of Hungary were compressed into a ghetto in less than a week's time.

Within the apartments, each room housed one or more families, a stationary version of the inhumanly jammed cattle cars that carried their doomed human cargo to the concentration camps. The ghetto in the center of Pest was walled and fenced in, and even the superior officers couldn't control the young thugs, who enjoyed unlimited power. Groups of them would pick a house at random and break into the apartments at night, screaming and slaughtering indiscriminately, then forcing those who were not killed to carry out the bodies to the yard or the street. Almost as many died of hunger, and the ones who could not bear to wait for the end escaped by choosing death, jumping out of the windows on the highest floors.

During the same period, the awesomely effective Raoul Wallenberg was able to make an agreement with the Szálasi government's minister of foreign affairs to designate a number of apartment houses for Jews, who would receive a *Schutzpass*, or safe-conduct pass, to be issued by one of the neutral governments. These buildings were officially designated "safe houses," each one marked by a Star of David. A limited number of passes were given out, by the consulates of Sweden, Switzerland, Spain, Portugal, and the Vatican, and the few who were able to obtain one had the right to move into a particular building. The Jewish tenants of the houses had to allow whoever had a safe-conduct pass to move in with them.

The tenants in each safe house organized an around-the-clock guard duty, but having no arms or authority, they couldn't stop the plundering Arrowcross from breaking in. For a while these *védett házak*, or protected houses, seemed to work, and quite a few of the blessed diplomats, Red Cross officials, and priests earned their canonization. In addition to Wallenberg, the papal nunzio Angelo Rotta must be in every survivor's nightly prayers. He had the skill of a superb diplomat, the resolution of a marathon runner, and the kindness of Saint Francis of Assisi. A large number of heroic Catholic priests and nuns did not follow the Church's official attitude of nonintervention, and put themselves in danger by saving Jews and others, during this shameful period of Hungarian history.

We didn't see any male adults who were not in uniform on the streets, and that made us feel even more vulnerable. An underground gas pipeline must have been hit nearby, and the combined stench of leaking gas and flame-melted asphalt gave us another preview of hell.

Finally we arrived at the Swedish protected house where Ágnes and her family were confined. After a nasty confrontation with two Hungarian military police, we entered the building, which was a fairly typical middle-class apartment house. It took time to walk up to the second floor, because every two or three steps were occupied by someone trying to rest on a backpack staring at the ceiling. After a confused search, I found Ágnes's mother and Mari, her baby sister. The three-room apartment was occupied by probably more than twenty people, huddled in a corner of the bedroom with only a single toilet and barely any water to drink—never mind bathing. There was no space between bodies; it didn't seem possible that they were able to stretch out at night.

At first Ágnes's mother, holding the baby in her lap, trying to stop her crying by dangling a little doll in front of her, barely acknowledged my presence. Finally she looked up at me, her eyes red from long hours of crying, and said, "*Gyurikám,* they took Ágnes away two days ago! I can't even kill myself because Mari needs me."

"Come with me," I pleaded. "I have false papers that prove you are a Protestant schoolteacher. I think it will work," I said, handing over the ID cards I'd received from the print shop.

"No, I'll stay here," she said in a hoarse, mournful voice. "Maybe the Swedish consulate will be able to protect us. How can I run with my baby?"

I wanted the details of what had happened to Ágnes, but I felt it would be too cruel to press her, so I left the room and tried to find out from others in the apartment what had happened. The only answer I got was that two nights before, a bunch of Arrowcross ghouls came in, brandishing guns, and gathered up a number of young women, laughing and shouting, "Now these Jewish bitches will learn what real work is!"

Back on the street, not knowing what to do next, we trudged along the Danube toward the next station of our Jewish calvary. For the first time since my days in camp and since we'd arrived in Budapest, my usually resourceful mind provided no possibilities. I felt naked among the cannibals.

Our nightmare continued as Satyú and I saw, from a distance, lines of Jews along the river, being herded by screaming Arrowcross thugs. They were making a game of frightening their victims—children with their mothers, and a few old men. They would shoot above their heads and in front of their feet, and if they accidentally killed someone, they argued about whose kill it was. An old woman carrying a bag couldn't keep up with the rest, and one of the despicable bastards smashed her head with the butt of his submachine gun and yelled, "I hope you have some gold in your bag!"

We tried not to look as she lay writhing and gasping on the frozen ground, and I was just about to pull out my revolver regardless of the consequences, but I remembered that when I had stolen it I had had so little time in the ammunition depot that I hadn't bothered to find the bullets for it.

I don't know how long we walked furtively along the blue Danube—the blue in those days was tinted with the blood of thousands of victims—before we got away from the Danube Corso to the adjacent blocks, lined with middle-class apartment houses, many of them aflame. We passed huge heaps of crumbled bricks and broken glass, twisted tram tracks, cadavers of horses, gaping bomb craters, and broken pipes oozing sewage.

Logic is an important tool, but it is a servant of complex forces within us that we cannot fully control, and often we are unable to explain the sources of our actions and motivations. Passing by a sign that read, JOIN THE ARROWCROSS BRIGADE, I turned to my friend and said: "Let's do it, I bet you we can get away with it!" The idea was so sudden and so absolutely absurd that he followed me as though hypnotized.

The second-floor recruiting office had obviously once been an apartment, though the slogans plastered all around the room, and huge pictures of Szálasi and Hitler, changed its character somewhat. An odious bunch of Arrowcross "brothers" were moving listlessly around, acting as though they were grocery delivery boys between errands, which was probably just what they had done before October 15.

I felt as if I were on the stage of our high school auditorium, far from the bloody scenes we had left on the street. I looked at them boldly, blurting out my lines, heedless of the fact that if I got a bad review, I would not get the chance to do another show.

"We escaped from the clutches of the Russian army in Transylvania, and we are ready to join you in fighting the bastards," I announced in a firm voice.

My declaration stopped the show, but instead of an ovation, silence followed. One of them opened the door to the next room and closed it behind him. A few minutes later we were ushered into this book-lined room. It was probably the study of the Jewish family who had lived there. We were greeted by an elderly man wearing an Arrowcross armband, a holstered revolver, and highly polished boots, yelling in the coarse accent of the lowest of the working classes, "Long live Szálasi!" And he raised his right arm in the Arrowcross salute. Then, in a voice loud enough so everyone could hear in the next room, he said, "If we get a few thousand more like you two, we will win this war in no time."

"Where do you come from?" he asked us.

"From Transylvania," I answered.

"Where in Transylvania?"

"We escaped from Battonya just hours before the Russians occupied it. We are Seventh-Day Adventists hoping to join the Great Cause." I thought of the Seventh-Day Adventist bit on the spur of the moment just in case they found out we were circumcised, which was only done to Jewish boy babies in Hungary. Mind you, I had no idea (and still don't) of the state of the private parts of male Adventists, but for the moment it felt a bit safer. As far as the location was concerned, I was stumped, but only for a couple of seconds, because I remembered that my father had told me about a village he had visited there with that name. Fortunately, neither of us knew that Battonya was not quite in Transylvania, but it sounded convincing enough.

"Both of you are to report to the adjutant of the Vannai Skull Brigade at the Károlyi barracks." He instructed a boy sitting in front of a big black typewriter to make out the order, and again went through the ritual of raising his right arm and extolling Szálasi, before retreating to his room, to do who knows what.

As the kid at the typewriter was looking for a form, we tried to engage him in conversation, which turned out to be quite easy. Although I was tense with fear, I forced myself to act friendly and tough at the same time. He told us that he was leaving the recruiting office and by the next day he'd be reporting to one of the Arrowcross outposts in Buda, on the right bank of the Danube. He was looking at us in a friendly way when his face lit up and he said, "Listen, I can make this paper out so both of you can report to the same place and we could get sort of together, if you know what I mean. . . ." As he spoke, he was watching for our reaction while looking at the closed door out of the corner of his eye.

"Hey, that's a great idea," we said almost in unison, and a short while later we were on our way to Mányoki Street, across the river. Still, no amount of self-hypnosis had been able to make me feel that I was not the same hunted person I had been a short while ago—even with documents bearing the Arrowcross stamp in my pocket. My instincts kept my warning signals at hair-trigger alert.

It took us a long time before we arrived at a handsome villa that—as we learned later—had been seized together with many others in the neighborhood, when their Jewish tenants were taken away. The villa was nestled on top of a gentle hill with the kind of view that usually exhilarates me. But it had no effect on me on that day. I followed the path to the door, and was apprehensive opening it.

There seemed to be very little activity inside, and we couldn't figure out the function of the dozen or so indolent guys, none of whom appeared to be over sixteen, who ambled in and out of the place. Even at dinnertime they just drifted into the kitchen, where an older woman was dishing out a bean-and-potato stew that seemed like a culinary masterpiece to us. Later we learned that she was the wife of the gardener, who was in the army somewhere on the front.

The next day our new friend arrived, and told us the purpose of the post. Apparently, shortly after the October 15 takeover, a few shrewd members of the Arrowcross Militia had decided to proceed to the section of the Buda hills where Budapest's wealthier classes lived. Because the Jews had already been taken away to the ghetto on the Pest side, each of these groups had moved into one of the handsomely furnished villas, where they were free to enjoy what they found there. They were charged to provide the militia with provisions they plundered, but by the time we got there, in mid-December, transportation had made that mission nearly impossible. So they just played cards, drank whatever alcohol they could ransack in the neighboring closed-down Jewish homes and stores, and, incidentally, pillaged everything from the surrounding villas, whatever was easily portable. A couple of the rooms and the entire attic were filled with paintings and other objets d'art, as well as clothing and other stuff—they didn't even know what they wanted, they just took everything. I spotted a few photographs in a garbage can, and it didn't take much time to figure out that their silver frames had found their way into the rucksacks of the "brothers."

The second day we split some wood for the cook and listened to the radio, which was playing nonstop Hungarian marches and spewing hate-propaganda; we could also hear the fireworks provided courtesy of the Russian military forces. I alternated between feeling guilty for playing at being an Arrowcross member and feeling lucky to be there. But then I always considered good luck my birthright. At night everybody tried to find a reasonably comfortable place, and since all the beds were occupied (the house had perhaps four or five bedrooms), my friend stayed in the kitchen, which was the warmest place in the house, and I hunkered down in a corner of the library. Later I stretched out and tried to sleep, without much success.

A young woman at the other end of the room was having the same problem falling asleep.

I broke the silence.

"My name is George Hegedüs. What's yours?"

She was startled at the voice coming from the heap at the other end of the room, and finally answered in a voice so tentative that I barely could understand her.

"Lili," she said.

Haltingly, with pauses between words and sentences, we began to talk about our worlds which had disappeared. She and her mother really were from Transylvania. I never learned how she got to this villa—we were both careful not to ask much about each other's former life. It was useless to pretend that we had any assurance of survival beyond the next few hours and this awareness doubtless had a bearing on what followed.

Suddenly I was ablaze with an overpowering sexual urge, tempered by a complete lack of knowledge of what to do—in spite of my post-adolescent braggadocio.

"You must be cold," I said. "Why don't you come here? Or should I move over to you?"

My voice cracked on the last word. She said something that I conveniently interpreted as "Yes," and I moved over to her corner, bringing the bedspread I was using as a cover. She was fresh and supple, shy and eager, and in this dark corner, surrounded by the monstrous world outside, to which neither of us had contributed, I lost my virginity.

If Satyú hadn't awakened me the next morning, I probably would have slept through the day. I looked around for Lili, but she was already gone. I've always hated unfinished works (with the possible exception of Schubert's), interrupted dreams, and uncompleted relationships. But this one couldn't be finished. Perhaps the incident revealed to me that in sex, the reality could live up to imagination, and that sexual fulfillment could, at least temporarily, remove me from the world.

The following day we were asked to bring back documents to the same recruiting place in Pest that we had come from, since by that time in the city, hand delivery was the only form of communication. With papers in hand, we passed the two guards at the building of the recruiting office and left the large envelope on a desk, sort of ambling in and out to avoid having to report on our activities at Mányoki Street. On the way back we were kidding about the fact that our new home was where, instead of saying "Hello, Mom," we saluted a mad dog like Szálasi. Our musings were interrupted by an air raid. The Russian planes were swooping down with an earsplitting roar, dropping bombs and spraying bullets from their machine guns. We were forced to run into the nearest building—by then, this action had become second nature. We waited a few minutes inside the doorway, but the nonstop explosions and gunfire made us run down to the basement of the building.

Just as the ghettos, *favelas,* and shantytowns throughout the world are more or less interchangeable, so were the look and smell of the honeycomb air-raid basements of Pest during those days. Everybody tensed at seeing two Arrowcross members enter the large basement, filled with what had become the standard arrangements of beds. It was early afternoon, and the only person who was in bed was a young girl. She seemed to me just a pair of huge, beautiful, dark-brown eyes, and unnaturally white skin, with the body of a ten-year-old. A woman was sitting by her, with a worried expression on her face. We had to do something besides smile uneasily. My friend took out his notebook to read it with great attention, and I ambled over to mother and child. It startled me that one of my favorite books, Montherlant's *Les Jeunes Filles,* was on top of her comforter.

The mother, unable to take her eyes off my Arrowcross emblem, told me anxiously that she was an unemployed maid and that Vera was her illegitimate child.

Talking to the girl was not easy. I could barely hear her, and as I stood next to her it became quite obvious that she was closer to fifteen than ten, closer to death than life, and very close to the ethereal beauty that does not depend on the eye of the beholder. Her name was Vera Kaunitzer, and she had tuberculosis. The mother chimed in, explaining to us that she had had pneumothorax, a condition arising from a puncture in the chest made therapeutically to collapse the lung in certain types of tuberculosis.

"Vera must have her medicine and her doctor. Otherwise . . ."

"Where is this doctor now?" I asked the mother.

There was a silence. Then Vera said, "The doctor is in a ghetto house on Hollán Street, and—"

The mother interrupted her. "You see, he is Jewish," she said uneasily, with a shrug and a forced smile. "Many of the doctors are," she added uneasily, trying to gauge our reaction.

When the air raid was over, Satyú and I agreed that he would go back to our Arrowcross base to make sure we could stay there a few more days, and that I would go in search of the doctor. What prompted me to take this insanely risky step may have been partly a romantic notion, but it was also my first chance to take action against the enemy.

By now I had developed a formidable technique of exuding authority, and the armed thugs in front of the ghetto house, after looking at my papers, let me in. The temperature inside the house was not much different from the outside. There was no glass in the windows; the bombings had taken care of that. Pieces of cardboard and wood collected from the wreckage had been used to try to stop the cold from coming in. I found the doctor, who must have been well over sixty, in the basement, taking care of a sick child with a glaucous hue to her face. It was so cold and airless that it surprised me that a candle had enough oxygen to burn. I told the doctor how urgent the situation was, and asked him if he would come with me.

Walking out of the ghetto was much more dangerous than entering it had been, and I held my empty revolver on the doctor as we passed the uniformed thugs at the door, to persuade them of my sincerity. Once we were on the street, I whispered to him: "Doctor, don't be afraid, I am a Jew too!" He must have been through a lot, or perhaps it was his nature, but he showed no reaction.

Instead of going directly to Vera's house, we went to Mrs. Felsenfeld's. She was still churning out the Arrowcross propaganda leaflets so that she would be able to continue her work with the underground. With a false ID plus some other official papers for the doctor, made impressive with a number of fancy Arrowcross stamps, we hurried back to the basement where Vera and her mother lived. My only thought as I saw Vera lying in bed was to do something, anything, to try to keep her from fading away. Her mother put up a sheet hanging on a line stretched alongside the bed to give some privacy while the doctor examined her.

"We must find a pharmacy," the doctor said, as matter-of-factly as if we were living in a normal time and another place.

To this day, whenever I find myself standing impatiently in line in a drugstore, I force myself to remember that visit to the partially bombed-out pharmacy we found a couple of streets away. The outer wall had collapsed, and the antique-looking maze of drawers, shelves, and labeled porcelain jars was surrounded by piles of pills and pools of spilled liquid.

But no one was there. No lines to get annoyed at, no pharmacist, just an abandoned, bombed-out store.

The doctor went searching through the rubble, and after a while announced that he'd found the medicine he needed. We went back to Vera, and he spent several hours with her, then left without showing any emotion. As we parted, he shook my hand and said, "Thank you for the papers. I'm going to try my luck in another basement. Maybe we'll meet after the war."

Vera, who was much smarter than her mother, obviously suspected me of being something other than a softhearted fascist, and after a short introduction we eased into my story and hers. Her father had disappeared in one of the labor camps in the Ukraine, and she and her mother were hiding with false papers, which didn't come as a great surprise to me.

War hath no fury like hunger. A chunk of a dead horse lying on the street was a prime ingredient for a feast, if you could get to the street between two air raids just after the poor animal had been hit by a bullet. Even dried beans and potatoes got scarcer and scarcer. But the doctor had said Vera should have some decent food.

It took me almost all day to get back to our uneasy base in Buda, but I made it, even though I slipped and fell on an icy patch of the road, a mishap that made me limp badly for days. I hoped that it would add to the general impression of a brave young fighter who had been wounded in battle.

My fellow Arrowcross comrades, meanwhile, were busy selectively emptying nearby villas, plundering what they thought was valuable. T'ang Dynasty horses were safe in their display cases, but silverware, clothing, and flea-market oddments found their way to the two adjoining villas, which they used as a kind of storehouse. And food, of course. There were plenty of sardines, all sorts of bacon, huge jars filled with sauerkraut, crackers, rice, jam—it looked to me as an oasis must appear to a lost traveler in the middle of the desert.

The next day, Satyú and I put some of this food into a couple of canvas bags we had found, and told the headman that we had been requested at headquarters to bring some provisions back. It was a pretty safe lie because there was no easy way to verify it, and the Arrowcross boys wouldn't have dreamed of leaving their cushy surroundings to check it out.

We gave enough of the food to Vera and her mother to last for a week, and stashed the rest in one of the empty apartments. We made this trip a few more times, until one day on the way to Buda, a young woman passing us on the street looked at us intently and then ran to a nearby SS soldier, pointing toward us excitedly. My friend recognized her immediately: she was the daughter of one of the janitors of the high school we attended in our hometown. Without missing a beat, and certainly taking a crazy chance, we jumped into the back of a passing military truck, and a few minutes later jumped off and ran into a building at number 13, Szent István Boulevard.

By now we were experts on basements. Life continued there on a thwarted, reduced scale, as though seen through the wrong end of the telescope. We forced ourselves to switch our actions and attitudes from those of the persecuted to the persecutor. I mentioned earlier that one of the games my gang used to play as kids was to enter a store we had no business being in, and then improvise a legitimate-sounding story to avoid nasty consequences. Entering these basement dwellings during the siege and impersonating an Arrowcross Militia member not only took a certain amount of insanity and a lot of guts, but also made use of the techniques I'd learned as a teenager playing our street games.

Our story was that we were fighting during the day and needed shelter that night, then we would switch to another basement and make the same case, navigating between three basements. This went on until opposing players forced an endgame to our charade.

One afternoon we arrived at 13 Szent István Boulevard to find a bald man on crutches talking to a young woman. They stopped in midsentence when they saw us, their eyes brimming with fear. I heard only the word "raid." I stopped and asked them what had happened while we were away. Walking toward the basement, he said haltingly, "We were just told to stay in our places with ID cards ready, because the Arrowcross police are coming to check on everybody."

"They are looking for Jews," said the young woman.

Just then, as if on cue, two young men with Arrowcross armbands passed by us on the way to the basement with a couple of other civilians, one of whom turned out to be the janitor of the building, interrupting our conversation.

Deciding to risk the worst, I confronted them fiercely.

"Do you have the authority to invade our territory, assigned to us by László Vannai himself?" We had heard this name several times at the Mányoki Street Arrowcross house, uttered always with fear. Vannai was the man who had put together the Vannai Skull Brigade, whose members, dressed in black, with a skull on their Arrowcross armbands, were renowned for their sadistic behavior in a roundup.

My question stopped the group for the moment. After a whispered consultation, one of them stepped forward and said, "How about joining us to conduct this checkup?"

It was chancy, but having no other choice, we agreed. During the inspection, when I saw someone who most probably had legitimate papers, I let the policeman look at the documents. We tried to be as canny about it as in a game when someone has to assume the characteristics of a person and the other team has to guess his profession. We took our toughest stance when we accepted the shoddiest, most obviously fake papers. Approaching the young woman I spoke with before, I pushed myself forward and asked for her papers. She gave me a birth certificate and an official-looking paper that said she had escaped from the city of Szeged in southern Hungary, which by then was occupied by the Russians. I immediately noticed that in the box where her religion was indicated, the key word had been scratched out and altered. Gruffly I handed the papers back to her, nodding approval, and moved to the next person. During the next half hour we found another half-dozen Jews hiding with false papers, but in this raid everyone passed inspection.

Later that evening she and her neighbor, the old man on crutches, invited us for a bowl of cornmeal mush, even though, as I learned later, it was the end of her supply. After the dinner, which should have prepared me to hate anything which can be eaten with a spoon, trying to make a party out of it, she wound up a portable gramophone and put on a record of the Mendelssohn concerto that eventually would play a decisive role on several occasions in my future.

First I just listened, infused with glorious music for the first time in quite a while. Then I felt my tear ducts getting full. I changed my seat to face the wall. All the controls were suddenly gone, the tough façade crumbled, and the feared Arrowcross militiaman became a silently sobbing boy. Mrs. Varga—that was her name—afraid I would be noticed by the neighbors, got up and said, "Let's go upstairs for a while." The four of us proceeded to her third-floor apartment and stayed there for a couple of hours before returning to the basement. I learned that her husband was in a labor camp, that she had given birth to a baby recently (who was with Mrs. Varga's mother in the ghetto), and that she was trying to get them out somehow.

I can't say that our lives became those of small-town civil servants, but getting food to a couple of dozen individuals and families foreshadowed my eventual life as a professional provider of food for people.

Through a friend of one of the Jews hiding in that cellar, I was able to connect with a small underground group, and on December 19 I met with Andor Breuer, another Jew in hiding, in front of the Café Upor. He told me that his group was trying to get into the ghetto one way or another, and bring out as many people as they could. They were armed, and he exchanged my bulletless revolver for a Frommer pistol with cartridges. The following day three of them accompanied me to my "home base" in Buda, where my pal and I packed as much food into three flour sacks as we could carry.

On December 24, during my last trip to the Arrowcross villa, we were told that within minutes the men there were going to leave with the German army, taking the only route of escape within the Russian ring around Budapest that was still open toward Germany. And, the leader of the small group added matter-of-factly, we should get ready too. Houdini (who was the son, incidentally, of Hungarian Jews) could have taken lessons from us. Our disappearance was instantaneous, clean, and undetectable on the way to the Pest side of the Danube. We could no longer feed the dozens of people we had kept alive. Every party must come to an end, but we still had a chance to join the advancing Russian army, by now in the hills of Buda.

During the next three weeks, the five of us organized rescue missions in a number of safe houses and yellow-star ghetto buildings, and our little group succeeded in bringing out a couple of dozen people without a shot being fired. To do so, we had to continue to emulate the behavior of the Arrowcross, screaming vile obscenities at the poor people we were dragging out of the ghetto: "You'd better keep quiet, or you'll beg to be shot to end your suffering." One of the ghetto police said, "Look, one has to carry out orders, but you don't have to behave like beasts." I was shaken by this incident, disturbed that my voice had become so like those of our persecutors.

On January 11, in desperation, Satyú and I decided to try to connect with the Russian forces in Buda. The Elizabeth Bridge was still standing, although it was full of holes. Running across the bridge, we dodged the usual machine-gun fire from Russian planes, while teenage Arrowcross fascists shot the helpless thousands of Jews on the banks behind us, afterwards pushing them into the indifferent Danube. When we got to the other side we waited until dinnertime, thinking that perhaps the Russian soldiers would have to rest every now and then, and hoping for a lull in the battle. But just when we were getting ready to run across the few blocks of no-man's-land, the Russians opened fire and we had to hustle back to the Pest side of the city.

Viewed from the distance of fifty-odd years, what I did was not heroic but unavoidable. I believe I inherited my resourcefulness from my father; I felt in the marrow of my bones what he would have done in similar circumstances. I remembered his cunningly resourceful ways—how he had survived by his brains instead of through brawn, only acting with unstoppable rage when there was no other way out.

Then our luck ran out.

On January 13, when Satyú and I got back to the basement of the building on Szent István Boulevard, we were confronted at the entrance by a group of half-drunk Arrowcross thugs. They jumped us, taking our guns and the two hand grenades I had stuck in my belt for extra effect, and shoved their pistols in our backs, herding us to the street. When my friend asked the reason why they were doing this to brother militiamen, they just snarled that we should keep our mouths shut while we still had mouths.

"It was reported what you did during the search for Jews! You two are either Communist saboteurs or Jews or both, and now you'll pay for it!"

"Let's take them to Andrássy Street for processing," one of them said.

They pushed us into an army truck to drive us to the showcase torture chamber of the Arrowcross movement. Between 1945 and 1956 the dreaded Communist ÁVO secret police used it for the same purposes—a sardonic illustration of history's enormous capacity to repeat itself. The truck stopped at the front door while one of our heavily armed brothers argued with the group guarding the entrance and the other kept his gun on us, just in case. Apparently there was no room at the inn and they were told to take us to 2 Szent István Boulevard, a reliable branch of the same chain, which offered the same services without having attained the reputation of 60 Andrássy Street.

The large room in the ground-floor apartment, which must have been the home of a civilized family who had lived there perhaps as recently as a few months ago, was stripped of all furnishings except the dinner table, which was cluttered with props out of a horror movie, such as heavy chains, huge iron clamps and nails, chisels, rolls of heavy rope, and jars of foul-smelling acids. To complete the grisly scene, four or five young men and women were standing, lying, or kneeling in the room, crying, screaming, or just gasping for air. It was not a sight to cheer us up.

The first thing they did was to strip us and examine our penises. Finding that we were circumcised, one of the more violent ones took up a thick metal club, ready to smash our heads.

I blurted out my usual line about being a Seventh-Day Adventist from Transylvania, and that our fundamentalist religion required circumcision . . . we were soldiers who escaped before the Russians took our positions . . . came to join the German army to fight the Russians. . . . But another young thug who was finished with his prey, lying in a corner, came over and hit me with his revolver. The blow broke a few of my teeth, and the next one broke my nose. But then, my profile was not my prime attraction.

Feeling something dripping, I thought that the sudden pain had made me pee, a reaction I had seen in the labor camp, but then I noticed the puddles of blood on my boots. The giggling kid was toying with the revolver he had just used to draw blood. I tried to hold back the scream of pain to deprive him of what he was waiting for, and almost succeeded.

As he was ready to start on Satyú, their commander—or whatever they called the only full-grown person there—shouted, "Stop!" A repulsive look of disappointment appeared on the face of my tormenter.

It's difficult to play a game with someone who holds all the aces, but I sensed that this moment was my only chance to stay alive—at least for a while.

"It's a horrible mistake you are making, and when Brother Vannai finds out, you all will be punished severely."

I knew, of course, that there was no way to find Vannai.

As if on cue, an air raid interrupted my monologue. They herded us down to the coal cellar of the building, shoving us into the almost totally dark space already filled with silent figures. After our guards left, there was a brief exchange of stories about how we got there, but none of us had enough energy left to talk more. We just sat there or moved our arms and necks as a form of exercise, or looked at the different shapes of each piece of coal, trying to force ourselves to sleep.

I sat next to a young woman by the name of Magda Hütterer, who had been there a couple of days without any food. I had a few broken pieces of cracker in my pocket, and I gave them to her.

On the other side of the cellar, Satyú had a chaste romance with a young girl who was caught hiding with false papers, a relationship of the sort that can only happen when both sides realize that the beginning contains the end.

I'd like to think that facing impending execution is different for innocent people than for criminals. Sitting there for long days without food or water made me think of what I would have liked to achieve, and of the few things I had done worth remembering. A condemned criminal, on the other hand, would probably be trying to rationalize his past.

Some of us were grieved about dying so young, while others tried to numb themselves into not feeling. Years later I understood that what we all shared was that we were trying to unbind what tied us to life.

I hesitate to recount the following incident, but it does perhaps illustrate the perverse obscenity of the times. When I tried to relieve myself at the back of the cellar, since they did not let us out all day, one of the young thugs opened the door and, seeing me urinating against the wall, started screaming: "How dare you do this in front of girls?" Then he hit me with the butt of his gun. The following morning he killed one of those same girls.

Remembering those nights, I think I was less afraid of what was to come after death than of the way I would die. At least I knew that I would not be buried alive, because my keepers were much too lazy to dig in the frozen earth. My mind became a slow-motion inventory machine, listing all the things I would have liked to do if I could have lived. Some of those thoughts I confided to Satyú, and it made it easier for me, knowing that he was barely listening. At the top of the list was the wish that I could have learned the Mendelssohn concerto the way it should be played.

I tried to talk to a young man about my age who sat next to me. His emaciated body had been beaten to the point where, when I asked his name, he could barely whisper, "Ernő Steiner." They came to get him a few hours later. Hanging him in front of the Vigszinház Theater didn't take very long, but I understand it takes almost seven minutes for the brain to die.

On the morning of January 19, they forced us to climb the stairs and move out onto the street. Only three of the Arrowcross thugs were still there, not the ones we had had the pleasure of meeting before. The rest had already fled. The remaining trio had obviously been assigned the job of executioners.

The street was completely deserted, but the sound of gunfire and machine guns was like a concerto for a thousand amplified solo percussionists. Knowing that the Russian soldiers were advancing and shooting from the Danube side, just about two blocks away, the three thugs yelled, "Go, run, meet your Russian friends. They love you too," as they pushed us toward the street corner.

I jumped in front of one of the thugs and screamed over the shattering noise, "Brother, we are here for stealing! We made a mistake! But now we are ready to fight the Russians and fight for the cause!" At the same time a few of our group ran toward the Russians, and when our executioners saw that the Russian soldiers had stopped firing, they ran to the corner and, with a seemingly endless burst of fire, shot our fellow fugitives in the back.

Decisive moments are the secret ingredients not only for taking great photographs, but for staying alive. Satyú and I and a couple of others from our group, taking advantage of those one or two minutes of distraction, fled across the street, into the basement of a building.

I don't know if it was minutes or hours later when the first two Russian soldiers burst into the basement yelling, "*Nyemtsi, Nyemtsi?*"— "Germans, Germans?" What I do know is that my first thought was that perhaps now I would get a chance to play the Mendelssohn the way it should be played.

CHAPTER 5

Double Exposure

THE MORAL OF A STORY usually comes at the end, but I will reverse the formula by quoting a fortune cookie that was recently presented to me with the check at a Chinese restaurant. It read, "In the Year of the Snake, whatever hits the fan will not be evenly distributed." It was not the Year of the Snake, but the statement fits 1945, based on the amount of the substance that the fan directed at me that year.

As a wartime soldier, one is caught between the roles of victim and executioner. Only from the distance of so many years am I able to understand the bestial behavior of the Russian forces after they occupied Budapest. They suffered some of their heaviest losses of the war from September 23, 1944, when they took the first village on the southeastern border of Hungary, until mid-April of the following year, when the occupation was completed. Their casualties numbered more than 100,000.

Yet even a saint whose sole responsibility is to absolve sins would have had difficulty understanding their behavior in post-liberation Budapest, which ranged from drunken and despicable acts to gestures of unexpected kindness. When Russian soldiers crashed into a basement full of frightened people, if one of them heard the cry of a child, it was as likely to be a loaf of bread as a revolver that he would reach for.

Among the first Russian words I learned—along with the other Hungarian civilians—were *"Davay chasi,"* or "Give me your watch," which, when spoken by a Russian soldier, were always accompanied by a look that said, "Your money or your life." Apparently watches were not manufactured in Russia at that time, and the soldiers were so fascinated by them that some wore half a dozen on each arm; I even saw a rapturous soldier carrying a grandfather clock on the street. I still wonder if he was able to take it back to Mongolia, where many of the occupying Tolbuchin army came from.

Satyú and I visited several of the people in Pest whose lives we had saved just a short while before, and they in turn saved us from starvation. We ate a few times at the home of Zsuzsa Varga, who lived with her sister, Mrs. Antal Bokor. As in the fairy tales of my childhood, when the hero saved someone from the jaws of a monster and that person turned out to be a king, who then rewarded him with the king's daughter and half of his kingdom, I learned that Zsuzsa, as a glamorous debutante, had married into one of the old and wealthy families of the city of Szeged.

"Why don't you come down and stay with us?" she asked as she and her sister were leaving to return to their hometown. When we said good-bye to them, we felt that perhaps we would be able to get out of the chaos and uncertainties of post-liberation Budapest. All around us, people were leaving the ghettos and safe houses with the few pieces of clothing and oddments they had, only to return to their apartments and find them occupied by another family. The dead had to be buried, buildings close to collapse had to be demolished, and food and medical services were scarce. The only joy was the reunion of family members and friends. We tried to find out about the fates of our parents and other family members, but the rumors changed daily.

Money had little or no value. Inflation was rising so rapidly that by the end of a dinner in a restaurant, you had to pay more than the menu indicated. It took a gold wedding ring to get a chicken or a couple of kilos of flour, brought from the countryside. For quite a few months, Budapest became a city of barter, reminding Latin-educated people that in the ancient Roman empire the name for money came from the word for cattle: *pecus*. Even in English, the word *pecuniary*, from the same root, still refers to monetary matters.

No job was too absurd for me. For instance, there was a law against selling new clothes and such at black-market prices. To make new shoes "old," I was hired to walk in the new shoes for a day so that black marketeers could then sell them as used. On my luckier days, the shoes were almost my size.

Taken in the spring of 1946,
shortly before I escaped to Austria

Walking on the streets of free Budapest had its perils. The Russian soldiers and military police would continually stop people and the second Russian expression everyone quickly learned was *malenki robot,* meaning "a little work." On occasion, Russian military police rounded up anyone who was walking down the street, perhaps for a garbage detail at a nearby Russian military camp. They indicated that you would be let go after a few hours of work, but many times the work turned out to be in a gulag in Siberia, and the few hours became a few months, in some instances years. A friend of mine recalled that he was walking on the street near the Western Railroad station when a Soviet military truck stopped, and a couple of Asian-looking soldiers pushed him into the back of the truck, which was already packed with Hungarian civilians. It took almost three weeks to arrive at a camp near Kovnov, not far from Moscow. After two years of hard labor, they were shipped back to Hungary. In 1961, when our reunion took place, he was still afraid to tell me about life in the gulag. He became permanently paranoid, not unlike some of my friends who returned from labor or concentration camps.

The Russians were collecting not only people but other things too. For instance, I had seen them rip up the parquet floors in an apartment. Such floors were a novelty for them, as well as the ultimate expression of Western luxury. Many of the Russian soldiers robbed, cruelly raped (a redundancy, I know, but there is an added viciousness when, for instance, a mother is deliberately raped in front of her child), and murdered during a rampage that went on for weeks after the occupation of Buda and Pest. This was one of the rare instances in history when people found it advantageous to be old and ugly. Parents would even mask the faces of young girls to make them look like *stary baba*—old grandmothers—dressing them in tattered clothes, and young men would let their beards grow in an attempt to look like unkempt old men on the verge of senility.

What was most demoralizing during this period in Budapest was being confronted with a world in which the rules of civilized society were totally ignored or turned upside down. The victorious Russian army had an unlimited capacity for alcohol of any sort, and gangs of soldiers would even break into museums and drink the ethanol formaldehyde the specimens were kept in, regardless of the contents of the transparent cylindrical beakers.

Our hometown still had not been liberated from the German forces, so we decided to take advantage of Zsuzsa's invitation to her home in Szeged. After waiting all day for a train we could squeeze into, we jumped on a narrow steplike platform when the train started to move rather reluctantly, and jumped off just before it got to each station. It gives me chills to think about how close our legs were to the wheels, but at the time it seemed a perfectly acceptable arrangement.

And then we arrived in Szeged. This second-largest city of Hungary, not far from the Serbian border, had escaped the war by wisely avoiding armed confrontation with the Russian forces, and so it remained a civilized place. I saw properly dressed children there coming home from school, stores open for business, parks, private cars on the streets, women with neat hairdos. What was normal seemed extraordinary, because by then wretched conditions had become the norm for us.

But it didn't take much time for this mental state to clear up. The switch controlling the density of fog in my brain box activated itself, and I quickly grew accustomed to the comforts and the welcoming warmth of the Varga household. It was easy to exchange the bare floors of the basement for a cushy bed and a duvet filled with enough goosedown so that the fairy-tale princess would not have felt a melon, let alone a pea, underneath.

But Satyú felt apprehensive, he had a shy nature and as soon as it was possible, he set out to return to our hometown, Székesfehérvár, which by then had also been liberated from the Germans. He promised me that if there was any news about my parents, he would get it to me somehow. I stayed behind mostly because I wanted to enroll in the famed University of Szeged. One of my favorite poets was giving a course at the university, and that was a compelling enough reason to take Hungarian literature as one of my major courses. To make my curriculum even more practical, I added philosophy. In high school, my performance in literature had been woefully erratic, but here I took the classes and the work assignments very seriously for the short time I was able to attend, and I probably would have ended up as a professor in one of the universities if the unpredictable director of my life had not had plans of another kind for me.

Meanwhile, I cautiously participated in the life of the university, enjoying the attention I was getting at the parties I was invited to. Women, as well as men, were fascinated with stories of my escapades. Success in the theater or in the drawing room depends, to a great degree, on a good plot.

Although I do consider my past affairs a very private matter, I think one of my unusual experiences in Szeged is worth recounting. Among the Russian military police there were quite a few women, and I became friendly with one of them, a robust woman who was a head taller than me. We finally got to the point where I mustered up my courage and invited her for a drink at a *kocsma*, the Hungarian equivalent of a tavern. If a sense of humor in a woman spoils a romance, I should've had the greatest one-night stand of my relatively young life. When I tried to be amusing between drinks, she would look at me as if I were someone trying to tell a joke at a funeral. Finally she lost patience and, grabbing my arm with both hands, pulled me toward the street, hissing, "*Davay, davay!*" "Let's go, let's go!" But in this instance it was a different kind of work I was required to perform. Since the rest of the affair is quite irrelevant to my story, the reader will have to imagine what happened in the room I was occupying at the Vargas' house, which fortunately had a separate entrance.

At one of those parties the hostess introduced me, in lieu of entertainment, as the "hero of the siege of Budapest." Two earnest-looking guys with short-cropped hair and open shirts kept encouraging me to talk about my days as an Arrowcross militiaman. At the end of the party, one of them asked me if I would come to police headquarters the next day to help them in their search for fascists in hiding. I didn't hesitate for a second to accept the invitation. A few days before, I had read in the local paper that Jews returning from concentration camps and ghettos were unable to find their birth certificates because the Arrowcross government had taken some of their records with them to Germany, while escaping from the Russians, and they were now being used by returning Arrowcross militia members in hiding.

The next morning I walked to the police station and asked for the man who had requested my help. They obviously knew about me, and took me up to a grim-looking room. I waited quite a while before a group of people, none in uniform, came in and surrounded me, to ask seemingly routine questions while a stenographer was furiously taking down every word I said.

Then one person who hadn't said anything until then got up slowly and, shaking his fist inches from my face, screamed, "So how many Jews did you kill?"

The startling realization that they thought I was a true Arrowcross member hit me so hard that I was unable to remonstrate or speak at all; the enormity of the accusation paralyzed me into silence.

When they showed me an already prepared document that ordered my arrest for war crimes, to be incarcerated for further investigation, I refused to sign it. I came away from this first confrontation unharmed, but I was taken in a police wagon to the notorious Csillagbörtön, the Star Prison, of the city of Szeged, which was, and probably still is, the Hungarian equivalent of Sing Sing.

The political prisoners awaiting trial had a separate section within the prison, where the cells were more like rooms. But as they locked the door behind me, I remembered vividly the line in an old movie when the protagonist said to himself, after the exaggerated click of the lock, "After this, I'll never be the same again." I had trained myself to be able to turn fear into a challenge, but at that moment I felt disoriented. Being ready to die was a primary reason I had been able to survive the fascist regime, but now, when my turn came to live like a full-fledged human being, I felt lost behind a locked door.

The next night a different group of interrogators woke me up, asking me the same questions over and over again. Not getting the answer they were looking for, they hit me for what seemed like hours, mostly on the bottoms of my bare feet, with a nasty bamboo cane. The single Russian in the group, who clearly ran the show, conducted the torture—he must have learned the technique at home, where it usually yielded the desired confessions for show trials in Moscow. I could see that they were competing to see who could make me talk. They acted like kids pulling the legs off of frogs—except that now it was my legs.

I felt threatened even more than I had during the fascist captivity and torment—after all, this was supposed to be the new world, which was governed by reason. Not having gotten what they were looking for, they returned me to the small room, fully packed with two bunk beds, a couple of chairs, and a small table. I was the fourth inmate and each of us had a number.

What was most disturbing was returning to my cell and enduring the sympathetic reaction of my cellmates. I did not have any proof concerning their activities as fascists, but there was a strong possibility that they were part of the world that had destroyed my family. During the day they were upstanding citizens, but in the middle of the night I could hear them spewing hate. It's a wonder that I was able to remain sane, inwardly hating those who were good to me in that cell and feeling a kinship with those who spat at me on the street when I was being taken from the prison to the courthouse by detectives of the political division of the police.

During the weeks that followed, my interrogators continued to try to squeeze out the confession they wanted to hear, and I had the unwanted opportunity to compare the Communist aptitude with the ingenuity of the Arrowcross Militia for inflicting pain. During one of those excruciating sessions, I realized that one of my roommates must be a planted spy, although he didn't have much to report.

But this was all part of the orchestrated pretrial "preparations" of the accused—ranging from crude psychological manipulation to even cruder physical means, and when they did not get immediate results, my jailers' reaction was increased anger—probably because they were afraid of being demoted to another post with less fun and games.

If I hadn't been so frightened, I might have laughed at the absurdity of the situation. I considered screaming "Let me go, you fools," during one of the torture sessions, but fortunately I was able to control myself. Thinking about it so many lives later, I am surprised that panic didn't choke me, and that I was able to survive without losing my sanity. During the long days and nights, I learned from my well-informed cellmates that by the time the trial took place, the accused usually was utterly broken in spirit. On occasion the presiding judge on a particular case would tip off the official Communist paper as to what the verdict would be, and it would appear in the paper even before the trial began.

"Last month they caught a big fish, and they even threatened his family as well, so he confessed publicly at the trial," one of my fellow inmates told me. What I never learned was whether or not this "big fish" had actually committed the crimes he was accused of, but that seemed irrelevant to my roommates.

The newly formed Hungarian government was not yet officially Communist (that came three years later, in 1948), but from the beginning it was dominated by the crushing presence of the Russian army, and the coalition government's key posts were taken by Communists. So-called People's Courts were established in the larger cities, and during those few years about 60,000 people were arrested, 27,000 were sentenced to prison, close to five hundred were sentenced to death, and 189 were executed for war crimes they were accused of committing. Maybe because my case didn't have any evidence to support it except my own admission that I had been a member of the Arrowcross, and no accusers came forward, it did not promise a great theatrical show, so luckily my torture did not go beyond inflicting pain without crippling me.

One morning a prison guard called my name, and I was taken to a room near my cell where an unfriendly, beer-bellied individual remained seated when I entered. Without shaking hands with me, he said, as if reading from a cue card, "My name is Dr. János Gajzágó, and I've been appointed by the court to be your defense lawyer. Tell me, in your own words, why you are here."

He didn't take any notes, but just listened to my torrent of words. Finally I was able to tell someone what a horrible mistake they had made when they arrested me. He didn't react one way or another to my story. At the end he informed me that my trial was set for May 22, which was a week away, and asked me if I could name anyone who could corroborate my story. When I began to enumerate dozens of names, he interrupted me to ask, "Is there anyone who lives in Szeged whom we could call as a witness, and who would tell the court about your actions during the siege?"

"I am sure Mrs. Vidor Varga and Mrs. Bokor would come, and they do live here," I said.

He made a note of these names, and as he was leaving he said to me, "Well, good luck!" It was a wish I could and did interpret anxiously in a number of ways during the next seven days.

On the morning of the trial, I got an extra slice of bread with my ersatz coffee. They put me in handcuffs and I walked between two guards to the courtroom. It was quite an experience, because, again, the ones who cursed me were cursing at a fascist, while those who were sympathetic were the ones I despised.

I entered the courtroom with my defense lawyer behind me. Looking at the six People's Judges, the presiding judge, and the prosecutor, I was reminded of something my father said once about a client who was very difficult during a fitting: "He's just like you and me, only worse."

When I noticed Zsuzsa Varga and Mrs. Bokor in the row reserved for witnesses, I felt like the hero in some of the adventure books I'd read as a kid, when, at the last minute, he is saved from certain death by his brave friends.

The cast of characters at the public trials of the People's Court consisted of a presiding judge, a prosecuting attorney, a court-appointed defense attorney, six People's Judges, and a court stenographer.

It should be noted again that I had not yet changed my family name from Deutsch to Lang, my mother's maiden name; thus, in the court records, I am György (George) Deutsch.

When I returned to Hungary sixteen years later, I hired an attorney in Szeged who was close to the Communist party, and he was able to obtain a copy of my trial transcript, sections of which are quoted below.

PRÉCIS OF FIRST TRIAL, MAY 22, 1945

The Presiding Judge warns the spectators and swears in the accused. The accused gave the following answers to questions from the Judge:

A szegedi népbiróság.

Nb. 119 / 13. szám.
   1945

A M A G Y A R   N É P   N E V É B E N !

A szegedi népbiróság mint büntetőbiróság háborus büntett miatt Deutsch György ellen inditott bünügyben nyilvános tárgyalás alapján meghozta a következő
           i t é l e t e t :
A népbiróság Deutsch György 21 éves, székesfehérvári születésü, szegedi /Tisza Lajos-krt.52.II.em.8./ lakos, magyar állampolgár, magyar anyanyelvü, székesfehérvári községi illetőségi, németül és franciáúl beszél, nőtlen, katona volt, munkaszolgálatos, gimnáziumi érettségi bizonyitványa van, szülei: Deutsch Simon és Láng Ilona, vagyontalan, bölcsésztanhallgató vádlottat, aki 1945. évi április hó 18. napja óta előzetes letartóztatásban van 1 rb. a Nb.nov.8.§-ával kiegészitett Nbr.13.§.3.pontjának 1.bekezdésébe ütköző háborus büntett miatt ellene emelt vád alól a Bp.326.§.1.pontja alapján felmenti.
A felmerült 2410 /kettőezernégyszáztiz/pengő bünügyi költség a Bp. 483.§.1.bekezdése szerint az államkincstárt terheli.
           I n d o k o l á s :
A népbiróság a vád tekintetében az 504/1945.nü.számu vádirat tartalmára utal.
A vádlott tagadta a bünösségét. Védekezését a 13.sorszámu főtárgyalási jegyzőkönyv tartalmazza.
A népbiróság a vádlott részbeni ténybeismerő vallomása és a főtárgyalás során kihallgatott Varga Vidorné, Bokor Antalné, Kauniczer Vera, Salcz Sándor, Hutterer Magda és Körösi Imre érdektelen tanuk vallomása, valamint a főtárgyaláson ismertetett okiratok tartalma alapján a következő tényállást fogadta el valónak:
A vádlott, aki 1944. március haváig Székesfehérvárott diákoskodott, de ott fasiszta ténykedést nem fejtett ki és akinek a szüleit 1944. évi junius hó 15. napján a magyar fasiszták deportálták és azóta nyomuk veszett, mint az egyik u.n. zsidó munkaszolgálatos állat tagja Komáromba került, ahonnét megszökött és 1944. évi decem hó 13. napján Budapestre érkezett. Itt előbb egy illegalitásban dolgozervezetbe akart elhelyezkedni, de miután kisérlete nem sikerült, a nála lévő leventeigazolvánnyal másnap - vagyis december hó 14-én - a "Hungarista Légió"-ban jelentkezett, ahova december 18-án fel is vették és az alakulat Mányoki-uton volt gazdasági hivatalában nyert beosztást. Nevezett már ebben az időben közölte az ismerőseivel, hogy csak azért lépett be a nyilas"Hungarista Légió"-ba, hogy magán és a szenvedő zsidó ismerősein segithessen.
Ebben a nyilas kötelékben a vádlott 1944. évi december hó 24. napjáig teljesitett g.h. irodai szolgálatot, de ezen a napon, amikor alakulatának tudomására jutott, hogy Budapest majdnem teljesen körül van zárva és már csak a Bécs felé vezető ut szabad, s igy az alakulat eltávozott, közülök megszökött és Hegedüs György névre kiállitott hamis pecsétü hamisitott igazolvánnyal különféle lakásokon bujkált.
Miután g.h. beosztásánál fogva élelemhez hozzá tudott jutni

A page from the court record of my second trial, indicating my acquittal

György Deutsch, single, born July 13, 1924, in Székesfehérvár, Hungarian citizen, mother tongue is Hungarian, speaks German and French, Jewish religion, unmarried, university student with philosophy major, was in the army, can read and write, graduated from gymnasium, indigent. Father: Simon Deutsch. Mother: Ilona Láng. No criminal record.

Presiding Judge notes that witnesses are present and asks them to leave the courtroom.

Court clerk is requested to read the indictment of April 20, 1945.

The accused gave the following answers to questions from the judges:

"I came down to Szeged because there was no food in Pest, but mostly to continue my university studies.

"While a member of the Hungarist Legion, I saved Mrs. Vidor Varga. I also brought her food to the cellar of St. István Boulevard no. 13. Another person I saved was Jenő Grosz, who had a 100-percent war disability. Someone denounced him to the Arrowcross security of his building, and I managed to get the assignment of checking him out.

"Another person whom I was able to help was Vera Kaunitzer."

Much more detailed testimony follows, essentially the same story and the facts as I recounted in the preceding chapter. Here are a few additional excerpts from the court transcript.

Under questioning by the prosecuting People's District Attorney, the accused gave the following answers:

"There are a number of other people whose lives I was able to save, including Mrs. Sebők, who was hiding under the name of Mrs. Kiss, and also her husband, who had false papers as a house painter.

"I was also able to bring a number of false papers to Andor Breuer, a citizen of Dunaszerdahely, who was a member of the underground cell.

[Answering questions:] *"I only met Magda Hütterer, who escaped the massacre of January 18, at the basement where we were all kept. I understand that she lives here and her younger brother is a soldier.*

[To the question of People's Judge Kárász:] *"I did try to escape through the front to the Russians when I went to Buda, but I was not able to do it because the Hungarians were shooting one way and the Russians the other way, and the chances of getting through were virtually nil."*

[To the question of the Public Defender:] *"I was in the labor camp when my family was deported."*

[Testimony of] Mrs. Vidor Varga, née Zsuzsa Schneer, 24 years old, born and currently living in Szeged, Jewish religion, married, mother of one, office worker, disinterested witness in this trial. After being warned, she made the following statement and declaration:

"I was hiding with false papers in the basement of St. István Boulevard no. 13, when I met the accused on the morning of January 3, 1945. He came to stay in the basement about that time.

"That same night, there was a roundup raid. The accused came at around 5 o'clock in the afternoon, and although Arrowcross special security people were making the rounds, the accused came with them. When they got to me, the accused took away the papers, looked at them briefly, and said to the Arrowcross people that they were in perfect order. The accused had an Arrowcross insignia and he wore black army boots.

"The only things I had were a birth certificate and a document indicating that I was a displaced person as a result of the war, but those papers were false.

"After the roundup, I complained to the accused that I was sick and I had no medicine, nor any food to eat. The accused then brought me medicine and food. He told me that he'd got it from an Arrowcross commissary."

[Answering a question:] *"I found out that the accused is Jewish because at one point, I put on a record in the basement featuring a violin concerto. While listening to the music, tears came to the eyes of the accused, and he told me that he couldn't take it anymore. He also confessed to me that he too was a Jew. He told me that he went to the Arrowcross recruiting office so that he could save himself and help other Jews as well. He also told me that there were others hiding in different parts of the basement.*

"No, the accused did not receive or accept anything for the food.

"Later, the accused was caught at our building at St. István Boulevard no. 13 by the Arrowcross police, and they took him and his friend away for interrogation. I did not divulge that I knew that the accused was Jewish."

[After the witness was confronted with her previous testimony:] *"In the political division of the Police, I gave the same details as I have done now at this trial.*

"The building I lived in, as well as the accused, had eighteen Arrowcross legionnaires.

"To my knowledge, the accused helped, among others, a Jew named Rappaport and a poor Jewish family from his hometown as well.

"Once, a woman looked me up who lived on Klotild Street, as well as another young woman. They told me that György Deutsch had brought medicine and food to them, and now they didn't know what had happened to him."

[To the question of the Public Defender:] *"When the accused returned from Buda in army uniform, he did not mention anything about participating in military action against the Russians.*

"That is all I'm able to say."

No one made other comments during this testimony.

District Attorney suggested that the witness should be sworn in.

Public Defender did not object.

The People's Court ordered Mrs. Vidor Varga, witness, to take the oath. After being warned, she did so.

Witness did not request compensation for appearing.

[Testimony of] Mrs. Antal Bokor, fifty years old, born in Szeged, citizen of Budapest, Roman Catholic religion, divorced with one child, milliner.

After being warned, she gave the following testimony:

"The only thing I know about the accused is what Mrs. Varga told me. In the beginning of January 1945—I don't remember the

exact date—she told me that she wasn't going to come to have some
food because an Arrowcross boy was bringing food to her.

"After the Russians came in, the accused occasionally came to our
house to eat, because he had nothing. When we left Budapest and
came to Szeged, we invited him to stay with us so he could straighten
out his life.

"That is all I'm able to tell."

Witness was sworn in after being warned of consequences
of false testimony.

The People's Court made the following declaration: they
will order the continued arrest for an additional thirty-day
period, and agreed with the Public Defender's request that
some of the many people whose lives the accused saved should
be summoned as witnesses for the next trial.

People's District Attorney did not object.

It was requested that the investigation should continue in
greater depth, and a new trial date should be set when the
investigation was completed.

Presiding Judge declared this part of the trial as over.

I kept looking at the mustache of the judge as he was talking, wondering if the scene would dissolve and I would wake up in my bed. The
combination of my arrest and being the subject of a monstrous plot with
an ending that could be the end of my life, made me so dizzy that I was
stumbling and had to be supported by the two courtroom policemen.
They hauled me out of the courtroom so fast that I didn't even have a
chance to say hello to the two women, but I saw Zsuzsa waving at me
trying to tell me something.

Back at the ranch, my three roommates bombarded me with questions, mostly trying to get tips on how to play the game and how to avoid
the evidence with which they would be confronted when their trials
came up.

During the night I kept telling myself that I was stronger than they
were. I knew the truth would win out in the end, and I would not make
their job easier.

For almost a week the prison officials let me alone, but then they staged a scary episode in their ongoing attempt to rewire my brains. I was taken to the old section of the prison, into a dark room with a bunch of prison guards lining the walls. There was no sound, no conversation; they just stared at me grimly. Finally the same prosecutor who had confronted me at the trial came in. He looked at me for quite a while without saying a word. Then he said in a very even, quiet voice, "My people will ask you again the same questions, and you'd better give the right answers this time." As he was leaving the room, I noticed that he gave an almost imperceptible signal to the prison staff.

I felt, instinctively, that these people needed the ecstasy that their power to hurt me gave them, and that if my response was not agonized enough, they would escalate the torture.

But it was a no-win situation. Steeling myself, I tried to endure the nonstop barrage of blows and the burning cigarette held against my feet (I had to remove all my clothes), while four of them tried to tear me apart by tugging my arms and legs in different directions. The worst was the last kick in my chest; I didn't think I would ever breathe again. Just when I was ready to confess to being a mass murderer, they suddenly stopped. My eyes were filled with tears, but I could hear that someone had come in. In a voice full of compassion, he told the men to stop and to bring me a glass of water. I tried to wipe my face, but just made it more bloody. I was surprised how salty my blood tasted.

He played the good-cop/bad-cop game flawlessly, explaining to me that these people, against his will, had been told to get the truth out of me, but that he was intervening to let me have a chance to think it over for a few days. I knew that he was lying, but I couldn't help liking him for his seemingly helpful, friendly attitude. It was like grasping for a speck of human kindness in a cruel, inhuman world.

I was brought back to my cell. A prison guard appeared with food, if you could designate a muddy liquid with some unidentifiable objects swimming in it as such, served in a chipped enamel bowl. I suspect that they put a purgative into it, and because they didn't let me go to the toilet when I banged on the door, I was forced to defecate in the cell. This is a time-honored tactic designed to destroy the identity and sense of dignity of the prisoner. They were well on the way to achieving this in a very short time.

I tried to think of good things in my past life, like the perfect day of my bar mitzvah, when my uncles came from different parts of the world

A portrait of me by a cellmate

for a great July garden party. I have often wondered since how long it would have taken before I cracked under such conditions, what was the limit of my endurance?

Because of Zsuzsa Varga and her sister, I didn't have to find out the hard way. They got in touch with a number of people in Budapest whose lives had intertwined with mine for a short while, and they hired a well-connected local lawyer by the name of Dr. Loránt to take my case.

Several things happened in rapid succession: I was put into a solitary but standard-issue prison cell; Dr. Lóránt came to talk to me, discussing the case in detail; permission was granted for me to receive daily luncheon from the outside, arranged by my friends, as well as to have a visitor twice a month. Dr. Lóránt told me that the People's Court was so overcrowded with pending cases that my trial might be delayed as long as several months. The best news he brought me was that they would allow me to receive books as long as the censors at the Csillagbörtön prison approved of the choice. During one of our meetings—which was monitored by a guard, fortunately one possessing minimal intelligence—he told me in subtle phrases that as the country was inching towards a total Russian-style Communist dictatorship, they would try to make the upcoming trial even more of a show trial than before.

Among the visitors I received were the Kiss sisters, two attractive and brainy teenagers I had met at a party during the pre-arrest days, when we played an innocent version of the grownups' ménage à trois. Our only commitment was to enjoy each other's company. The three of us would spend several pleasant hours in the local park and museums, where the expenses were just right for my pocketbook. I was just about to make a choice between the dark-eyed beauty, almost a woman, and the pert blonde, when the Csillagbörtön prison called me away. During the prison visit they played out their fantasies of bravely visiting the persecuted hero, making me even more eager to become free again.

Instead of the court-specified one month following the first trial, the second took place on September 6, 106 days after the first one. It was assigned to a larger courtroom, and I was surprised how full it was when I entered between two armed guards. I almost cried out when I saw so many of the people whose names I had mentioned during my interrogations—they were real, and not just figments of my warped imagination, as even I had begun to suspect by then. I learned later that twelve of them had hired a small bus to come from Budapest to Szeged, a major undertaking in those days.

Of the six People's Judges, only one was the same as at the first trial. The presiding judge, Dr. Sándor Csaba, remained, as did the prosecuting district attorney, but this time Dr. László Lóránt conducted my defense. The audience was warned not to express their opinion one way or another. Then the prosecutor made an impassioned speech, making me out to be an evil mass murderer, who must be punished by being sentenced to death as an example for the future.

I was called to the stand, where I gave my testimony, which, according to the transcript, was virtually identical to what I'd said at the first trial, with some additional details. Following my testimony, Mrs. Varga and Mrs. Bokor were sworn in as witnesses, and again they related their encounter with me between December 1944 and January 1945.

Then a fragile, almost transparent apparition of a girl took the stand. It was Vera Kaunitzer, in a prim school uniform, with her braids almost reaching her waist.

What follows are a few excerpts from the extensive official court transcript:

[Testimony of] Miss Vera Kaunitzer, 15 years old, born and lives in Budapest, student, disinterested witness.

"We were hiding with my mother at Szemere Street no. 17. He brought us food, and even found vitamin pills.

"The accused, appearing like a real Arrowcross lad when I was sick for two weeks living in the basement, brought out, in the midst of the heaviest bombing attacks, Dr. Marcel Rózsa, a physician from a building in the ghetto, clearly endangering his life. The accused behaved toward us in an exemplary manner."

The next witness was Sándor Salacz, 32 years old, born and lives in Budapest, married with one child; profession, sculptor; disinterested witness.

"I'm aware of the fact that the accused escaped from the labor camp in order to save Ágnes Weisz, and to find false papers for her.

"I consider the accused an extremely decent person."

The next witness was Imre Kőrösi, born in Székesfehérvár, lives in Budapest, merchant, married, and disinterested witness.

[Answering a question from a People's Judge:] *"Yes, I am aware of the fact that he helped quite a few Jewish people in hiding. A number of people told me how many times the accused brought food and helped in every possible way."*

Presiding Judge (after official procedures, declarations, and such) considered the testimonies to be completed without calling other witnesses since the Court had heard and received enough evidence about the activities, character, and history of the accused.

People's Prosecuting Attorney in his statement continues his original premise about the accused's guilt.

The defense attorney, recalling testimony of witnesses, requests a verdict of not guilty.

Following a period of deliberations during which the Judges of the People's Court weighed the evidence, the Presiding Judge declared in a public session the enclosed judgment, including detailed reasoning thereof.

VERDICT.

Based on the investigations and witnesses' testimony, it is unquestionable that the accused became part of the Arrowcross Legion and performed insignificant activities therein.

Based on all facts, however, the activities of the accused were directed exclusively toward helping his despondent fellow humans living under abject conditions, bringing medicine, doctors, and food to them, and these activities certainly did not help in the continuation of the power of the Arrowcross movement—which was the main point of the charges.

Furthermore, his activities were actually instrumental in the cessation of the Arrowcross power.

The decision of the People's Court is that, in addition to these facts, a compelling and imperative emergency situation justified the actions of the accused in joining the Arrowcross Legion; thus, based on applicable laws, no guilty action exists.

Therefore, the People's Court unanimously declares that the accused committed no crime of any kind, and for the lack of criminal action based on Bp 326&.1., it acquits him.

Szeged, September 6, 1945

Signed by six People's Court Judges,
As well as the Presiding Judge and the
Court stenographer.

In spite of the request of the District Attorney not to release the prisoner, the People's Court ordered the immediate release of the accused, and considered the proceedings final.

Addendum: The 1,600 plus 1,750 pengő expense, was assigned to an existing budget for such purposes.

What was left out from the official record was the fact that the Presiding Judge, before delivering the verdict at the end, asked me if I had anything to say. By then, my fear and apprehension had turned into an embittered frustration tinged with bravado, and I made the following short statement, looking each judge in the eye, one by one.

"Although I am not a Christian, I consider Christ a great philosopher, whose ethical teachings should be followed by the entire world.

"I do *not* agree, however, with the prayer that includes the plea, 'Lead us not into temptation. . . .'

"Without having been tempted to abandon the Judeo-Christian ethic in order to save your life, none of you can ever know how you would have behaved, what you would have done, just to survive. Yet you are sitting in your chairs judging me, who withstood this temptation."

The spectators began to cheer at that point, but the guards' threatening motions stopped the demonstration cold, as well as my speech, and the Presiding Judge began to read the above sentence.

While I was collecting my belongings at the prison office, I was pulled aside by an officer whom I had not seen before. He asked me in a very low tone if I would be interested in joining a division of the secret police just being formed. Struggling to control my anger, I just mumbled something about wanting to return home.

CHAPTER 6

You Can't Go Home Again

*A*FTER THE TRIAL, there were toasts and hugs, and stories about the most un-Christmaslike Christmas we had all lived through. The celebration went on until midnight, when the last guest left the Vargases' living room. Saying good-bye to Zsuzsa, I felt that, on the whole, to be is better than not to be, even though my future looked bleak at the moment.

In prison, I had had no way of finding out whether my parents or any other members of my family had survived and returned home. I was overwhelmed when the Budapest contingent offered to take me to my hometown on their minibus. Even before I had put my few belongings down at Satyú's place, I ran around town to try to get some news about my parents. I found only a few people who had come back from Auschwitz, and one of them was able to tell me about my parents' fate. The story took most of the night.

"You know the brick factory on the outskirts of the town," my informant began. "This was the place where we were herded. Your father tried to convince us that the Hungarian government and the army would save us from the Germans, and the brick factory was only a step in that direction. He felt that we would make it somehow."

Actually, he was almost right. If he had lived in Budapest, his optimism would have been almost justified.

As I learned the details of the deportation during that night, it became clear that the devil's paymaster must have recruited a few people to stand along the streets while my parents and the others were herded toward the brick factory. Quite a few of the townsfolk who had lived and worked with them all of their lives committed the crime of cruel indifference, and others spewed their repressed hate at this inhuman procession.

If the voice of the people is the voice of God, it's one more proof that God cannot be trusted, I thought as I heard the accounts.

"Your mother could not bring herself to touch the few bites of food they had thrown to us during the weeks before they took us to the cattle cars. She said that eating nonkosher food would betray everything she believed in, even though in Jewish law it is permitted to disregard *kashrut* 'to save a life.' By the second week she was hardly able to get up from the bare ground where we all slept inside the compound. The foreman of your father's tailor shop, István Halvax, smuggled in some vegetables and fruit, which kept her alive.

"When we arrived at Auschwitz, they lined us up, and those who were too weak to work were sent to the left, to their death. Your father wouldn't leave your mother, not even for a minute, and even though they told him to go to the right, which would have meant survival, he moved with your mother to the side of death, leading directly to the gas chambers."

I have always known that my father couldn't live without his beloved Ilonka. I know that their love endures somewhere.

There is a monument in Székesfehérvár, my estimable and doubly cursed hometown, bearing the names of the martyrs who were executed on October 15, 1944, when the Arrowcross terror began. István Halvax is listed along with other good people, bless his memory.

Early in my adolescence I had trained myself in the art of selective hearing—it was part of my survival technique—but I was never able to learn the art of selective feeling. Even after learning about the details of the last weeks of my parents' lives, I refused to accept it as a finality, and I would wait for their return. It was an aching, day-to-day and night-to-night subsistence and my hopes would be strengthened when a member of someone else's family did come back. A half-century later there are still moments when I feel that they are waiting for me somewhere.

A result of my self-torment was that I had an almost nonstop pain in my solar plexus, the kind of pain I used to feel when I received a blow there during my short period of amateur boxing. The doctor I went to see had no answers beyond the obvious references to my recent ordeal, and it took about a year before the pain disappeared.

In the fall of 1945, for the first time living in my hometown as a full-fledged citizen, I encountered a few people who seemed sympathetic, but it stopped the minute I quietly asked for the return of what had been ours. I found our house occupied by a mailman and his family. When we sat down in the front hall, which my father kept as a year-round indoor garden, overlooking the big acacia tree shading the round marble table we used for outdoor dining, the mailman looked at me and said portentously, "We have suffered too. . . ."

Nations have short memories after they have occupied other countries' territories for a time, and individuals have a similar penchant for self-delusion about rightful ownership. Having lived in our house for over a year by then, this family felt it was their home, and when I took legal steps to reclaim it, they considered me an intruder (typical of my race) who was trying to take it away from them.

Looking at his children running around in the playground of my childhood, and seeing his wife cooking in the kitchen, cooled my resentment. In a way, I saw that family as my own, and felt a measure of sympathy. Some of our furniture was still there: my father's prized walnut bedroom armoires, the depleted bookcase that looked like the mouth of someone with lots of missing teeth, my mother's framed Gobelin that was the only art that graced the dining room wall. Remembering her working on it for long months, usually after we had finished dinner, was a disquieting feeling.

During the next few weeks I visited a few of my gentile schoolmates, trying to bridge the gap between us. I was not expecting them to weep for the six million, but only for my parents, whom they had known well. Several of them behaved like compassionate friends, but as I listened to others, it became clear that they had clung to their prejudices. I found that in my hometown everybody had some rationalization for doing what they did during the war, and good conscience in postwar Hungary was mostly the result of poor memory. They didn't compare their feelings and behavior toward Jews with fundamental ethical values, but with the national pattern of anti-Semitism around them.

One evening while I was visiting a neighbor of mine, we tried to reconstruct the past, and the subject came up of my parents and friends who had not returned from concentration or labor camps. His teenaged son asked the inevitable question: "Why did it happen?" The father was a teacher in one of the local high schools, and he explained to his son that the Jews in Hungary had led, prior to the war, lives relatively free of the sort of persecution that was common in neighboring countries, but that the Germans had changed all that. A sensitive person, he added that Auschwitz was not only a Jewish tragedy, and that the perpetrators were affected even more. Part of me was desperately seeking for reasons to be able to forgive, but at that point I couldn't. As the Hungarian poet Magda Székely wrote, "Whom can I forgive for a crime that no one owns up to?"

After much hesitation, I decided to hitchhike my way to Mezőko-márom, my father's village, to reclaim my violins. The benevolent wheat had kept them in good condition, and my father's childhood friend returned the double violin case to me. Of my mother's jewelry, only a gold bracelet remained; the rest had supposedly been taken by Russian soldiers. Anyway, I hadn't expected him to return everything, and he came through.

While waiting to move back to our family house, I stayed with child-hood friends who had returned from labor camps and moved back to their families' homes. I found myself moving again from house to house, but at least I didn't have to worry about being a hunted specimen in the jungle, and I achieved a minimal subsistence by selling my mother's gold bracelet. It was a couple of months before I received the court order, and still more time before I was able to move back to our family house. It was an eerie feeling, being alone there, without my parents, without the usual sounds, smells, activities, arguments, and exchanges of affection; in other words, without the life of our family. I was not sure whether I should try to bring back my childhood or run away from it, but I did attempt to gather fragments of my family and my own past.

As I walked around our neglected, abandoned, and forsaken garden, it seemed to me like another relative who had died. At the end of the gar-den my father had built a little shack for his gardening implements. It was overflowing with broken furniture and decomposing refuse, and that was where I found a faded, brownish photo of my parents' wedding, with my maternal grandfather sitting in the front row, wearing a top hat. Now, fifty-three years later, it is the dedication page of this book.

I desperately yearned to get back to a great violin teacher. After a strenuous audition, I was fortunate to receive a scholarship from Imre Waldbauer, a chamber music professor at the Academy, whose legendary string quartet had introduced Bartók's first quartet. Once every couple of weeks I traveled to Budapest for my lessons, practicing diligently in between.

One happy day, I learned through a former classmate of mine who had gone to grammar school with me and who had been in Auschwitz, that my cousin Évi had returned, and was living in Budapest. Our reunion was joyous, but as we tried to cope with the loss of both sets of our parents and grandparents, and of her little sister, Győrgyi (Georgina), our joy was tempered by the unspoken understanding that we both had to learn to accept what is unchangeable. I am still amazed that in the attempt to acquire a kind of artificial insensibility, we were able to retain our sanity. While I was still in prison, our uncles in America, through the American legation, had located Évi and sent not only some money but the kind of love and concern that was an innate part of our family, which was a powerful panacea in our lives.

For a long time it had troubled me that my family name, Deutsch, meant "German," and during this period I went through a long process with the Ministry of Interior to change it officially to my mother's family name: Láng. Its Hungarian meaning has no relation to the Anglo-Saxon *Lang—Long—Laing;* in Hungarian, Láng means "flame."

The first and only letter I received during this period came from my labor-camp savior, Sergeant Lengyel, who knew my home address. He got in touch with me after I returned from Szeged, and we corresponded even after I got to America, and I used to send CARE packages to him. The envelope I received from him contained a letter that Ágnes, my

Vera Kaunitzer in Budapest, 1946

piano partner and girlfriend, had written me; I had given her Lengyel's home address when I was in the labor camp.

Looking at the yellowed pages in front of me, I tried to imagine the chain of little miracles that must have occurred so that I could receive this parting outcry from Ágnes, on her way to Bergen Belsen. It was one of the few pieces of paper that I kept with me on the voyage to America, and I was distressed later when I thought I had lost it.

Then, a few days after I decided to write this story of my life, I was standing on top of the rolling ladder of our library, in order to get down an anthology of Hungarian poems. As I was searching for one of my favorite stanzas, two sheets of paper fell out of the book and floated down to the floor, twenty feet below. It was Ágnes's letter. Here is my translation of it:

1944, Day of Santa Claus

Dear Mr. Lengyel!

I would very much appreciate your giving these words to Gyuri Deutsch.

My dear Gyuri darling, I am in Komárom, in a wagon at the railroad station. They took me away from Mom and Mari. I left them standing there alone—my heart is going to break!

I was waiting for you! Or at least a letter!

My hands are in dire condition, and I don't know if I ever will be able to play the piano.

I vaguely remember you once quoted: "There is nothing more painful than remembering beautiful times during bitter periods." Now I really understand Dante's words.

As many of us as there are, we are scattered in that many directions. What's going to happen?

Gyuri, you said good-bye forever in the doorway of Park Street. I could do this now with a reason which is much more real. But I won't. I won't!!!

I trust fervently that we will have a happy reunion.

Gy! I want awfully to live. TO LIVE!

Gyuri! . . . well now . . . I am saying good-bye again. I don't know where or when, but I am positive that we will meet again!!!

With a horribly anguished heart I embrace you.

Ágnes

The Verdi Requiem is with me, and the Bible . . .

CHAPTER 7

Lifting the Irony Curtain

S A KID, I ALWAYS tried to see any movie that starred my hero, Tom Mix, and I watched with admiration as he was always in the right place at the right time, holding his never-miss guns with nonchalance as he eliminated the bad guys. But by the age of twenty-two, I learned that—in the language of gamblers—it is not holding a good hand that is important, but playing a poor hand well. Fate had dealt me a lousy hand in my native country and with every new day I felt that I would have to try my luck elsewhere. The most logical place was America, as I had two uncles living there, so I quietly began to make plans to emigrate somehow, and as soon as possible.

Soon after returning to Budapest, my cousin Évi, who had wondrously survived Auschwitz, married Victor Aitay, the concertmaster of the Budapest Opera House. The CARE packages and several money orders we received from Uncle Lajos and Uncle Eugene, who had emigrated to New York, made our lives more agreeable, though occasionally perplexing. We couldn't understand, for instance, why tea was packed in such tiny bags, and we would open up every single tea bag to pour the contents into a self-respecting canister. The chocolate, welcome as it was, seemed a bit salty to us, but we found the canned corned beef splendid.

Victor Aitay, in addition to his position in the opera house, had a fine string quartet that bore his name, and when he received an invitation from the radio station of Vienna, as well as the U.S. occupation forces, all the musicians, and, of course, Évi, traveled from Budapest to Vienna in February of 1946. This event was what triggered my resolution to get to Austria—as a first step to America—one way or the other.

It took me quite a few weeks to connect with a group that was in the dangerous business of smuggling people across the border into Austria. When I started to negotiate the price with the leader in the doorway of an apartment house, he told me that he had been a border guard before the war, and that the way they operated was to use a hearse—the least likely vehicle to be stopped along the way. When he told me how much it would cost, I realized I didn't have that kind of money, and asked him if we could meet again. In the meantime I managed to raise the bulk of the money by renting our family house for half the going rate, but demanding six months' rent in advance. I also managed to find my father's prized sewing machine at a tailor's shop, and after much cajoling and even some physical threats, the tailor reluctantly bought it from me, at a fraction of its value. I had to sell my oak desk with its hidden drawers, which my father had bought me at an auction, and with the remainder of my share of the money our uncles had sent us from America as my bankroll, I was ready for Austria.

I had been waiting for these unsavory characters for a couple of hours at the same doorway where we had met before, when finally two of them arrived, looking around furtively. They asked me for the money, but instead of giving it to them right then, I asked the ringleader a couple of questions.

"Please tell me the route you will take. I also want to know what will happen when we get there." By now I had enough experience to know that in any venture the likelihood of success was fair if the plan was flawless, and nil if even the slightest details were left to chance.

For this meeting, my original contact brought one of his pals with him, and they told me we would be driving on the highway leading to Graz, and would arrive near the Szentgotthárd border at around three in the morning. "It's all arranged. The guards on the Hungarian side receive a cut from each of our 'deliveries,' and they in turn share it with the Austrian border guards when they meet once a week in no-man's-land." It sounded like a plausible scheme. They insisted on getting all the money up front. Realizing that this might be the only chance I would have to get out of Hungary, I gave it to them as I was getting into the shabby hearse.

They stopped somewhere outside the city, on a small side road, and told me to get inside a black-painted pine coffin.

"We have made it as comfortable for you as possible. When we get to the border, you'll get out of the coffin, and we'll make certain that the Hungarian guards allow you to leave and that the Austrians will let you in at the official border crossing point."

I asked them to take care of my violin and a small papier-mâché suitcase I brought with me, which didn't fit in the coffin.

I tried to look through the holes that had been made in the coffin so one could breathe. We were passing by Székesfehérvár, and I wanted to take a last look at the house I grew up in on Palotai Street. But unfortunately the only thing I could see through the two-inch round holes was the blank wall of the rear of the hearse. The coarse sackcloth lining in the coffin made my skin itch all over, and being too cramped to be able to scratch added an extra element of creepiness to the voyage. Hours, or—as it seemed to me—perhaps days later, the hearse stopped and the top of my coffin was opened. The night was totally black. The stars and the moon were cooperating by hiding behind thick clouds, so I felt that nature was assisting me in my disappearing act.

My companions gave me my violin case and the little suitcase, and returned to the front seat of the hearse to start up the engine.

"We brought you to a safe place to cross. There are no guards or barbed wire at this stretch of the border, so you can stroll across, and in a short time you'll be saying good-bye to Hungary and hello to Austria. Good luck!"

I was stunned.

Never having been outside of Hungary, I had only seen in movies and read in books about the formalities of crossing from one country to another, and I was expecting to see uniformed officers checking passports and visas and custom guards inspecting luggage, while armed border police eyed every traveler with suspicion.

Desperate and bewildered, I blew up. "I thought you had arranged it so that I could go across as though I had official papers, that's what we agreed on! And now you break our deal and leave me here in no-man's-land!"

It didn't take much for their tone to harden.

"Don't give us any trouble," said the one who did all the talking, with a menacing glance as they started to drive away. He looked back and yelled over the roar of the engine, "And watch out for the land mines!" I'll never know whether they were grinning or not.

Now I understood why no one was guarding the border; only a fool would attempt to play Russian roulette on a live minefield. I numbed the part of my brain that activates or blocks one's actions, and without weighing my chances, I began the longest kilometer of my life. I have always believed in my luck, even when there was little reason to do so.

I noticed a path leading toward the Austrian side, but avoided it, reasoning that it must be a trap. That's all I can recall of this deadly walk. I was disoriented as I straggled ahead, forcing myself to keep going. About two hours later, as the sun began to make its regular morning appearance, and my endurance was exhausted, I found myself in Heiligenkreuz, a small village in Austria.

I was overwhelmed at the idea of being free, even though this part of Austria was still occupied by Russian forces. Where I came from, "freedom" was a word just thrown around by poets and politicians. It took months, years, decades to understand what it meant—that I was free to try, to succeed, to fail, to go left or right or nowhere, and to say whatever came into my mind—as long as I accepted the consequences.

When I asked someone if there was a railroad station in town, he told me to keep walking to the nearby village of Jennersdorf. I got there in another couple of hours, and stopped a friendly-looking chap, asking him in my paprika-flavored German where the railroad station was. To my surprise he answered me in Hungarian, looking at me with a combination of sympathy and curiosity.

"Yes, there is one, let me show you."

One of the curses of living in a totalitarian country is that you become suspicious, even of your own mother. My concern was unfounded; the station he took me to was the railway's, not the police station. Along the way, he asked me where I wanted to go, and it turned out that we were not far from the city of Graz, where I could easily find a train to Vienna.

It was hours before the train arrived. Since I was the only person in the waiting-room café, the waiter and I started a conversation. I only had my uncle's dollars with me, but I couldn't even buy a cup of coffee and something to eat, although the dollar was the most powerful ally one could have in those days. I ended up exchanging a few of my dollars for a quantity of schillings, and at last I had a satisfying cup of coffee with a number of buttered *Kaiser-Semmeln,* as those crisp rolls are called. I told the waiter that I was hoping to get to the American occupied zone, but that made him nervous and he left me to tend to the suddenly urgent cleaning of the coffee maker.

At that time, Austria was divided into four sections by the Allied powers, and to get from the Russian zone, where I was at that moment, to the American zone, one needed a "pink pass," which was not easy to get, but I had decided to improvise somehow. When the train arrived, I boarded it, remaining in the corridor instead of taking a seat. I had enough schillings left to buy a ticket, and I asked the conductor about the schedule, mentioning to him that Vienna would be my last stop. He looked at me warily, as if he considered me one of those Hungarian clowns from the nearby Burgenland, a formerly Hungarian county ceded to Austria at the end of World War I.

He answered me snidely that the train was going from Graz to Salzburg, and not to Vienna. I was disappointed to hear this news, thinking about my plan to meet my cousin in Vienna, but I recovered quickly when I learned that Salzburg was in the American zone as well.

My primary problem, however, was not the train's destination, but what would happen when it stopped at the point between the Russian and American zones. In my extreme anxiety, I racked my brain for a feasible way to avoid the border military police. Like a hunted animal, I acted instinctively. When the train stopped, I jumped off to look for a water fountain. In the meantime, everyone's passes were checked, and when the train started to move again, I simply jumped back on, this time taking a seat in a compartment.

I shared the train compartment with a family of four, and they told me they were going to a wonderful spa-village called Badgastein. I figured that as long as I wasn't going to Vienna, I might as well try my luck in a place where I might be able to pull myself together. So in Salzburg I changed to a local train.

When we arrived at the Badgastein station, the highest point in town, I could have shouted for joy. My first vision of the village below, with its imposing waterfall, framed by the lush Alpine scenery, gave me an unbeatable thrill. Feeling I was on a lucky roll, I walked into the local hotel, where I was greeted at the front desk by a rather plain-looking young lady. In my halting German I indicated to her that I had just come from Hungary and was looking for a room—a very, very reasonable room. I was carrying my violin, so, not surprisingly, she asked if I was a violinist. In return she told me that her name was Ilse, and that she was the daughter of the owners and was just helping out for a few hours.

"We are not very full at this time, and I could give you a little room on the ground floor," she said. When I asked the room rate, she gave it to me in schillings. I paused to mentally convert it into dollars (it was the equivalent of a single dollar), and seeing that I didn't respond right away, she added, "Including breakfast and dinner, of course."

Then she showed me to the charming little room. A line of Heine's came to mind: "... *und mein Liebchen was willst du noch mehr?*"— "... and, my dear, what else could you wish for?"

A couple of days later she helped me call the Collegium Hungaricum in Vienna (collect, of course), which was a kind of Hungarian artists' colony where Évi and Victor and the quartet were staying. Triumphantly, but trying to be casual about it, I told them that I had arrived, found a great place, and would make the necessary arrangements in this hotel if they would like to join me. I also mentioned that I had found out that the first ship to America was going to leave from the German port of Bremerhaven sometime during the late spring, which was another reason for us to be together. By the end of the week, Victor called back and told me that not only were they coming to Badgastein but Janos Starker, the cellist, who had also received an invitation for a command performance in Vienna, and his wife, Baba, were joining us, as well as another member of the quartet.

The hotel was quite empty, so it wasn't a problem reserving these rooms, but I felt it was my duty to show my gratitude to Ilse, since I couldn't do much for her parents. We had several pleasant dates while waiting for the troops to arrive.

When they arrived, great times were had by everybody. Our get-together became a kind of nonstop talk fest, the conversation ranging every night from important issues like spiritual movements as they relate to sound perceptions, to creating new endings to well-known books. We threw around so many ideas that in the next half-century, whenever we met again, we would smugly say, "Oh, we already solved that question in Badgastein!"

We didn't take seriously at the time the fact that Badgastein's natural thermal baths—which had attracted rich kings and eventually equally rich peasants since the Middle Ages—were saturated with radioactive elements, and we luxuriated for hours in the sunken marble tubs. What we needed more than the healing waters was a concise guide titled *How to Live Like a Count on the Resources of an Indigent Musician.*

The Starkers turned out to be an important part of the Viennese contingent; Baba was a young woman of wit and refreshing unpredictability, and Janos was already the pride of Hungary. To say that Janos Starker is a cellist is like describing a great sculptor as a stonecutter. The Good Lord takes a few pounds of minerals, amino acids, and other unexciting ingredients, and on rare occasion turns them into human beings of exceptional qualities. The process of the creation of a great performer is even more mysterious, and it would be pointless for me to try to analyze what makes Starker what he is.

Within a very brief period we recognized each other as friends, and after fifty years we still get together every year in some part of the world to argue, laugh, grouch, rejoice, banter, wisecrack, and just let our brains play hopscotch. Ours is—to some degree—the opposite of an unqualified friendship; we do not agree on a number of important issues. But friendship requires almost as much talent as playing an instrument well, and Janos is as good at it as he is on the cello. In a way, I took the place of his two brothers, who died in the Holocaust, and he became the brother I never had.

As the only unready instrumentalist in the group, I decided to enroll in the famed Mozarteum in Salzburg, for lessons with Professor Müller. I would make the trip on the railroad once a week. I don't really think that the good professor taught me much, but the walls of this musical-history-saturated institution did.

In the meantime, Évi, Victor, and I kept in close contact with HIAS, a Jewish refugee organization, as well as with our uncles in the United States, and when the call finally came from the U.S. consul's office, we were ready.

Recently, when I was ransacking storage rooms I haven't looked at in years, I found the black corduroy pants my father made for me before I went to the labor camp. I stroked them affectionately and, reaching into one of the pockets, found a little brown-covered calendar from the year 1946. The very first page contains the chronology of our voyage to America in my handwriting:

The arrival of the S.S. Marine Flasher *in
New York harbor, July 15, 1946*

June 19—Appointment with U.S. Consul
June 24—CIC (Bureau of Investigation)
June 29—Transport to Bremerhaven
July 4—Pick up tickets for ship
July 5—Board SS *Marine Flasher* (Bremerhaven)
July 15, Monday—*Szabadság szobor* [Statue of Liberty]

The SS *Marine Flasher,* the ship we boarded at the heavily damaged north German port of Bremerhaven on July 5, 1946, was a rickety Liberty ship—one of the very first to ferry refugees to America after the war was over. On our first ocean voyage, Évi, her husband, and I were among 865 DPs, as displaced persons were called in those days. The amenities on this ship, which had originally been used for transporting U.S. troops to the Pacific, were not quite up to the level of Cunard's *Sea Goddess,* but it didn't matter to me. The daily buffet was what we would today sneeringly call a cafeteria line, but then it overwhelmed us with its variety. Even so, like modern versions of the Tantalus of ancient mythology, we were not able to eat because of our incessant seasickness.

Even the sailors aboard were frightened and sick from the monumental storm that lasted almost throughout the voyage. The angry ocean formed giant mountains, alternating with precipitous valleys. The savage waves brutalized our toylike ship—and our stomachs—while making threatening, crashing noises.

One day while lying on my bunk, trying to mesmerize myself into not feeling or thinking, I heard shouts in all kinds of languages, but the one English word that was on everybody's lips was *liberty*.

I ran up to the deck.

Hundreds of my fellow refugees were crammed together into a single cheering crowd. With a few of them, I climbed to a small platform on the deck, and there she was, the Statue of Liberty, seemingly within touching distance.

Together, Évi, Victor, and I stepped ashore. I had my trusty violin and my papier-mâché valise (tied with a piece of string), and I was wearing a tie, since I felt that I should be properly dressed for the occasion.

CHAPTER 8

Manhattan Graffiti

WO UNCLES, TWO AUNTS, and two first cousins were waiting for the three of us on the pier and my first thought was that the nine of us represented the vast majority of what was left of our family. Uncle Lajos (who had since Americanized his first name to Louis) had been a physician in a Slovakian town which was formerly part of Hungary, and had come to America on what he termed (as did so many others) "the last ship" in 1939. Uncle Jenő (by then renamed Eugene) was already waiting for Lajos and his family, since he had arrived in New York about ten years earlier. In 1929, Eugene had been encouraged by his parents (my maternal grandparents) to leave town, country, Europe, anything, to avoid marrying Ila, his attractive first cousin. *Amor vincit* and all that—in any event, she followed Eugene across the water and the marriage, which lasted fifty-five years, produced a wonderful daughter, Leila.

Members of my mother's family were always anointed by her as sacred, each possessing all the virtues of the Old Testament prophets. She would visit her parents, who lived forty miles away, as often as her busy life allowed, and since we had no telephone, she wrote a postcard to them at least once a week. As far as the rest of the family was concerned, even third cousins twice removed were considered candidates for the Hall of Fame and Perfection. Since her two brothers were already in America, they were far enough away that I could grow up believing in my mother's exalted image of them.

Évi and Victor Aitay and I on Broadway,
four days after our arrival in 1946

Still, the fact is that my uncles were quite human, complete with all-American midlife crises. But Uncle Lajos's wife was so eccentric that she was convinced she heard paintings talk, while Uncle Eugene's wife was such a hypochondriac that she complained that her hair hurt while growing during the night. I called Uncle Lajos "the pen Napoleon," because he would often tell me to my face that I was making the right career moves, and then return to Elizabeth, New Jersey, where he lived, and write sizable epistles informing me that unless I changed my ways I would never have steak on my plate, or a knife to cut it with.

Uncle Eugene was as loving and lovable as my mother. Still, it was difficult to take seriously the counsel of someone whose professional activities ranged from journalist to concert impresario to bank official to manufacturer of artificial pearls, at none of which pursuits was he very successful.

The first week in America I stayed with Eugene and Ila in their comfortable Washington Heights apartment in New York. As I think about Ila and my first days in Manhattan, I've decided that she invented Jewish

Zen by having the soul and head of a nagging yet innocent child. The second day after we arrived, she gave me some money and asked me to go to the grocery store on the next block, to bring back bread for dinner.

"What kind?" I asked.

"Any kind you like," she answered.

"But I can't speak English."

"You can just point, can't you?"

So I went out and brought back a loaf of rye bread.

"Gyuri, I wouldn't put this bread in front of your Uncle Eugene."

The next day, the same scene. I returned from the store and presented her with a different type of bread.

She was chagrined. "This just won't do. Your uncle would never touch white bread!" So I pulled out a pumpernickel loaf, then a whole wheat, followed by a strange-looking thin loaf. Her shock turned to uncontrollable laughter, and from that moment on we understood each other.

My relatives, in their loving effort to protect me, made me feel like a kid who must account for every minute of his time. It was claustrophobic! So by the third week I borrowed some money from my Uncle Lajos, and moved myself to West 49th Street, where I shared a tenement apartment with a fellow refugee from Hungary to whom Uncle Eugene had introduced me.

HIAS, the Hebrew Immigrant Aid Society, which had been instrumental in bringing me to America, had a bulletin board in their offices filled with job offers. During my first year in New York I had several jobs, often simultaneously, making a few dollars at each. One of the more lucrative was as a busboy at the Reuben's twenty-four-hour restaurant on West 57th Street. The night chef, who was German, took a liking to me, probably because I could speak his mother tongue after a fashion, and chose me to bring him his huge daily bucket of beer after the rush hour was over, sometimes rewarding me with special snacks.

One night, when the people were pouring in after the theater, and the waiters were running around anxiously trying to take and deliver orders ("One Cary Grant on Rye"), I rushed through the kitchen, and Chef Kurt told me to come back in exactly ten minutes. When I returned, he gave me a stunning-looking lobster platter while barking instructions in machine-gun-fast English, forgetting that I didn't speak the language. The only words I understood were "go" and "fast." In pure logic worthy of Kant, I surmised that he was telling me to go down to the employees' cafeteria and eat this fast, before the boss saw me.

About fifteen delicious minutes later I came upstairs and passed through the kitchen, suddenly noticing that the huge din had subsided and everybody was looking at me in a peculiar way. The chef quietly asked me in German, "Did you eat the lobster platter I gave you?"

"*Danke vielmal,* thank you very, very much, it was absolutely delicious," I replied, wiping my mouth.

At that point the chef went berserk. Fortunately, a waiter of Hungarian origin, who had become my pal, walked by and whispered to me to run out through the back door as fast as I could, and he would talk to me later.

The next day I learned from him that apparently what the chef had told me was to take the lobster platter—fast—to the captain, who was working at Claudette Colbert's table. I was scared to go back to get my back wages, and as far as my clothes are concerned, I wouldn't be surprised if they are still in one of the locker rooms somewhere.

I couldn't afford to be out of work for more than a couple of days. Fortunately I remembered that another busboy at Reuben's had mentioned to me that there were jobs for unskilled workers at the Western Union center downtown, so I took the subway there and offered my services. Luckily they had an opening. That was where I met an artist who became a friend, and who introduced me to nonrepresentational art, which had until then been incomprehensible to me.

Whenever I looked at art in museums, I always felt that it made the disagreeable things in my life disappear. Doing some drawings in my free time increased this feeling of release, especially when my style was liberated as a result of seeing my Western Union colleague's skillful but prudently abstract art.

Searching for jobs remained an ongoing activity. Once, passing by a sign that read, EXPERIENCED CUSTOM TAILOR WANTED, I walked into the shop and asked for the job. For a few days I felt as though I were back in my father's tailor shop. Unfortunately it soon became obvious that my modest skills were not adequate for fine custom tailoring, and I had no interest in operating one of the scores of sewing machines in a bra factory for more than a few days—a job I got through an ad in the paper—even though it gave me good material for some (even then) politically incorrect remarks.

Years later, when I could afford it, I chose for my first bookplate one of Botticelli's circular drawings of heaven, and combined it with the motto VARIETAS DELECTAT: "Pleasure in variety." The dizzying multifari-ousness of my early jobs in America fits the spirit of my *ex libris*.

One of my father's choice after-dinner stories was about Ferenc Pol-gár, a friend of his, who had the knack, even as a young man, of being able to hypnotize just about anybody who was a willing subject. He had moved to New York during the early 1930s, and I called on him shortly after my arrival. Uncle Eugene told me that he had become a well-known showbiz-type personality who gave illustrated lectures at colleges. Polgár received me like, if not a son, at least the son of a friend, and told me stories about my father that activated the painfully sweet recall-button in me.

I attended a couple of Polgár's lecture-demonstrations, which went far beyond demonstrating and explaining hypnosis. Among other seg-ments in the two-hour performance was an astonishing memory act in which he was able to quote almost verbatim any story from that morn-ing's *New York Times* that someone in the audience suggested. Since I eventually became one of his trusted allies, I can vouch for the fact that it was mnemotechny at its best, and all on the up-and-up.

That's why I was so surprised when one day he asked me to assist him on an important live TV show. He explained to me that the problem he was facing was that he had only four minutes to do an especially tricky hypnotic act, and the directors insisted on its being the closing segment. This meant, of course, that if his subject turned out to be difficult or impossible to put into a hypnotic trance, the failure would affect his future bookings.

We rehearsed for an entire afternoon. When the show went on, I was sitting in the front row of the studio, and I eagerly volunteered on cue. Within a few seconds, surprise, surprise, I was under hypnosis and ready to respond to his commands. I became a two-year-old child crying for my bottle; I was ready to strip—"jacket only, please"—believing I was in the middle of a steaming jungle, then I was shivering in Alaska, with my chattering teeth sounding like castanets in the amplified mike. His repu-tation was saved, the commercial was cued on time, and I was richer by fifty dollars, which at the time meant the equivalent of two weeks' income. Shortly afterwards, hypnotic acts were outlawed on television by the FCC.

The violin, of course, remained my love, although the affair pro-gressed rather slowly, with mostly one-night stands. The most bizarre of these was a television appearance on the Arthur Godfrey "Talent Scouts" show. As a parlor trick, I had developed a novel technique of playing two violin bows by using one as a violin and the other as a bow. I became the Paganini of the métier. With the help of a microphone, the sound was quite loud, like a chorus of bees groaning the "Anniversary Waltz" a capella, which was exactly what I was playing. I wish I could report that I won first prize, but that went to a winsome young lady whose singing was swinging.

There have been cultures without painting, or bereft of the wheel or the written word, but never a culture without music. For me, life would have been utterly meaningless without music, especially during this early period of my life. My passion was supported by my conviction that I had the makings of a top-notch violinist and that I would make a major career. I had an exceptionally large and warm tone, a sense for the big line, and whatever it took to hold the attention of the listener. What I did not have was seamless technique, and I chose to play certain compositions that showed my strengths to advantage, like the Mendelssohn— alas, the first movement only—and the first two movements of Bach's G Minor Solo Sonata, among others. Consistency was not my forte, either: *capriccio* would describe my method of practicing six hours one day and leaving my violin in its case for the next two days. In 1946 it seemed that I might have the kind of a career that is often expected when a prodigy grows up, provided that a forceful and effective teacher would take an interest in my development.

The way I connected with Madame Vera Fonaroff, who became my violin teacher, is a bit bizarre, perhaps even on the slippery border of legality. During the war, my aunt Ila had worked in New York in the office of government mail censorship, and one day in the course of doing her job she read a letter written to Madame Fonaroff by the famous violinist Joseph Fuchs, in which he recalled pre-concert working sessions he had taken with her years before that had helped him on his way to the top.

A few months after I arrived, my aunt remembered this bit of intelligence and called Madame Fonaroff to arrange an audition for me. When I entered her small but impressive duplex, where the walls were covered with signed photographs of all my musical gods, saints, and prophets, I was greeted by a five-foot-tall elderly lady in an old-fashioned dress, with long gold chains around her neck, her head crowned by a snow-white braid of hair. Without preliminaries or small talk, she motioned me to the violin stand and asked me to proceed.

After I finished one of my warhorses, Franceur's *Sicilian and Rigaudon,* she said in her pungent Russian accent, "You do have a lot of talent, but if you keep playing like that, you'll end up like most of the rest. If you are ready to work hard, I will take you on as a full-scholarship student at the David Mannes School."

"By the way, how old are you?" she asked me.

"Twenty-two," I answered, knowing full well that it was like a heavyweight boxer saying he was forty-two.

"I will also give you some lessons here in my studio. You don't have much time left," she added quietly.

Madame Fonaroff had been all business till then, so I was taken aback when she said, "You look kind of hungry. Come, I'll buy you tea and some sweets."

The elevator took us down to the lobby, and we entered a restaurant unlike any I had been to before. I couldn't take my eyes off the shapely nude girls almost jumping off the murals that lined the walls. As I concentrated on not looking at them, I dropped a spoonful of whipped cream on the trousers of my only good suit.

That was my first encounter with the Café des Artistes.

Although I never discussed my financial state with Madame Fonaroff, she must have known that it was a precarious balancing act. She introduced me to Árpád Sándor, a noted professional accompanist who had played with Heifetz on some of his early recordings, and I supplemented my lean income by turning pages for him, and eventually others, mostly in Carnegie Hall.

The job took more than just being able to read music and turn when the pianist nodded. I had to anticipate, learn little signals of each pianist, and of course, I had to be quasi-invisible on the stage. I only had one disaster with Sándor. He was playing with a noted violinist by the name of Odnoposoff, and one of the pieces was the first performance of a composition by a contemporary composer. Just as in many of the dishes of today's young, ambitious chefs, this musical work had too many ingredients—in this case, notes. It was a complex piece, and even the final rehearsal in Sándor's apartment was a bit bumpy.

On the night of the concert, all three of us were rather nervous. The last movement was marked *presto,* and the piano had to race through tricky, high-speed passages. Sándor, who had had to learn this piece laboriously, as opposed to most of his repertoire which he knew by heart, gave me the page-turning signal only at the very last bar on the page. I turned with equal speed, pulling down the entire manuscript, which was written on endless accordion-folded pages, and the paper skittered across the stage of Carnegie Hall. The waves of laughter in the audience turned to disappointment when the artists took it from the top.

Through Victor Aitay, my cousin's husband and fellow refugee (who eventually became concertmaster of the Chicago Symphony under the legendary Fritz Reiner, and later under the equally celebrated Sir Georg Solti), I got on the list of a booking agent who specialized in pickup musicians. Within a single year, among all my other activities, I played quite often with wedding bands. The first thing I had to learn was how to pick up the tempo just before the contracted four-hour booking was up, so that the host would be obliged to ask us to stay overtime to keep his guests happy. On a couple of Mondays, when the *primás* (lead violinist) was off, I substituted for him in the gypsy band at the Csárda Restaurant in the Yorkville section of Manhattan. I am glad to be able to report that I didn't play either "The Singing Canary" or any of Brahms's Hungarian Rhapsodies during these gigs.

Once I was even called as a substitute in Toscanini's NBC Orchestra, but to my regret, it was on a day when Toscanini was indisposed.

Working intensively with Madame Fonaroff, I was on the way to learning to play the violin "as a serious discipline," as she had phrased it during our first meeting. On very rare occasions, even my good friend János Starker had mumbled something to the effect that "you played— hmm—almost acceptably . . . ," which in his vocabulary was high praise.

In a student recital, I played the Bruch Violin Concerto with my new friend Jacob Lateiner, the budding concert artist. He was a student of another legendary Russian teacher, Madame Vengerova, who taught many of the young hotshot pianists of the time on a wholesale basis.

I certainly couldn't complain about burnout from monotony; for a couple of weeks I was even a fill-in at Billy Rose's Diamond Horseshoe. What I remember most about this overblown nightclub was the women guests dressed up like sequined handbags, and their escorts with three-piece suit façades. As part of a group of string players, I would stroll around the room in a carefully rehearsed fashion. It occurs to me now that many experiences of my early life came full circle later—for in time I did become a part of Billy Rose's coterie of friends and a member of Carnegie Hall's Board of Directors.

After moving out of my aunt and uncle's apartment, I had to find a grocery store near my 49th Street apartment. Bread was always a staple of my life, and I did find a shelf of parcels deftly wrapped in shiny paper that looked very much like the bread I'd bought for my Aunt Ila. I purchased a loaf, hoping it was ready to eat. (I was permanently hungry in those days, a sensation that hasn't ceased.) Back home, I eagerly opened the package only to see layers of a downy white substance fall out. Biting into a piece, I found it had the texture of a cotton-filled cushion. It was nothing like my mother's balloon-high bread with its potterylike glaze. At the time I had not yet formulated Lang's Law—If in doubt, toast it— but since I didn't even have a toaster then, that option wasn't available anyway.

When I had some money and didn't feel like cooking on my two-burner hot plate, I would go down the block to a diner at Eleventh Avenue and 49th Street and order meat loaf, the specialty of the house. It probably contained more bread than meat, but sprinkled with Tabasco sauce, my latest discovery, it made a satisfying meal. Culinary history seems to repeat itself, and meat loaf is again in fashion, but the price has gone up in today's restaurants, where it is served in different shapes and herbaceous flavors, often with lumpy garlic-mashed potatoes.

Whenever we felt the need for solace, my roommate and I would walk to a tiny drugstore on Eighth Avenue, near the old Madison Square Garden. There we sat down at the counter on green-vinyl-covered chrome stools and sipped the best egg cream soda in New York. While making it last as long as possible before my straw started to make slurping noises, I pondered how this glorious drink, made with Fox's U-Bet chocolate syrup, milk, and fizzy water, had acquired its name, since it contained neither egg nor cream. Another puzzle I haven't solved yet.

One night I stumbled upon one of America's most original contributions to the ritual of public dining, in the self-service cafeteria perfected by Horn and Hardart. After an especially nerve-racking page-turning evening on the stage of Carnegie Hall, with the five dollars I had just received getting restless in my pocket, I passed by a large, brightly lit restaurant that looked more like a market. I took a chance, entering through its center door. For a minute I didn't know whether I had stepped into a palace or the big hall of a railroad station. I watched an elderly man approach a glass-enclosed wall divided into small cubicles, take a coin from his pocket, and drop it into a slot. To my astonishment, he opened the little glass door and removed a doughnut. I took a closer look at the many brass-framed glass boxes, each containing some kind of food. So, after changing one of the dollar bills I'd just received, I, too, made my choice.

I don't think one of the goals of automation was to entertain while reducing as much human intervention as possible, but to me it was easily as good a show as a flaming dish must have been to a turn-of-the-century gourmet in a grand restaurant in France. Also, I had the comforting feeling that by removing one of the rolls, I was liberating it. It cost me a nickel, and I had a feast by dunking it into the ketchup and mustard conveniently placed at the center of each table, and sprinkling it liberally with pepper. Some of the best things in life are indeed free.

Almost from the beginning, I discovered the thrill of being able to visit Italy, the Middle East, Russia, Central Europe, Scandinavia, and Brazil—without crossing the ocean. Searching, together with another refugee who had come over with me on the SS *Marine Flasher*, for the most exotic experience the city had to offer, we took the subway to Chinatown. Upon emerging from the subway station, we were totally lost, and by the time we found Mott Street, we were ready to exchange the most amazing experiences for a cup of soup. Still, the tumultuous conglomeration of restaurants with glistening, dark brown roasted birds hanging in the windows, the store windows containing strange objects, the teeming sidewalk stalls selling something we suspected was meant to be eaten, and the banks and theaters with Chinese signs made a deep impression on me. We ended up in a restaurant called Lum Fong on Canal Street, which probably seemed just as strange to a Chinese as it did to me.

Drinking wine in those days was a form of lottery, with only a few winners. The selection in most restaurants was absurdly limited. Italian places in Greenwich Village sold straw-covered Chianti bottles containing a purple liquid that stained your teeth temporarily and your clothes permanently. Restaurants of other ethnic persuasions pushed the slender bottles of white wine known generically as Liebfraumilch. As later scandals revealed, it was at best a blend of cheap German wines, and at worst a mixture containing Austrian plonk. But, surprisingly, it could range from acceptable to what my father used to call a "three-man wine": two men had to hold you so that a third could pour it down your throat.

Sometime in that first year I ventured all the way to the East Seventies, into a neighborhood called Little Hungary. In those days it was populated by Hungarians who tried to avoid speaking English, and whose English was functionally indistinguishable from their native tongue. My favorite restaurant was Debrecen, a congenial place with a little garden on 79th Street near First Avenue. It served caraway soup with poached egg, huge portions of Transylvanian stuffed cabbage, vanilla-and-rum-flavored chestnut purée hiding under a mountain of whipped cream, the kind of food that to this day I call normal. A decade later I used to take my good friend Jim Beard there for his favorite golden dumpling cake (see page 364 for the recipe). Our usual waiter, *Józsi bácsi* (Uncle Józsi), was famous for his insults. Once he greeted a regular who came in after a few days' absence with "Should I still call you *Elnök úr* [Mr. President], or did you get a job?" But even he was awed by Jim's larger-than-life presence and the casual yet elegant manner in which he polished off several huge portions of golden dumpling cake.

Once in a great while I was taken as a guest by American-Hungarian friends of my Uncle Eugene to dinner in a Broadway restaurant called Dempsey's, and this adventure always revealed a number of strange customs. To begin with, the fruit cocktail was served as an appetizer, but it resembled neither the fruit I knew nor cocktails I had read about. During the next course, my host covered his steak liberally with a strange dark-brown sauce, and switched his knife and fork from the right hand to the left hand and back again with each bite, which seemed strangely inefficient in the country where time-and-motion studies were invented. Our glasses were continually refilled with ice cubes and ice water, which I drank until my mouth was numb. At one point all the waiters surrounded the party at the next table to sing a song, loudly interrupting everyone's conversation. Afterward, we proceeded to a stretch of 42nd Street between Broadway and Eighth Avenue that was filled with movie theaters, all quite respectable back then. That block served as a kind of Berlitz school for most immigrants. You could stay as long as you wanted for twenty-five cents. On a rare day when I didn't work, I could see two double features in adjacent movie theaters and still have enough money left for a hot dog and a glass of Orange Julius, that pleasantly sweet mystery drink.

One of my first dates in America was with a comely young violinist. After rehearsing a Bach double concerto together (always a good ploy for a sexually hopeful young male violinist), I persuaded her to go to dinner with me that night. But once we were in the taxi, I had no idea where to take her, so I started a conversation with the driver in my sketchy English. His proficiency in the language was about the same as mine, though with a Slavic flavor, but he assured me he knew "the goodest place."

He took us to the Lower East Side, to a Second Avenue nightclub-restaurant called Moscowitz and Lupowitz, owned, as I learned years later, by a man named Anzelowitz. It served Russian-American-Jewish food, not exactly spa cuisine. After devouring herring, pot roast, potato pudding, and orange ice, we listened to a trumpet, drum, and piano trio playing Piaf's latest hit, "La Vie en Rose." We decided to stay off the tiny dance floor after watching two rotund ladies hoof with great abandon; a collision with them might have had serious consequences. When it came time to pay, my date insisted on going Dutch, which saved me from washing dishes there for several weeks. About five minutes after we'd paid, the owner passed by and growled, "What's the matter, are you renting the place?"

Of course, by the time I arrived I was convinced that I already knew everything about America, even though I didn't speak more than three or four words of English, each flavored with an accent making them incomprehensible. I also knew that America was the home of the free and the land of the brave and every now and then the natives stuck their tongue out while speaking, when their words began with the *th* sound.

I was always annoyed by Americans who asked, "And what language do you speak in Hungary?" Some years later, during a discussion about the relative merits of languages, I informed an especially obnoxious individual that Hungarian is so precise that it has different words to distinguish sexual from nonsexual love, unlike a primitive language like English, which forces you to elaborate on whether you're expressing affection toward your mother or your girlfriend.

Back in 1946, the words I spoke were a new language, one that helped to create a new person within me. Nearly every refugee thinks he is ready for America, although probably the last foreigner who really understood this country was de Tocqueville. As a child, my main source of information about the United States had been a Hungarian translation of *The Last of the Mohicans*. And a film I saw in the early 1940s taught me that in the United States, parents dutifully obey their children. Some of the misinformation I chalked up to tall tales of the New World. No one in my hometown would have believed that any native-born citizen had a chance to become the president of the United States; that you only had to work forty hours a week; that some people actually changed their professions within their lifetimes; and the most astonishing hearsay, that ice cream was served throughout the winter. But I still wasn't prepared for the surprises I encountered in Manhattan.

Before I came to America, I didn't know, for example, that like horses, humans could eat standing up. It was an almost extraterrestrial experience to enter a brightly lit store and hold in one hand a hot dog lying in state inside a woolly crustless roll badly in need of additional baking, while in the other hand balancing a tabloid newspaper printed with removable ink—and then act as my own busboy!

I marveled at the lack of ritual in the daily life of Manhattan. When I went into a store, no one said hello, or good-bye when I left, and in between it wasn't customary to tell the clerk the reason for coming in to begin with. And male customers didn't even remove their hats.

On the positive side, I soon learned that in New York a stranger didn't have to know what was expected of him and act accordingly. I felt that I had found a place where it was easy to live in my own way, and half a century later I haven't changed my opinion.

The city was saturated with the creative juices of such composers as Leonard Bernstein, John Cage, Walter Piston, Peter Mennin, and Roger Sessions. There were premiere performances in 1946 of works by Bartók, Stravinsky, and Hindemith. Balanchine's *Nightshadow* ballet had its world premiere in Manhattan, Martha Graham introduced her *Cave of Heart*, and Gian-Carlo Menotti's *The Medium* opened during the same year.

Mind you, the New York of those days was far from heaven. Along with 70,000 other residents, I had no private toilet in my Hell's Kitchen railroad flat. Others were worse off, living in Union Square without a roof over their heads. My roommate, Morris, slept on a couch in the only real room of our apartment, and left at five o'clock every morning to work in a vegetable-and-fruit store in Brooklyn. We cooked, ate, and relaxed in the kitchen. I had a room of my own, which must have been built by putting walls around a small bed, and to get into bed I had to dive from the door.

A few months after my arrival I felt lonely (though never homesick), especially when I walked down from our fifth-floor apartment and noticed other tenants opening their mailboxes and tearing open letters on the spot. On January 2, 1947, I too opened up my mailbox and found the following letter—in Hungarian, of course:

> *Dear friend!*
> *I wish you from my heart a happier and more agreeable New Year.*
>
> *Your devoted,*
G.

It felt good to read it, even though I had written it to myself a couple of days before.

Decades later, when I read a little poem by Irwin Copeland, I felt, along with all those who were lucky enough to get here, that it was especially written about my passionate attraction to New York, the city of unlimited diversity.

> *Shining towers, in the sky*
> *The Torch of Liberty, lifted high*
> *Blazing lights, of the Great White-way.*
> *Spelling glamour—bright as day!*
> *Flitting traffic—everywhere*
> *Bridges hanging in the air*
> *Tooting tugboats, never still—*
> *Sights and sounds which bring a thrill!*
> *That's New York, where dreams come true*
> *Her magic skyline welcomes you!*

It certainly did.

CHAPTER 9

Decisive Moment

OLLECTING MY THOUGHTS about my first great summer in America is like having only the faded segments of a puzzle at hand, and trying to assemble them by dim candlelight. If put together accurately, the picture would be of a musical Elysium in New England. Tanglewood was in its early years, and after I auditioned to be accepted as a student in its famed music school, I received a full scholarship. To me, this summer music festival was the very idea of heaven.

The Place: A bucolic park, dotted with concert sheds, rehearsal gardens, and other ingredients designed to please all the senses.

The Magnet: The Boston Symphony, with Serge Koussevitzky conducting.

Musical luminaries on hand that summer: Honegger, Copland, Piatigorsky, Primrose, Serkin, and the young Leonard Bernstein, surrounded by even younger artists such as Walter Hendl, Lukas Foss, Lilian Kallir, Jacob Lateiner, Gary Graffman, William Kapell, and dozens of others who have since become important members of the society of musicians.

A couple of times Koussevitzky conducted the student orchestra, and I had a chance to collect firsthand a couple of original "ku-bits," as we called them. One time, for instance, during rehearsal he tapped vigorously with his baton to stop the orchestra and said to us, in his heavy Russian accent, "I told you before, children, to play better and better, and yet you play *badder and badder.*"

Chiba admires Janos Starker's Bach

And when I got tired after a demanding rehearsal, or shuttling among several performances which were going on at just about any time of the day or night, together with a few colleagues I would climb a hill, swim in the placid lake, or hike on the winding trails. The evening discussions were like what might have taken place in ancient Greece, if music had been the main concern of the philosophers of the day. I still remember Lenny Bernstein's lucid arguments on the subject of experimental music. He pointed out that no composer starts out planning to compose music that is experimental, and therefore there is no such category. Of course, he had a vested interest in the subject.

Later, when we got to know each other, I suggested to him that he compose music appropriate for different occasions, such as the *aubade*, the wake-up music for French royalty. I was embarrassed when he pointed out to me that Telemann had already written his *Tafelmusik*—table music to eat by, in the early 1700s.

He was well versed in foods and wines, and it didn't surprise me when, years later, a friend of ours gave me a copy of his *Four Recipes*, which he wrote for the legendary soprano Jennie Tourel. They sure beat anything on the Food Channel. . . .

The female students of Tanglewood fascinated me, and not only for the obvious reasons. A Hungarian humorist wrote in the 1920s about a man who is first disturbed, then becomes unhinged, when he realizes that his favorite radiator is giving warmth to others as well. In Hungary, when a girl smiled at me and asked what I was reading at the moment, it was a clear sign that her interest went beyond getting a good tip about literature. At Tanglewood, the healthy, smiling openness of the young women and their easy acquiescence to taking a walk with me, as well as with others, made me feel the way the abovementioned gentleman felt about his promiscuous radiator.

I—or at least a part of my body—became a minor pinup celebrity toward the end of my summer at Tanglewood. A few months earlier, Heinz Weissenstein, who was the exclusive photographer for the festival, had taken a picture of my left hand on my violin. To my pleasant surprise, one morning I found a two-by-three-foot enlargement in the music shop, and my hand gained the kind of popularity I wished that I had had.

In those days Manhattan was filled with creative young people eager to meet one another; the obnoxious idea of networking was still decades away. Before going to Tanglewood I had been invited to a party where I met Dorothy Caplow, one of the early Bennington College products. She was a pianist-singer-performer who'd had parts in Broadway musicals and in a radio soap opera. She had made records and, as a student of Theodore Roethke, had written elegant poems; she also played Brahms on the piano on the same high level as she did Gershwin. Like most Europeans, I was awed by the wealth of New York, but I sneered at what I thought was its cultural emptiness, so I was overcome as she opened up the world of American literature and visual arts to me.

Without being aware of it at the time, I was looking to replace my family, and her parents were civilized and loving people. Also, she was Jewish, which was important to me after the war. And the fact that she was beautiful didn't hurt either.

We got married in the spring of 1948, and it was fortunate, during those lean years, that she could always do a gig as a cocktail pianist when the larder was empty.

After Tanglewood, I felt that the time had come to test my wings, and my first tentative flight took me to an audition for the Dallas Symphony Orchestra. In a couple of weeks I received a note that I had been accepted and should report for the upcoming season. Some years later, Walter Hendl, who was the musical director there, and another of the triple talents in the Bernstein mold, told Starker the story of my audition.

"After a bunch of mediocre violinists, in comes this young guy who plays the Pugnani-Kreisler *Preludium and Allegro* almost like one of the big boys. I could hardly contain my excitement, and I asked him to sight-read the first violin orchestra part of the Beethoven violin concerto. Stumbling along the way, he played the entire section in D minor, although even our stagehands knew it was written in D major. Because of his big, warm tone and accurate intonation, I hated to lose him, so I compromised and put him at the last stand of the second violins."

I did advance within the section eventually, but heaven and I knew I would never have become a concertmaster of a major orchestra. There is a photo in my "Crazy File" of me playing the violin with a saw instead of a bow, which will give you an indication of how I felt about playing in an orchestra for a living.

Since in Dallas we didn't have enough money to furnish our apartment with well-designed furniture, I made our place unique by resourcefully transforming inexpensive or even discarded furniture and objects into playful yet functional designs. Pictures I painted were framed with thick climbing ropes; one-inch-thick wooden rods were pressed into a coffee table held by glass blocks; two-sided bookshelves became mobile room separators; and an abstract painting I did on glass was inserted into a wooden box and became a light fixture on one of the walls.

Doe and I used to invite to dinner some of the people we met at social events connected with the orchestra. The first time, we invited three couples and they came dressed in the casual elegance of Dallas society at the time. After dessert was served, we got up to have coffee in the living room section, and all of the guests had a bold, horizontal black stripe on their trousers or dresses where they had come in contact with the bottom edge of the dinner table. Apparently I hadn't realized that the paint I had used to paint the table had to be thinned; in its concentrated state, it took months to dry. Fortunately everyone was gracious about it, and one of the wives joked that she would have someone design a dress with the black stripes.

Another time, I decided to cook a Hungarian paprika chicken dinner. To my dismay and amazement, in the only—excuse the expression—"gourmet shop" in town, no one had ever heard of sour cream.

"But why would you want to turn good cream sour, young man?" was the reply to my inquiry.

Sawing away. One of my rope-framed pictures
is in the background

During the spring of 1949, I wrote quite a few letters, some containing only a paragraph or a clipping, to friends in Hungary. It was clear from this correspondence that I was astonished by what I had found in Texas, which Communist propaganda labeled a cultural wasteland; it had more first-rate symphony orchestras, theaters, museums, and colleges than all of Communist-dominated Hungary. The real irony was that some of my former schoolmates became Communist sympathizers despite our Thomas Mann–influenced student days.

Toward the end of the season, Doe received word that she had been awarded a Fulbright scholarship in music, and a couple of months later we were on our way to Rome on a transatlantic ship that bore no resemblance to the *Marine Flasher*, which had brought me to America just three years earlier.

Soon after arriving in Rome—once the shock of novelty wore off—I realized that this city was similar to New York in that one had to love the city in order to like it. Fortunately, it was love at first sight, smell, and taste—if not sound. I did have difficulty tolerating the Romans' second-most-popular sport after soccer: *fare rumore,* making noise. But when you go to a new country, you are either a pebble in the water or you can become part of the water. It didn't take much of an effort for me to emulate the behavior of the good citizens of Rome.

Shortly after our arrival, I auditioned at the Accademia Santa Cecilia, and for my first piece I played one of my favorite openers, the Veracini-Corti *Largo,* a majestic, soaring piece that has to be performed with controlled passion in order to be effective. The professor who was presiding, together with two others at the audition, was an elderly gentleman. After I finished (with a vibrato that was a bit wider than I had intended), he complimented me: "I am pleased that you have played my piece so well." I was a bit taken aback, knowing that Veracini had lived in the first half of the eighteenth century. The mystery vanished when I learned that this man's name was Corti, and he had written the transcription that bore his name decades before, and it had since become a standard part of the violin repertoire.

The music-making and teaching at Santa Cecilia were not on the level of my Budapest, Salzburg, or New York experiences, but I never received as warm a reception anywhere else as I did during my first recital there—opening, naturally, with the Veracini-Corti *Largo.*

For a while we lived in Rome, and on very rare occasions we satisfied our daily pasta quota at a small trattoria, usually ordering spaghetti all' Amatriciana, the spicy, angry-red specialty of the nearby village of that name, which at that time cost the equivalent of fifty cents. We would hang our coats against the wood paneling, and we became quite friendly with the unflappable waiters. In some countries, reading a menu makes you feel like a birdwatcher focusing a pair of binoculars on an interesting but strange specimen, but in the trattorias of Rome everything seemed familiar and comfortable, although I had not tasted many of the dishes before. Italian cuisine has never lost its popularity because Italian cooks are masters of the art of keeping up with the flavors of yesterday. My all-time favorite became *arrosto di maiale,* the young pork, roasted with rosemary and garlic, that is sold on the streets.

I used to visit the Trastevere section of the city and sit on the Piazza Santa Maria to observe the life of real Romans. Eventually, as we learned the local customs, we would go to small trattorias in this area on Sunday mornings to avoid the tremendous rush when church let out. I guess we were too early one Sunday when we ordered a specialty of Rome, *abbacchio*—the consummate dish of a roasted young lamb, no more than a month old, which has never tasted grass, and has the texture of a young chicken—because it was not quite ready. So the cook cut off a couple of pieces and finished it *alla griglia*—with slices of thick bread, also charcoal-grilled, to be dunked into the juices of the meat. Wisely, I never tried to reproduce this resourceful improvisation in any of my eventual restaurant ventures.

Nowhere will you find more culinary chauvinists than in Rome, and those in the Trastevere section top them all. Supposedly, the philosophy that guides the locals is *Acqua e pane, vita da cane*—"Water and bread is a life for dogs only"—and that notion is more important to them than the glorious past and the uncertain future. Most of the restaurants had similar menus, all using liberal quantities of good olive oil in their cooking. According to local wags, one of the restaurants here was once hit by a bomb, but the enormous amount of olive oil that was used in its cooking caused the bomb to simply slide off it instead of blowing up.

Because I have always loved cityscapes more than landscapes, the sidewalk cafés of Rome became permanent garden parties I could attend every day without receiving a special invitation. I could listen to ongoing arguments, which were amusing if you were not involved, meditate like a sidewalk Buddha when they let me, and get tanned by the glare of the glittering diamonds of the nouveau riche tourists passing by. Café Rosati was the ultimate setting, offering an unobstructed view of life on the street. To Romans (and Italians in general), the street is a parlor and the stage for 2,687,000 non-union actors. One of the secrets of happiness is first to have something and only then to want it. For me, the Roman sidewalk cafés were a good illustration of this principle.

I would be less than honest if I didn't admit that much of my culinary knowledge and instincts developed years later, after countless visits to Rome, doing research for articles and working with chefs there. I learned to my great surprise that, by and large, food in Italy had been arrested in time, circa 1800. The taste gestures are often broad yet subtle, primarily by-products of the superb ingredients. In other European cuisines, chefs are apt to superimpose on their creations, insisting on something new for the sake of newness. But in Italy every dish must be in tune with the environment, which makes it safe and comfortably predictable.

I learned a lot about art from the Hungarian expatriate sculptor Amerigo Tot, who became a friend after I met him at his home in Via Margutta. There were times when I was convinced that he loved only his own creations, and when you made a comment about his sculptures, it was advisable to watch your words. In one period he sculpted only preg-nant women, claiming, "I am the first who has done it since the Etrus-cans." When a visitor, a Hungarian philosopher, put one of Amerigo's cats inside the plaster cast of a ready-to-give-birth lady, saying, "Imre [his Hungarian name], finally you have *life* in your sculpture," he was ready to break a few bones. But Tot wasn't fast enough, so he chased his friend down four floors to the street and across the Piazza del Popolo, disregarding the small detail that he was wearing only underpants.

Listening to his ideas about art, I could believe even such fanciful theories as the one he told me one day when we were looking at ancient Greek sculptures at the Museo Barracca di Scultura Antica. "You see, George, by admiring the marble figures carved by the great sculptors, after a while Greek mothers began to give birth to babies with similarly perfect shapes."

Whenever I look at the bas-relief built into a wall of my bathroom in New York, I remember his insistence that pebbles, formed by the ele-ments for millions of years, were the most perfect pieces of sculpture, and quite a few were strewn around his substantial ladies. He was a great enough sculptor to have created a new brass door for the Vatican, and the façade design of the Stazione Termini in Rome, but he was proudest of the Madonna of Csurgó he made and donated to the little Catholic church at Fehérvárcsurgó, the village where he and his family were born and lived.

After the first few months, Doe and I moved to Castel Gandolfo, one of the villages of the Castelli Romani. The natives can't seem to agree on how many of these small, ancient villages lie in the vineyard-laden hills southeast of Rome, but thirteen is the most commonly accepted number. None of the communities is more than forty-five minutes from Rome by car or train, and they are all minutes away from one another; you have to be careful not to lose any in the crease of your map.

I commuted to my violin lessons and social activities in Rome from Castel Gandolfo, where we rented the ground floor of a discreetly shabby villa directly on Lake Albano. Every morning I used to admire the palace across the almost-too-picturesque lake, and feel sorry for Pope Pius XII, whose view was our decaying terrace. The popes have spent their summers there for many centuries, blessing the townspeople and visitors after Sunday mass from the window of the sprawling seventeenth-century palace designed by Maderna, the Philip Johnson of his time.

A local girl came once a week to simulate the motions associated with housecleaning. One day she told us tearfully that her family had decided she couldn't marry her boyfriend because she was from Marino and he was from Albano Laziale—villages almost directly adjacent to each other. There had not been any intermarriage for a long time, she sobbed, because of a feud between the two villages, although nobody knew when it had started or what was the reason for it. Also, she added, "They eat funny stuff." That really surprised me, because I hadn't detected the slightest difference in cuisine between the two villages—but of course I wasn't a native. In this case, however, love conquered all, and the couple married anyway.

In June, another nearby little village, Nemi, held its annual Sagra delle Fragole, or "wild strawberry festival," and I learned a startlingly delicious preparation there which is still one of my favorites: ripe straw-berries sprinkled with a good red wine vinegar and a bit of sugar.

One day, while returning from Rome, I sat opposite an obviously American couple, and we soon realized that we lived right next to each other in Castel Gandolfo. They were Carson McCullers and her husband, Reeves, and they became good neighbors of ours. Her Italian, steeped in heavy Georgian syrup, amused us no end. One day they were supposed to have dinner at our place, but they had to cancel because she became ill. The following day, on the way back from Rome, I passed by the flower stands of the Piazza di Spagna and bought a single flowering almond branch, remembering how she had talked yearningly about the almond tree that grew in their garden in Georgia. I had to stand on the bus to the station, as well as on the train all the way to Castel Gandolfo, in order to remain vertical so I could hold the fragile branch and my violin case as well.

I could hardly wait to see her stroke-damaged face when she looked at the tiny blossoms. Her reaction was heartbreaking for all of us.

"Oh, George, the flowers on our almond trees had a color of their own, and . . . and . . . and . . ." She broke down and left the room. Color, especially when combined with fragrance, can create an intense connection with our past. That night we drank much more of the local Goccia d'Oro wine than our usual quota, each of us with his or her own agenda— to forget or to remember.

I have always loved the printed word, and I have always loved discovering every street in a new city. One day my wanderings through the streets of Rome led me to a small antiquarian bookstore where I was greeted by an elderly, pewter-haired proprietor, who could have been placed there by Central Casting. After my violin lessons, I used to visit the shop, where I would climb up to the dusty shelves, and when I found something I wanted to buy, the owner would quote me an absurdly low price, knowing that I would not accept the book as a gift, nor would I have any money left by the middle of the month if I bought it for the regular price.

One day, doing a balancing act on the wobbly ladder, I pulled out a book from a very tightly packed shelf, and several volumes fell on me. My Italian at the time was not quite up to a profuse apology, and as I picked up the books as fast as I could, I kept muttering, "*Scusa, Signore Longhi. . . .*" One of the slim, fragile books that had fallen to the floor was bound in a yellowed vellum, and when I opened it to its title page, the first words that hit my eyes were: *Cardinal Aldobrandino.* I got very excited because just a few days before, we had visited the Villa Aldobrandino in Frascati, a village next to Castel Gandolfo. The book was written, as I found out upon looking at it more closely, by the chef of the cardinal's household in the year 1610. Naturally, I had to buy this book, which transported me into the very kitchen where for centuries dinners were prepared for the Aldobrandinos and their illustrious guests. Whenever I remove the volume from one of the shelves in my New York office, I fantasize about sitting at the villa's great table and being served a gilded bird perfumed with rare spices of the Middle East, while a musician plays a Gesualdo madrigal on his viola da gamba.

Decades later, while doing research in a Roman archive, I learned that the fourteen-year-old Catarina de' Medici, when she married the future Henri II, brought master chefs from the very same kitchen to France, and they infused old forms with new energy, turning the folk-art of bourgeois cooking into the high art of the *Cuisine Classique*.

The year went by much too quickly before we had to return to the realities facing us in America. The first week back in New York, I was sitting in the cheapest section of the now-extinct Lewisohn Stadium in New York, listening to Jascha Heifetz playing the ubiquitous Mendelssohn concerto. A kind of musical epiphany came to me after he had completed the cadenza at the end of the first movement—the revelation that I would never be able to play like that.

I was so stunned that I walked like a somnambulist toward the subway, but during the endless night that ensued I worked out how to face the morning with renewed hope. Or perhaps as an avid reader of Bergson, I forced myself to believe that to exist is to change, to change is to mature, and to mature is to go on creating one's self endlessly.

Strings can be lethal or vital. The title of the late Hungarian violinist Joseph Szigeti's memoirs is *With Strings Attached,* a perfect description of his oneness with the violin. At that point in my life, the same line could have applied to me as well, but for different reasons. Since grammar school, I had been traveling on the bumpy side of the road leading to concert halls. That night, realizing that my time had run out, I finally cut the strings with which I was attached to the violin. (During the early 1940s in Budapest, Professor Rados had stated that if a child did not have seamless technique before he or she reached puberty, the chances of his or her making it were rather small.)

In the morning I awoke overwhelmed by a good feeling about a new life. Perhaps I would be able to choose a profession in which, just maybe, I could be a Heifetz. I took my violin from its battered case and looked at it with affection, wiped it clean of its rosin dust, closed its lid, and put it in the closet.

The last time I played the violin was for my son Simon's first-grade class. After a few variations on "Old Macdonald," I played the cadenza of—what else?—Mendelssohn, and I got almost as much satisfaction out of their pleasure as Mr. Heifetz must have felt that night after receiving a standing ovation in Lewisohn Stadium.

CHAPTER 10

A Cook's Progress

CHANGING PROFESSIONS at the age of twenty-six can be wrenching. Shortly after my epiphany at Lewisohn Stadium, I took the subway to Warren Street in downtown Manhattan. The Roosevelt administration, full of good intentions, had tried to simplify the job-seeking process for the multitudes of unemployed during the Depression by creating a single building jam-packed with various employment agencies. It certainly saved time and subway tokens, but the effect of being rejected dozens of times within a single day could be depressing and humiliating. It offered a first chance to some of us, and loomed as a last resort for others.

I walked around on each floor, reading the lists of jobs offered on bulletin boards, stands, and posters, sampling the wares, and, every now and then, forgetting that I was the merchandise. The possibilities I considered included jobs as a janitor, stockroom clerk in a publishing house, and a florist's assistant. Then I passed by a notice for a *commis saucier* in a private club, and I was puzzled: Why would they want a Communist cook? But I considered myself an accomplished cook who could make even a Spam schnitzel taste good, so I embarked bravely on this venture although my stomach was in close proximity to my heart.

I sat down in the cramped little waiting room in the employment office until a gentleman with dusty blond hair, perhaps in his thirties, asked me to come into his cubicle, which was fully packed with a desk, a file cabinet, and a chair. I admired his leather vest and the self-assurance that emanated from him.

"My name is John Comerford. Please sit down."

Then he looked at me with an almost disturbing gaze and, without any preamble or the standard questions, said to me in a strange accent, "So you want to change your life?"

My English, after three years in America and one in Italy, was still rather shaky (I had a colorful list of excuses, none of them valid), and I wasn't sure I understood him correctly.

After he repeated the question, I told him about my life as a budding violinist and a little about my background. I also mentioned that I was interested in the cook's job. I will never know why he responded to me in the way he did, but he looked into my eyes and said, "Now listen to me. I will tell you where to go, whom to see, and what to say. I will also call the chef and tell him that you will be a fast learner. You have a good chance of being hired. The rest will be up to you."

The chef did hire me, mostly because I spoke Italian with him. The job, my first in a professional kitchen, was at the Columbia University Club, on 43rd Street off Fifth Avenue. I was put at an easy station as a *commis potager* (I finally learned that *commis* means "assistant"), endlessly peeling vegetables, making *roux,* the flour-and-fat thickening, in enormous pots, and skimming the marmite, the steam kettle, that was kept simmering at all times as a base for broths.

A few days into the job, I became careless and cut my finger pretty badly. I was working the industrial-sized mixing machine, drizzling oil into the vat, when I noticed Chef Panteleone watching me. What I also noticed was that the sizable bandage covering my self-inflicted wound had fallen into the mayonnaise I was making. I stopped the huge mixer and desperately tried to fish it out with my other hand, and when the chef walked over, watching my motions with puzzlement and alarm, I improvised: "I learned this technique of alternating the motion of the machine with hand-stirring—it makes the mayonnaise much lighter and airier." He was not sure what to make of this, but to my great good fortune I soon found the bandage and, with closed fist, lifted it out of the gallons of almost-ready mayonnaise. I survived many similar near-disasters—most of the time using my improvisational skills and guessing how to do a job seconds before I had to do it.

My undoing in the kitchen of the Columbia University Club was caused by Signore Bibieni, a baroque stage designer—and I am sorry if this statement sounds as though I am reaching for the esoteric.

My friend Janos Starker had just made his first U.S. record, the *Boccherini Concerto*, and when he told me what the record company was planning as a cover for the record, I decided to do something about the aesthetic part of the package. So, after lunch, I walked over to the 42nd Street Public Library, which was just a block away. After an hour or so, with the help of one of the librarians, I found a charming eighteenth-century pen-and-ink drawing of a stage by the aforementioned Bibieni, which was an ideal background for the cover and would express the spirit of the music.

I ran back to the kitchen, rather pleased with myself, and to my shock, the chef was standing at the door. He was six feet tall, and with his starched, bone-hard *toque blanche*, he looked like a vengeful larger-than-life angel.

As I greeted him, trying to pass by him, he growled, "Youuu firedeh!!"

Although my job was a so-called split shift, from 10:00 a.m. to 2:00 p.m. and from 4:00 p.m. to 8:00 p.m., he expected me to stay after lunch, as was the custom in those days, to do additional chores. Since there was no higher tribunal to take my case to, I got my belongings and left after four months in this kitchen.

While waiting for the next opening, through another Warren Street employment agency, I was sent to the 2,800-room Hotel St. George in Brooklyn as a temporary. There my job was, with two co-workers, to clean and prepare oven-ready frozen chicken all day. I tried to make this chore less depressing by figuring out shortcuts and dividing the work among the three of us cleaning the thousands of damned birds from morning till night. After a week, my hands became a bloody and painful mess from the razor-sharp frozen bones, so I was relieved when I heard the good news about my next job.

I wasn't planning to get an American college education by working in university clubs, but the next kitchen Mr. Comerford, my protector at the employment agency, eased me into was that of the Yale Club. The food they produced at that time was on a high level, far above the kind of fare usually associated with university clubs. Chef Soulier was also a good

The Yale Club buffet in 1950; I'm on the right

leader with well-calibrated taste, and I learned a lot from him, finally working up to the position of a real *saucier*. The highlight of my six-month stint there occurred one morning when I substituted for the breakfast cook, and the chit presented to me by the waiter was signed by Thornton Wilder, whose *Bridge of San Luis Rey* had been an important part of my war years. I not only understood the message of that book, but accepted it: You'll die whenever you've completed your mission on Earth, not before and not after. I'd like to think that the sunny-side-up with extra-crisp bacon was to his liking. By the way, he was never charged for it, because I kept the slip of paper with his signature. I hope that this single dastardly act of mine did not contribute to any financial difficulties of the Yale Club.

The low point of my "Yale education" came a week before Christmas. The *chef garde-manger*, the head of the cold kitchen, became sick, and at the very same time his assistant got the top job elsewhere, so there was no one to do the elaborate decorations for the Christmas buffet, which was an important tradition of the club. Mr. Broun, the chef-steward, called the union and asked if they could send someone as a temporary replacement, but neither the union nor the employment agencies could produce anyone on such short notice.

Because I was used to staying after hours to learn this fading skill, I had developed the ability to create better-than-acceptable pieces, some of which were quite inventive. Knowing this, as a last resort, Broun asked me if I would stay nights after my shift as a *saucier* and act as the *decorateur* for the big display pieces.

Two days later I received a visit from the business agent of our union, who warned me not to moonlight. He also informed Mr. Broun that unless I stopped, the union would form a picket line in front of the club's entrance. When he was confronted with the fact that the union had been asked to send us a temporary substitute but was unable to do so, he just shrugged, repeated his threat, and walked out of the kitchen. I don't know what buttons were pushed by whom, but nothing came of the union's bullying. I kept working feverishly, assisted by two others in the department, and no one had to cross a picket line.

As for the *pièce montée*, as these decorative set pieces used to be called, it was made with a huge salmon covered with the gelatin-based *chaud-froid* designed to look like a fisherman in a boat. I made the scales of the fish with a "paint" made of black truffles. Completing this piece was a lot of trouble, but nobody knows the truffles . . .

One day when I returned to the Warren Street agency, Mr. Comerford was not there. His successor called me into the same small cubicle Mr. Comerford used to occupy and, in a halting voice, asked me to sit down.

"Your friend, Mr. Comerford, has disappeared. It turns out that he was a member of the IRA, and the FBI was after him. By the way, his real name was not Comerford."

I also learned that he was a playwright, and that a one-act drama he had written under a pseudonym with the title—of all things—*Kaddish* (which is the Jewish prayer for the dead) had been performed some time earlier by an off-off-Broadway group.

I felt as though I had lost a good friend. Although our lives had just brushed past each other's while taking different roads, I will always remember him with affection. During the next few weeks I called the agency a couple of times to inquire about him, but no one ever heard from him again.

Keeping to my agenda, I worked in as many different kinds of kitchens as I could get into, ranging from small East Side French bistros to the Café Chambord, an acknowledged temple of French haute cuisine at Third Avenue and 49th Street. A 1938 restaurant guide (with an introduction by the inimitable Lucius Beebe) indicated that it was "favorably known to discriminating diners-out . . . and the preparation of food is not treated casually." The kitchen was famous for a Gruyère omelette and fresh truffles cooked with champagne, but to my great shock, I found that the dozen or so fancy sauces, each christened with an impressive-sounding French moniker, were all doctored out of a single basic *fond de veau,* a kind of all-purpose French brown sauce—which was the antithesis of the true classic preparations in the repertoire of French cuisine. This practice, by the way, was the rule and not the exception in the French *grands restaurants* of New York in those years.

When I look back, some of the experiences I had then seem like something out of a slapstick movie. For a few weeks I worked at the famed Copacabana nightclub as a temporary roast cook. One night the eccentric impresario Julie Podell (who was supposedly a front man for the mob), in a drunken, melodramatic gesture, took me and two others from the kitchen into the club, and plunked us down in the front row to have a look at the well-rounded, pink-haired showgirls doing their bathing-beauty act. I must say I had a great time watching this spectacle; showgirls in those years weren't concerned about diets and other losing propositions. When we returned to the kitchen at the end of the show to prepare the pseudo-Chinese food the Copacabana specialized in (like chicken breast coated with chopped walnuts and served with a sweet-and-sour sauce), Mr. Podell, who usually liked to sit on a high stool in the kitchen near the entrance to the dining room, opened our stainless-steel wall refrigerators, screaming, "Everything is a mess, you are pigs, you are motherfuckers!!" and began furiously throwing tomatoes, eggs, and containers filled with sauces to the floor and at the cooks. I was pummeled only with a few pieces of fruit—the melons, fortunately, were kept in another walk-in refrigerator.

We just went on working. No one quit. We all needed our jobs.

When, in 1953, I finally managed to get into the kitchen of the legendary Hotel Plaza, as a *commis-saucier,* my excitement was hard to contain. I felt as if I were a member of one of the world's all-star soccer teams, positioned between the seemingly endless range on one side, and on the other, the forbidding sight of the great *chef de cuisine* Humbert Gatti.

Working in such a super-organized kitchen as the Plaza's, where each department was an autonomous entity, yet interdependent with the others, I learned how to create systems that became a basic tool in my profession later as a consultant. To learn as much as possible, I worked for (or at least watched) some of the fine craftsmen at the Plaza's kitchens, such as Aldo Fattori, the *chef garde-manger* of an especially gifted brigade, and I would stay many hours after my shift was over, furiously taking notes.

Top professionals in many disciplines like to dazzle each other with pointless technical tricks. I learned, for instance, how to make a *pomme en cage,* an imprisoned potato ball within a potato cube carved out of a single potato. After I perfected this arcane skill, I used to frighten young apprentices by telling them that they must make a couple of dozen to be fried for a party of ten within thirty minutes. Those were the days when superannuated dowagers lived in plush suites at the Plaza and would give recipes to the room-service manager, who in turn passed them on to the chef, and we had to prepare these dishes to be served in their parlors. I had to cook, for instance, a breast of baby chicken, cut into precisely half-inch cubes, in a light cream sauce and put into a specially baked, hollowed-out, large-sized brioche—at exactly 6:00 P.M., to be served to one old lady by selected room service waiters at 6:15 several times a week.

I loved to watch the creative process of the *chef de cuisine,* Gatti, to whom skill came first, and inspiration only later. He would direct his kitchen—based on French classic cuisine—with supreme confidence, and on occasion he cooked something for "the family" of cooks. I tried to reproduce his vegetable soup, but it never quite came out like his. He cut onions in half, browned them directly on top of the range, and then combined them with diced potatoes, turnips, chopped tomatoes, julienne of leeks, fennel, shredded lettuce, and a julienne of chicken gizzards, all of which he would cook in a chicken-and-beef broth. Afterwards, everybody was instructed to put a slice of cheese toast into his (there were no female cooks in the kitchen) individual soup bowl, and to break in a raw egg. Then we ladled the soup on top of the toast. The egg, of course, was cooked by the heat of the broth. Finishing the last spoonful, it occurred to me that simplicity may be one of the signs of perfection in all the arts. But then, maybe it isn't. . . .

Not only was the à la carte menu extensive, but the management was proud of the fact that it would serve almost anything a guest requested— within reason. If someone ordered *haricots verts,* the French string beans that are indeed string-thin, I would go into the refrigerated walk-in box and take out an already half-cooked little bundle tied with the green stalks of leeks, and finish cooking them in a little broth. Naturally, they lost some of their character and flavor, and the dish was a bit far from the taste nature had endowed it with. After an exceptionally demanding rush hour, I made a vow: if I were ever in a position to create menus, I would not offer dozens of vegetables and garnishes, because too many short cuts are required to produce such a variety. But I did admire the cuisine of the Plaza, which was so classically oriented at that time that even a simple cream pie ended up as Carème Pie.

Almost everyone working with me on the line was either Italian or French. Most of the French cooks came from Gourin, a small town in Brittany—as a matter of fact, two of them had been neighbors there. I had to switch my hours for a couple of weeks because one of these *sauciers* was on his honeymoon in Brittany. When he returned, he told me about his wedding dinner, which was held in a place on the Lower East Side called Chateau Gardens. He also told me that the lady who made the arrangements for their wedding, when she learned that he was a cook at the Plaza, had mentioned that they needed someone to help organize their kitchen.

Timing is one of the keys to an actor's delivery, a musician's interpretation, and even great sex—knowing when to stay and when to move on. After eight months at the Plaza, I realized that making the switch from behind the range to management would be the essential next step on my path upward *ad Parnassum.*

Hearing the aforementioned bit of information from my colleague, I was so excited that I could hardly wait until the following Monday, my day off.

CHAPTER 11

Bowery Follies

I DRESSED UP in my double-breasted dark blue suit, with a conservative tie, a well-starched white shirt with French cuffs, and a handkerchief with just an inch showing—ready for an interview for my first management job. When I mentioned to a friend of mine the address where I was headed, he mumbled something about it being in the Bowery, a location that seemed to him unusual for a banquet hall, but it didn't diminish my enthusiasm during the long subway ride.

Chateau Gardens looked like a muted version of Frankenstein's castle circa 1898. As I learned later, the building had originally been a Greek Orthodox church. When, years before, the church had closed its doors, the city, or perhaps the Church, hadn't known what to do with the building, and so the couple who interviewed me had taken it over for a token sum. (It would eventually be torn down to make space for the rebuilt and enlarged Houston Street and Second Avenue subway station.)

Stepping through the imposing portal, I was greeted by an old man with a scraggly mustache, wearing a chauffeur's cap and an ill-fitting suit. Giving me a professional grin, he took me to the office, where I found a woman who seemed to be in her forties and who used makeup with great abandon. She introduced herself in an unstoppable torrent of gabble:

"IamMrs.HildaKayeandwhatisyournameandwhereisyourbrideyou-areluckythatyourweddingwillbeinthemostbeautifulballroomintheworld-and . . ."

I waited her out. When she finally had to take a breath, I told her I was there to talk about a job.

The smile disappeared from her face.

"So why didn't you tell me before? The person you have to talk to is my husband."

With this, she hit a bell on top of her desk. In a few minutes, a fragile-looking creature came in with a baleful expression on his face, which—I had a chance to observe later—was permanent. He reminded me of Mr. Rudbányai, a rich merchant in my hometown, about whom my father had once said that he probably went up to the attic every morning and laughed for half an hour so that he could cry for the rest of the day.

"So, why do you want to work for me?" was the first question he asked me. What do I say to someone who is wearing a heavy coat in July, flutters around the room like a bird on a hot roof, and has just asked me a question to which the only answer could be that, having no qualifications whatsoever for a management job, perhaps I could learn to shave on his beard, so to speak.

After half an hour of continuous questions, many of which were repeated several times—most likely to see if I was consistent in my pre-varications (which he probably presumed would be an advantage in selling his banquet rooms)—I was shown around the building.

"Mr. G," as he was known, had divided the cathedral-height space into four levels, making each into a banquet room. To create the fifth ballroom out of the basement space, he had hired a designer whose taste matched the market he was aiming for. The result was the Palm Room and the Hollywood Terrace, dotted with fountains and palm trees made of an array of materials from lacquered papier-mâché to colorful sheet metal, a few of which supported strange-looking birds and glittering *tchotchkes*.

At the end of the tour he turned to me and said: "So don't be late tomorrow. We start at eight in the morning."

And thus it was that I made the big switch from the kitchen to a coveted management job—a challenge that turned out to be much more than making the kitchen work more efficiently.

I had already observed in Italy that the two high points in people's lives were their weddings, which happen to most people, and their funerals, an event in which participation is universal and obligatory. And I eventually discovered that in New York the best part of the wedding for the engaged couple was their visits to a minimum of three, and perhaps as many as ten, wedding halls or hotels to find the dream place for the wedding dinner.

At Chateau Gardens it was rarely an intimate affair. The ground-floor ballroom could accommodate as many as five hundred under its swaddle-draped ceiling, and the smallest room held two hundred people. Eventually I surmised that the two families would buy a map of the area they lived in, draw a circle around it, then simply invite everybody within that circle. Because of the huge weddings, many of the couples had to choose the cheapest place. So it was not surprising that some of these turned out to be fêtes worse than death.

History often records even the people who are responsible for marginal inventions, but we will never know who came up with the idea of the package deal for weddings. Chateau Gardens offered a dozen types, and the most comprehensive one included, in addition to the meal, the orchestra, twenty-five percent off at a particular jewelry store and at wedding gown and tuxedo shops, tips for the waiters, and even the limo from the church. The most brilliant format was the "sandwich wedding dinner." Four or five kinds of popular sandwiches (such as prosciutto, provolone, and roasted red pepper in a heart-shaped roll) would be displayed on an elevated, shiny plastic version of a large *compotier* in the center of the five-and-a-half-foot round table seating ten people—rather tightly, I might add. Huge pitchers of beer and red wine were served—no limit on consumption (all included in the basic price of the dinner), yet I can't recall many occasions when anyone got drunk or disorderly.

The bride and groom would sit in fancy carved armchairs, and as guests came to wish them eternal luck and numerous (male) children, they would produce an envelope containing their monetary contributions to the newlyweds. The bride usually put each under her elaborate gown; it surprised me that toward the end of the evening she didn't actually tower over her groom, owing to the mountain of stuffed envelopes she was sitting on.

The Main Ballroom of Chateau Gardens, 1954

No royal wedding banquet was as solemn and orderly as when a mafioso's daughter got married. It was quite an experience to observe those beefy guys with scarred and permanently scowling faces standing around the room, wearing close-fitting suits and never saying a word to anyone.

My multifaceted job would begin in the morning when I telephoned prospective brides or their mothers, whose names I received from the priests of neighboring parishes. These friendly priests were on our payroll, although we couldn't tell—nor did we care—whether they kept the kickback or whether it went to the church. The busiest time was during lunch and after business hours, when the brides were free to shop around. I would introduce the slide-show presentation, showing them how glamorous the event would be, instead of trusting my verbal virtuosity to paint a picture that would evoke the wedding of a princess in a bygone era.

As a young man I was always impressed when the stunning female lead in a movie walked down a curving staircase, lightly touching the velvet railing. One of my first contributions to Chateau Gardens was to re-create such a set. I got hold of a carpenter, who built an impressive staircase

With colleagues at Chateau Gardens, 1955

inside the ballroom near one of its side entrances, covered with white carpeting. It was designed in such a way that the bride could go up the twenty or so steps unnoticed behind the scene. When she arrived at the top, a spotlight would pick up first her profile, then her gowned body, and her glamorized shadow that filled one of the walls. After the guests made the proper admiring noises, she would walk slowly down the steps, whereupon a pink spotlight turned every one of the brides into Sophia Loren.

A heavily retouched photo of the bride and groom was plastered everywhere, from the menu and place-cards to the back-label on the Asti Spumante magnums. A wedding cake with three or more tiers was displayed throughout the evening on the "sweet table," flanked by a fancy chromium fountain spouting purple fruit punch. Mountains of Italian cookies in beribboned gilded baskets completed the sweet excess on this lace-covered table.

Word of mouth did its job, and soon the five ballrooms were booked almost every weekend. On occasion we had ultra-Orthodox Jewish weddings as well, complete with the cutting of the bride's hair, a practice I was aware of, but that still shocked me. The rest of the week could be anything from the Chicken Neck Cleaner's Union's bingo party to the Haitian Communist Party's get-together, or Celia Adler (of the famed theatrical family of Stella and Luther) reciting something appropriate to a Jewish anniversary party.

In addition to selling these parties, my duties included producing the meals, beginning with purchasing the ingredients, receiving them, hiring and training the personnel, and figuring out ways to save money. The first lesson I received from Mr. G took place in the bathroom of the Grand Ballroom.

"George, pull the toilet paper!" he demanded. I was baffled, but pull I did—or, rather, I tried.

"You see," he said, "I had this fixed so that it's difficult to pull. We save on toilet paper this way."

During my first tour with Mr. G, he carefully avoided showing me the kitchen, which was in the basement of the former church and wholly deserved its forbidding name: everybody called it "the dungeon." And a dungeon it was.

We had only a couple of permanent employees, and had to hire as many people as I needed on Thursdays. The lineup started by five or six o'clock in the morning in front of the building, although we only opened the delivery entrance at eight. The applicants knew that they had to come sober; for them it was perhaps the only time of the day when this was even a remote possibility. Without inhaling the cheap fragrance of sentimentality, I grew to like these people and instead of judging them or, worse, condemning their way of life or death, I tried to help them as much as I could. I would be a hypocrite if I said that they were all fallen angels, but certainly at one time in their lives they'd had a chance—which they missed. It took me a while to understand that inebriation was the only state in which they could enjoy the comforting delight of hopelessness, where nobody told them, "Keep trying, you can do it"—where they could escape the rat race. The Bowery was a place where they couldn't get lower on the social ladder. The rest of the world scorned failure; here it was the norm.

One is supposed to drink to celebrate when one is happy, or simply has a thirst for a good glass of wine. But most of the denizens of the Bowery I got to know drank because they could not bear any kind of responsibility, as I learned eventually. They rarely harmed anyone except themselves. Many of them were victims of their World War II experiences, and they fought their last battles with bottles on an eleven-block-long skid row. Getting to know a few of them well, I came to the obvious conclusion that what, how, and how much someone drinks is not really important; the key is *why* they drink. What made them drink? For them it was the sweet poison that unmanned the man. Sinclair Lewis (and he should have known) put it this way: "A man takes a drink, the drink takes another, and then the drink takes the man."

I reorganized the kitchen by reclaiming unused storage spaces and setting up simple assembly lines for the task of making sandwiches, or anything that could be broken down into steps. I also introduced a system whereby anyone who came to work for four consecutive weekends would get a small bonus. Unfortunately, this reward didn't affect our payroll seriously.

These down-and-outs were a rich resource for missionaries, columnists, sociologists, or someone doing research for a doctoral dissertation. Little by little I learned about the world of the twenty-four-hour nightcaps, populated by derelicts, winos, and panhandlers. During the first three decades of this century, the Bowery had been filled with intimate Chinese, Yiddish, and Italian theaters, beer gardens, concert halls, and burlesque theaters, but they had disappeared during the Depression. By 1954, when I became a player there, the rows of tenements were dotted with flophouses, a Salvation Army hotel, liquor stores, and bars. But even here, there was a *Guide Michelin*–type star system distinguishing the flophouses that had a toilet on each floor, a separate cubicle lit by a single bare lightbulb, with a locker, a cot, and a blanket, from those that offered nothing more than a dump to sleep off a drunken stupor until the morning, when it changed to a sober stupor. The bars offered their "regulars" the first drink of the day free, even if it was midnight by the time they got to the bar.

Selling one's blood was a common practice in those pre-HIV days. A few of the old-timers specialized in getting hit by a car, picking small ones that were going slowly, and developed a technique so that they did not get hurt fatally. If they survived, ambulance-chasing lawyers handled their cases, taking most of the compensation money. And whatever these shysters handed over to the poor bums, they in turn gave it to their trusted bartenders in order to be able to draw on the sum like a kind of bank account. It usually took just a few days before the barkeep declared the account closed, and the deadly game began again, until a careless driver finally dispatched the man. Everything was stacked against these broken creatures. The liquor and the cheap wine were often spiked with ethyl alcohol to make it more potent—a rotgut vile enough to kill even those with steel-lined stomachs.

I became very fond of two guys who worked at Chateau Gardens almost every weekend. They were as different from each other as could be.

The older man was a white-whiskered vaudevillean character who dreamed about occasional small pleasures. "Monday ah'm gonna go to Coney Island, ah hope, ah hope, ah hope . . . get a hot dog at Nathan's, ah hope, ah hope, ah hope . . . and a big pitcher of beer, ah hope, ah hope, ah hope. . . ." He was an accomplished artist of anticipation, and I hope that he actually got to Coney Island on occasion before he was taken off to that great Nathan's-in-the-Sky.

The other, Captain Cummings, could easily be the subject of a book, but sadly all that will ever be remembered of him is contained in the following few paragraphs. He was probably in his fifties, a gaunt, rather tall person, not unlike an out-of-work Shakespearean actor. His erudition was limited to special pockets in literature (his hero was Francis Bacon, who, according to him, wrote everything attributed to Shakespeare), music (he knew the madrigals of Gesualdo, complete with the details of how he murdered his wife upon catching her *in flagrante delicto*), and the history of old New York's newspapers (his favorite was *The Ledger*, which published serials by Mrs. Harriet Beecher Stowe). He could recite poetry when he was sober, and probably made some up when he was not. I must have heard from his lips a dozen times a couplet by Robert Burns which sounded as if it were written about him:

> *God knows, I am not the thing I should be*
> *nor am I even the thing I could be.*

The most surprising segment of his knowledge was about the Cabala, perhaps because he could interpret its "thirty-two paths of wisdom" any way they suited him.

Then came a June weekend that was so heavily booked with weddings I had to hire a large group of people to work during the week as well, in order to be able to prepare the food for the ten luncheons and dinners. Little by little, I gave more and more responsibility to Captain Cummings, and he was in charge of the people who were roasting dozens of turkeys and hundreds of chickens. Friday was the key day when everything had to come together, and the workday started at 6:00 A.M.

Six o'clock came, then seven o'clock, then eight o'clock, but Captain Cummings was nowhere to be found. Desperately I sent several people to different flophouses to search for him, and finally one of them reported back that he had found him. I was so upset and disappointed that I went immediately to this miserable rooming house, a few blocks away, to give Captain Cummings a piece of my mind. I found him upstairs, at the end of a row of prisonlike cages, behind a wire screen, lying fully clothed on a filthy mattress, empty jugs of cheap wine his only companions. He didn't even try to get up; he just looked at me while I was trying to hold my temper.

"How could you do this to me? I was counting on you!" I said, without raising my voice.

He sat up with some difficulty and, slowly measuring his words, said: "How dare you lay responsibility on me, trying to reform me? It buried me in my previous life, and this is the place where I came to escape it. To hell with your clean shirt, clean living, sense of duty, and conformist's way of life."

Then he pulled the grubby covers over his head, and my last sight of him was his scaly feet with their long, broken nails. The cover was just not long enough for Captain Cummings.

Not many days after this incident, which had a profound effect on me, I was walking on the Bowery when I passed a wino I didn't recognize, lying in the gutter. He opened his eyes and in a cheerful voice greeted me: "Hello, Mr. Lang!"

That was the moment when I knew I must leave the world of Chateau Gardens.

CHAPTER 12

Dais Without End

I DON'T RECALL whether it was a few days or a few weeks after the encounter with the wino that my wife, Doe, who at the time was performing at the Hotel Pierre's fashionable Café Pierre as a pianist/singer, was asked by Stanley Melba, the booking agent, to come—as a guest—to a small post-opening party honoring Maurice Chevalier's return to the Waldorf-Astoria's Empire Room. The agent explained to her that after the coffee was served, Claude Philippe of the Waldorf, who was hosting the party, would ask her to sing something. Philippe, he said, minutely calibrated every event, and felt that an intimate party needed impromptu entertainment by a decorative, cultured guest—someone who, for example, could casually sit down at the piano and sing a few French *bergerettes* with style.

When, at the end of the party, Philippe thanked Doe, she mentioned that her husband arranged banquets too, and suggested that perhaps he could use him on his staff. A few days later I received a call from Ann Viccaro, his personal secretary, to come to see "Monsieur Claudius Charles Philippe" at 9:00 A.M. in his office two weeks hence.

What I learned only later was that one of the big boys in the building trade, whose daughter's wedding I had arranged at Chateau Gardens, had attended a ballroom function at the Waldorf the following day and, during a conversation, had teased Philippe by saying that his daughter's wedding was even more spectacular than the Waldorf party. Philippe, always ready to hire new slaves, asked him who had arranged the wedding, and the rest is (my) history.

The Waldorf-Astoria opened its art deco doors just as the Roaring Twenties were suddenly turning into the Groaning Thirties. The forty-seven-story structure stood six hundred twenty feet and seven inches high, combining the ultimate in luxury on an unprecedented scale. It was designed and built by the finest architects and craftsmen of the day, with a kitchen on each floor so that the *chef d'étage* could satisfy the wishes of the guests twenty-four hours a day. The money used to build the hotel had been deposited shortly before the Crash, and the investors could not withdraw it. They *had* to build it. So there was this dinosaur of a hotel with a receptionist on each floor, not to mention a Starlight Ballroom with a retractable ceiling that could open the room to the sky, renting its luxurious rooms for five dollars a day.

When I read *Confessions of a Grand Hotel: The Waldorf-Astoria,* by Horace Sutton (which had been published the previous year, 1954), it made me feel like a village priest reading about the Vatican. I hastily reread the book, especially the passages that had originally impressed me the most.

A guest staying at the Waldorf could have a chair upholstered and on the same morning buy a sapphire diamond necklace for $43,000. Later on he could undergo minor surgery and, before checking out of the hotel, bump into a former king of England, one of the two living ex-presidents of the United States, or General Douglas MacArthur, all of whom lived on the premises.

If there had been a television game show in those days, I wonder how many contestants would have guessed which two cities had the same size telephone system and police department as the Waldorf had at the time. (Miami Beach and Poughkeepsie would have been the winning answers.)

The immense size of the edifice is the source of some bizarre trivia. For instance, someone with a penchant for pointless statistics once figured out that the hotel used enough steam every year to have kept an average-sized house warm from the time of the Crusades to the present.

On the day of the appointment, as I entered the awe inspiring grand lobby of the Waldorf and thought about these awesome facts, I almost turned back. But I took the elevator to the fourth floor, where the banquet and convention department was located. I had to pass several secretaries before I was asked to wait in one of the reception rooms. I waited and waited. And waited some more. I couldn't leave the room for fear of missing the interview. Finally, about four hours later at around 1:00 p.m., a secretary opened the door and, with a French accent, said, "Monsieur Philippe is ready to see you."

As I walked into the opulent corner office, I saw a hard-featured, middle-aged man with a prominent nose and alert eyes behind thick, horn-rimmed glasses that bored through me. He was sitting behind an impressive period desk flanked by two secretaries not very subtly concealed behind plants. Without any preamble he said to me, "Tell me about yourself."

By then I was not only famished but angry as well, and I said, "I am thirty years old, and I think that my most valuable asset is that I can deal with eccentric people."

He got up and walked to his private bathroom at one end of the large office, and his next question came through the door: "Tell me about your other qualifications, besides having the gall to talk to me like this."

I was taken aback—imagining his activities in there—but I forced myself to go on, and our interview continued.

When, about a week later, I received a call to contact the hotel's personnel department to fill out some forms before starting to work in the banquet department, I felt like someone who had just won the grand prize in the lottery of life.

Reading a daily function sheet of the list of parties and other events there, it would seem that in the 1950s, if New York was the center of the world, the Waldorf was the center of New York, and Philippe controlled the heartbeat of the Waldorf. Whether you were the president of the United States, the queen of England, the premier of the Soviet Union, or a tycoon of immeasurable wealth, you needed a guiding hand at the Waldorf, either as a guest or as a host, and Philippe's hand was very firm. It would have been difficult not to become arrogant in his position as vice president in charge of all of the hospitality services of the Waldorf, a post that had been held by the legendary Oscar of the Waldorf before him.

A dazzlingly accomplished performer, Philippe was able to dictate in French and English to two secretaries, talk on the phone, and, at the same time, sell a party to the person sitting in front of him, promising that it would be the affair of the year or—if they were willing to sell the family yacht—of the decade. To make sure that he had something to do with his hands, too, he would be signing letters while a secretary systematically fed him the pages. He also edited his assistant's letters and menus, and these were sent out under his name, with the assistant's name in small letters in parentheses on the lower left side of the page—only as an interoffice reference. His signature, which read, "Philippe of the Waldorf," was quite accurate. He *was* the Waldorf.

At the beginning of my first week, a colleague took pity on me and told me before we went into the weekly Friday 8:00 a.m. meeting, "Mr. Philippe on occasion tells a—supposedly amusing—French story. I warn you not to laugh loudly because he'll think that you're a sycophant; don't smile because he'll think that you're laughing *at* him; and if you remain serious, he will think that you didn't like his story. Now at least you know what not to do."

Equally arrogant in a number of languages, only on very rare occasions did he meet a worthy opponent. According to a made-to-order legend, one day Philippe, as usual, was juggling two phones, making notes about an upcoming event, and, at the same time, giving directions to one of his assistants. Unfortunately, all this was happening while the chairman of the board of a large company was sitting in front of him waiting to discuss an important banquet he was arranging in the Grand Ballroom.

"I want your undivided attention, Mr. Philippe, this is most important to us!"

"Oh, yes, yes, certainly," Philippe said. "Try that number in Paris again," he instructed one of the secretaries hidden behind the foliage.

"I insist that you put down those telephones, Mr. Philippe," growled the chairman.

At that moment, one of Philippe's calls was connected and he said, "Oh, Madame, everybody is hoping that you will join the committee for the Debutante Ball. We simply can't do it without you . . ."

At that point the chairman turned red, got up from his chair, and pulled the telephone wires out of the wall.

The reactions in the room varied from suppressed laughter to shock, while Philippe stood there holding two telephones with dangling wires.

Most people in his position would have thrown the man out, but Philippe didn't even deign to comment. Smoothly, he began to talk about the chairman's party, partly because he obviously had respect for someone who could be as outrageous as he had been, and partly because he refused to lose a ballroom event just because of a couple of telephone wires.

Among my Waldorf mementos, I treasure one of my party arrangements on which Philippe wrote, "Good work"—the ultimate compliment one could possibly receive from him. He used to say that since the brain was nothing more than another muscle, if dumb jocks could develop their muscles, why couldn't we do it with our brains?

He was one of the few truly great creative men in the world of banquets. His day started at eight in the morning, and once, when I came in ten minutes late (disregarding the fact that I had left the hotel at eleven o'clock the night before), he greeted me with "Good afternoon, Mr. Lang."

I found memos I sent him that surprise me even now (at a distance of four decades), wondering how I had the guts to write, "I hope our future staff meetings will not be like the ones we have had in which people who cannot do anything get together to decide that nothing can be done."

He used to invite people like Lena Horne, Marlene Dietrich, Maurice Chevalier, Victor Borge, and Harry Belafonte to Watch Hill Farm, his country estate in Peekskill, and I recall seeing him sitting on a barstool in the kitchen, directing everyone, including me, on how to wash the lettuce, tend to the fire under the grill, or open and serve the wine from his wine cellar, which was filled with historic vintages. Only Grace Kelly looked upon the scene with a kind of detached hauteur, and took no part in the dinner preparations.

Philippe enjoyed acting like a cross between a benevolent dictator and a kindly father at his Lucullus Circle dinners. It was he who organized this dinner society of about fifty gentlemen, quite a few of them residents of the Waldorf Towers, and one of the basic rules he established was that politics, religion, and business were not to be discussed. I had the privilege of arranging many of these black-tie occasions, and there was no limit on what I could do with them. I could come up with any theme and be as extravagant as I liked, as long as I could get someone else to pay for my ideas—for example, suppliers indebted to Philippe. When I suggested a dinner based on the rich culinary tradition of the city of Lyon, remembering that it had also been the center of the silk industry for centuries, I was able to get on loan—with Philippe's help—a rare array of silks from various museums and individual collectors to cover the walls of the Jensen Suite, where the dinner was always held. From a private source in France, I borrowed wineglasses that were so thin they

With King Saud at the Waldorf, 1957

would break if you looked at them too hard. The insurance on them turned out to be more expensive than all the food we served at the dinner, but in those glorious days the only limit was my imagination.

Working with Georges Blanc, the *gros bonnet* [literally meaning "big hat," or head of the kitchen] of the Waldorf at the time, and his team gave me an opportunity to research the menus of the past masters of French *grande cuisine,* the only codified system of gastronomy in the world. Looking back, I realize that the collection of menus of the Lucullus Circle—the majority of them composed by Philippe—could also add up to a veritable kaleidoscope of a new golden age of gastronomy.

Taking care of royalty, including sultans, rajahs, and other potentates, was also part of my job. The visit of King Saud turned out to be quite a challenge. In February 1957, the "Talk of the Town" column of *The New Yorker* offered an amusing report about Saud's stay at the Waldorf; the following excerpts afford a glimpse of the royal circus that occupied seventy-five rooms of the hotel.

> *The King's entourage numbered seventy-six and included three sons, an uncle, a cousin, a prince officially described as Royal Intimate, the Director General of Press, Broadcasting, and Publications, the Chief of Protocol, the Royal Interpreter, three private secretaries, five bodyguards, the Royal Purser, the Royal Steward, the Royal Barber, the Royal Laundryman, and two Royal Coffeemakers.*
>
> *The Waldorf had been led to believe that King and party would arrive with four hundred pieces of luggage and was ready to handle all four hundred in jig time; nevertheless, the staff was a tiny bit relieved when King and party showed up with only eighty. (The rest of the royal luggage was shipped straight to Washington.)*
>
> *George Lang, the assistant banquet manager, is a dynamic young man of the true Waldorf stamp. "We learned two weeks ago that King Saud wished us to provide a reception for eight hundred and fifty in the Starlight Roof and the Palm Room, and a dinner for eighty immediately afterward," he said.*
>
> *"All the arrangements for the reception and dinner were in our hands. How to preserve the King's dignity at a reception for eight hundred people! How to seat him and eighty other people at a single banquet table and still obey protocol! Where to put Cabot Lodge! Dag Hammarskjöld! Krishna Menon! Oh, how the problems mounted! In the end, we managed to solve them all. As soon as I saw that the banquet was going well, I left the hotel and went for a walk along the river, to calm my somewhat excited nerves. I love this work, but I think that to do it well one should combine the head of a scientist with the heart of an artist, the ingenuity of a used-car salesman with the energy of a marathon runner. There is never any respite."*

No one within miles of the hotel believed in moderation. For one of King Saud's parties, in the center of the long table occupying the length of the entire Jade Room, we installed a toy-train system, the wagons of which were filled with fake jewels. Naturally, the king—like a child at Christmastime—controlled the traffic. The next day, one of the King's aides-de-camp reported to me that the king was very pleased, but requested that the next time he would prefer to use real jewels.

A gold pocket watch was King Saud's standard gift to someone who had especially pleased him, and I must admit I was somewhat disappointed when I received only a cigar-sized fountain pen the following day. Thinking that I might exchange it for a set of studs, I took it to a friendly jeweler, and was taken aback when he asked me how many sets of studs I could use, as the pen was made of solid gold.

When I had the first meeting with the *chef de protocol* of King Mohammed V of Morocco, I suggested that if the king would like to get the kind of favorable publicity he was hoping for, he should, instead of inviting the usual dignitaries, give a party for five hundred New York City schoolchildren, and the hostess should be his young daughter Lalla Amina.

The menu I concocted was somewhat outside the routine of the Waldorf-Astoria's chefs, but it was prepared with as much care as if it had been a Chevaliers du Tastevin dinner.

MOUNTAINS OF SANDWICHES IN CENTER OF TABLES

Peanut Butter with Currant Jelly

Chicken Salad on Whole Wheat Bread

Cream Cheese and Iceberg Lettuce on Nut Bread

Chocolate and Vanilla Dixie Cup Sundaes

Served in Praline Cups

Individual Uncle Sam Hats Filled with Brownies, Popcorn Balls,

Candy and Chocolate Bars and Sugar Cookies and tiny toys

Milk, Chocolate Malted, and Banana Milk Shakes

A photograph taken at the party, of Eleanor Roosevelt sitting with the princess and Zippy, the chimpanzee of TV fame, appeared in newspapers all around the world. Of course, my secret agenda was that my seven-year-old daughter, Andrea, could attend the party, which she did. The king received loving notice even from the most hard-boiled columnists in New York.

It is easier to figure out what one should give to someone who has everything—a burglar alarm, perhaps—than to invent parties for hundreds of food editors who have already tasted, seen, and written about everything and everybody. One of the ideas I came up with for Gerber Baby Foods featured a stage split in half. On the left side was a 1920s mother with one child, and on the right side of the stage was a modern-day mother with—if I remember correctly—eleven children, each going about the task of preparing a meal for her offspring. By the time the 1920s mother was through with cooking, mashing, and straining the food for dinner for a single child, the other mother's eleven kids had all been fed—with guess what brand of food? The most difficult part was to find the mother with that many children who would be right for the role. But, fortunately, this was not my problem.

Another party, hosted by Robert Smallwood of the Lipton tea company for the same gathering of food editors, was based on a seventeenth-century engraving I had in my collection. I reproduced the menu and the interior of the room, complete with waiters wearing wigs and period costumes, while the Pro Musica Antica played incidental music from Purcell's *Love Triumphant*. How could anyone, after a party like that, drink any tea but Lipton?

It was during this congress in 1956 that I also met James Beard, who turned out to be one of the most influential people in my professional life. When Evan Jones interviewed me for his superb biography, *Epicurean Delight: The Life and Times of James Beard*, I told him about my first encounter with Jim. I was called in to Philippe's office, and there was this large gentleman. He was like a Turkish pasha who knew the essentials of life. Philippe was sitting at his Louis XV table. I was taken aback when he introduced Victor Borge the entertainer as Borge the breeder of ViBo Rock Cornish hens. But it didn't take an investigative reporter to solve the mystery, when Borge mentioned that he would like to serve his rock Cornish hens to the food editors. Jim then suggested we do something amusing with the little birds—have a party featuring these hens, boned and filled with a dozen different stuffings. We hit it off right away. Later we thought it would be fun to transform the Waldorf ballroom into a Midwest country tavern with a barbecue.

On the night of this singular event, Jim was at stage center, cooking spareribs and hamburgers on an open grill. Neither he nor anyone else had given thought to fire problems. When torchlike flames shot up toward the high ceiling of the ballroom, some of the guests began to panic, but Jim had seen too many open fires to show any reaction. While the fire department was being called, he was calm and kept on cooking with a smile, even though the flames were five feet high. His self-possession was enough to keep the evening going. By the time the fire department came, things had calmed down, though the following day we received a warning and had to pay a stiff fine.

I had a few other disasters, too, some of them quite colossal. For "A Night at Antoine's," I was able to get a few of the chefs from this legendary restaurant in New Orleans, and the menu we served, as well as the reproduction of its interiors, was quite authentic. The host kept mentioning the need for nonconventional entertainment in addition to a jazz band from Preservation Hall, so I called a few booking agents, and one of them suggested a witty pantomime act featuring a New Orleans street scene. I should have been suspicious when they moved in their props. The performers reenacted a red-light-district episode *à la Créole*, ending up with a stylized but rigorously athletic finale on a bed. The accompaniment of a jazz trio synchronizing its beat with the movements of the couple didn't help matters, and the host and I, not to mention his wife, tried to figure out how to stop the show. Finally I was able to get the attention of the actors, and mercifully they left the mini-stage before the climax. (No pun intended.)

Ever since then, I have made sure that I audition the entertainment ahead of time.

This was the era of the big bands, and the music made people forget for a while their problems outside the doors of the Waldorf. I remember one night having to check on parties in four different ballrooms. In the Astor Gallery, guests danced to Xavier Cugat's orchestra; in the Sert Room, Benny Goodman played "Sugar Foot Stomp," while Artie Shaw and his band performed on the stage of the Ballroom. Count Basie was barely noticed at the dinner dance arranged for Standard Oil executives, during which each lady was served a real pearl, nesting in one of the oysters she received for the first course. Unfortunately, I can't recall whose band was playing in the Empire Room.

It's easy to understand why Cole Porter, who lived in his own "townhouse in the sky" in the "A" suite on the thirty-third floor of the Waldorf Towers, wrote:

> *You're the top!*
> *You're a Waldorf Salad.*
> *You're the top!*
> *You're a Berlin ballad.*

When Philippe booked Dorothy Dandridge into the Empire Room for a two-week stint, several of the Waldorf Towers fossils called on him to protest. But with his French charm and a bit of strategic arm-twisting, he overcame their outrage at having a black performer at the Empire Room. By the time the great Lena Horne came, she was fêted by one and all.

As I peruse my Waldorf files, the array of parties seems endless. One I must mention was a birthday party for the grande dame of New York, Mildred Hilson (who, coincidentally, lived in the Waldorf Towers), at which Laurence Olivier sang "Happy Birthday," with Richard Rodgers at the piano. It wasn't easy to convince Mrs. Hilson that the invitees needed a bit of titillation, but she finally acceded to my idea of getting a classy stripper for the finale. When it came to the part where the young lady was to remove her G-string, as she pulled it off, through an ingenious device, she was fully clothed again in a film-thin fabric rolled up in the G-string.

During this period I became a tolerated member of a small group that emulated those groups that used to meet in the coffeehouses of Budapest, a world I had experienced mostly as a young man only through windows and from a few friends who were old enough to remember the days in Hungary before World War II.

Perhaps no one was more qualified to represent *Homo cafeaticus* outside its habitat than my elder children's "adopted grandfather," as he called himself, Alexander Ince. I was so eager to meet this legend of my youth that when I noticed his and his wife's name on the seating list for a theater party I had arranged in the Grand Ballroom of the Waldorf, I went to their table and introduced myself. As an awkward opening gambit, I said, "I beg your pardon, but are you the legendary Sándor Ince?"

He shook his head and, with a puckish grin, looking like an undersized Buddha, said, "No, I am sorry, I am not. But I used to be. Now I am just a poor relative of his."

He had started publishing *Szinházi Élet* (*Theater Life*) in 1910, the first magazine of its kind in any country, which served as yeast for the rise of the Hungarian theater. When he came to the United States in 1939, he tried to duplicate this seminal publication with the creation of *Stage* magazine, but he was never able to recapture the excitement of the first fifty years of his life. He did succeed, however, in assembling a Manhattan version of his Budapest roundtable, which used to meet in the Taj Mahal of coffeehouses in Budapest, which went by the unlikely name of "New York." Eventually I became a member of the group, and some of the most delectable times of my life were spent at this displaced roundtable, where even the salt shakers must have contained sarcasm ground to a crystalline form. The stories told there reflected, if not the virtual reality of yesterday, at least the piquant overtones of the politically incorrect; all conversation was based on a kind of skewed but delicious Central European logic.

Ferenc Molnár, the legendary Hungarian playwright and wit, was gone by then, but occasionally Ince, Billy Rose, Gilbert Miller, Al Hirschfeld, or perhaps Alexander King would quote one of his lines, just as if he had uttered them the night before.

Playing self-invented games was a serious part of the group's activities. One day someone would be talking about the first words he learned in English, then each of us tried to come up with an amusing line, breezily bypassing the truth. None of us, however, was able to top Molnar, who claimed that his first English words were, in the interests of self-defense, "Separate checks, please."

Going with Ince to an opening night on Broadway (on the rare occasions when I was able to get away from the Waldorf) was an education for me. He produced a number of plays on Broadway with the renowned Gilbert Miller (including *Gigi*). Instead of watching the stage during the premiere of one of his shows, he would concentrate on the reaction of the critic from *The New York Times*. During intermission he explained the finer points of critic-watching: "The danger sign is not when a critic looks at his watch; you know the show is in trouble when he looks at it and then starts shaking it."

Ince took me backstage after one of his plays. While we were waiting in front of the leading lady's dressing room, he whispered to me that she was totally miscast and he didn't quite know what to say to her. When we finally entered, he embraced her ebulliently and gushed, "Darling, are you happy?"

It was always a pleasure to spend time with Sándor, and the two of us had a standing weekly dinner date for years. Life for him was a party only occasionally interrupted, and I rarely saw him sad, with the exception perhaps of one morning in the early 1960s, a few years after the 1956 Hungarian Revolution. Noticing how downcast he was, I asked him the reason. He sighed and replied, "I was just told that you *can* send money again to Hungary."

Sometime in the mid-1950s, Ince and I were walking into the steam room of the Gotham Health Club, near the theater district we used to frequent—the same location where, these days, people are sweating for different reasons in a steel-and-glass office building—and we both noticed a mutual friend sitting on one of the wooden benches. To my surprise, Ince didn't say a word to him. After leaving the sweat-box he explained to me that a couple of nights before, this person had insulted him in his dreams, and before he talked to him again he would have to receive an apology—in another dream. Later I heard this story attributed to several other Hungarians, but a good scene doesn't have to be original to be enjoyed.

At least one out of every three incidents with Ince and his friends involved women. For example, an octogenarian member of the round table spent months wooing a young showgirl, trying to get her into bed, promising her everything, including a trip to the Côte d'Azur. One day he stormed into the Oak Room, and even before sitting down he exclaimed, "Which one of you was the pervert who told her to say yes to my proposal?"

Trying to emulate their style, I have kept the most delicious story for the closing act of this reminiscence. One night, after we'd finished a good bottle of Sándor's favorite Schloss Johannesberg, he told me about the time he met a former girlfriend—an actress, naturally—in Paris and invited her to his suite at the Ritz for an after-theater supper. "And after the Grand Marnier soufflé, which was her favorite, and plenty of Cristal champagne, we undressed and she looked at me critically and said, 'You invite a guest *for this?*' "

There was no one quite like Sándor; they must have broken the mold *before* they made him in 1889.

Like most of my musician friends, I consider teaching as important as performing, and in 1956 I created, at New York Community College, the first banquet management course ever offered. Until then, nobody had considered it a real profession worth teaching. During the first lecture, I explained to the students one of the ten basic challenges of selling banquets: "Once a canny old hotelman told me, 'There is a big difference between magicians and banquet salesmen. The magician can pull a rabbit out of a hat, if there is a rabbit nearby, but a good banquet manager has to do it even if there is no rabbit. Sometimes,' he added, 'there is not even a hat to pull the rabbit out of.'" Fortunately for the students, I supported my rhetoric with a systematic presentation of the technique of selling and arranging banquets.

I learned a lot of the rabbit-pulling from Elsa Maxwell, who lived at the Waldorf Towers. Her hobby was collecting people. Born in Keokuk, Iowa, she had dreamed of glittering balls filled with beauty, power, and fame. She was a dumpy little woman; Dorothy Kilgallen, the gossip columnist at the New York *Journal American,* once quipped that Elsa Maxwell had come into the ballroom during an April in Paris Ball riding an elephant, but Kilgallen couldn't tell which was the elephant and which was Elsa. Her small suite at the Waldorf—for which she paid a fraction of the actual rental, courtesy of Philippe—was the headquarters for plotting the revival of Monte Carlo (by turning it into a chic summer destination instead of just a winter playground for the rich), as well as for planning the April in Paris Ball, which at that time was the most extravagant, opulent peacock show on earth. This was also the place where she wrote her newspaper column "Party Line," keeping the glitter-to-go scenes lively, as her readers feared ennui more than communicable diseases.

Elsa Maxwell was the first hostess of her day to mix society, show business, and real business. Nobody before her had dared to mingle Hollywood stars with CEOs, royalty, writers, actors, and amusing eccentrics.

Elsa's feud with the Duchess of Windsor became the juiciest ongoing grist for gossip columnists and café (or Nescafé) society; it provided the stuff of which pop myths are made. I imagine they both needed something to shore up the lagging interest of the public. When Elsa told me that by coincidence she and the duchess would be traveling together on the *Queen Elizabeth II* to Europe (I didn't believe the coincidence part), I suggested she turn the voyage into a high-profile international event: *The Duchess and the Queen of Society make peace with each other.* At about that time I met the renowned writer and journalist Cornelius Ryan, who was between assignments (later he wrote *The Longest Day*), and since he was planning to go to Europe anyway, I gave him the idea that he should travel on the *QE II* and do a story about the *rapprochement.* The rest is the kind of history that is used to wrap fish and chips in England.

Elsa considered me her protégé, and I was flattered momentarily when she called me, in her column, "the Hungarian atom bomb," but the thrill was gone by the next day, when I realized that it was just part of the disposable myth-manufacturing process, retail and wholesale.

Many years before, she had met Jim Beard in Paris, where she had worked as a society hostess in a nightclub called Les Acacias. The three of us collaborated on quite a few spectacular parties, each of us providing a different part of the show.

When Elsa died, in her two small rooms in the Waldorf Towers, she left only a bunch of dresses that the famed designers of the day had made for her, a few books, the large imitation emerald ring she always wore, and the memory of a one-of-a-kind woman in our homogenized society.

Her closest friend—if she had one—was Cole Porter, her Waldorf Towers neighbor, who dedicated "Miss Otis Regrets" to her. I consider it more of a distinction than most of the coveted honors one can receive in life. George Bernard Shaw summed it up best for me when he said: "Elsa Maxwell is the eighth wonder of the world."

Every day at the Waldorf we would put on a different show, each with a different cast of characters. In one of these morality plays, Grace Kelly had the lead. On the surface you couldn't find a more unlikely match than the young movie actress (whose previous romance had been with the young, handsome Mohammed Reza Pahlavi, the Shah of Iran), and Philippe, who was far from handsome and ruled only one block on Park Avenue—and even there, he had to answer to the general manager.

It was years later, in 1956, that Grace Kelly returned to America as a princess, on the arm of her prince, pregnant with Caroline, her first child. I was standing in the Park Avenue lobby of the Waldorf watching the scene intently as she and Claudius Charles Philippe, ruler of the House

*With Princess Grace and Prince Rainier in 1956—her first
return to the U.S. as a princess; she was pregnant
with Princess Caroline*

That the Astors Built, confronted each other. Prince Rainier was walking beside her and, to my disappointment, Princess Grace and Philippe looked at each other as if they were meeting for the first time. It was as good a show as any of her movies.

There are enough biographies of Ms. Kelly to supply the seemingly endless appetite of readers. The main reason she has a walk-on role in this chapter is that I arranged a luncheon in the Empire Room on September 13, 1956, at which she was the honored guest of the Overseas Press Club, with intriguing consequences.

The menu for this luncheon had to be simple, since the OPC only paid five dollars per person, including gratuities, a bargain-basement price even in those days. Naturally, as at most parties, the little-known Bessarat de Bellefon champagne, from one of the several vineyards in which Philippe had a financial interest, was served (but only at the head table). There was nothing inventive or subtle about this menu. It had to be cost-efficient, and the lunch had to be served within forty-five minutes, leaving time for the question-and-answer period (the prime reason for the event), and there had to be just an indication in the menu that it was tailor-made for the event. It was the same old soup/chicken/ice-cream formula, but dressed up as Philadelphia pepper-pot, breast of chicken Monégasque, and an ice-cream bombe made with a lining of vanilla ice cream, a raspberry sherbet interior, and served with a *sauce fraisette,* which I named—rather flatfootedly—*La Bombe Glacée Princess Grace.* Still, everybody seemed to like the luncheon, especially Georges Blanc, the *chef de cuisine,* whose monthly food budget was not seriously affected. I had discussed the menu and the arrangements with a small committee of the Overseas Press Club, but my main contact was a decisive chap given to understatement named William Safire. With enough research, it was possible to discover how 3,800,000,000 years ago, two cells fused to form a new organism. It would be much more difficult, perhaps impossible, to discover why two people with completely different backgrounds, educations, and characteristics take a liking to each other, but that's what happened when we met each other, and we have kept our friendship in good standing for the last forty-two years.

The morning following the luncheon, Bill and I had breakfast at the Norse Grill in the Waldorf (where the Marco Polo Club is located today). During our conversation, I mentioned that the one thing that bothered me in New York was that everybody associated with people of the same or similar profession, whereas in Budapest young writers, scientists, actors, lawyers, doctors, musicians, journalists, entrepreneurs, and restaurateurs on the way up formed bonds of various sorts. Then I suggested we should gather together a few men of similar age, perhaps between twenty-five and thirty-five years old (we were both in that category at the time), each from a different profession and, most important, with a sense of humor.

Bill told me that he and a couple of his friends were already planning to do something like that, and ten of us had our first get-together the following Wednesday, again at the Norse Grill. The Wednesday Ten, which by now numbers twenty-five men, has been meeting continually for dinners ever since. We talk about subjects that interest us, and since our members are by now at the top of a dozen disciplines, including medicine, communications, politics, entertainment, publishing, finance, law, and journalism, we have a chance to look behind the scenes, often before events occur. We used to invite a guest to each dinner, and after plying him or her with enough wine, we would proceed to take the guest apart. One month, for example, Bill Safire invited Roy Cohn, and I retaliated the next month by bringing Alger Hiss. The guests ranged from cabinet ministers and Nobel Prize winners to Gypsy Rose Lee and Betty Friedan. Everybody always performs a bit during these dinners, but with a certain ease that can only come with three hundred or more rehearsals. One thing is certain: If anyone was the subject of national or international news the week before, the following Wednesday night he would still be just one of the gang.

The rules? Everybody pays his share of the check. Period.

One Wednesday night I brought into the group a noted Swedish sociologist who was teaching at Columbia University at the time. During one of our sessions, he analyzed our Wednesday Ten group, using the impressive-sounding hyphenated terminology of his discipline. His bottom line was that the group had no real reason to exist, and that therefore, after a rather short period, it would "unbind and dissociate." The sociologist unfortunately passed away before he could discover that certain coteries are outside of the clutches of sociology, and we have since celebrated our fortieth anniversary. There are people who believe that the good life is conditioned by love, music, and a fine meal. Although I am

You'll find "Nina" on my left ear

an aficionado of all three, I propose to make a quartet out of this trio by adding time spent with friends.

The Waldorf brought me many pleasures, but to survive it one had to be like an Olympic high diver who plunges into the water with style but without making an unnecessary splash. Whoever worked for Philippe had to perform smoothly to survive the pool of the Waldorf.

A Cautionary Tale

IRST LET ME give you the answer: Yes, a company with two bosses can screw up even the best deal.

Casting stones at people who are not around anymore to give their version of an argument is not fair. So I'll cast cheesecakes instead. Brass Rail cheesecakes, that is.

Early in the twentieth century, a generation of immensely talented immigrants from Russia and eastern Europe managed to build mega-businesses here by simply applying common sense. They understood elementary truths about the behavior of large groups of people (such as how to fulfill consumer demand), and combined that with determination and the guts to take all sorts of risks. None of these people climbed the corporate ladder on the way to the top.

For example, the Levine brothers came to America in 1914 with fifty gold rubles in their pockets, and started slicing pastrami in a little deli they opened at Seventh Avenue and 49th Street. By 1930 they had enlarged this tiny space, and their restaurant, which occupied several levels of the building, became the first Brass Rail. By the time they approached me at the Waldorf in 1959, they had a highly respected and profitable company. The foundation of the diversified organization was a chain of solid family-style restaurants. Eventually, mammoth multi-facilities were added, with extensive banquet facilities, restaurants at such places as Orchard and Jones beaches, Central Park (Tavern on the Green), and airports (the Golden

Door at Idlewild—today's Kennedy—Airport, which also did in-flight catering). The Executive-Employee Food Service Division managed— among others—the Ford Foundation, Columbia Pictures, and Socony Mobil's dining rooms. One could say that the Levine brothers built a several-hundred million-dollar business out of cheesecakes.

I couldn't and didn't resist their offer for two very good reasons: I realized that I had reached a dead end at the Waldorf, despite the glory that came with the job, and I felt that the salary package the Levine brothers offered me could buy a larger chunk of happiness. My vaguely defined new job description was vice president of just about everything.

No one knows—or cares, for that matter—whether the real, traditional New York cheesecake was developed by Lindy's, the Turf Restaurant, Junior's, or the Brass Rail, but the fact is that in the 1950s the Brass Rail sold several hundred of those irresistible golden cheesecakes every day. The recipe called for a certain type of fresh pot cheese instead of cream cheese, which (as far as I know) was the base of all others, and it produced a superior cheesecake.

A few minutes after I moved into my new office at the Brass Rail, I heard two male voices arguing loudly from an adjacent office. Not being used to such a ruckus, I stepped out to the corridor, where I saw Julius and Ed Levine at each other's throats. They were clearly enjoying the argument, and it looked to me like some kind of ritual. The minute they saw me, they stopped, and Mr. Ed, who was the business end of the partnership, said to Mr. Julius, who took care of operations, "So why don't you ask Lang to investigate. Let's see if this big shot can solve problems and not just smile at celebrities at the Waldorf."

It took a bit of time to untangle the story, which was about a flood of recent letters of complaint involving the Brooklyn branch of the Brass Rail, one of the largest restaurants in the borough.

In a voice that was just one decibel below theirs, I said, "Let me see the letters, and I will check out the situation."

Julius and Ed looked at me as someone who had spoiled their daily workout. But soon thereafter I did receive a bunch of letters and calls, mostly from people who had bought Brass Rail whole cheesecakes to take home.

The Brass Rail organization didn't abide by formalities, so I didn't have to coordinate a meeting with the Levines' secretaries; two days later, when I bumped into Julius and Ed in the men's room, I gave them the gist of my findings.

"The assistant manager, who is in charge of requisitioning food at the Brooklyn restaurant, miscalculated the number of cheesecakes they would need for Mother's Day, which was a month ago. As a result, they ended up with many, many unsold cakes. He was afraid to report the miscalculation. So from that point on, the fresh cheesecakes were put aside until they sold the old ones, but of course they couldn't catch up. So customers have been getting cheesecakes that are three or four days old. That's the reason they've had a flood of complaint letters. Anyway, I told them to give the several-days-old cheesecakes to a retirement home and start from scratch, so that they can sell the fresh cakes each day as they come in from the commissary."

They approved of my solution grudgingly, but I realized that I would have to perform a more impressive act as my opening number. Remembering the lesson I had learned at Chateau Gardens about the irresistible allure of getting something for nothing, I used up almost the entire advertising budget of the catering department working with our ad agency to put full-page ads in the tabloids. The copy blazed across the page:

You will be our guest for the first day of your honeymoon
FREE at ANY HOTEL IN THE WORLD.

How could we do it? Actually, it was quite simple. Just about any hotel is pleased to get a good number of extra bookings. But the hitch I devised was that the honeymooners would have to stay seven days. Although the one night was "with the compliments of the Brass Rail," the hotel simply gave seven days for the—probably padded—price of six. Within a short time, a flood of bookings followed.

For a while I enjoyed life at the Brass Rail because I learned to live with the unexpected. I also learned from the Levine brothers how to make a company with thousands of employees seem like a family. One of my responsibilities was to create and open new facilities, and this included working on airport restaurants. While designing the Panorama Room for the new Pan American Building at Idlewild Airport in 1960, I had to take into consideration that the renowned Najeeb Halaby (whose daughter later married King Hussein to become the queen of Jordan) had created an airline that was not for people who shopped at Woolworth's. Working on the pre-opening party, I felt that to gain attention in the national press I would have to take a slightly zany approach, verging on the irreverent. So I persuaded Ludwig Bemelmans, the legendary author and artist, to be the star of the show. On the day of the party, my friend Henry Sell, of *Town & Country*, had lunch with Ludwig at Le Pavillon restaurant and plied him with enough champagne so that he agreed to change into a Santa Claus costume in the nearby Sherry Netherland hotel. Then a Pan American helicopter flew him to Idlewild, landing right in front of the building. A group of children, after consuming Christmas-tree-shaped ice-cream cones and marzipan turkeys, were delighted. They surrounded him, thrilled to see Santa arriving, undoubtedly from the North Pole, while he mumbled, through a champagne haze, with tears in his eyes, "Please, children, don't believe in me. I am just a sham! You must wait for a real Santa who will come to you!"

Whenever I read his classic *Madeline* to my children, I remember his gentle smile and this surrealistic scene at the airport.

Each generation has a list of its eating and drinking preferences, and the restaurateur who can get hold of this list has a good shot at creating a successful place. Giving customers what they want seems an absurdly simple task, especially if you have the talent of the Levine brothers. They were born with an instinct for creating restaurants that fulfilled every guest's wish list. The large-scale rooms of the Brass Rail restaurants were a cut above what had been known as family restaurants, but they did not challenge the guests with trendy innovations. The menu offered not American but Manhattan foods, such as freshly carved meat sandwiches packed with three inches of filling, and coffee made from beans roasted and ground on the premises—certainly not the rule of the day. Understanding mass psychology, the brothers invented all sorts of package deals, twofers, contests with prizes, and other irresistible marketing devices. The bar with the famous brass rail, where you could spend several hours if you wanted to, served honest booze and big drinks, always with a smile. And if you felt like having a fancy dish for a special occasion, you could order stuffed lobster tails.

Unfortunately, by the time I arrived on the scene, the Brass Rail format and the entire chain's ability to change were deposited in a large ice block resting inside a Brass Rail freezer.

And this is where our cautionary tale begins.

Early in the 1960s, my secretary told me that someone at the reception desk would like to talk with me about an important matter. By then I had learned to act like an executive, and in order to maintain at least part of my sanity, usually insisted on prearranged appointments; but this man turned out to be so persistent that I gave up and asked my secretary to bring him in.

A portly gentleman sporting a goatee and wearing a white suit entered and, shaking my right hand vigorously with both of his hands, gave me a smile that was more than a stretch of his mouth. He seemed to me to be a mix of actor, patent medicine salesman, and kindly grandfather, but his accent was so thickly breaded and Southern-fried that I had difficulty understanding him. The conversation went something like this:

"Son, you look like someone who likes to eat chicken, am I right?"

"I guess most everybody does," I replied noncommittally.

"I knew it! I heard about you and this great company of yours, and I want you to come and taste a fried chicken like you've never tasted before!"

During the next half hour I learned that he had perfected a method and a piece of equipment for cooking Southern fried chicken in a way that yields a crisp, flavorful bird that melts in your mouth; this contraption was said to seal in all the taste that God (who was quoted, or at least mentioned, several times) put into the little birds.

"I am from the great state of Kentucky and I want to find a nice group of people who would open a fine place for my chickens in New York. And nothing on the menu but my chicken, that's very important, son, you understand?"

I learned that he had rented a small warehouse space in Queens and had set up his equipment there.

"How 'bout coming for a little chicken tasting tomorrow?" he invited me.

I was fascinated with him and with the idea, so we made an appointment. This outpost of a laboratory approximated a kitchen, and his invention turned out to be a kind of pressure-fryer instead of the usual type of pressure-cooker that used steam. The fried chicken, using his secret recipe for flavoring, was delicious and reminded me of the picnics of my youth. I told him how I felt—it was easy to be enthusiastic, especially after I learned that huge quantities could be made in a relatively short time, cutting down the cooking time from thirty or thirty-five minutes to a mere seven.

Later I discovered that he guarded his spice formula so closely that he had different suppliers for each of the many spices and herbs. Naturally, the "secret" recipe added cachet to the product.

I thanked my host and told him that I would get back to him after I discussed it with my bosses, who, in addition to the two Levine brothers, included David Burge, a capable executive vice president who had his own opinions.

Back at the ranch, I corraled the decision-makers and presented my findings. Mr. Julius was appalled by the whole idea; he didn't want to cheapen his restaurants. Also, going head-to-head with the big fast-food boys scared him—which was not unreasonable. But Mr. Ed thought it was a concept we should try. His idea was that, instead of planning a free-standing building or even a separate store, we should test it first in a separate room in one of the existing Brass Rail restaurants. He added that the most logical place would be the giant 49th Street and 7th Avenue unit, transforming the existing Sea Grill Room into a Brass Rail Southern fried chicken place. One of the reasons he suggested that location was undoubtedly so that he could keep an eye on the firstborn baby.

At the end of the meeting, everybody accepted Mr. Ed's suggestion as an easy-to-live-with compromise. I didn't show my disappointment when I brought back the news to our inventor, who by then had become an ally. But he was thrilled. He loved the association with the large company in the Big City, and enthusiastically went along with the plan, even though it didn't coincide with his original idea.

I don't remember the next three months in detail, but fortunately, as I am writing these pages, I have in front of me the draft of a memo I wrote at the time. Here are a few segments:

SUBJECT: SEVENTH AVENUE CHICKEN PROMOTION

8. PROMOTION:

   c) Seventh Avenue window to be decorated with the help of the Poultry Association of America; probably with pre–Civil War menus, recipes, and figures, and our radio program should introduce the new concept and its creator.

   g) Tie-in with the State of Kentucky: inviting the Governor for a colorful party; menu cover to feature the Grand Old State of Kentucky.

The last paragraph of the detailed outline dealt with the all-important question of the name.

> New name for Sea Grill must be chosen, decision must be reached whether we are going to make a reference to Kentucky, a Southern plantation, or [by now you have guessed]—Colonel Harland Sanders.

The place closed after three months. It was the wrong place, at the wrong time. And we missed the point completely.

Understanding human nature is an art and not a science, and Colonel Sanders was an artist. However, Pepsi Cola turned out to be the "scientist," eventually acquiring the company in 1986 for $840 million. Today, Kentucky Fried Chicken takes in around $7 billion annually in worldwide sales.

CHAPTER 14

The Restaurant as Entertainment

WHILE I WAS PERFORMING my attention-grabbing acts at the Brass Rail, I kept hearing and reading about Restaurant Associates, a group that was rewriting the rules of the restaurant game. By 1960 they had created and were operating the Forum of the Twelve Caesars, arguably the first so-called theme restaurant. There are those spoilsports who claim that Ernest Byfield's Pump Room in Chicago has that distinction, but regardless of chronology, the Forum was the first restaurant ever that was systematically created like a perfect Christmas tree, with decorations, lights, and other details supplied by a team of historians, architectural designers, witty scriptwriters, chefs, and food historians—all supported by a cast of public-relations experts.

And, of course, Restaurant Associates had created The Four Seasons, which opened in 1959, back when canned pimiento was still in the fancy-food section of the supermarket.

I wasn't exactly a rookie then, but when I received a phone call from Abe Cox, the astute but wily head of personnel for RA, I felt as if I were being drafted by the big leagues. I was a bit taken aback, though, when he told me the address of RA, near Eleventh Avenue on 57th Street; it just didn't seem a likely location for the headquarters of such a company. My second shock came when I walked into the shabby building, located right next door to a garage. And I was even more perplexed when I entered Cox's office, which was filled with furniture that even the Salvation Army would have rejected.

I was still curious when I was taken to the office of Jerry Brody, who was the president of the company, since I was expecting the kind of attention to detail I had admired at The Four Seasons. Only later did I understand that, just like any other decisions RA executives made, the choice of office location and furniture was the result of a carefully thought-out strategy. When banker types came to these shabby offices, they would think that these people spent all their money on the product—the revenue-producing restaurants—and virtually nothing on their offices. It would disarm them, even before their meetings began.

Another man came in to join us from an adjacent office, one that I found much more *simpático*, since, for me, even the cage of a hippopotamus would be agreeable if it was lined with books.

"I'm Joe Baum," he said, shaking my hand. Throughout the meeting, he kept looking at me with singular attention.

The technique the RA executives used was admirable, and obviously the result of an agreed-upon strategy: one of them asked a question, and after my response, the other two shot follow-up questions at me. They had certainly done their homework, and I was surprised at how much they knew about my life and work.

Baum, for example, questioned me about the Panorama Room of the Pan Am Building, where I had tried to create the illusion of an oasis in space. Then he asked me who had designed the waiters' uniforms. I told him that I had sponsored a contest for the students at the Parsons School of Design, and the prize-winning costume was implemented in the restaurant. He seemed pleased by the answer.

Joe Baum thought less of the menu, which he felt was too convoluted and esoteric—an uneasy mixture of science fiction and reality. I had worked on this futuristic restaurant with John Morton Levine, the talented son of Ed Levine; our aim was to make guests "experience a new vision through the mirror of their eyes and palate," to quote the menu cover. The eight main courses—both the food and all the tableware—represented the eight segments of the world that Pan American serviced at the time. My belief in this restaurant was supported by its uncommon success, and I defended my ideas vigorously, although today, almost forty years later, I admit that I would agree with Joe's point of view.

The conversation then turned back to more practical matters, and by the end of the lengthy interview they asked me if I would be interested in joining them as head of new projects. The first one, Brody explained to me, was a restaurant and private club on top of the Time-Life Building that was supposed to open in ten months.

I had difficulty containing my joy. As I continued the meeting with Cox alone, however, I outlined my conditions, which included all the trappings a wonder boy should get when invited to become a member of the all-star team. The next few days of waiting were not easy, but three weeks later I moved into my shabby little office next to Joe Baum's.

Working with Joe was an uncommon experience that included much time spent in trying to find one's way through his labyrinthine thought process. Joe always knew that he was destined to succeed, but that he had to work to achieve that destiny. There was a form of dictatorship in RA, but we were all its accomplices. We believed that our business was one that offered the maximum pleasure with the minimum effort to the largest number of guests. Everything else, including staying within budget when opening a new restaurant, was someone else's business. As a result, despite our unprecedented successes and the fact that we introduced the idea of more than one seating per evening, the bottom line was rather meager. But our compensation was that we knew we were writing the next chapter in the history of restaurants.

To build the Time-Life high-rise at 49th Street and Seventh Avenue as part of Rockefeller Center, the two giants, Rockefeller Brothers and Time, Inc., joined forces by forming Rock Time, Inc. Gustav Eyssell, the president of Rockefeller Center, who understood self-made destiny (he had started his career as an usher in Radio City Music Hall) had already worked with RA when the Forum was installed in the Rockefeller Center complex. Enjoying the reflected glory of its success, from that point on he favored Restaurant Associates over every other aspiring tenant.

The first time I took the elevator to the forty-eighth floor of the Time-Life Building and was confronted with the astonishing view, I remarked to a colleague in charge of the design department, "Lee, I guess we can reduce your budget and just use the skyline for decoration."

When I began to work on the concept and details of the new sky-high restaurant, I was faced with a real problem. The forty-seventh floor of the building had eight small private dining rooms, seating from ten to forty people each, and the main dining room, on the forty-eighth floor, was able to accommodate 210 people. But the available space for kitchen, storage rooms, and so on was not adequate to service such a complex of dining facilities.

The concept of the Tower Suite was to serve dinner without a printed menu. This idea had evolved from necessity before I came on the scene. Because there was only enough space to create a very large version of a home kitchen, with a few professional additions, this unusual super-elegant banquet-menu was the logical conclusion reached by Joe Baum, Jerry Brody, and their team.

I am strongly influenced by first impressions. The first image that came to my mind as I was faced with the commanding view from the top of this high-rise building was that I had just arrived at my imaginary uncle's luxurious Manhattan penthouse. He is well-traveled, loves art and good food, and has a well-stocked wine cellar—and, incidentally, I am his favorite nephew.

From that point on, the rest was as easy as pie. Or, rather, I should say as easy as a *Gâteau Chamounix,* that dome-shaped cake glazed with apricot marmalade and filled with kirsch-flavored chestnuts and surrounded by fruit cream. I had unearthed this spectacular dessert from the 1893 edition of *The Epicurean,* written by the chef of the legendary Delmonico's, and we eventually served it at the Tower Suite.

A curator at the Museum of Modern Art chose the paintings for the Tower Suite (Franz Kline, Soulage, and the like), and the interior was underplayed so as not to compete with the view. The lighting was a problem. We experimented with dozens of different table lights until we found a candle that was bright enough to read the menu by and gently illuminate the guests, without distracting from the skyscape. Since this was well before the time when lighting could be adjusted by a computer, the dining-room manager had to dim the room lights about every ten minutes to adjust it to the sunset, ending up with a light low enough that by the time the sun disappeared, the lights lining the avenues below had no competition.

We opened on December 6, 1960, and from that day on, the two seatings were sold out every night. The two leading members of New York's culinary Supreme Court, Clementine Paddleford of the *Tribune* and Craig Claiborne of the *Times,* gave rave reviews to the restaurant, which was not a common occurrence in those days.

The "Today's Living" section of the *Herald Tribune* had a full-page photograph of the stylish miniature appetizers we served at the beginning of the dinner, with the caption:

"A Lang specialty: The array of bite-size off-beat ('kaleidoscopic' in his word) hors d'oeuvre."

There should be a special phrase for getting credit for something you didn't do and at the same time attributing your ideas to someone else. For instance, the elimination of toast or a similar bready base for miniature non-canapé appetizers was not my idea. It came from Albert Stöckli, the immensely talented master chef of the RA.

At the same time, dozens of other touches of the evening *were* my invention. For instance, when a butler in a black tailcoat and a maid in a soft green dress and fluffy apron—in the manner of the stage maids of the 1920s—came to the table, they introduced themselves by name: "I am John, your butler, . . ." ". . . and I am Mary, your maid." That was my way of identifying my "uncle's" servers. It may turn out to be one of the many reasons I will end up in restaurant hell, because "I am Bruce and I will be your waiter for the evening . . ." has been echoing throughout the land now for thirty-seven years in a multitude of pretentious eateries.

One of the many other little touches I introduced for the rather formal dinner at the Tower Suite was restoring the alcohol-flavored sorbet that had been served for centuries in the middle of the dinner. Considering my musical background, the word I used for this, *Intermezzo,* was a logical choice and certainly easier for both the guests and the butlers/maids than ". . . and the *trou de milieu* for tonight is, . . ." or—heaven forbid—*trou Normand,* which can be a double entendre for a French guest.

Even before opening the Tower Suite, I realized that the very format— my uncle's aerie—would be ideal for a Sunday brunch that stretched from ten in the morning until three in the afternoon and offered the luxury of unstinting abundance. The seemingly endless array of dishes became first the talk of the town in New York, and then traveled to other towns, too—so much so that, during the first few years, the Tower Suite brunch became the hottest ticket in town. Here are a few samplers from our 1961 repertoire:

Avocado Filled with Lobster and Grapefruit Salad

A Planked Smoked Fish Selection Accompanied by Hot Bagels

Crab Thermidor

A Platter of Kitchen-made Sausages

Chicken and Sweetbread Terrapin

A Basket with Six Types of Biscuits Accompanied by Three Types of Butter

Baked, Stuffed Pears and Whole Fruit Compote

Fresh Figs in Cream, Stemmed Strawberries with White Chocolate Dip

During the day, the Tower Suite became the private Hemisphere Club, and the forty-seventh-floor private dining rooms were leased by various companies. The largest of them became the boardroom of Time, Inc. The first time they held a board meeting there, Henry Luce almost lost his cool because a huge *Newsweek* sign was visible from the south windows.

Depending on the Time-Life function for which their boardroom was required, various sizes of conference tables were called for. The largest, which was about six by twenty feet, had a polished rosewood top made in such a way that it could be lifted off its base and fitted flush against one of the walls, paneled with the same wood. Each little private dining room had its own butler's pantry so that the food could be kept fresh, and the butler and maid entered the dining room only when it was necessary to serve. I used to consider it a sign of luxury to be surrounded by unnecessary space, but I adjusted my definition: Luxury is having as much privacy as you want or need.

The series of strange coincidences that I experienced throughout my life continued at the Hemisphere Club. I became quite friendly with Bob Keilt, an executive of the advertising agency Kenyon & Eckhart, and during one of our post-luncheon chats (I never sat down at a table, of course), realizing that I was of Hungarian origin, he told me that he had been on several bombing missions over the country toward the end of 1944.

"Can you remember the date and the place?" I asked him.

"Not exactly, but I kept some of the photos we took, and if I can find them, I'll bring them in tomorrow."

The next day he arrived before his guests did, so he could show me the pictures. As he was removing the large black-and-white photos, I knew that I would see the oil refineries of Almásfüzitő, near Komárom. The backs of the photos had the date and the name of the oil refinery where I had experienced my full measure of hell from the sky as a labor-camp inmate. Rockefeller Center, in 1961, on the forty-seventh floor of the Time-Life Building, was about as distant a place from that burning Hungarian oil refinery as the moon. Yet, as I was looking at the pictures, the wall-to-wall-carpeted floor seemed to tremble violently under my feet.

On February 20, 1962, when John H. Glenn came to New York to be honored as the first American to orbit the earth, he was given a private party in the Tower Suite. As I was riding up with him in the private elevator cab operating between the forty-sixth and forty-eighth floors, I apologized for the absurdly slow ride. He smiled and said, "That's all right. After the fastest vehicle in the world, it's good to be in the slowest. And besides, I hear the view is just as spectacular."

This remark was so perfect that it seemed tailor-made for our PR department. Or would it seem that I had made it up? In any case, I never gave the story to the press.

The one problem I had with the Brody-Baum team was that in our initial agreement, my job description was given as head of new projects and project development, yet I was cajoled into the directorship of the Tower Suite/Hemisphere Club after it opened. Finally, about a year later, I got the green light to hire someone, and I was fortunate to lure my friend, Tom Margittai, away from the Mark Hopkins Hotel in San Francisco, where he was working as a banquet manager.

Six months after his apprenticeship with me (his first position in the restaurant business), Tom took over as director of the Tower Suite and then hired Paul Kovi, another Hungarian protégé of mine, who had worked at the Waldorf in the banquet headwaiter's office during my days there. It would be an exaggeration to say that I knew at the time that I was the casting director for this highly effective team who eventually bought The Four Seasons; Tom and Paul would each ultimately have become very successful anyway, though perhaps through different routes.

CHAPTER 15

Fun at the Fair

IN 1961 ROBERT MOSES, who for forty-four years was the autocratic emperor of the city and state of New York, became the president of the New York World's Fair Corporation, and managed to create the only such fair in history that was open for two years instead of one. I got along well with him, even though his actions were often outside of the democratic process. But at least he could find solutions to seemingly insoluble problems.

Once I was present at a press reception, just before the opening day of April 22, 1964, when a reporter asked Moses to define the purpose of this World's Fair. In addition to uttering some pompous clichés, such as "Olympics of progress" (probably given to him by one of his speechwriters), he called it a great summer university where Americans could overcome their provincial insularity. He added that this was not inconsistent with having fun at the fair.

When Restaurant Associates decided to participate in the 1964–1965 New York World's Fair, I was the logical choice to head up the planning and eventual operation of a mixed bag of restaurants under the RA flag. About two years before the scheduled 1964 spring opening, we had agreed to create and operate a large number of restaurants, executive dining rooms, cafés, and, as the official caterer of the fair, to open the food facilities in the Administration Building. We also signed an agreement to create a prime restaurant in the American Gas Association's pavilion. The gas industry had a big stake in the restaurant business, and was willing to spend quite a few million dollars in order to create an impressive showcase for what they called "a gourmet restaurant."

In those days the much-abused word *gourmet* was applied to Manhattan restaurant-goers who could afford to order dishes obliterated by sauces (which covered up undesirable tastes and unrefrigerated foods) and fancy preparations flambéed by captains wearing tuxedos. And to play it safe in this high-risk business, chefs throughout the land synthesized formulas and dishes that had made other restaurants successful.

At Restaurant Associates, at the very beginning of a new project, we would usually go through an initial period of search/destroy/search, and, after endless but fertile sessions, try to zero in on the one single right concept. In this instance, one of our goals was that each of our restaurants and snack bars would fill a lack that had been found in earlier fairs. For instance, reading the press about American world's fairs, beginning with the Crystal Palace Exposition in New York in 1853, at the intersection of Sixth Avenue and 42nd Street, made it obvious that there was a need for an American restaurant that would combine the richness and breadth of our heritage with all the niceties and luxury we had for too long attributed only to European cultures.

Not surprisingly, Brody, Baum, and I came up with exactly the same—almost inevitable—idea: to create a restaurant based on the indigenous cuisines that had developed in this country, drawing from America's almost inexhaustible variety of foods.

Then the research began.

I still have my first attempt at working out a menu, which focused on dishes the early settlers brought with them and then later were adjusted using the foodstuffs they found in the New World. Within a day or two I received comments from James Beard, who was the hired hand, or rather the hired palate, of Restaurant Associates. Actually, he was the high priest of the cult we fervently believed in, and Jim was in his element when it came to American food. Even though Beard's vast gastronomic knowledge knew no bounds, in his inner core he remained a citizen of Oregon with the wish list of an always-hungry American.

Beard made his points by clipping a page to my proposed menu outline, bearing the following message:

Two friends: Jim Beard and Joe Baum

Dear George!
Where are
   The American classics?
   The American grand hotel's specialties?
   The best from the cookbooks of the 19th century women's auxiliaries?
                                      Regards, Jim

    Then Joe Baum reviewed my suggested menu and Jim's comments. What I think he said, in his cryptic manner, was that we were not going to resuscitate a dead body in suspended animation. His main observation was that what Jim and I had suggested should be part of the final menu, but we must fuse it all into a contemporary American cuisine for contemporary American sensibilities, including imaginative West Coast salads and sophisticated New York appetizers. The style and content of the menu of Festival/64 (and of Festival/65 the following year) reflected all of our approaches.

The two most important developments in contemporary food preparations are the stove and the refrigerator. Early in the nineteenth century, Thomas Moore, one of the fathers of food refrigeration, said that refrigeration reduces the necessity of using lots of wines and spirits, because food spoilage does not have to be covered up. At Festival/64 we remembered his words and tried to use as little additional flavoring and spices as possible, with the exception of fresh herbs.

My search for the true story of American cuisine took me on a fascinating journey through early cookbooks, menus, and manuscripts in archives and my own library, providing me with authentic material ranging from Lincoln's inaugural luncheon to the favorite dishes of James Buchanan Brady, better known as "Diamond Jim," a man who was designated by one of the contemporary restaurateurs as "the best twenty-five customers we ever had."

The key personnel of the Festival/64 Restaurant were a mirror of America: a Swiss chef, an American-born Armenian *sous chef,* an Irish and a German manager in the dining room, and a displaced Hungarian as its planner and general manager.

The opening menu was a bold and convincing answer to the ubiquitous question I received whenever I mentioned to European journalists that we were opening a restaurant featuring American food: "You mean hot dogs, hamburgers, steak, and apple pie?"

The magazines and newspapers were uncommonly positive, mentioning that while the cooking was contemporary American, many of the recipes were adopted from regional specialties of great originality and imagination. They picked out some of my favorites, such as Convent Broth (chicken and beef broth with finely ground vegetables flavored with fennel, a specialty brought back from the 1920s); Shaker Herb Soup; Baked Shad with Roe Soufflé; Glazed Sweetbread under a glass bell resting on a slice of Kentucky Ham (it was served with a crouton shell filled with fresh peas and two boiled new potatoes, scraped but not peeled); Georgia Country Captain (an Early American chicken curry, which first appeared in a cookbook in 1857); Frisco Frittata with Artichoke Hearts; Berry Flummery; and Crisp-Fried Sugar Bush Pancakes (made with maple sugar and served with maple syrup).

Customers could also replicate authentic dinners by ordering complete menus that included "Dining with Jefferson at Monticello" (featuring pan-fried young pheasant with cornmeal square and fresh peach chutney as its main course), "Ward McAllister's Dinner Menu" (which he served at Delmonico's for the society he named "The Four Hundred"); "A Nantucket Beach Clam Bake," and "Lyndon Johnson's Texas Barbecue." The "First Ladies' Dinner" was based on courses that six different first ladies favored for their family dinners at the White House, such as Boston lettuce with sage cheese dressing, served at Jackie Kennedy's table.

The entire restaurant was conceived as an unending garden, indoors and out. The dining area was enclosed by hung glass windows without frames. It afforded an unobstructed view of brilliantly colored islands of flowers in the tranquil pool surrounding the dining room, in which the building appeared to float, and of the continuous festivities in the walkways beyond. Herbs were a part of the landscaping, not only as the decor, but to supply the kitchen; after they were picked, they were replanted nightly.

The talk of the fair was our fleet of mobile cooking carts, fueled by liquid gas, that cooked smokelessly right at the table; each was manned by a waiter and a chef. The overhead infrared burners reached peak heat almost immediately, and broiled steaks and chops in less than six minutes. It was awe-inspiring to see about twenty chefs all working at the same time in their white uniforms in the 225-seat restaurant. The chefs would remove the raw ingredients (for instance, a fillet of pompano) from the refrigerator at the bottom of the cart (which was cooled by the same liquid gas used for the cooking) and cook it under the broiler located on the upper section of the mobile wagon.

A couple of months after the opening, *Gourmet* magazine began its review with the following sentence: "I am convinced it will be a great pity if after the fair closes on October 17 [1965], some arrangement is not made to transfer to Manhattan The American Restaurant, now located at the Fair in The Festival of Gas Pavilion." Alas, it didn't work out that way.

During the second year we were asked to provide some refreshments for the donors of the World's Fair Blood Bank Drive. Recalling Robert Moses' point about having fun at the fair, when I got together with my cohorts, one of our managers reminded me of the old European chef's custom of drinking the blood from roasted meats; it was considered a super-restorative. So we decided to experiment with this idea, and came up with the novel cocktail of clarified roast beef blood, blended with lightly spiced fresh vegetable juice and a hint of horseradish, served well chilled.

*At the wheel of the minivan in which I got around
the grounds of the 1964 World's Fair*

I don't recall whether the blood donors liked it, but word about this bloodiest of all Marys got around, and it became the favorite of the World's Fair executives. A few weeks later I had to put a stop to it because I found out that the cooks kept roasting beef just to have enough blood for this drink, and our food costs were going through the roof. It should have taught me a lesson. Fortunately, it didn't.

Ex-president Truman, who visited our Festival restaurant on April 26, 1964, enjoyed an eclectic luncheon of kippered sturgeon and roast stuffed lamb, and finished his meal with plum pudding served with plum ice cream, washing it down with a cup of chicory coffee. Former president Eisenhower had two hot dogs and a glass of iced tea at our Missouri Snack Patio. But my plans did not work out when Governor Scranton of Pennsylvania visited our Festival/64 restaurant. We had prepared a historic menu for him based on Pennsylvanian specialties, but the governor declined in favor of New York and New England, ordering New York State trout stuffed with mousse of Kennebec salmon from Maine.

My priorities got me into trouble on occasion, such as the time when I was arranging a huge breakfast party at the Ford Pavilion. According to a carefully arranged schedule, four thousand freshly baked croissants were due to be trucked through a fair gate at exactly 7:30 A.M. When I called our pastry shop, which supplied The Four Seasons and The Brasserie, I was told that the shipment had left on time, exactly at 6:30 A.M. By 8:00 A.M. I became frantic. The guests waited and waited. Their coffee got cold. Ford executives looked at me as if I were a saboteur hired by General Motors.

Finally one of my assistants brought the news that the pastries were being held up at the gate.

"By what?! By whom?! What for?!" I screamed.

"The *Pietà*, Mr. Lang," answered the disconcerted youngster. "I was told by a guard that all traffic is being held back until Michelangelo's *Pietà* arrives safely at the Italian Pavilion."

Frustrated, I cried out, "I can't believe it! They are holding up our truck just because the goddamned *Pietà* is arriving! And for this we will have to serve soggy croissants!"

Fred Feretti, a journalist of the "Front Page" school, happened to overhear my extravagant reaction, and the story became part of his Sunday article in the August 29, 1965, issue of the *Herald Tribune*. Fortunately, this happened towards the end of the Fair, because from that point on I became the subject of endless ribbing and the *Pietà* had acquired a rude adjective.

As soon as the plans for the Festival Restaurant were set, I felt a longing to escape somewhere to forget the Flushing Meadows bedlam. I was having a meeting in my office, taking notes, while holding a mug of coffee in my left hand and trying to sort out the differing opinions of my fellow inmates, when it hit me: I'd love to be sitting in a coffeehouse with a "small black" on a little round marble table in front of me, reading the morning papers or looking through the great plate-glass windows. But I would have been enraged at *Népszabadság* (*People's Freedom,* the official Communist paper in Hungary in 1963), so instead, within a couple of days, I was on my way to Vienna.

I arrived in Vienna on December 17, 1963, but I never got to my favorite café, the Café Sperl. I had just checked into the Hotel Bristol and hadn't even had a chance to unpack when I received a call from the president of RA, asking me to proceed to Jakarta as soon as possible. He told me that the Indonesian ambassador had been in touch with him to find out if we would be interested in creating and operating an Indonesian restaurant at the World's Fair, five months hence. They had agreed on the terms, and he promised the ambassador that they would send me to Indonesia immediately so we could adhere to this absurdly short schedule.

At the time, my main source of information about Indonesia had been Miguel Covarrubias's book about Bali, written in the 1930s, and a fascinating study I had read by Margaret Mead. My limited knowledge included bits and pieces about gamelan music, batik cloth, the famed dish called rijsttafel, and unconfirmed stories about the political situation.

After getting a visa the next morning at the Indonesian consulate in Vienna, I flew to Zurich on the first available flight; then changed planes to fly to Teheran via Tel Aviv; took another plane to Bombay; and flew yet another airline to Colombo and Singapore. One scene I'll never forget in Teheran: The plane developed engine trouble and couldn't take off. All the passengers were stuck inside the plane for three hours in the middle of the night, until finally we were allowed to stagger off, dizzy from exhaustion, at which point I noticed the pilot and a couple of mechanics standing with a flashlight and a diagram, peering uncertainly into the engine, wondering what the hell to do. It wasn't a reassuring sight. But after three days and five airlines, I did finally land in Jakarta at five o'clock in the morning, December 21.

No one came to meet me at the airport, and I was without a single rupiah in my pocket. I leafed through the entire Jakarta phone book trying to find the number for a David Chang, who was supposed to be my contact. Since Jakarta, at that time, had a population of three million people, of which one million were Chinese, trying to call the right Chang (or Tsiang, Cheng, Chung) and getting, at best, every now and then a dial tone, was not exactly rewarding. After a futile hour in the phone booth, I decided to go to the hotel, commandeering, with considerable difficulty, a four-wheel rickshaw whose operator charged ten times the going rate, which I had to pay in dollars.

In the midst of the most unbelievable squalor stood a typical modern, interchangeable Intercontinental Hotel. Goats and beggars grazed nearby, and the whole scene was as unreal as a mirage. When I tried to check in at the front desk, a bunch of hotel employees informed me that

One of my many arrivals in Djakarta

they had never heard of George Lang, Restaurant Associates, or New York City, and only vaguely of the United States of America. The fact that I was garbed in winter clothes, appropriate for the freezing weather of Europe, added to my general discomfort in the steaming jungle climate of Jakarta. But eventually I broke through the communication barrier and collapsed in the room they assigned me.

The next morning I was still deeply asleep when the shrill ringing of the telephone woke me up. The concierge was calling to tell me that a delegation was waiting for me in the lobby, and that I should come down as soon as possible. Half asleep and dizzy from the punishing trip, I took a hasty cold shower and dragged myself down to the lobby. After identifying myself to the concierge, I was shown a group of people led by a Chinese gentleman who turned out to be the very David Chang I had tried to contact from the airport. When I was introduced to everyone, I was certain that remembering their names would be the most difficult part of my mission. But eventually, names like Burhan Pranatyo, Gamba Sukotjo, Djawad Sudadju, Hadidirto, and Hersubeno became as easy for me as Joe Smith.

After the introductions, I felt like asking Mr. Chang if they had known when I was arriving and why no one had come to meet me at the airport, but for diplomatic reasons, I kept quiet. At the time I didn't know this was a country where nothing was to be expected but the unexpected.

Trying to find out what they had been planning so far, I became quite frustrated; I didn't yet know that meetings in Indonesia tended to go on for days. Even brilliant people with double diplomas would maintain the style of tribal village meetings that were held in large, thatched structures covered with palm leaves, where decisions were reached only after many hours of circuitous dialogue.

I did learn that the food would have to be authentic Indonesian, and that there was an architectural plan for the pavilion, but there were no details regarding the restaurant. At the very end of the meeting I was told that the entire World's Fair Committee had been dismissed by President Sukarno two weeks before I arrived; only Chang had survived.

During one of my subsequent trips to Jakarta, one night my taxi passed by a structure that looked exactly like the Indonesian Pavilion we had opened a few months before in New York, and it seemed so improbable that I wondered if I had drunk too much *brim*, the delicious Balinese rice wine. The apparition—as I found out later—was an exact model of the building, but they had forgotten to show it to me during my first three visits.

I was eager to get to one of the open-air food markets I had heard so much about, and the next morning a lively young man picked me up, a trained guide who spoke a number of the languages of the different islands, in addition to the official Bahasa. Just before we arrived at the Djalan Sudirman market, my guide told me not to respond to beggars "or you'll have twenty of them surrounding you in the next second. They are naughty children—they won't stay on their reservations."

"Their what?" I asked, to make sure I'd heard him correctly.

"Reservations. Our great president set up reservations for children with no families, but they still come out to beg."

The open-air food market was a large area, about a quarter of a square mile, with scores of stalls, like a very low-budget version of a state fair in the United States. Rickety tables and homemade chairs were grouped next to crude cooking equipment, and the vendors' carts, many of which were simple affairs mounted on bicycle wheels, offered more kinds of merchandise than could be found in our large shopping malls.

The sound of bargaining was unmistakable, and the squealing pigs and the powerful smell of dried fish are still vivid in my memory.

I needed my well-developed ability for rationalizing and my strong professional stomach to be able to taste the extraordinary variety of fascinating and mostly delicious food, and to try to take notes and make sketches in the midst of the unappeasable hunger and appalling misery that seemed to permeate the whole city. At a kerosene-lit cart, I tasted *martabak,* a sort of egg roll that was filled with lamb, onions, garlic, pickled vegetables, and eggs. The filling was cooked on a griddle like a soft omelette, then folded into egg-roll skins, fried, and cut into squares. I wanted to see how they were made, so I ordered several more and then asked the man to give them to the children. They crowded around eagerly while he wrapped the *martabak* in palm leaves, then, as he handed them out, the children grabbed, laughing happily. Eventually *martabak* became part of the menu at the World's Fair restaurant.

I couldn't resist any of the exotic gallimaufry of tastes, textures, and shapes, and I sampled almost everything. One vendor made me a delicious *saté ayam* (marinated chicken bits on skewers) on a miniature kitchen that he carried on his shoulder. At another little stand I sampled *ajam tuturuga,* a chicken stew made with turtle sauce and a huge variety of little side dishes.

As I was walking out of the labyrinth of the market with a lovely palm-leaf and flower arrangement in my hand, planning to photograph it in a less hectic spot, I noticed that all the girls were giggling at me, and that some of the men lustily spat on the ground when I passed by. I was puzzled until I learned that the flower arrangement I had picked up was one a girl receives at the official ceremony after she reaches puberty, when she is proclaimed a woman.

I will never forget the sounds and sights of the street that first night: the faint chink of *betyak* bells mounted on three-wheeled vehicles with painted sides, driven by gaunt, barefooted men, and the self-important horn occasionally tooting—in a major third—and the beauty of the people with their luminous smiles, seemingly unaware of the squalor around them.

On the way back to the hotel (by then it was way past midnight), I ambled into a small, garish amusement park with food stalls, shops, and a dance hall with taxi girls for a hundred rupiahs a dance. A somnolent orchestra was playing 1920s-style European music, and there was a sign advising patrons that the twist, rock and roll, and boogie-woogie were strictly forbidden by order of the government. By then it was clear to me that one had better listen to the words of Big Daddy Sukarno.

Everywhere I went, in shops, in houses, on the streets, the president's picture was prominently displayed in various sizes. This show of the people's affection seemingly belied the rumor I heard that there had been five assassination attempts on Sukarno in 1962 alone, and that seven of his bodyguards were killed while trying to protect him.

The highlight of the first forty-eight hours was still to come: an official courier brought me an invitation to a private party at Sukarno's summer palace, indicating that I should leave at 4:30 p.m. in a car that would be waiting for me and proceed to Bogor, about an hour and a half's drive from Jakarta. Kumaraswami, my Indian driver, told me that, properly speaking, the ride should not take more than half an hour, but since President Sukarno traveled by helicopter, the roads had not been repaired, and during the rainy season some of the holes were easily as big as a car. At the time, Indonesia was in a state of near-war with Malaysia (which explained the tight security controls), but after the fourth checkpoint, I began to think that they were overdoing it.

The Bogor Palace, which had been built for the governor during the Dutch administration, stood in the midst of a magnificent several-hundred-acre botanical garden of rare tropical plants and flowers and enormous banyan trees; exquisite miniature deer ran about the garden like playful kittens. The entire estate was impeccably manicured; there was clearly no shortage of servants. The palace itself was of white marble—in a style one might describe as Grandiloquent Colonial—and surrounded by thirty-foot-high slender columns and imposing twenty-foot-high doors. Crystal chandeliers lit the Greek friezes and bas-reliefs on the porticoes; it was designed to impress and delight.

Inside, wandering around the rooms surrounding the ballroom, I noticed that the walls were covered with a strange mixture of paintings ranging from traditional Balinese to 42nd Street–style "art store" nudes and melodramatic works in a *Sturm und Drang* style.

As I entered the oval ballroom, a strange sight greeted my eyes. In the inner circle, approximately fifty girls were seated primly next to one another, as in a dancing-school lineup. At the extreme end were eight armchairs, a cluster of microphones, and about twenty high officials grouped behind them, including—as I was told—Chairul Saleh, the powerful chief of the army, the navy, and the entire cabinet.

At the other end were a few selected journalists, from a Red Chinese agency, the Associated Press, and *Newsweek*. Thomas Morgan was there, writing an article for *Life* magazine, and a CBS crew was filming the proceedings. As I learned from Bernie Krisher, the bureau chief of *Newsweek,* the reason for the gathering was not a major political announcement, but the official selection of twenty-five Indonesian girl guides (out of a group of fifty-five semifinalists) for the New York World's Fair. After about a half hour, everyone stood up at the order of the chief of protocol, and in walked President Sukarno with a retinue of about ten people, including one of his wives. Wanting to make a note to myself, I pushed the button on my ballpoint pen, which made a rather loud clicking noise. Instantly I was surrounded by a bunch of secret-service agents reaching for their pistols. I decided, then and there, to use a pencil—maybe forever.

Sukarno was dressed in a dark civilian suit and a black Indonesian-style *pitji* hat. He ambled in at a slow, cocky pace, looking salaciously at the girl finalists as he passed them and headed toward the "throne." His face looked like a professional fighter's after moderately successful plastic surgery, yet he projected enormous charm, which he could turn on at will, spreading it hundreds of feet around him.

His forty-five-minute speech was apparently, for him, a short one. One of the women was assigned as my interpreter, and she translated some nuggets for me: "The American imperialists and colonialists have distorted Indonesia's reputation by saying that Indonesia is a rotten country full of savages," he said. "New York will be a good place to show the true picture of our great country." A short excerpt from the speech eventually appeared in the *Jakarta Daily Mail,* which was the sole English-language newspaper available in Jakarta, but the accusations against America were left out.

When he finished, he walked up to the line of girls, picked one, and led her to the microphone, where he asked her a few questions in English, some obvious and some tricky ones, to test her linguistic knowledge and intelligence.

He then invited foreign guests and newsmen to question her. One of the wire service correspondents asked what kind of food she would suggest be served at the Indonesian restaurant at the World's Fair. The young woman, tightly wrapped in a colorful sarong, her jacket and shawl folded across her shoulder and her glossy black hair worn in a bun, said without hesitation, "Rijsttafel! There is no food as wonderful as our rice surrounded with an array of different dishes, both mild and spicy."

Everyone seemed to be pleased with the answer except Sukarno, who said in a rather aggressive tone, "The idea was stolen by the Dutch. We had the great *Hindangan Nasi Indonesia* hundreds of years before they occupied our land. That is the name this dish will be known by throughout the world, after we introduce it at the World's Fair."

The guests were seated in five different areas of the hall, and I had the honor of sitting opposite President Sukarno, next to a girl named Andrini. Little did I know that she was a member of the official greeting group—whatever that meant. Sukarno called over a number of girls, giving them bits of snacks and asking them questions, patting them here and there.

Ten minutes later I was called away by the chief of protocol, whose chief qualification for his post must have been that he was the only Indonesian almost six feet tall. He whispered to me, "Don't get too friendly with that girl, she's very close to the palace," and winked significantly.

Later we all returned to the main ballroom, where dancing—interspersed with traditional folk songs—resumed. Several of those songs were sung by the president himself, with more gusto than voice. His manner was so compelling, however, that I could see why he usually got what he wanted.

The last part of this seemingly endless affair was the hardest. After the president took off his shoes, he started an improvised folk song in which the same melody went on for nearly an hour with varying rhymes. He would point to someone, who then had to get up and improvise. After the two-hundredth repetition of the same brief melody, a few of us Westerners were ready to start a palace revolt.

Finally it was over. Chairul Saleh approached the president and announced that the representative of Restaurant Associates from America, who was the consultant to the government of Indonesia for its World's Fair pavilion, was here to greet him. This was the moment I had been waiting for, but by then I was so tired I was slap-happy.

Still, I found the proper style and tone, talking artfully for a few minutes in bland generalities. I must have mentioned several times the idea of the great nation of Indonesia and Restaurant Associates joining forces. Beaming his famous smile, he thanked me, saying that he had heard a great deal about my company and was very appreciative of our efforts on behalf of the Indonesian Pavilion. He ended with a wink, remarking impishly, "I do hope that we will earn money as well as accolades." For a moment I was tempted to say, "Not if we emulate tonight's style of cuisine and entertainment," but then I came to my senses and just mumbled the expected civilities.

He shook my hand with a firm grip, and departed through a back door followed by his retinue, shaking hands with some of his cabinet ministers as he passed.

Later that night his press secretary told me that one of Sukarno's conditions for participating in the Fair was to have the Indonesian Pavilion placed midway between the United States' and the Soviet Union's, as a symbolic statement.

Thus ended my second day in the Land of Three Thousand Islands.

After ten days of strenuous work in Jakarta, I decided to continue my research in Bali. Even though we arrived early in the morning, the traffic was chaotic. Our car had to navigate between wagons pulled by huge water buffaloes, women walking to the market carrying fruit-filled baskets on their heads, and naked children chasing the hundreds of homeless dogs. It was difficult not to stare at the young women wearing tightly wrapped batik skirts, walking with grace, unaware of their loveliness.

So that I could experience an evening in a Balinese home, I was invited one night to the house of the widow of the Belgian painter LeMeyeur, who was the Gauguin of this island. Polloh Alliney (she kept her maiden name, as is the Balinese custom) had married the already elderly artist when she was thirteen, and had posed for most of his luscious nudes. Still a very handsome woman in her late forties, she was a sort of local institution. The house where she lived had been given to her for life by the government, and declared a national monument. It was a small, typical Balinese house at the oceanside, with intricately carved paneling in black, gold, and red covering all the walls. I was immediately struck by the way the dining table was decorated with flat woven baskets made of palm leaves and filled with flowers. This skill of arranging flowers is part of every Balinese girl's education, since they decorate their shrines daily with flowers.

When I subsequently returned to Jakarta, I proposed to the officials I dealt with that the Balinese girl dancers and the guides coming to the fair should—as part of their job—spend one hour each day arranging flowers for the restaurant. Thus we were able to duplicate Polloh Alliney's table decorations quite authentically.

The ten of us guests sat around a table bearing a centerpiece of a coconut shell filled with coconut oil and provided with a burning wick. One serving boy dressed in white would enter gracefully with a dish and bring it to a low, festively decorated sideboard; another would place it at the center of the dinner table. Altogether about twelve dishes were served, accompanied by a vessel filled with rice. As is the custom, everything was at room temperature.

The stylish dinner began with *ikan goreng ayam,* which consisted of a platter of small fish fried, then marinated in coconut milk and local spices, and served with a sauce made out of the marinade—it reminded me of a more complex version of the Italian *anguilla marinara.* Next was *lawar,* an intriguing Balinese specialty of flavorful shredded beef tossed with finely cut unripe papayas, followed by the best suckling pig I have ever tasted, with a skin so crisp and glittering that it caught the shine of the moon. The deep golden color was helped—as I learned during dinner—by bathing the suckling pig in turmeric before roasting. I was grateful to the local gods that in Bali the predominantly Hindu-Balinese religion permitted the consumption of pork. I also found that it didn't take much effort to fall in love with *kepiting isi,* the small, stuffed crab shells that seemed to me almost like an eccentric cousin of New Orleans deviled crabs, and with the *saté lillit,* chicken bits flavored with garlic and lime, and threaded onto bamboo skewers.

Es apokat, the avocado ice cream, was presented on an intriguing avocado-skin-clad decorative base and covered with a bitter chocolate sauce. We served this glorious dessert a few months later at our restaurant in New York, enhancing it with a spoonful of a variation on zabaglione, made with coconut milk whipped with egg yolk at tableside.

The Balinese specialty, *brim,* a very light, pleasantly sweet rice wine, was offered as one of the beverages, but one needed an adventurous palate to appreciate *tuwak,* the strange-tasting palm wine, almost like an alcoholic pickle juice, especially, as I learned later, when it was kept too long.

When I look back at the triumph of the Indonesian Theatre-Restaurant, with its dazzling, centuries-old dances of the islands, the end product was so inevitable—at least to me—that I have difficulty recalling the grueling months of going from island to island to learn about the cuisine, folk art, and music of the different regions.

It took three more trips before the opening to accomplish all the jobs that had to be done—for example, selecting gamelan orchestras, and working with artists and artisans and with the directors and stage managers of the Indonesian ballet and the *wayang kulit,* the indigenous shadow-puppet theater. The entire pavilion had to be redesigned, and a kitchen planned that would accommodate the traditional cooking methods and yet be able to produce five or six hundred complex luncheons and dinners every day; and, of course, working on standard pre-opening restaurant requirements such as graphics, uniforms, service accoutrements, and promotions.

Selecting personnel turned out to be much more convoluted than the election of a congress in a banana republic. We also had to solve the enormous problems of selecting, packaging, transporting, and obtaining U.S. permits for the importation of essential foodstuffs, spices, and fruits on an ongoing basis. According to the agreement, the housing of personnel was not our responsibility; unfortunately, it didn't turn out that way.

At the time I must admit I felt like Marco Polo, introducing foods of this almost wholly unknown culture to millions of visitors to the fair. I was lucky to meet Fritz Schild, who eventually would be the man primarily responsible for the quality of the cuisine at the Indonesian Theatre Restaurant. A quiet, mustachioed man with flashing dark eyes and a warm smile, he was not only an accomplished chef but also well educated in both Western and Indonesian cuisines. After the World's Fair, I became a consulting editor for the Time/Life Foods of the World series, and I worked with him on the Indonesian section of this series.

Fritz Schild's father, also a master chef, had lived in Indonesia and married there a part-English and part-Indonesian woman. When I met Fritz in 1963, he was recovering from cancer, after a brilliant career as a chef and a restaurateur. Although he has never even visited Germany, I felt that for the sake of ethnicity he should change his name to the Bahasa equivalent of Schild, and thus he became well known during the World's Fair as Chef Tameng.

Step by step, I managed to learn from Chef Tameng the ritual and technique of eating rijsttafel: First one is served the *satés,* the little bits of fish or meat charcoal-grilled on delicate bamboo skewers, accompanied by their mild or pungent sauces. If you ask your server, he will bring your soup—which is the next course—when your *saté* brazier is on the table. He told me about *asinan,* a salad course with a very light dressing made without oil, which has a function not unlike the sorbet in French *grande cuisine:* to refresh one's palette before the important courses arrive.

He described how at an authentic rijsttafel, or *Hindangan Nasi Indonesia,* the server places a large dinner plate in front of you with a steaming, perfectly shaped rice mound in its center, and how a variety of different preparations are then brought to your table one by one, placed in quarter-moon-shaped side plates, and you mix each with a little bit of rice and proceed to the next, tasting as you go. Chef Tameng also taught

*The Indonesian Pavilion at the 1964 World's Fair, with its two
ornately carved towers and the roof ornament shaped like
a five-petaled flower, symbolizing "Pantjasila," the
five basic principles of the Republic of Indonesia*

me that salt and pepper were never part of the table setting. "The *sambals*
will take care of the additional pungency."

Sambelans, or side dishes, *atjars,* or marinated fruits and vegetables,
and, of course, an array of *sambals*—to make your food as hot as you
choose—provide a whole orchestration of tastes, textures, colors, and
aromas.

The sumptuous repast (the number of persons served can range from a minimum of ten to as many as three dozen) usually ends with an enormous variety of fruits. If the Garden of Eden had *rambutan, duku, sawo,* and *nangka*—to mention just a few—indeed our ancestors made an unfortunate mistake. I also learned that beer seems to go well with this food, but Dutch connoisseurs I spoke with favored a spicy Alsatian Gewürztraminer wine as an accompaniment. To me, a neutral and soothing hot tea served throughout the meal was the perfect beverage, with strong Javanese or Balinese black coffee at the very end.

I learned to eat by holding the fork in my left hand and the spoon in the right, but I also tried the old-fashioned way of eating with the right hand—without utensils—in which case, finger bowls were presented to me several times during the meal.

We worked hard on the first official tasting session (attended by Sukarno as well), and to my shock it turned out that none of the Indonesians had ever experienced a dinner that represented a sampler of the seven major culinary regions of Indonesia. In the end, each person considered the dishes from his own region authentic and excellent, and criticized the rest as the result of typical Western manipulation.

Chef Tameng recruited another of the key figures in the kitchen, an uncommonly talented *bumbu* woman, a true artist at grinding, blending, and mixing the herbs and spices that were used in the vast array of dishes to create a heightened sensation of textures, colors, and aromas. I also asked for ten outstanding female cooks, wanting to add homey authenticity to the food, but unfortunately they sent us the wives of prominent officials, who had just come for the ride.

It was a much bigger blow to us when a large ship arrived three weeks before the opening of the fair, filled with Indonesian herbs, spices, vegetables, and beverages, all of which had to be discarded at the Manhattan pier after health officials found the vessel infested by rodents and other strange creatures chewing on the stuff. Fortunately, by pushing the right buttons, we were able to secure another shipload of foodstuffs—this time properly handled—and we received the shipment a couple of days before the opening day.

Finally, the great day arrived and the Indonesian Theatre Restaurant, seating 350 people, opened its elaborately carved portals. From the very first moment, we cooked and played to packed houses.

One should remember that in the 1950s, Americans' favorite foods were surf and turf, luaus à la Trader Vic's, groaning pseudo-smorgasbords, fondue, beef Wellington, flaming shish kebabs, and dishes known as "continental" that were not too disturbingly different from Americans' accustomed fare. But after the 1958 recession, the early sixties became an era of prosperity and affordable travel to faraway places, which stimulated restaurant-goers and restaurateurs alike. Americans have always been adventurous people, and by the time we opened up this restaurant in the Indonesian Pavilion, the middle class had begun to recognize cooking as an art form; American cookbooks, which had been largely catchalls, became skillfully written manuals; and emerging young professionals had begun to seek out authentic experiences.

The theatrical part of the evening was equally exciting. Twice a night, after each dinner service, we would present a show based on ancient tales of Java and other islands, and on Hindu-Balinese mythological stories from the Ramayana and the Mahabharata. The group consisted of twenty-five dancers, girls and boys trained from early childhood, and they gave brilliant performances, showing astonishing technique and a bewildering variety of experience ranging from intense terror to low comedy, from rituals of birth and death to the eternal conflicts of good and evil.

For special parties, guests were dazzled by a traditional shadow play, the *wayang kulit*, in which the silhouettes of puppets cut from stiff buffalo hide were projected onto a large white cotton screen by strategically placed spotlights. Drums and ethereal bamboo flutes would accompany the voice narrating the story, as in a European medieval morality play.

Just as the dances and shadow plays had infinite variety, so did the gamelan orchestra accompanying them. Modulation, the change of key within a composition, does not exist in gamelan music—nor, as a matter of fact, does melody based on a fixed-key note. Interestingly, those familiar with modern atonal works seem to appreciate more readily the intricacies of this music. The orchestra is driven by large bronze gongs and bronze-keyed xylophones. The music adheres to a "sacred geometry" reflecting the Balinese cosmology, from the number of beats in a given piece to the order of the dynamics. The ecstatic frenzy of the *ketjak*, the "monkey dance" of Bali, with the counterpoint of chorus and gamelan orchestra, created an unforgettable experience. I might have thought that listening to it nightly should have muted my passion for this music, but the more I heard it, the more it penetrated my heart and mind.

When the dancers took their final bow on the opening night of the Indonesian Theatre Restaurant on April 9, 1964, I was so ecstatic that I had no energy left to feel tired. The *selamatan* feast we served clearly indicated that, as in the manner of French and Chinese cuisines, the art of Indonesian cooking is able to play hundreds of variations on a handful of themes.

The nightly feast-cum-dance-performance became the sensation of the fair, and it took possession of me like the capricious mistress I never had. On April 24, two weeks after the opening, the *New York Times* reported:

> *Once inside the Indonesian Pavilion the aroma of exotic oriental spices wafting from the Indonesian restaurant above, accompanied by the haunting strains of a native Gamelan orchestra, will suggest tarrying long enough to sample the authentic regional and provincial dishes served at lunch, dinner and supper by waiters in colorful native costumes.*

With just a bit of understandable exaggeration, I can say that it was one hundred eighty days of the most enriching, frustrating, and thrilling time of my professional life.

CHAPTER 16

A Change of Seasons

IT MUST HAVE BEEN in early 1967 when I was invited to a meeting in the office of the new president of Restaurant Associates (whose last name was Brody, the same as his predecessor's, although they were not related). Joe Baum was there too.

Without any preamble, Joe looked at me and said gravely, "George, we feel that The Four Seasons—after eight years of operation—needs you, and we would like you to take it over immediately."

Brody added a sentence that was so startling I wasn't sure at first I'd heard him right. "And you should think about perhaps putting together a group to buy it for you eventually."

I felt flattered because I had enormous respect for this restaurant. But back in my office, the pleasure was mixed with an uneasy feeling about getting back into operations, which I equated with a daily relentless grind, as opposed to creative work—although at The Four Seasons, even the routine had a measure of diversity. As far as buying it was concerned, I saw that as a very long shot and I wanted to remain a free agent if and when I ever left the company.

At our second meeting, which was a couple of hours later, I accepted the challenge, but I insisted on keeping Paul Kovi, who was then the rock-solid director of the restaurant. And that same evening I was ready to greet the rich, the famous, and those who would do anything to belong to either group, namely the guests at The Four Seasons.

To some people, 1959 will not be remembered as the year Nixon had his famous "kitchen debate" with Khrushchev. To a sizable group of discriminating people, that year was significant for the opening of The Four Seasons in New York City. At best, the early reviewers, such as the estimable Craig Claiborne, displayed admiration spiked with scorn. I still remember one Francophile guru who complained, "There is no excuse for such an odd combination of foods, and besides, the rooms don't even have any decorations—it looks like they ran out of money." It would be several years before The Four Seasons' architecturally superb spaces, filled with luxury without excess, would be appreciated.

To really understand The Four Seasons, one has to look at the restaurants of nineteenth-century New York to see why it has taken so many years to achieve proper recognition. The beginning is perhaps the most glorious part of the story. Delmonico's, which opened its doors in 1837 at its first location, was designed not only as a club for superachievers and the socially prominent, but also as the home of the first serious cooking in this country. Charles Ranhofer, Delmonico's famed chef, refused to prepare certain dishes during the off season when he felt that the ingredients would not "cook well," a dictum followed by Albert Stöckli for his menus seventy-five years later at The Four Seasons. A November dinner in 1838 at Delmonico's, for instance, began with a soup of Purée of Young Rabbit, followed by Baked Sole Italian-style, with Rack of Venison as the entrée. Then came roasted Teal Ducks with Hot Potato Salad, and, to finish, Soufflé Fritters Medici-style, capped by a frozen Biscuit Diplomate enriched with kirsch-laced candied fruit, crushed macaroons, and whipped cream tinted with purée of strawberries.

Just as Lorenzo Delmonico had the wisdom to rent penthouses in the center of New York City to grow baby vegetables that were harvested only hours before being served to the guests, the young Four Seasons rented hothouses to grow baby vegetables for its kitchen.

Delmonico's cellar contained the most prized wines of Bordeaux— the Lafite Latour and Margaux fetched the steep price of two dollars a bottle.

When Oscar Wilde came to New York in 1882, he went straight from the pier to Delmonico's, where Mark Twain and Bret Harte also habitually gathered—just as the literati did (and still do) in The Four Seasons' Grill Room.

After Delmonico's closed in 1923, many people dreamed of creating its successor, but until Henri Soulé, the patron of the French Pavilion at

In front of the famed Picasso curtain
at The Four Seasons in 1967

the 1939 World's Fair, opened his Le Pavillon on East 55th Street in
Manhattan, no one came close to achieving this goal. Like eager students
seeking the strict discipline of an absolute authority, a certain segment of
society was looking for this teacher/father figure who would set the ultimate standard in a restaurant. "Papa Soulé" established, just as Lorenzo
Delmonico had, an unbending set of rules in manners, tastes, and customs for decades to come.

Nature and restaurateurs abhor a vacuum, judging from the endless
string of French restaurants in Manhattan that followed Le Pavillon.
Many of them were decked out in carbon-copy elegance and run mostly
by former headwaiters with operatic emotions, catering to patrons who

loved the overdone and the obvious. French boilerplate "specials" were
featured even at the most celebrated restaurants: "Gratin de Crabmeat
Princess" at Quo Vadis; "Mousse au Salmon" (*sic*) at Le Chambord;
"Bisque de Homard" at Laurent; crêpes Suzettes at The Colony; and
"English Sole Dugléré" at Voisin.

The five-letter adjective *theme*, as applied to restaurants, is justifiably
considered a four-letter word these days where up-scale establishments
are concerned. But The Four Seasons, with its resolute concept, is perhaps the only theme restaurant in history that had an honorable goal and
gave an explicit description of its intended mission to the restaurant-
going world in its very name. My mother certainly would not have been
surprised by this restaurant's mission, which was to serve foods only
when they are naturally available—produce that grows in fields and
orchards, fresh birds and game and prepared foods and specialties
indigenous to the current season. For my mother, this was not a self-
imposed rule, but rather one imposed by nature: in those days she could
only serve us pea soup during the few weeks that peas grew in our garden. She took her culinary cues from nature automatically.

This seems like an obvious idea, but most restaurateurs try to fulfill
their customers' desires by offering almost unlimited choices on their
menus. It is a well-known axiom in the restaurant business that educat-
ing the customer is a very expensive proposition. In a highly civilized
way, this is what The Four Seasons set out to do by basing its philosophy
on the biblical observation that "to every thing there is a season, and a
time to every purpose under the heaven." The Four Seasons flew in *fraises
des bois* from France, fresh grouse after the "Queen's shoot" in Scotland,
oysters from five different countries, wild boar from Wisconsin, and live
fish from Marseilles. They used twenty-two kinds of olives at a time
when only the tasteless California blacks were generally available. All
this and much, much more, only in their season.

Reading the opening menus of The Four Seasons of 1959, one
quickly understands why this establishment, which could have been created only in New York, influenced so many chefs and restaurants in the
first ten years of its existence. A few random selections from those early
menus were Minted Lobster Parfait, Smoked Salmon Soufflé and Onion
Sauce, Bouillabaisse Salad, Julep of Crabmeat in Sweet Pepperoni,
Kumquat Ice Cream, and Violets in Summer Snow.

At that time, when few restaurants outside the Napa Valley served
California wines, the selection of American wines at The Four Seasons

equaled the best French wine list in the most eminent restaurants of the land.

A few of the firsts at The Four Seasons' kitchens included portion-sized vegetable steamers, soufflé ovens, separate saltwater and freshwater fish tanks, a beeper in each waiter's pocket to inform him when an order was ready to be picked up, and so on.

Matching the gustatory with the visual was the second half of the homework required of the creative team. In addition to the food, every-thing—well, nearly everything—changed four times a year: the paint-ings, through an exchange program with the Museum of Modern Art; the elaborate plantings in the Grill Room and the Pool Room; the server's uniforms; the upholstery of all the furniture; the show plates, linen, menu presentation, and all the graphics; and dozens of other details. And precisely on March twenty-first, the secretary had to switch the color of the ribbons in the typewriters to spring green.

One of the intellectual dandies of the day compared the excesses of The Four Seasons' quarterly changes to a young couple who choose a painting to match the sofa in their living room and then, when the uphol-stery has to be changed, start the process all over again. What the critics didn't understand was that such a sweeping, overall visual statement can't be expressed with a few touches here and there; The Four Seasons, during those days, became a veritable cult with its own mantras and symbols.

A little knowledge is not dangerous as long as it makes the guests and the waiters more knowledgeable about the food they choose or serve. The quarterly calendar served this purpose well. It was a challenge to come up with interesting bits of historical trivia, especially because everyone in the restaurant became an instant critic.

Here is a sample of one of my attempts to inform and amuse at the very same time:

AUTUMN 1968

THE FOUR SEASONS CALENDAR OF EVENTS

SATURDAY, SEPTEMBER 28

Birthday of Confucius On this 2,519th Birthday of China's great Philosopher, we will serve the traditional Chinese Pearl Soup (chicken broth, flavored with ginger, creamed corn, shredded ham, tiny peas, bean thread noodles, strips of pimiento, and "clouds" of chicken breast previously marinated in beaten egg white and sherry). Presuming that Confucius had a first-rate cook, he must have loved it.

THURSDAY, OCTOBER 3

The Incomparable Duse was born in —— (you are not supposed to tell a lady's age). To commemorate her genius, *our* genius, the Chef, will prepare "Sole à la Duse"—stuffed, folded Filets of Sole, poached in Savarin mold, lined with saffron rice and cheese. The center of the dish is filled with Shrimp in Lobster Sauce.

THURSDAY, OCTOBER 10

Verdi was born in 1813. To commemorate his birthdate before, or instead of, going to the Metropolitan Opera, try our "Noisettes D'Agneau Verdi"—which is two little Lamb Medallions topped with foie gras and Sauce Madère, and garnished with croustades of Duchess Potatoes, tiny carrot balls, and braised lettuce,

SATURDAY, OCTOBER 12

Columbus Day   Probably the first time it was celebrated with elaborate festivities, was 99 years ago in San Francisco. To commemorate this event, The Four Seasons will serve a "Columbus Cake," which will contain a variety of spices he was hoping to find.

THURSDAY, OCTOBER 31

Hallowe'en   In the last century, "Snapdragon" was a popular Hallowe'en game. Raisins were placed in a bowl of brandy and the dish was set aflame. The trick was to extricate the raisins without getting burned. The Four Seasons will serve a Brandied Raisin Soufflé, which can be enjoyed without any risk.

MONDAY, NOVEMBER 4

St. Hubert's Day   Hubert was a great hunter, and many countries have an annual deer hunt on this date. Wafers, used in the mass, were made especially for the occasion, and imprinted with a hunting horn. The Four Seasons, as part of its Game Holidays, will serve the traditional Venison Cutlet St. Hubert, served with Lingonberry Compote and Gnocchi of Maize.

FRIDAY, NOVEMBER 15

This is the National Day of the Proclamation of the Republic of Brazil. A Frozen Coffee Mousse is in order.

THURSDAY, NOVEMBER 28

Thanksgiving Day   347 years ago, Governor Bradford of Plymouth Colony proclaimed a formal Day of Thanksgiving, and dedicated it to the Feast of the Wild Turkey. In addition to this, you will be able to order Priscilla Alden's special dishes: Pigeons and Partridge; Venison and Stuffed Wild Turkey; Fish, Clams and Oysters.

DECEMBER 10

A day of mourning—GROUSE SHOOTING ENDS!

By now, just about everybody has put in his claim to having created The Four Seasons, including a deli owner I met in Hong Kong. The credit really belongs to a team that only happens once in every hundred years, so I guess we will have to wait another sixty-odd years for a repeat performance. The team was led by Joe Baum, that man of uncommon vision, who was able to combine a selective use of the past in marriage with the flavors of tomorrow. He also had the ability to inspire and to be inspired. The two people who were the inspirees were Albert Stöckli, one of the most inventive chefs I have ever known, and Albert Kumin, who was a veritable wizard in the pastry department. The so-called revolutionary *nouvelle* French chefs of the 1970s blithely disregarded the fact that their "original" creations were simply variations on early menus of Albert Stöckli at The Four Seasons.

Being Swiss was a great advantage for Stöckli. Having grown up with different languages and cuisines, he—like so many other Swiss chefs—carried less of the baggage of gastronomic chauvinism than did most European chefs. Albert was both curious and conservative, a poet and a peasant of the kitchen, considerate and boorish, original and imitative—just for starters. But the two characteristics that made Stöckli the ideal choice for the position of chef of The Four Seasons were his ability to imagine a taste and the talent and skill to be able to reproduce it. His wife told a few of us that during his sleep Albert once had a dream of a bold yet subtle sauce that fused many flavors. He got up from bed excitedly, went to the kitchen, and experimented the rest of the night until he could taste the sauce he had dreamed about.

Albert was a burly man, sometimes violent, with a voluminous girth and a domineering presence. He had a coarse sense of humor, especially when he mixed his nightly gallon of beer with a more potent poteen. Once he gave a lecture to a new apprentice, who was full of himself, about the importance of the correct temperature of a chicken *before* you start roasting it, and the poor lad was instructed to put the thermometer into the rear ends of several dozen birds and tabulate the results.

The Four Seasons enjoyed a measure of fame and success in its first eight years of operation, but I was brought in as its new director to win the plaudits of the arbiters of taste. While I did manage to elevate the level of consistency in the kitchen (always a problem in any restaurant), I succeeded only marginally in changing the clientele. The main reason was the way The Four Seasons had been promoted throughout the world. Old New York money and those who liked to be shaded by their family trees didn't want to mix with people whose money and power had just recently been acquired, or with the hundreds of people from around the world who filled The Four Seasons' Pool Room during its two nightly seatings. Also, only traditional French cuisine bore the upper-class stamp of approval, so the four or five restaurants in New York that were French-owned and French-managed remained the quasi-club for the "right people," and those who liked food and wine. It seems odd today, three decades later, that the celebration of the best of nature's bounty was considered an unnecessary culinary rebellion by the very class we were trying to attract.

I inherited other handicaps, too. Much as I appreciated The Four Seasons as a superb instrument to play on, from the very beginning I realized, with a heavy heart, that such an establishment cannot be operated on an optimum level within the autocratic system of a large company. With every change I tried to make, I managed to step on someone's pride of authorship.

For instance, when I used plants to separate the superbly designed bar from the rest of the Grill Room (which eventually made it possible for the Grill Room to become the luncheon-encampment of New York's power elite), everybody, from the architect Philip Johnson (who was responsible for the overall design concept and some of the details of the interior of the restaurant) to Joe Baum, acted as if I had strung Christmas lights around the restaurant.

I won a few battles here and there, but the skirmish of the floating flowers was not one of them. From the very first time I saw the large, white marble pool dominating the main dining room of The Four Seasons (hence the Pool Room), I felt that its emptiness was an exaggerated understatement. The creative decision-makers of RA were programmed by the authoritative minimalists of the day who would never consider the possibility that, on occasion, less amounts to less. I felt strongly that a few petals of flowers in the bubbling water would soften the austere architectural design element and add a festive touch to the surroundings.

The day I instructed our florist to make the arrangement (after trying out several variations), the comments of our guests were uniformly wonderful. But the command center's reaction was swift and decisive: "If you like flowers, move to suburbia or become a milliner."

In those days The Four Seasons was a gathering place for creative people from every part of the world, though fewer book deals were closed at its tables then. One of the many amusing incidents I remember occurred when Yevgeny Yevtushenko came to dinner. He told me that rich dishes were not for him; he had the tastes of a simple Russian poet.

"I'll just have some wine and cheese," he said quietly.

Then he proceeded to choose the French Brie de Meaux and one of the great wines from our wine list, Château Lafite-Rothschild 1945.

Arthur Rubinstein, the preeminent pianist, had been one of my idols since childhood. I was awed when he came to lunch, and I took his order myself. He started with lobster, went to a pot-au-feu, and finished with a frozen soufflé.

"This will make me four pounds overweight," he beamed. "When I lived in Paris and Berlin, I never had enough to eat, and ever since then I am happiest when I am four pounds overweight," he added.

On occasion I allowed myself the luxury of having some fun with our guests. When eighteen members of the Long Island Fishermen's Society had their annual dinner in one of our small private dining rooms, each was served the fish he himself had caught. When they entered the dining room, they were quite surprised at how far they were seated from each other, but I announced to them that instead of being seated twenty-four inches apart, as is customary, they were six feet apart so that they would have enough space to spread their arms to show the size of "the one that got away."

The staff had a sense of humor, too. For my forty-fourth birthday they presented me with a cake in the shape of a globe. It was precise in every detail with the slight exception that the entire world was covered with one single country: Hungary.

The child in me always wants to be amused and to amuse others, and when Brother Justin of the Christian Brothers asked me to plan a Wine Harvest Dinner, I proposed that we develop a menu in which every course would be prepared and/or garnished with the same grape that was in the accompanying wine. He was delighted with this idea. The main course, for instance, was Scotch grouse, the accompanying Pinot St. George was a red varietal from Christian Brothers' vineyards, and the Pinot grapes were incorporated into the stuffing of the grouse. The turtle soup (the turtle had been captured in the Virgin Islands for us) was served with Christian Brothers' cocktail sherry, and the poached Petrale Véronique, a delicate fish from the Pacific, was accompanied by their Sylvaner Riesling wine and garnished with its grapes, adding up to the classic Véronique preparation. And the light-as-a-cloud Soufflé Château La Salle had fine slivers of Sémillon grapes embedded in it.

During the same period I was in charge of the off-premises catering division of Restaurant Associates as well. Some of the parties were as simple to create as a one-piece jigsaw puzzle, but others, such as the Brown Brothers Harriman 150th anniversary party, celebrating that October day in 1818 when John A. Brown, the founding father, pronounced himself an importer of Irish linens, was a puzzle of several hundred pieces. Since the original partners were all immigrants, I thought that, as a setting, Pier 13 on the East River at the foot of Wall Street would be in keeping with the founding spirit of the early nineteenth-century company.

Pier 13 was used regularly by banana boats, but that week one of them was delayed because of a storm, and instead of Tuesday at noon, we had to install our entire little portside village after midnight the following day, for opening the same evening. It was close to impossible. But we made it.

We re-created an authentic-looking old waterfront, complete with shops, little booths, benches, a calliope, and several fountains, while a group of musicians entertained the guests in the park pergola. Itinerant banjo players, nickelodeons, sea chanteys sung by an old saltwater tar, and "Professor Lang's Live Medicine Show" livened up the evening. Vendors, from their traveling carts, dispensed everything from buttercup boutonnieres to gingered lemonade. The guests received wooden nickels, with which they could buy all sorts of souvenirs, from doll-house furniture to nineteenth-century magazines and slides for their stereopticons.

The recipe for the Brunswick stew, which we served from a huge cast-iron pot, came from Moreau D. Brown, a descendant of the original family.

If nothing else, this party proved that money *can* buy happiness—at least for a few hours.

Although we didn't need a great chef for this waterside party, we certainly did for The Four Seasons. By the time I took over, Albert Stöckli was mostly involved with the new restaurants the company was opening, and I felt the need for a chef whose sole responsibility would be our kitchens. After considerable searching, we found Maurice Chantreau at the Seattle World's Fair, where he was the *chef de cuisine* of the official French restaurant. After working with him, I was reminded of something I'd muttered years ago in one of my exasperated moments: "If you hire a French chef, you deserve it." He was a superior practitioner of his art, but to get that extra something out of him, I often had to resort to convoluted stratagems. One day I asked him to reproduce a complex nineteenth-century dish made by deboning a whole oxtail, then stuffing it with a marrow-dumpling farce and serving it as part of a pot-au-feu. Chantreau attempted to make the dish for weeks before he perfected the technique. Not wanting to die by being stabbed with a twelve-inch French cook's knife, I never told Chantreau that I had never actually seen or heard of such a dish.

One of the most entertaining moments of my professional life also occurred during my Four Seasons reign. I should preface the story by admitting my allergy to winecompoops, who confuse good wines with those from fancy chateaux. A small group of members of the Chevaliers du Tastevin, a society formed to celebrate the virtues of Burgundy, gave a gala dinner in one of the private dining rooms of The Four Seasons. We served two wines with each of the six courses, and to make sure that the right wine accompanied each course—as we usually did at similar dinners—we stuck different numbers of silver or gold stars on each bottle. Halfway through the dinner, Charles Mabille, who was in charge of the service, ran up to me, redfaced and almost apoplectic.

"Mr. Lang, I don't know how, but one of the wines we served with the venison was a Bordeaux! It needed decanting and no one noticed the mixup. Please! Make an announcement! They all know you, and you can do it."

"Thank you for telling me. I'll see what I can do," I answered uneasily.

I realized, of course, that admitting the error would dent our invincibility, but on the other hand, if I didn't say anything . . . I decided instead to wait until the venison course had been cleared by the waiters, at which point the acting host of the evening, as part of the ritual, would ask several people to critique the wine.

I still recall a description offered by one of the oeno-snobs: "It carries the perfumed scent of a sixteen-year-old vegetarian virgin." At the end we were relieved that every member of the wine society critiqued the Bordeaux as a considerable Burgundy of typical characteristics.

As a discreet restaurateur, I have never told this story to anyone, but I guess after three decades it is safe to share it.

There was one person in the world of gourmet societies who would have known instantly that we had made a mistake; what's more, he would have described every detail of the Bordeaux, maybe even the date of the harvest. His name was Gregory Thomas. I suppose I liked Gregory so much because we shared a great number of likes, dislikes, and prejudices. But he became rather difficult to deal with when I was arranging one of his Chevaliers du Tastevin parties. As president of Chanel, with his six-foot-five-inch frame and all-encompassing knowledge, especially if it had something to do with gastronomy, he was one of the most formidable people I have ever met. His wit, often tinged with sarcasm, was so dazzling that once I took out a pad to make notes of the way he devastated my suggested menu.

During my Brass Rail days in 1959, when the Golden Door at Idlewild was under my jurisdiction, I wanted to make my mark, so I took extraordinary pains to obtain a swan to serve to Thomas and his party. In his after-dinner remarks he said, "George Lang served us a roasted swan, for which he should be commended. Unfortunately, it tasted like a roast turkey. Perhaps next time he can serve us a turkey which tastes like a swan."

Recently I found a letter I sent Thomas after one of the several tastings we had before an important Tastevin party he was arranging at The Four Seasons. During the luncheon I had tried to keep to the practical aspects and avoid getting involved in the interplay between Gregory and the two other members of the wine society who were present, each determined to offer his learned judgment. As they were leaving, I promised to send Gregory answers to his questions regarding the problems we faced with importing foods for his dinner, and a few other points as well.

December 18, 1967

Dear Gregory:

I hope the following paragraphs will answer some of the issues which came up during last week's tasting sessions. Perhaps I'll go through the points in order of service.

1. *The Quilcene oysters may not come in because of the bad weather on the West Coast—in which case, unlike Vatel, I am not going to commit suicide, just substitute them with the best of the local products.*

2. *The Bouchées will be filled with the coxcombs and testicles of the cock in a very light Madeira sauce. (By the way, they are supposed to be an aphrodisiac.) While they have a certain relation to the classic Financière preparation, this must have been an ingenious simplification served to one of the financiers while the market was down.*

3. *Oxtail Royale in the Double Consommé is mentioned by Urbain Dubois in his nineteenth-century book, although he doesn't give a recipe for it. As you suggested, we'll try to keep a balance between giving an oxtail taste and yet retaining the characteristic texture of the Royale.*

4. *You shouldn't worry about the Lobster Americaine served in an edible pastry shell! Emil Valdez, our pastry chef, has been experimenting with so many different shapes and types of dough that I think at this point he considers himself an industrial designer.*

5. *The story of the smuggled Poulard de Bresse could be material for the next James Bond movie. Some of the bare facts are as follows:*

In spite of the great difficulty as a result of coordination problems, transportation, etc., we do get these magnificent birds from France quite regularly. A day after our tasting, we got a cable from our supplier, Monsieur Pedaux, informing us that he could not get the U.S. permits, so he was unable to ship the fowls (by the way, they come chilled, not frozen). I called him and told him that we had to get them, and asked the reason for the sudden change. After several more phone calls and cables, we found out that we couldn't bring them in at Kennedy because the American officials were afraid that the chickens might be being used for smuggling narcotics. I am pleased to report to you that by pulling all sorts of strings, we did receive the shipment yesterday, so if any of you gentlemen feel especially elated after the roast, perhaps the hallucinogenic agents are responsible.

6. *The haricots verts came separately to make sure that we have them even if the birds should be confiscated (just as husband and wife are supposed to take different planes, I guess). By the way, the saga of how we finally got the chickens through customs must remain a secret, if heroic, chapter. The only thing I'd like to mention by way of justification is that even our premier gourmet, Thomas Jefferson, sometimes employed not-quite-legal methods. According to contemporary accounts, "The young Jefferson had inconvenienced and even endangered himself . . . he had smuggled Lombardy rice out of Italy in his pocket at a time when the exporting of rice was punishable by death."*

7. *The cheeses are coming in from France also, and by Tuesday morning I will give you a list of the ones we decide to use after tasting them. We certainly will have a large Brie de Meaux, and I know you will be interested in my recent discovery that in Charlemagne's time the brioche was made with Brie, and* hocher *means "to stir"—hence the name* brioche. *(It's an interesting bit of trivia, even if it is the product of a trying-too-hard gastro-historian.)*

8. *We decided to keep the traditional dessert of Buche de Noel, knowing that there is a special section in culinary hell for those who don't show the proper respect for such sturdy traditions. To provide a playground for Invention—the beautiful*

*and rebellious daughter of Tradition—the pastry chef created
a Nebuchadnezzar-sized single log, and filled the sugar baskets with forest mushrooms made of lemon ice cream stems
and meringue caps.*

*Although Tom Hoving tried hard to break precedent by opening
the treasure house of the Met for a private party, apparently it would
take several months to get the approval of every member of the
Board, and there was insufficient time to go through the process.*

*But fortunately we were able to borrow magnificent figures and
candlesticks for the decorations. I guess "private collection" is as good a
description as any of the source. Suffice it to say they are not from the
Met, and they are not smuggled! (Detailed description is enclosed.)*

*I hope you'll find some of the above germane. En passant, I'd
like to share with you the recently found (by me) sentence of Brillat-
Savarin, in a letter to a friend: "All of us should profit by the aid of
the cook except the apothecary."*

Your devoted friend,
George

As a postscript to this Christmas party for forty gentlemen, I should
mention that we had obtained photographs of all the guests through
their secretaries, so that every single waiter or captain in the dining room
could identify and greet him by name as he arrived.

Sometimes there was a very thin line between whimsy and silliness,
as the following story illustrates. A friend of mine who was a regular at
the restaurant told me about his problems with his girlfriend.

"I am trying to break up with my girlfriend, but she's so sensitive that
I don't know how to approach it."

Jesting, I said, "Why don't you invite her to an all-black dinner?
Surely she'll get the idea."

His eyes lit up, and he told me he would call me for a reservation.

Unfortunately, I couldn't use black linen in The Four Seasons (it
would have been *my* funeral), but I did purchase a couple of black china
platters to match the black-sprayed flowers. The dinner began with a
whole roasted black truffle, followed by polenta made with a puree of
black olives; then came *seppie*, the Italian cuttlefish, cooked and served in
its very own ink, on a black dish to dramatize the image.

When it came time to serve Cahors, the wine that they call *vin noir*,
accompanied by goat cheese in crust of ashes and midnight-black grapes,

the lady had left not only the table and The Four Seasons, but her gentleman friend as well.

I wish I could've solved my impending divorce with a single dinner. Truth is a moving target for a divorced person, and I certainly do not intend to reinvent my past or to show it in a flattering light. Our marriage was held together for eighteen years by our genuine fondness for each other and our love for our two great children. Life was neither heaven nor hell—not even purgatory. It was one long conversation checkered by alternating interruptions as we shifted between the roles of teacher and learner.

Sadly, the longer we were together the more the balance of love and forgiveness changed for the worse.

One morning after breakfast, I said good-bye to Doe and left our West End Avenue apartment, never to return. But I will never be able to divorce my memories: the first smile of Andrea, the sight of little Brian with his pet sheep in our country house, and the pleasure of playing Mozart sonatas with Doe.

It took time before I could forgive myself. I learned a lot from her.

CHAPTER 17

A Bunch of Asparagus

IT WAS A GOOD THING that by the end of 1969 it was too late for me to be driven to an early grave, because the situation at Restaurant Associates would surely have done it. On a particularly disagreeable day, I received a call from Bethesda, Maryland, from someone who introduced himself as the secretary of J. W. Marriott Jr. She told me that her boss would be coming to New York the following day and would like to meet me.

"Why don't we meet at the Peacock Lounge of the Waldorf for a cup of coffee?" I chose that place because it was close to The Four Seasons.

After a few seconds of hesitation, she said, "Mr. Marriott doesn't drink coffee or alcohol. But he will be there at three o'clock in the afternoon. Please be on time."

The very same day, during luncheon at The Four Seasons, I greeted Bob Tisch, half of one of the great brother acts of all time. After settling on a menu, almost as an afterthought he mentioned to me that Loews, their hotel division, was going to build a number of fine hotels in Europe within the next few years, and asked me if I might be interested in working for them to open exciting "magnet" restaurants that would attract customers to stay there.

I said that I would get back to him soon.

On the same afternoon, back at my old haunt, the Waldorf's Peacock Lounge, a young man introduced himself as Bill Marriott, with a hint of a smile and a hearty handshake. I would not have known him, but obviously someone in his office had dug up a picture of me. Later I found it was a standard practice of his—something started by his father—to learn all he could about his employees—even prospective ones. The Marriotts would always ask the doorman or room clerk in whatever hotel they were visiting how their children were doing, knowing them all by name. It was all a part of running the organization like a family, even when they had more employees than the population of a good-sized city.

Wearing a dark suit, a white shirt, and a conservative tie, Bill Marriott looked like a college student dressed up to look like a businessman. But from the minute he opened his mouth, he exuded the authority of a person who had absorbed it with his mother's milk. Just like Bob Tisch, he came to the point without wasting any time:

"George, what do you know about our company?"

I was a little taken aback, being accustomed to the European way of using one's first name only after having established some kind of familiarity. Fortunately, I had made a couple of phone calls before this meeting and I was able to tell him about the Big Boy coffee shops, the Hot Shoppes restaurants, which his parents had started, the Roy Rogers chain, Marriott's in-flight catering, and the fact that just then his airline catering division had started serving the brand-new Boeing 747 jets. I said that their hotels were as American as apple pie is supposed to be. He looked as if he wasn't sure whether my comment was a slur on the pie or their hotels, or if I had intended it as a compliment.

"Yes, but what do you know about our restaurant division?"

I had to admit that I knew absolutely nothing, outside of its coffee shops and fast-food chains.

"George, we would like to enter the upmarket restaurant field, but in order to do so, we have to explore ways to do it."

I learned a long time ago the technique of keeping my mouth shut in order to force the other person to talk. After an uncomfortable silence, he said, "Would you like to join our organization?" I was so flabbergasted that the only thing I could say was that I would get back to him.

I felt elated at being approached by two of the most prominent men in and out of my profession. I also felt scared—scared that I would not be able to make the most of these opportunities. I stayed up most of the night, going over and over a number of scenarios.

The next morning I went to the New York Public Library and researched both companies before making any decision. I didn't have to do

Working with Bill Marriott in 1975

much research on Loews, because I had known Robert Preston Tisch quite well since my Waldorf years. Larry, his older brother, and Bob formed a singularly effective team, and their ventures, which ranged from insurance companies to hotels and real estate, were all eminently successful.

The story of J. Willard Marriott Sr. was like a folk legend. The son of a poor Mormon sheep and cattle rancher, at the age of twelve he had packed a pistol and worked with the shepherds who tended his father's flocks. At twenty-seven he obtained the A&W root beer franchise for Washington, D.C., and opened his first snack bar, incidentally on the day that Lindbergh flew across the Atlantic on May 20, 1927. Recognizing what the automobile was doing to America, he started the first curbside service, and to supplement the root-beer business during the lean winter months, he and his wife introduced chili, tacos, and tamales to the menu, which became the basis of the chain of restaurants they would call the Hot Shoppes.

I really perked up when I got to the part about his son, Bill Marriott Jr., who in 1964, at the young age of thirty-two, became the corporation's president. I was flabbergasted to read that they operated some one thousand food outlets in addition to airport hotels, gift shops, specialty restaurants, and other divisions. It was clear to me that Bill junior's plans would take the company into dozens of other businesses.

During the next few days I changed my mind on an hourly basis. In the end I chose not to think about it for a day.

The next morning it hit me: Why shouldn't I work for both? Why not form a "company of one"! Instead of a salary, I would take a fee. I would have an office with my own name plate, make my own schedule, and perhaps I could even take on other jobs as well.

In a medieval codex, perhaps this event would have been illustrated as "The Angel of Hospitality Offering a Revelation to Lang."

That was how I became a consultant.

Unfortunately, it was not this imaginary angel but I, as a full-fledged consultant, who was expected to work miracles in both companies. I tried to appear sure of myself as I presented my plans to both Tisch and Marriott, hoping to sound convincing enough that they wouldn't change their minds. During the separate meetings, I told these gentlemen that I would leave RA, form my own company, and be ready to start within a month or so. I never asked for a contract. Our handshake agreements lasted for over ten years.

I was not of voting age when my parents chose my first name, and—except for the time, after the war, when I changed my name to my mother's maiden name—this was the first opportunity I had to choose a moniker. I could not call the company Temptations Incorporated, and General Foods was already taken.

I talked with George Lois, who had come up with some of the most inventive advertising copy for Restaurant Associates, and after I stated my problem, he blurted out, in his inimitable style, "You horse's ass, the only thing you have in your miserable life that's worth anything is your name. Use it!"

So I had half of the solution to the puzzle. I still needed the other half, which would be the visual message of the logo.

The Four Seasons was the right place in those days to meet guests who have made a difference in our time. Milton Glaser was such a person. Through his graphics he has changed the way we see the world around us. I took an instant liking to him, and as the ultimate expression of my feelings, I served him an extra portion of white truffle shavings over his risotto. When I mentioned to him that I was forming my own company and that I still needed the visual message of a logo, he asked me

Milton Glaser happy in a taxi

a few questions. Then he pointed out to me that whatever was chosen must have the following characteristics: "It must be appropriate; it should convey the nature of your activities; and it must be a food you love." Then—to my surprise—he offered to design it for me.

During the coming week, I couldn't stop thinking about the food I love that would lend itself to the logo of my company to be. A goose liver just wouldn't do it, or even a perfectly ripe Comice pear; I was toying with the idea of making a seal out of an artichoke, looking at its open petals from above.

When I saw Milton's dazzling bunch of asparagus, it was like a revelation—as though someone had presented me with the answer to a problem I had been trying to solve for my whole life.

By that time I was married to Karen Zehring, whom I had met while she was visiting Budapest as a tourist. I had been having dinner in a restaurant there when I overheard a hopeless non-dialogue between the waiter, who didn't speak a word of English, and two young women who spoke French and English but not a word of Hungarian. I am not sure whether the moral of the story is that one should or should not volunteer either in the army or in a Hungarian restaurant, but eventually I ended up married to one of the two charming guests at that restaurant, who could have been cast in a European movie as the pretty, blonde American.

With my asparagus collection and my cat, Truffles

The marriage, which lasted about seven years, was doomed from the beginning, though no one would have predicted it at the time except my former wife and Karen's father. Our union had a lot of reasons to last, but I guess not enough of them. We couldn't keep to the rules of the marriage game, which require the players to love each other's faults as well as their virtues.

While adjusting to my new life, I also had to find an office for my company. Marriott had just bought the Essex House on Central Park South, their first venture in New York City, and Bill offered me a room on the 58th Street side of the lobby, which originally had been a barber-shop. Within a couple of days I had transformed this space into my office, which felt like an extension of the home Karen and I were furnishing on Riverside Drive. I lured my secretary away from RA, and in no time at all the George Lang Corporation was in business.

Restaurant consulting was a new profession then, and one could ask why there was a need for it.

Restaurants, until the end of World War II, had been mostly mom-and-pop operations, and nobody had really applied to them the multiple skills and the kind of research that goes into large-scale business ventures. If a chef or a maître d' hôtel accumulated enough money to open a restaurant, or maybe if one of their wealthy customers provided the financial backing, the fare was usually based on French cuisine or whatever kind of cooking the chef was familiar with. Refugees new to this country, who were not burdened by knowing too much about the restaurant world here, contributed much by opening their own dream places.

And, of course, America had changed after the war; people traveled, and they wanted the same kind of exciting and authentic eating experiences at home that they had discovered abroad. Before the 1950s, one had to have a special reason to go to a restaurant—for a celebration or a business event, or perhaps because it was the maid's night out—but by the time I began to work as a consultant, restaurants had become an agreeable form of entertainment. They were not only suddenly big business, but—depending on which statistics you read—hospitality had become the second or third largest industry in America.

Sitting in my Essex House office, shortly after the very unceremonious beginning of my role as a restaurant consultant, I realized that I would have to start from the very beginning. I knew what my goals were, and it was clear to me that first I would have to forge my tools.

Within a year I was able to staff the George Lang Corporation with a graphic and industrial designer, a kitchen planner, and several top-notch restaurant experts. We always began our research with a survey of the environment of a particular project. Then we studied the history and the habits of both the local population and transients; we visited the markets to observe the local produce and other products; we called upon labor unions to check out the supply of help and the restrictions of the unions, if any; we examined the costs of transporting foods from other regions or countries and dozens of different areas. Any of these factors could affect the eventual success of the venture. During my work, I tasted everything that was edible—and some things that were inedible—ruminated with cabdrivers in Hamburg, shopkeepers in Boston, and farmers in Macedonia to gather as much information as I could. The paradox was that, for all the research, the creative process had to be spontaneous. Nor was the amount of preliminary work necessarily indicative of the final result. For instance, the Beverly Center in Beverly Hills (where the owner, Sheldon Gordon, was part of the creative team) took months of research before we came up with the right mix for a giant boutique and restaurant complex occupying the entire eighth floor; on the other hand, the idea of the round-the-world cruise for the *Queen Elizabeth II* occurred to me on the spur of the moment during a meeting with their executives. Each time I proposed a concept, I had to be sure that its time had come. I always reminded myself of André Gide's line: "Heaven help the man who comes up with an answer for which the question has not been asked!"

Several top professionals and I dealt with that problem in a three-day seminar I organized at the Hotel St. Regis for the leaders of the hospitality industry. During one of the heated debates about how to focus and aim at a particular group of consumers, I characterized a "tablecloth" restaurant's clientele as people who come there in order to: cheat on their diets; cheat on their spouses; tell their dates why they can't get a divorce just now; feel important; satisfy their curiosity about seeing how the other one percent lives; or take a trip down nostalgia alley.

Although this list was offered as an ad-lib intermezzo, it is not far from the truth.

In 1981, Charles Bernstein wrote, in his book *Great Restaurant Innovators:* "Today food service consultants are so plentiful that—like some segments of the food service operations themselves—the field may face its own saturation dilemma. But in 1970, Lang was the first to offer creative help to operators on a wide range of services."

Within a few years, many instant consultants opened up shop, but only a few survived. The reason was simply that the one who fills the restaurant calls the tune.

I learned much during those first couple of years, and here are a few of the verities:

- As a consultant, you don't have the right to be wrong.
- Unless you have a contract to supervise a restaurant after its opening, don't go back there, because the chances are that you will feel like a father whose daughter has become a prostitute.
- To guard your professional reputation, choose your clients as carefully as they choose you; being a consultant to some companies is like being a purser on the *Titanic*.
- Don't think that you'll get rich. Consultancy is supposed to be based on prophecy, but unfortunately most consulting companies are "non-prophet" organizations.

For a consultant to advise against opening a restaurant may seem like Reebok advertising that one shouldn't exercise, yet throughout my consulting life I have made cautionary speeches and written articles to those who are infected with the most curious illness of our time, *restaurantitis*. Alas, opening restaurants became as common as adultery (and just as dangerous), with one of the highest mortality rates of all businesses in the United States. But I do believe that working with a skilled restaurant consultant can reduce the risk; it is a form of insurance, and the premium is usually worth it.

At one of the "Table Two" dinners that we host on occasion (which, not surprisingly, take place at our round table designated No. 2 at the Café des Artistes), a friend of ours expressed outrage that a few nights before, he had paid thirty-five dollars for a plate of pasta at a fancy East Side place when other restaurants charge half that amount.

Then I asked him if the thirty-five-dollar pasta at this restaurant, owned by a famous chef, was better than the others.

"Yes," he answered, "but not that much."

"My good friend," I replied, "you pay double or triple in all walks of life for that extra ten-percent edge."

That ten-percent edge is another service that a good consultant can supply. And that is what we did for the Marriott Corporation. The more I got to know young Bill, the more I realized that underneath the boyish grin, he had inherited his father's drive and austere perseverance. Within forty-eight hours' time, I received half a dozen assignments. One of them involved the Essex House, which Bill wanted to remake in Marriott's image. For my first working meeting, I went down to their headquarters in Bethesda, Maryland. I was expecting a full-scale session with a dozen specialists of his team. To my surprise, I was ushered into his office, and without much preamble he got down to business. He told me that he and his brother felt strongly about an upscale version of an English tavern on Central Park South, inspired by the name Essex, which evokes an English connection.

On the way back from Washington to New York on the shuttle, which from that point on became my crosstown bus, I was so excited that I made notes on an idea that had come to me the minute I had left Bill's office. "Tavern . . . Samuel Johnson . . . Boswell . . . eighteenth-century England . . . something about the tavern chair which is a throne . . ." No one could talk to me during the next couple of days without getting a quote from one of those two worthy gentlemen.

In my initial report I wrote, "Samuel Johnson loved the tavern life and stated, 'A tavern chair is the throne of human felicity.' He observed that prescriptions which used to have fifty ingredients now are compounded of five, and the same thing could be done in cookery if we chose the highest-quality ingredients and learned the proper techniques of cooking them."

Bill called me shortly after he read the report, and told me that I was on the right track. I suggested that we go to London with George Jenkins, a friend of mine with whom I had worked at the World's Fair, and who was now the contract designer for Samuel Goldwyn. I remembered that at one time he had also made a study of English inns and taverns, and he could be an enormous help to Marriott's in-house architects and designers.

This was before the Marriott Corporation made their first move to extend their hotel empire into Europe, and Bill was not in the habit of jetting to London. Yet within two weeks we were visiting ten to fifteen pubs, taverns, and inns together with George Jenkins. The first place we checked out was George Inn, near London Bridge, where apparently Dr. Johnson frequently raised a tankard of ale by the open fire. We also amassed a lot of relevant information about the public houses during the reigns of George I and George II, even stretching our mark toward the third of the Georges since Johnson was still living and writing his *bons mots* well into the latter's tenure on the throne.

As a model for the Boswell Room at the Essex House, we found a handsome eighteenth-century paneled room with a stylish marble mantel and chimney piece, doorways, corner cupboards, and so on. Jenkins also knew someone in London who would coordinate tailor-made changes, and find additional lighting fixtures, credenzas, rugs, porcelain-ware, and other furnishings.

We wanted the menu to be quite authentic, but not so much so that we would miss the market we hoped to attract. After a while we could almost taste the veal-and-ham pie (a favorite of Dr. Johnson's), the apple stuffed and baked with plum pudding, and the afternoon tea in the Georgian manner.

When I returned to New York, I received a call from Bill quite late one night, and I knew immediately that something must be wrong.

Something was.

He told me that his father had just heard about our plan for the Essex House, and was squarely against it.

"George, maybe you can bring him around. If you can't, no one can."

The next day I went to Bethesda to accomplish Mission Impossible. The meeting was rather short, perhaps three minutes. J.W. senior told me to forget the whole project and get things done instead that were vital for the company right now.

No one would ever talk about the elder Marriott's reasons for being so hostile to our idea. But as I got to know him, it became obvious to me that he had created his empire by consistently avoiding any kind of concept that was not based on probable acceptance by the largest possible segment of the market. Also, he let other companies experiment with new concepts, and would then improve on the few that succeeded. This turned out to be a safe and highly profitable formula.

It was the only time something like this had happened at the Marriott corral, and I was able to work for ten good years—without getting involved with J.W. senior—on dozens of original restaurant prototypes and hotels, including a restaurant group in Rome, several amusement parks, shipping companies like the Sun Lines, and such fine resorts as the Camelback Inn in Scottsdale, Arizona.

The Tisch family saga had its beginnings just after World War II, and there were no cowboys and shepherds. While the brothers were still in their mid-twenties, they had purchased a small resort hotel in Lake-wood, New Jersey, and turned it into one of the most successful vacation hotels in the Northeast. By the time I began to work with them, they owned and operated the Loews Theaters, the Loews Hotels, Lorillard, and a home development company, and the annual income of the company topped $800 million. All in less than two dozen years, starting with that small hotel in New Jersey!

Loews Plaza in Hamburg, which opened in the spring of 1973, set a number of records. It was the first hotel in Europe for Loews, and with its thirty-two stories it was the tallest hotel in West Germany. In America, until quite recently, dining in a hotel was the last refuge of the tired traveler, and hotel operators considered restaurants simply a service for the guests, and didn't expect them to bring in any money; in fact, they felt lucky if a restaurant broke even. Bob Tisch was not particularly interested in food or wine, yet he was among the first American hotel magnates to realize that hotel restaurants should not be relegated to a mere supporting role.

The more I read, interviewed people, visited the existing restaurants, and dined in private homes, the more I realized that what a nineteenth-century English trader wrote, that "Hamburg and London seem to be different sections of the very same city," was still true a hundred years later. The menu of the English Grill, which we opened in Loews' Hamburg hotel, was based on a passage from Kettner's *Book of the Table*, written in 1877: "It is curious that the most ancient and most simple mode of cookery should be in some respect the most perfect and certainly the most esteemed. The first cooked food that man ate was broiled." Eventually the grill rooms of German and English cities added a limited selection of other specialties to their menus, and the dining rooms of the Loews Hamburg Plaza featured some of those dishes as well.

In an effort to emphasize the importance of its wine cellar, I bought a simple machine that the sommelier could use to engrave a *Stammkundschaft*—that is, the regular customer's name—on the *tastevin* cup used to taste the wine they ordered. These cups were displayed in a velvet-lined display case, naturally with the engraved part on view. Soon, quite a few prominent local citizens booked tables just so that they could show off their names as they entered the dining room.

For the menu at one of the restaurants, Vierländer Stube, Milton Glaser used an eighteenth-century drawing of a winsome young woman, wearing voluminous skirts, to create a charming and masterfully practical design. To our dismay, one of the reviewers groused about it, complaining that "the guest has to lift up the skirt of the young lady to be able to read the menu."

I never found out who took care of the situation, but after a brief storm-in-a-schnapps-glass, the lady decorating the menu cover continued to submit to the innocent skirt-page-turning.

We had barely finished this hotel when we began to work on the restaurants of Loews Monte Carlo. Even before I started my research, I knew about the culinary chauvinism of the locals. So instead of entering a race I was sure to lose, I created a highly successful niche in the local restaurant scene by opening an elegant Argentine steakhouse, a variation on a *churrasqueria*. Considering the anti-American feelings of the French, an American steakhouse would have failed, so this was a perfect alternative for a clientele that cried out for great roasted or grilled beef. The menu we presented was in the form of a stylized leather gaucho apron (complete with pockets), the steak knife was an honest-to-goodness gaucho knife, and the bread we served was baked in a ceramic oven in front of the guests.

The presentation of a new project usually took place in my office, where the walls were lined with more than ten thousand cookbooks. After I outlined a probable financial scenario, I would always put on a full-scale performance with renderings, three-dimensional maquettes, and servers dressed in the proposed uniforms, and I would offer a few of the characteristic food specialties on the specially designed tabletops. For the nightclub at the Monte Carlo hotel, I suggested a theme that seemed a natural to me. Stravinsky's *Petrouchka* ballet had been premiered in 1911 by the Ballet Russe de Monte Carlo, with Nijinsky dancing the title role, and I thought Petrouchka would be the perfect name and provide lively visuals. I lost this bout, however; instead, at the suggestion of Bob Tisch, the name of the nightclub became Folie Russe. I guess he must have been right, because it is still operating happily as a Monegasque version of the Folies-Bergères. But at least after the presentation, he complimented me on the only mobile office garden in the free, democratic world. I had designed an earth-filled eight-by-six-foot container on wheels, filled with flowers, plants, and fifteen-foot-high trees growing in its center under the skylight. We would roll it against the rear wall of the office to create a large enough space for the theater-style presentation.

I was troubled by being given only a tiny kitchen for the Folie Russe. But then I decided that plenty of caviar and vodka would take care of things. *Zakouski* is the classic Russian hors d'oeuvre, and almost every selection was topped with caviar; even the consommé that followed contained vodka. Since the hotel had a high-traffic casino, the winners could always afford to pay for the *assiette des hors-d'oeuvre Moscovite* while the losers would console themselves with a glass of vodka offered in a festive cup.

Eventually other hotels followed, in different cities. I am still pleased that after so many projects, we have never repeated a concept.

We would always keep refining our preliminary research technique and conceptual work before we made our so-called Phase One presentations. But when something unexpected happened, it killed the entire venture. A painful example of this was when I was asked by a highly successful entrepreneur, Charlie Stein, to create a prototype for a chain of imaginative, casual restaurants to be called Orient Express. I had prepared a thorough feasibility study for him and his illustrious partners, bound the results in a book, and we had even picked the locations for the first three units. As the second part of the presentation, I staged a tasting of the highlights of the menu in our home, three floors above my office, which has a very large kitchen furnished with professional equipment. The principals were in a great mood, sipping a special nonalcoholic Orient Express cocktail and anticipating a pleasant evening.

Suddenly we heard a cacophony of screaming voices and an earsplitting clatter of pots hitting the tiled floor. I ran into the kitchen to see what was happening. As I opened the door, I saw the Malaysian chef in a fit of rage, with a cleaver in his hand, chasing the Chinese chef through the other kitchen door leading to the living room, screaming what was probably a pungent description of his colleague's ancestors.

One of my assistants, who must have been a linebacker in college, tackled the raging chef and we all piled on top of him. Even my secretary got into the act. Everybody tried to make the best out of a shocking scene, but even when we switched to the alcoholic version of the Orient Express cocktail, it couldn't save the evening. The mortified partners considered the debacle a bad omen, and despite their positive feelings about our concept, the entire project was canceled the next day.

CHAPTER 18

The Failure Factor

SOMETIMES I THINK of my life as a consultant as not unlike
that of a compulsive mountain climber who not only has to scale the
existing, cloud-capped, difficult-to-reach peaks, but also needs to create
his own mountains on occasion, just to have something to climb. In the
fifteen-year period between 1970 and 1985, I was busy manufacturing a
great number of mountains on several continents, although sometimes
my associates and I ended up with interestingly shaped molehills.

If the world of restaurants were built on pure logic, most of my professional life would have been spent in a very special heaven. Alas, the
best-planned restaurants are not necessarily the most successful, and failures are often the result of correct assumptions and methodology. On the
other hand, great successes are often achieved with built-in mistakes and
accidents or by playing on the lowest common denominator of human
nature.

On January 2, 1972, I received a telex that contained news to touch
the soul, stir the blood, and warm the pocketbook of a passionate consultant. It had been sent by the Hong Kong–based design office of Pat and
Dale Keller. They asked me to call them immediately in connection with
a large resort compound in Greece.

Within forty-eight hours I was on my way to Athens to participate
in a critical meeting. I had met first with the Kellers and Apostolos

Ziros, who acted as a representative of the client, Yanni Carras. They familiarized me with the architectural plans and other details of a seaside resort within a Macedonian-style village on the Aegean coast of the Khalkidhiki peninsula. The location was about a hundred kilometers southeast of Thessaloniki, on a small bay opposite the tiny port of Néos Marmaras. The land embraced 4,500 acres of pine forest, almond orchards, olive and lemon groves, secluded coves, and fine beaches. Ziros, who obviously knew the history of his country intimately, commented that ancient books pinpointed this location as the place where the gods and evil giants fought for the supremacy of the earth. Trying to make a good impression, I held back the comment that the results were still not in.

In a large conference room I met with the high-powered team that had been put together to implement the idea of this village and resort compound, including the famed Gropius-founded TAC architectural group, the designers Pat and Dale Keller, the noted Bordeaux oenologist Emile Peynaud, and quite a few other specialists. I was told that my role was to plan, organize, create, and open a number of different types of restaurants, including the food and beverage facilities of a hotel, an inn, and—as a separate project—all of the food-service facilities of two luxury class cruise ships. Fortunately, the only work that had been done so far was to locate the hotels and restaurants within Porto Carras, as the new village was named.

I could hardly wait to meet Yanni (John) C. Carras, a Greek shipping magnate whose Herculean idea it was to build this entire village. He probably wanted to size me up, so he made me sit next to him at dinner that night. We were still sampling *mezéthes* when I asked him what made him start this vast undertaking. I guess this was the last topic he expected from an American restaurant consultant, but he took the question seriously and told the story to the entire table:

"A few years ago I was checking out one of my oil tankers when I passed the yacht of a fellow Greek ship owner; we greeted each other from a distance. That night, before going to sleep, I started thinking about the fact that I was not getting younger. Remembering my friend on his splendid yacht, all dressed up and surrounded by jolly company, I asked myself, 'What am I going to leave behind after I'm gone?' The more I thought about it, the more I felt that I wanted my legacy to include more than ships, money, villas, yachts, and a bound volume of photographs of great parties. Little by little I realized that my bequest to the world should be an ideal village in Greece that would retain a close link between the man-made and the natural. By keeping the groves of olive and citrus trees, I could make it a self-contained oasis where art and culture would have their place alongside the yachts and the villas."

I was so taken with his dream that if he had asked me to work with him for nothing, I probably would have said yes.

John Carras was a remarkable person who represented the ancient Greek model of *kalos kagathos,* a human being who is close to the ideal. He inherited his passion for the sea from his family. His grandfather had been a simple boatman in the nineteenth century, and John had become one of the legendary ship owners of Greece. One of John's own sons, Costas, was part of the often exciting process of developing Porto Carras.

The style of the village was to be a contemporary version of the architecture of the nearby Mount Athos—houses with rough-cast, dazzling white walls, gray slate roofs, and balconies with dark-timbered balustrades. What we were really planning was the ideal instant village, including shops, tavernas, museums, an amphitheater, art galleries, and—we hoped—real life in the village square. The entire village was to be situated around a marina, which also had to be designed and built; the backdrop to all of this was the green hills of Khalkidhiki.

The marina of Porto Carras was designed by the eminent British specialist Sir William Halcrow, and by this time his people had been working on it for more than three years, creating a rectangular basin with 180 moorings, so that the two planned Carras cruise ships and other visiting vessels could anchor directly in front of the village. A giant dredger was brought from the United States to carve out the port itself, and complex machinery was installed at the exit of the port to renew the water in the marina periodically. There were no shortcuts on this project; every part of it was done to last for many centuries. It was a playground for grownups, with toys too expensive even for F. A. O. Schwarz. One day, for instance, we all gathered on the outer edge of the port when a helicopter dropped huge balloons to outline the proposed shape of the marina.

After completing my feasibility study, I worked closely with key members of the team and we made a presentation of my concept of the array of restaurants.

Over the years, in my capacity as a consultant, I have found that every client becomes an expert during planning sessions. John Carras, looking at the room layouts for the Hotel Meliton at one of the design presentations, remarked that there didn't seem to be enough space for steamer trunks. The rest of us looked at each other, wondering who was going to tell him that the days when people traveled with monstrously bulky movable armoires were over.

There is a panel from an old comic strip, "The Little King," that has always reminded me of my life as a consultant, and I have it framed next to my desk. The rotund Little King is standing on a balcony, making the following declaration: "The golden rule is that he who has the gold makes the rules." John Carras could have supplied this line to Mr. Soglow.

Of the many restaurants, tavernas, and formal dining rooms I planned at Porto Carras, my favorite was Farma-Yanni, named after Yanni Carras. We designed the restaurant to look like a typical Greek agora or market, with a farmlike environment to be supplied by bowls of fresh vegetables from the garden behind the restaurant, and olives from our own trees. A tureen filled with Greek country-style soup hung in a copper kettle over an open flame; whole roast suckling pig and lamb turned on a spit. Côtes de Meliton (Château Carras) wine was standing proudly on each table in traditional carafes. It gave all of us a good feeling that the place was true to its name: most of the food came from Yanni's farm.

In my master plan, I recommended a restaurant that would be based on the culinary glories of the Byzantine Empire and would represent *deipnosophis,* or connoisseurship. The entire restaurant was a stylish fantasy overlooking the port, with a series of tall, slitlike windows covered with latticework frames.

On the calligraphy-embellished menu (written in several languages), a short paragraph from the *Banquet of the Learned* (by Athenaeus, after A.D. 192) was quoted: "For when you write a book on Cookery, it will not do to say: 'As I was just now saying,' for this Art has no fix'd guide but opportunity, and must itself its only mistress be."

Guests of the Bosphorus received a sumptuous five-course repast that included a whole fish bathed in aromatic herbs and baked in live coals, and cheeses of the Byzantine Empire presented on a tiered epergne with Greek sun-dried fruits; the feast concluded with coffee as served in Constantinople or in the style of Antioch, or tea perfumed with rose petals.

In 1991 I returned to Porto Carras to participate in a week-long international food festival and seminar series, arranged by the Greek Tourist

Board. One night, after the last glass of ouzo, I remembered an early planning meeting in John Carras's office in Athens almost twenty years before when I'd asked what I considered a key question regarding the viability of this mammoth complex.

"Excuse me, but, based on the weather, how many months of the year will this place be usable for tourism?"

The expression on everyone's face suggested that I was an idiot who didn't realize that Greece is the land of eternal summer. They humored me by showing me elaborate meteorological charts indicating that the village could prosper all year.

A month later I flew to Thessaloniki and drove from there to the tiny village of Néos Marmaras. As I was standing at the future site of Porto Carras, holding a huge plan, every now and then I had to rub my hands together and put them into my pockets to make sure that they would not snap off, frozen, at the wrists. One of the strongest recommendations I made, following this visit, was that an underground convention center be built in addition to the existing plan, but the idea was unanimously rejected. I must confess that I too was so caught up in the excitement of this once-in-a-lifetime creation, feeling like one of the builders in the entourage of a modern-day Medici, that I discarded my misgivings. Alas, when Porto Carras did open a few years later, climate was one of the several reasons why this resort did not fulfill its original promise, though poor management and utterly misguided marketing were also factors. In plain English, you could say it bombed. And as I said in my speech at one of my seminars, one of the built-in drawbacks of the creative process is that when you want something badly enough, you will indulge in the art and craft of rationalization.

Simultaneously, as I was developing the plans for the restaurants of the cruise ships, I asked myself a vital question: What are the primary reasons most people go on cruises? The first of my many answers was that cruise ships are like clubs with short-term memberships, and passengers can belong for a week to this club where most of their wishes will be fulfilled. The problem I had to deal with was that their predictability provides their appeal *and* their ennui. There are many ways one can treat this malaise. Ideally, restaurants on cruise ships should be like the theater, each venue a stage set capable of being changed completely according to the occasion and time of day.

Naming restaurants or cruise ships is a game everybody likes to play. Finally, about six months before its maiden voyage, after several changes,

A partially completed Porto Carras in 1976

one of the ships was named *Danae*, after the daughter of Perseus, and the other became *Daphne*, the nymph who escaped Apollo's advances by turning into a laurel leaf.

Having covered every detail, including the availability of worry beads in the boutique, finally, toward the end of 1976, we were ready to make plans for the debut of the SS *Danae*, a trip that would start in southern France and continue on to Asia. On virtually every cruise ship, especially in those days, the cuisine tried to emulate the menu of a five-star hotel—already an oft-revised, unsatisfactory imitation of French *grande cuisine*. On the *Danae*'s maiden voyage, the theme I chose for each dinner was based on the port where we would dock the next day. The night before the ship arrived at Heraklion, for example, I planned a Cretan fisherman's holiday repast, featuring *kakavia*, the great seafood soup-stew from that part of the world, an aromatic member of the bouillabaisse family. The rest of the menu was based on what a local fisherman would eat perhaps once a year, on a special holiday. Another example: shortly before we docked at Istanbul, a great Ottoman dinner was offered to the guests.

In order to join the *Danae* midway on its maiden voyage, I flew from Athens to Bangkok on what seemed an endless plane trip. But the first

With Greek shipping tycoon Yanni Carras on the S.S. Daphne, *1977*

sight of the ship made up for it—there it was, looking like an elegant, sleek private yacht, a 17,000-ton, 532-foot-long vessel with 220 staterooms. I felt like the proud parent of this brand-new baby.

During the first twenty-four hours aboard the *Danae,* observing, analyzing, making detailed notes on what had happened to my ideas when put into practice, I remembered Janos Starker's counsel to his artist/students: "You have to be good enough that eighty percent of your best is still on a high enough level." I thought the premiere came in at above eighty percent. Fortunately the glittering list of passengers did too. Everyone quaffed a lot of champagne, the mostly Greek staff was spirited, and the food, thanks to some sure-fire presentations, was praised by everyone.

The captain of the ship assigned me one of the plush staterooms, which had a little balcony. The first day out at sea, I got out of bed while the rest of the passengers were still asleep, opened the door, and stepped out onto the balcony to fill my lungs with the bracing air. Just then the ship bounced on top of a playful wave, and the door closed behind me. I stood there naked, unable to get back into my cabin.

Two painters were doing final touch-ups on the ship, and, not having much choice, I started waving at them. They didn't quite know how to react to a full-grown, totally nude passenger. Was I a fugitive from an asylum, or a sex maniac? They just grinned at me uneasily and threw up their hands.

Finally I did succeed in communicating to them what had happened, by pantomiming the incident, and they came to my rescue.

During the voyage, Prince Souvanna Phouma of Laos was on hand to give a few history lessons on modern China, offering his slightly biased version of the past and the present. Chinese musicians played a dinner concert, and for anyone who wanted to learn more about Chinese art, there was an artist aboard who not only talked about the subject but also gave a splendid demonstration of classic Chinese brush technique. The reason for all this *chinoiserie* was known only to me and a few of the officials of the Carras-Delian line: there was a good chance that the *Danae* would be allowed into the People's Republic of China. I was all keyed up about this opportunity to see China. As the ancient *Book of Han* (A.D. 200) says: "To see once for oneself is better than to hear a hundred reports."

Even now, almost twenty years later, I remember feeling like one of the first astronauts on the way to the moon, when, during the night of Wednesday, February 24, 1977, Captain Filipoussis of the *Danae* received radio signals from Chinese officials announcing that the ship would be allowed into Whampoa, the port of Guangzhou (Canton). But there was a last-minute hitch, when a monsoon developed suddenly in the South China Sea, which forced our captain to reduce speed to under eight knots. The Chinese officials were curt and clearly inflexible in their instructions that the ship must arrive in Guangzhou exactly at midnight on February 26 to meet the Chinese officials. But because of that monsoon, we were delayed, and until the last night, no one was sure whether we would get permission to dock. As it turned out, we made up the lost time and docked at the Chinese pilot station at the mouth of the Pearl River with fifty minutes to spare.

When we came close to Whampoa, the Chinese pilot boat debarked fifty-three Chinese officials without a sound or an unnecessary motion. It was an impressive performance. After boarding and taking over the *Danae*'s controls, communicating with their own pilot ship, they navigated the *Danae* up the very narrow river in the middle of the night, in thick fog, without using radar or sonar. In the meantime the Luxingshe Chinese tourist officials and armed customs and immigration officers worked until five o'clock in the morning checking out the papers of the ship and the crew, and searching every inch of the ship to make sure that there were no passengers with Israeli, Portuguese, or South African passports.

Before embarking in Bangkok, I had bought a few bottles of a particular Thai hot pepper sauce that was—and still is—a favorite of mine. When morning came, at my suggestion we invited the Chinese crew to a breakfast, and I offered them (with aching heart) my orange-red liquid treasures. It was like serving a 1949 Château Petrus in magnums to a French crew. After the breakfast they became easier to talk to, realizing that perhaps not every occidental is a *gweilin*—a foreign devil—without tastebuds.

The French author Dominique Lapierre and his wife (whose first name is, confusingly, the same as his) were passengers on this inaugural trip, and within a short time it seemed as if we had known each other since childhood. In the late morning of February 27, 1977, the three of us disembarked together, talking about the fact that we were part of a history-making voyage, since it marked the first time in twenty-eight years that a Western cruise ship had been permitted to dock at a mainland Chinese port. We wondered if in 1841 (the year when China ceded Hong Kong to Great Britain) the first Western gunboats had gone up the same route, trying to take over China.

As we stepped onto Chinese soil we were surrounded by the blaring of loudspeakers, broadcasting kitschy Chinese music punctuated with Chinese and English slogans about the infallibility of the Revolutionary Committee.

When we reached the streets of Guangzhou—a city that, at that time, housed a little over three million people—busloads of factory workers lined the roads, fighting for space with swarms of bicyclists, hand-pulled carts, and pedestrians that filled every inch of public road. And because every single person was wearing an identical dark blue Mao jacket, only the hairdos gave a clue to the gender.

I had heard about the brand-new thirty-three-story White Cloud Hotel in the center of the city, so I asked one of our guides if that was where we would be staying. He somewhat reluctantly told me that by mistake they had built the ceilings too low for Western tourists. Instead, we were bused to the 1,800-room Tung Fang Hotel, across from the Canton Fair, where we were taken to our rooms without the usual check-in process. The furniture was a good approximation of secondhand Grand Rapids style circa 1930, except that my bed was surrounded by a mosquito net. Packages of cigarettes and matches, a calendar, a lamp, an ashtray, and stationery were all placed on the desk, plus a bottle of glue to be used for sealing envelopes. It reminded me of the joke, circulating around Budapest at the time, that Hungarian stamps did not stick to the envelopes because people were spitting on the picture of Rákosi (the Hungarian equivalent of Mao) instead of the sticky side.

There were no door keys, since hotel rooms in China were never locked. Stealing was only done on a monumentally large scale by the state after everything was nationalized in 1949, but personal burglary was virtually unknown even as late as the 1970s.

On my first night there, thinking about Marco Polo, Richard Nixon, and the fact that I might be the first American restaurateur to visit mainland China after the Communist revolution, I entered the main banquet hall of the Tung Fang Hotel all keyed up for the official state dinner given by the city's Revolutionary Committee and high officials from Peking. I was expecting the greatest dining experience of my life. But the mai-tai toasts that occurred with increasing frequency could not sweeten the bitter experience of a mediocre meal which is not even worth detailing here. As the endless courses progressed, it seemed to me that a funny thing had happened to the Chinese on the way to the revolution: they'd lost the art of dining. The service, however, was most attentive, and each table of ten was attended by six waiters. I couldn't help observing to my table companions that it was no wonder there was no unemployment in China. I was surprised that each guest brought his or her own chopsticks, just as in medieval times in Italy, when everyone carried his own silver flatware.

The women at the banquet unfortunately wore loose, baggy trousers to deemphasize the female form, probably as part of the party's drive to reduce the population explosion.

While I was there, I often tried to have short conversations with some of the hotel employees, using a Chinese phrase book.

Q. What made you decide to choose being a waiter as your profession?

A. I was told that this is what the Party needs, and I'm happy to serve the Party.

Q. Can you leave this job and take another?

A. Why should I? I am happy here.

Q. Do you get good tips?

A. We consider tipping an insult, and would return it.

Q. What would you like to do ten years from now?

A. Whatever the Revolutionary Committee decides.

Q. If you have an idea about improving something, do you tell it to someone, or just do it?

A. What do you mean, improve?

Q. For instance, to cut an orange a certain way is more attractive and makes it easier to eat, like this. [I demonstrated a simple technique.]

A. If something can be done better, our comrades in the provincial central committee will tell us.

After such frustrating dialogues I decided to talk to someone who was in a decision-making position. I had to go through much string-pulling and button-pushing, but finally I was seated in a reception room on the seventh floor of the Tung Fang Hotel with Mr. Chou, the hotel's sixty-six-year-old chief cook, who had worked in the kitchen for thirty-nine years, and Mr. Lo, my interpreter-guide. Some of the questions I asked produced heated, or at least animated, discussion between the two in Chinese, the translation of which was often a curt sentence.

Q. Do cooks specialize in certain types of cooking?

A. There are mostly three categories: general cooks, dim-sum cooks, and hot-bread pastry cooks. But in the past, many cooks could excel in all. [After this sentence, the translator realized what he had said and tried to change it. Any comparison between the new regime and the old one is a highly sensitive matter in China.]

Q. Are there famous chefs today whose names are known, as in the past?

A. We are all the same, and we try to follow the ideology set by Chairman Mao: Everyone should do his or her work, and there is no place for individualism or cult of personality in the kitchen.

Q. [Approaching it from a different angle.] Are there highly paid chefs in Guangzhou?

A. Yes, in this city, which we think has probably the best restaurants in China, there are about ten.

Q. How much do you earn?

A. One hundred yuan [fifty dollars] a month. [He was one of the ten.]

Q. How many dishes can you cook?

A. About four hundred, including all types of courses.

Q. How many do you think exist in the Chinese repertory?

A. I don't know, but an old chef who was eighty when I was an apprentice in the kitchen once said that someone many years ago compiled seven thousand basic dishes, but this number did not include the many variations of each.

Q. Has anything changed in the past couple of decades, as far as restaurant kitchens are concerned?

A. Yes, in 1958 the state mobilized a task force to develop one hundred new dishes to be served in restaurants. [It turned out that this group developed recipes that simplified existing preparations and called for inexpensive ingredients.]

Q. During the prerevolutionary period [before 1948], was the style of eating different in any way?

This last question caused a lengthy discussion between them in Chinese, which, when translated, boiled down to the following:

A. Yes, during the time of the Kuomintang gangsters, the people starved, but now everybody eats very well.

During my stay, I tried several times to get permission to visit a restaurant kitchen, but to no avail. So when Chef Chou asked me if I would like to see the hotel kitchen, I eagerly accepted the invitation. A built-into-the-wall, very primitive tiled refrigerator with exposed coils was shown to me first, with great pride. Apparently the hotel workmen and the cooks had made it themselves, and I complimented them on their resourcefulness. The kitchen itself was huge and airy, with windows looking outside. Ten or so good-sized stone-topped tables were placed around the large room in addition to chopping blocks, pastry boards, cooking ranges, steam-cooking stoves, and racks of all sorts. An interesting glass-topped, three-by-four-foot flat box near the cooking area held the spice and sauce jars and containers. Steamer baskets, woks, pottery dishes, and various kinds of vessels were hanging all over, which gave the room a lived-in feeling. It was a pleasant place to prepare food, compared with several of the basement kitchens where I had worked in the Western world.

I was surprised to learn that in Canton, people still cooked with coal and charcoal. Gas, so essential to produce the furnacelike flame needed for Chinese cooking, did not exist at the time. I discussed this with Mei Mei Lin, the daughter of Lin Yutang, the famed Chinese philosopher. Mei Mei, who knows as much about Chinese gastronomy as anyone I ever met, told me that in the past the fire would be started early in the morning, and that by mealtime it had built up to such an intensity that it was a veritable blowtorch. Because keeping the fire going all day was considered wasteful in Mao Zedong's China, the food that was cooked in the woks often ended up as a stir-braise rather than a stir-fry, which diminished the quality of many dishes.

When I returned to the *Danae* at the end of my visit, and my fellow passengers asked me about my gastronomic experiences, I answered by paraphrasing Lincoln Steffens's famous line: "I have tasted the future, and it needs seasoning."

The only souvenirs I brought back from China were a copy of Mao's "Little Red Book" in Sanskrit, and one in Hungarian. The books became valuable additions to the "Cockamamie Collection" I keep behind my desk in my New York office, which includes a tin of coffee-flavored tea, honey gathered by killer bees, and a wooden hand that drums on the table when I crank its handle. Such things justify trips to the remotest part of our universe.

One day when I was back in Manhattan, a conservatively dressed gentleman by the name of Jerry Castle came to my office at the suggestion of a mutual friend, while his bodyguard waited discreetly in the hallway. His visit started a new chapter in my consulting life. With a little smile, he started the conversation even before we sat down.

He told me that he wanted to open a restaurant that would surprise and maybe even shock people. The place should be fun, a bit crazy. Next to great French dishes on the menu, for example, he would like to have a matzo-ball soup, and then late at night would turn the place into a disco. I couldn't believe my ears when he described what he had in mind for the interior: for instance, he planned to buy for the men's room one of the van Dongen paintings "where women are balling each other." He also wanted to have palm trees growing on the sidewalk outside the front door. As an afterthought, he mentioned that the bartenders might be midgets, "serving Dom Perignon from giant double magnums."

I had learned years earlier from Jim Rouse, the creator of Baltimore's Harbor Place, who was the most original entrepreneur I have ever worked with, never to react negatively to an idea, no matter how absurd it seemed, and even before Castle finished, I was thinking about how I could wrap the roots of the palm trees with warming electrical wires to keep them alive for a while, replacing the trees every six months. The idea for this offbeat restaurant was just insane enough—in our super-prudent world—to arouse my interest.

At that time Harry Helmsley owned the Ritz Carlton Hotel, at 61st Street and Madison Avenue, which he had renamed the Carlton House, and Castle and I agreed that this spot would be the ideal location for the restaurant, which we were now calling La Folie. My client headed a large company called Penn-Dixie, and he insisted that Harry Helmsley should come to *his* office, which gesture he felt was as important as the deal itself. Helmsley was interested only in closing a deal, and went along with the—for him—pointless charade.

Even monumental cathedrals were designed by single architects, but my client told me that he was bringing in three interior designers for different sections of this restaurant/disco. One gentleman represented period elegance and the other a more hard-edged contemporary look with fashionably super-cool overtones, and the third one was supposed to add the "crazies."

The final total investment in this project ended up as perhaps the highest cost per square foot in all of restaurant history; La Folie became the classic case of a project that started out with an unlimited budget which by the time the doors were opened had been far exceeded.

I obtained the services of some of the most accomplished people in various fields, such as the famed Broadway theatrical lighting designer Abe Feder. Saul Bass, a leading Hollywood titles specialist, eventually designed the logo of La Folie: a cheetah with the extended sexy leg of a woman and its front paw in the shape of a provocative fork.

Some of the more bizarre touches that were built into this elegantly wacky establishment included a vibrating brush device so that when guests came through the entrance door the bottoms of their shoes were cleaned; a wall covered with framed pictures of celebrities as children, ranging from Jacqueline Onassis to the Kentucky Derby winner Citation as a colt; a bar, inspired by a table owned by the Duchess of Windsor, which had as its base dozens of pairs of mannequins' feet, each wearing a different pair of real shoes (naturally, the most expensive designer footwear); a rack in the bar containing many of the great newspapers of the world, including the *Irish Echo,* the Communist *Daily Worker,* and the Jewish *Forward;* a jukebox clad in an eighteenth-century cabinet, in the style of the restaurant's Malachite Room. In addition to the loud rock emanating from it, I insisted on Caruso singing the World War I hit "Over There" and some early records of Fats Waller chatting with the audience as he played the piano. A large eye (complete with false eyelashes) was painted inside each toilet bowl, and penis-shaped light fixtures stood at full attention in the men's room, courtesy of one of our designers.

I never discovered the reason for all this unbridled eccentricity, but I must admit I had fun; I felt just like a kid who doesn't have to harness his fantasies with good taste. The seventies were a time when extravagance was the norm, and it was often practiced by self-made men whose passion was to open their own restaurants. J.C. had the hunger to be seen and respected, and for a brief time La Folie made him the talk of the town, although the talk was not always the kind he was looking for.

At this circus, where one of the rooms boasted real malachite walls, the food had to be at least as impressive as the appointments and the guests in the dining room. I was fortunate to hire Bernard Norget, a chef at the Connaught Hotel in London, who was a combination of a thoroughly trained professional and someone with a remarkable palate, not a common occurrence.

An exciting innovation at La Folie was the first champagne-and-caviar bar in New York, and as a lure and a folly, we charged for the luxury only its cost price. The result was, of course, a hugely increased bar business, because word of mouth spread speedily among the New York foodies. The Dom Ruinart Blanc du Blanc was paired with a bite of lightly smoked veal tartare topped with American caviar, the Schramsberg Cremant was accompanied by caviar dip and champagne wafers, and the other nine champagnes had their caviar partners as well.

In the restaurant we pampered the guests during dinner by offering an array of miniature samplers of a basic ingredient such as ham (Virginia, York, Westphalian, Sugar Baked, Bayonne, Parma, San Daniele, etc.), and we introduced on the menu a selection of nine different stuffed vegetables, including my favorite Stuffed Savoy Cabbage (see recipe on page 348). The chef learned how to make the featherweight matzo balls that the proprietor had envisioned, floating them on a heavenly chicken soup. We even had some fun with China Garden Chow Mein and other similar super-basic Chinese dishes prepared by a Chinese cook and served on standard cheap Chinese restaurant dinnerware.

Some of the finer contemporary restaurants in America feature first-of-the-season specialties, but I was proud of the idea of having an end-of-the-season section in our menu: vegetables that were just going out of their prime season, or, for example, shad from the Columbia River at the end of May.

To be true to the overall duality of the character of La Folie, we had a Bloody Mary soup as well as a Virgin Mary soup. If anyone asked for condiments, we presented a lazy susan with Tabasco, horseradish, ketchup, and A-1 Sauce, *plus* Alka-Seltzer. Some of my whimsies included our tartare steak, which was wrapped in paper-thin slices of carpaccio-style raw beef that made it look like a steak. We also had Chewing Bones on the menu, for the guests who wanted to gnaw on a roast-beef bone. We concocted our own vinegar from leftover wines, so there was a chance that a guest might well be tasting a decades-old Premier Cru Bordeaux. Traditional blue and green glass Good Health seltzer bottles were available for each table.

The playful—bordering on crazy—list of desserts included a chocolate-covered Giant Fortune Cookie containing small fortune cookies, with special messages for preplanned parties, and a Candy Apple served upright on a special stand with holes in its base that were filled with lollipops in the shape of amusing public figures.

I waited anxiously for the *New York Times* review late on a Thursday night, and opened the Friday, April 8, 1977, newspaper to Mimi Sheraton's rave three-star notice. As usual, she did not equivocate:

> It has been a long time since we have sampled a progression of dishes as stunningly, ethereally delicious as these. . . . Home-cooked artichoke bottom crowned snowy lump crabmeat in a piquant remoulade sauce and a terrine of duckling with its insets of duck liver and its light perfuming of brandy, were perfection. The three outstanding specialties among the hors d'oeuvre were genuine masterpieces: snail pot pie Bourguignonne, each plump shallot-scented snail nestled in a ceramic pot de chambre topped with a round of buttery puff pastry; Tourte Picardie . . . and Oyster au Champagne et Caviar . . . the best quenelles of pike we have ever had in this country . . . crackling crisp grilled duckling with prunes, noisettes of

veal with tender slices of kidneys inlaid in each and devastatingly rich sweetbreads in puff pastry packet (Ris de Veau Perigueux) *were among the faultless selections.*

The place was a hit from the start, and the first year indicated La Folie would have a long and happy life. People from different walks of life, who felt that living without a measure of silliness is not as great as it's cracked up to be, came to enjoy the mixture of heavenly cuisine and put-ons. But by the end of the second year, little by little the social arbiters made no secret of their philosophy that too much fun is suspect. It became painfully clear that those who took food seriously did not feel comfortable in a place which was a *folie,* a high-wire act. The mixture of humorous conceit and serious food was hard to swallow. A *Daily News* review that came out a year after the opening of the restaurant put the point squarely on the table: "Lang asks the question: Is New York sophisticated enough to support a restaurant of the true *haute cuisine* that can also playfully turn itself into a disco late at night?"

The answer turned out to be negative.

The story of the next fiasco had already begun in 1969, years before La Folie had its finale, and stretched into the mid-seventies.

As an apolitical person (my father taught me that "an honest politician is one, who after you buy him, stays bought"), the closest I'd ever got to Washington was the main reading room of the Library of Congress. But all that changed during the first four years of the 1970s, when I became a player in one of the year-long national festivals that occur only once in every one hundred years.

When I was studying for my citizenship examination back in 1948, I became fascinated with every aspect of the Declaration of Independence and the Constitution. Like a convert who is often more passionate about his new religion than those who are born into it, I read everything I could find about America in the second half of the eighteenth century, especially after I could finally understand the dismayingly long words. So it isn't surprising that when I received a discreet call in 1969 from Leonard Garment, a special consultant to President Nixon, asking if I would be interested in being named a public member of the Bicentennial Commission, I responded enthusiastically.

For the next five years I spent a great amount of my time in Washington as chairman of Open House USA, working with the Performing Arts, Creative and Visual Arts, and Invitation to the World panels. I felt good that in addition to a lot of inspiring phrases and several thousand plans, at least a couple of dozen of them became a reality: the artist-in-residence programs, the Bicentennial inventory of American paintings, the youth athletic exchange programs, and a program of home hospitality in which Americans opened their homes to other Americans and visitors from abroad.

Because I am an aficionado of world's fairs, it may seem surprising that I was the one to discourage the president from having a fair during the Bicentennial year. It stunned the press, and especially the 1976 Bicentennial Corporation in Philadelphia, the last and only city left in the running. But I was convinced that a world's fair would bankrupt Philadelphia, and that eventually the federal government would foot the bill.

My real concern, shared with a number of my fellow commissioners and panel members, was something we didn't make public. The 1970s were a period of student unrest, and at just about the time when our committee was deliberating, the Ohio National Guard opened fire on students at Kent State University who were protesting the widening of the war in Southeast Asia, killing four of them. We felt that a world's fair in an American city would offer the perfect stage for a chain of similar events, and that that would have disastrous effects on the celebration throughout the year.

But it was the Watergate scandal, not civil unrest, that destroyed many if not most of the plans our commission had wrought during five years under the chairmanship of David Mahoney. The members of the commission felt that we would not be able to continue our work effectively, so we unanimously decided to resign. Almost at the same time, each of us received a "thank you for your great contribution" letter from Nixon, indicating that a Bicentennial Administration would take over the job of the commission. The timing of the letters was interesting: they were posted eleven days before Nixon was named as a co-conspirator in the Watergate break-in.

During the second half of the seventies, the George Lang Corporation was working on a variety of restaurants. One of them was in the St. Regis Hotel. By now we had our own interior design department, and in 1977

we completed the restoration of this room, which still featured the famed Maxfield Parrish mural of Olde King Cole and his court jesters. The tables were laid out in the King Cole Room so as to give everyone a ringside seat; the original dance floor was restored, and an aura of cozy grandeur was brought back. I considered this room my last stand against the T-shirt society, and the beginning of the road back to elegance.

Something known as a "contrast bath"—a therapeutic immersion of the body alternately in hot and cold water—could have been the metaphor for my life in those days. One day I was approached by a most *simpático* gentleman by the name of Mahmud Alghanim, who was a member of a highly respected Middle Eastern family that had a number of different businesses in several countries. He asked me if I would be interested in working with him and his associates on a private club in Riyadh, Saudi Arabia, and on a chain of family restaurants in Kuwait. I was eager to experience a part of the world that was new to me, but there was a small problem: at that time you were not allowed to enter Saudi Arabia if you were a Jew, and the U.S. government's Passport Division discouraged going there because of the dangers. As a consultant, one of the mottoes I have lived by is "Get the job done first, and then practice heroism if you must," so I arranged with a Catholic priest friend of mine to give me a document stating that I was a member in good standing of his Roman Catholic parish. I am sure Father Paul was troubled by my request, but I guess he felt that God would forgive him, considering the circumstances. He is past eighty now, doing his work with the same enthusiasm as before, so I trust the Good Lord closed one of his eyes.

After all this effort, it took me only a few days in Riyadh to come to the conclusion that even if I could break through the oppressive darkness of Saudi Arabian authoritarianism, it wouldn't be worth it.

Onward to Kuwait, to the sheikdom of Sheik Jaber El-Ahmed.

My digging during the next weeks turned up facts that were vitally important for formulating the right concept. I found, for instance, that non-Kuwaitis (about half of the country's population of one and a half million at the time) would make up much more of the future restaurant's clients than would Kuwaitis, since both middle- and upper-middle-class natives have one or two maids, plus one or two cooks (in addition to a gardener and a chauffeur), and stay home for meals. Because alcohol was forbidden, we decided to install a freestanding juice bar and surround the restaurant with a small farmer's market, where freshly cut fruits and glass jars filled with fruit syrups would be displayed. We had to consider alternate sources for foods, because Iraq supplied most of Kuwait's produce, and the relations between the two countries were so bad that one couldn't depend on delivery. On the other hand, we were pleasantly surprised that the cost of air conditioning was always included in the rent, gasoline being so cheap.

The owners named the restaurant Shehi, an Arabic word meaning something pleasant and delicious. The idea was that the guests would not only enjoy savory foods but bask in an atmosphere of a family living room—the only kind of entertainment allowed by the strict Muslim authorities.

Alan Reyburn, my trusted chief of staff, continued the work in Kuwait, masterfully dealing with the enigmatic world of the Middle East. As consultants we had learned that problems are like messages, and the messages we were receiving—while doing our research there—were not very reassuring as far as our active participation was concerned. So, after our presentation, we suggested to Mahmud Alghanim that he open and operate the first prototype, based on our fully developed concept—but without our participation.

While this was going on, I had to immerse myself in a historic project in Manila.

At the time I knew only a few things about the Philippines: I was aware that more beauty contest winners came from there than from any other part of the world, and that a vile-tasting liquid called *patis*, made of fermented fish, was produced there. I also knew that President Marcos was a more-or-less benevolent dictator, and that the definition of his benevolence depended on whom I talked to. The project I was asked to do was the renovation of the venerable Manila Hotel, one of the last grand hotels in Asia; it had served as headquarters for General MacArthur after World War II. It was badly in need of restoration, and I was pleased to learn that President Marcos, on the advice of a wise local architect, had decided to retain the original hotel and to add a new wing behind it.

I made it part of my agreement, which we drew up in New York, that I would visit every region of the Philippines to learn about the country's gastronomy and way of life. To understand the culture was essential in renovating this historic hotel, which had been built in 1892, and had been the scene of some of the most elegant parties in Asia.

First, accompanied by a hotel executive, I visited Legazpi, in southeastern Luzon, which is famous for the only spicy foods served in the Philippine Islands. One dish they gave us at a tasting luncheon that particularly fascinated me, since I am always hooked on historic or geographic connections, was *adobo monoksagata,* a comforting chicken-and-coconut dish that is very basic to the Philippines. Learning that the word *adobo* indicates marination of some sort, I realized that the dish was related to sauerbraten and that both were derived from the ancient Chinese practice of tenderizing meat by marinating it in some kind of vinegar. In this particular case the key ingredient of the marinade was palm vinegar, which, along with singed garlic cloves, gave the *adobo* its distinctive taste.

Then came the Bicol Express, which finally brought the message to us that we were in a one-alarm chili country. This zesty relish, based on a number of local chilis, peppers, onion, and various spices, can stand proudly next to the other spicy chutneys, *sambals,* and hot sauces of the world. Combining it with the ever-present rice, I almost made a meal out of it while everyone at the table was surprised at a Westerner's appetite for spicy foods.

The several-hours-long midday sampling came to an end with a fascinating dessert made of *pili* nuts. A *pili* nut looks not unlike a baby eggplant. Its flesh has a kind of chestnut texture, and a flavor not unlike baked pumpkin. Inside the kernel is a white nut that is used in many ways; on this occasion the chef had caramelized a batch to make a kind of *pili*-brittle that was so delicious I couldn't stop eating it. I quickly decided that a marriage between *pili*-brittle sauce and a toasted brioche would be a union made in gastronomic heaven, and eventually I sneaked it onto the menu of one of the restaurants, which we named Ilo-Ilo.

I had the opportunity to visit quite a few islands. In Davao, under the watchful aegis of the Apu volcano, I finally gathered the courage to ask to taste the famed durian, which is either the horror or the delight of culinary Southeast Asia, depending on where you stand. At the Insular Hotel, where we were staying, I had noticed a sign prominently displayed in all bedrooms: PLEASE DON'T EAT DURIAN IN YOUR ROOM! THE MANAGEMENT. When I asked the manager, Mr. Mascumana, about this, he told me that one day a guest had called the front desk to complain about a dead rat in his room, so the housekeeping department went to investigate. They soon found the source of the problem: a happy Filipino had been eating durian in his room, and the air conditioner had picked up the scent of this overpowering fruit and carried it to all the rooms. Then I understood why, after our fine meal, when I asked to taste a durian, it was suggested that I try it on the garden terrace.

The fruit was brought out ceremoniously, and a young man carrying a twelve-inch kitchen knife was summoned. The smell had already started to ooze from the unopened fruit. While I waited eagerly and, I must admit, nervously, the durian-carver continued to search for an invisible seam in the skin. After a minute or so he found it and revealed the inside, which contained yellow, creamy, round objects, each the size of a chicken egg. Mr. Mascumana's daughter, a stalwart durian fancier, told me never to use a utensil, only my hands. Displaying exemplary courage and bravery, I bit into the fruit. One of my theories is that everything that tastes exquisite is on the borderline of tasting foul. Just think of a very ripe Brie cheese, sea urchins, and the pungent aroma of a white truffle. So my reaction was an uneasy mix of delight and surprise, alternating with suspicion and unease.

After the third bite, I decided not to add durian to my wish list.

We continued our culinary journey on to Zamboanga, a region in the southern Philippines, which embodies perhaps the last remaining Kiplingesque way of life. Zamboanga City is a teeming port of endless markets where you can find unsuccessfully hidden Muslim treasures, disposable dentures, and anything wearable, edible, or usable, including suitcases that cannot be closed, and socks with unremovable price tags soldered on, and maybe even a vegetarian vulture for a pet.

We dined at the green-lanterned oceanside terrace of the Hotel Lanatak, watching and being watched by the sea gypsies who alternately slept, ate, and peddled their woven mats and baskets and exquisite coral and shells, and we listened delightedly to the music provided by small native groups. After a repast of local seafood wrapped in tree leaves, and prawns saturated with unexpected flavors and served from charcoal grills by teams of white-jacketed young men, I understood why the Spanish stayed for four hundred years. I inquired about the native brew I had heard about called *lambanog*, a luscious palm wine that comes from the province of Batangas, and it turned out to be as satisfying as a good Sauterne, especially if one has it instead of dessert.

How many millions of people throughout the decades have trekked religiously to different regions of France to experience a variety of great cuisines? Or gone from Tuscany to Abruzzi to enjoy the titillating diversity of Italian foods? Yet few would make a gastronomic trip to the Philippines, where the cuisine, influenced by Chinese, Malay, and Indian traders, the Spanish, and even us Americans, is so varied and complex.

After assembling information about every aspect of the country and its culture, I began to put together concepts for the various restaurants and the nightclub in the Manila Hotel. I hired Paula Wolfert, a young, unknown, but remarkably talented cook (who has since become one of America's most renowned cookbook authors) to come to Manila and work with the executive chef of the hotel to test and develop scores of native recipes. During the months she worked, she adjusted many of the dishes, maintaining their authentic character and at the same time introducing subtle changes to make them suitable for a five-star international hotel. One day, during one of the annual monsoon floods, I found her in the test kitchen standing up to her knees in water. She had just gone on cooking through the deluge.

On occasion, an international food consultant needs other kinds of courage and endurance. One time I tasted a Philippine delicacy called *balut,* a hard-boiled duck egg with a partially developed embryo inside. When I asked my host what he enjoyed about it, he replied with great surprise, "You mean the tickling of the fuzzy hair as you swallowed it didn't give you pleasure?" Since I was his guest, an honest answer would have been unsuitable, so I just changed the subject.

One morning, back in Manila, I read in the English-language daily: "We hear that the American designers and consultants, planning the new addition to the Manila Hotel, want to put gold bathtubs in the luxury suites, which we certainly think is outrageous these days." During the next couple of weeks more and more items appeared about fabricated goings-on at the Manila Hotel, edged with insults or insinuations. It was obvious that the columnists and the papers knew that Imelda Marcos, who was half of the Philippine dictatorship at the time, was building her own hotel, the Plaza, and they were playing up to her by disparaging our restoration of the old Manila Hotel. We all became quite concerned that these carefully orchestrated attacks might have serious consequences, knowing that you can't prevail over a dictator's wife in her own country. And we were right. It wasn't long before I was tipped off one morning by a government official I had befriended that I and two of my associates would be arrested within the next couple of days on trumped-up charges. I quickly thought of the American corporate system, in which one pushes a distant button to affect another, which in turn will take care of the one you really want to activate.

So I called a Filipino friend who had close contact with a good friend of President Marcos, and luckily the last button in the chain averted our impending arrest. I never saw the inside of a Philippine prison (although it might have been interesting to compare it with the one I visited at length in 1945 in Hungary), and a few months later my team and I had an extra dose of satisfaction when we opened the Manila Hotel before the Hotel Plaza made it.

The concept of the Roman Forum has always fascinated me, the way it reduces the chaos of life to a manageable architectural space. Its illegitimate offshoot, the suburban shopping mall, has become so much a part of the lives of its denizens that by now they can't imagine existing without it. Until quite recently, city life in New York, with its endless shops and amusements, didn't seem to lend itself to the concept of malls—although one, the first, did open in 1933 when John D. Rockefeller splurged on a shopping arcade underneath his Rockefeller Center.

When, in 1975, a Citibank executive called me and asked if I would be interested in working on an urban shopping center as part of their new headquarters on East 54th street in Manhattan, I could barely let him finish his question before I said yes. He asked me to familiarize myself with the location, architecture, and so on, and then submit my proposal within a month's time.

I learned that Citibank already had a crop of consultants developing an overall retail concept, which ranged from a fashion center to a leisure/amusement arcade complex—a sports center was another possibility—but those in charge didn't feel right about any one of them.

It took me ten days to put together a proposal, and I didn't mince words when I said, "I very strongly feel that it *must be a gastronomic center* where virtually everything must be related to eating, drinking, and the pleasures of the table."

At the presentation I was expecting opposing views, remembering the fate of the other consultants, but the Citibank people must have realized I had done my homework with regard to the four "C" words: Conspicuous Consumption Carefully Considered. The George Lang Corporation was hired on the spot.

The location where the market would be was a three-level space clustered in and around a seven-story-high skylit atrium inside the fifty-nine-story, slash-topped Citicorp tower. The building stood on four columns, making it seem like a free-floating, weightless monolith hovering above the street. The pioneering design contained a Rube Goldberg–type invention: a 410-ton block of concrete held by springs, floating on a film of oil on top of the tower, a device that counteracted the swaying of the building to reduce the possible danger that a once-in-a-hundred-years windstorm might inflict.

At the time when I was working on the Citicorp project, my daughter Andrea told me that she was engaged. She confessed to me that she would love to be married in a place where no wedding had ever been held before, and never would be again. Her wish was fulfilled when I received permission to hold the ceremony on the top floor of the tower. Its interior at that time was not completed, so her desire that no one else ever be married there was also realized, because afterwards the space became the super-expensive penthouse office it was intended to be. Andrea was an imaginative artist, and she designed an invitation that the fortunate invitees could fold into a three-dimensional replica of the Citicorp building.

At one point I had great difficulty in communicating with Hal de Ford III and Robert Dexter, the vice presidents acting as project managers for Citicorp, two capable professionals who usually returned my calls within a couple of minutes. At the time I didn't realize the magnitude of their other concerns. William J. Le Messureir, one of the world's leading structural engineers, had designed, in addition to the floating concrete block, another inventive defense against the swaying of the tower in case of severe winds. This took the form of forty-eight braces, like giant chevrons, located behind the aluminum-and-glass walls of the building. A letter from an engineering student, who used the building as a subject for his dissertation, precipitated an investigation. It was discovered then that the braces were bolted instead of welded, and under certain conditions might not be strong enough to withstand the immense force of diagonal winds. I certainly didn't know at the time that one night De Ford and Dexter even had a meeting with the American Red Cross's director of disaster services for New York and with the mayor's emergency forces to put together an evacuation plan for the building and the surrounding neighborhood. Naturally, when I complained to whoever would listen at Citicorp about the need for decisions regarding a number of problems, I was talking about subjects that at that point were about as important for them as the temperature of the food served aboard a plane when a couple of its engines were on fire.

My working relationship with key members of the Citicorp team passed all kinds of tests, even though their approach to the Market's design, and to their choice of tenants for it, was much too conservative in my judgment. After an especially heavy-duty meeting with top-level Citicorp executives, a number of the prospective lessees and their attorneys and I were leaving at the end of the all-day session. As we were waiting for the elevator, Hal de Ford said to me, "George, we would very much like you to be as fully involved in the Citicorp Market as possible, in a way that goes beyond consultancy. So how about opening your own restaurant here?"

I was so taken aback that I sort of mumbled something instead of giving him an answer. Then he continued, "What kind of restaurant would you like to open, considering the other restaurants in the space?"

Since he'd told me at one of our past meetings that I looked at everything from the point of view of a restaurateur, a marketing person, a designer, and, he had added with a wink, a "professional Hungarian," I quipped, "As a professional Hungarian, obviously I would open up a Hungarian restaurant here, and call it Hungaria."

To my surprise and shock, on the ride down in the elevator he said to me, "All right, George, let's start talking about it tomorrow."

During the negotiations, when the bank indicated that they would advance all the money in the form of a loan, I disregarded the rigorous process of starting out with a due diligence study, as I always did on other projects, and I also put out of my mind the advice that I had given to hundreds of clients and friends not to open a restaurant in which the interest combined with the return of the borrowed money would be bigger than any profit it could possibly earn. Hungaria, with its extra-large pre-opening expenses, imported chefs, and special design costs, surely belonged in this dangerous category.

I was also influenced by the fact that the legendary chairman of Citicorp, Walter Wriston, who envisioned the Citicorp Market as symbolic of New York City and setting new standards for urban achievement, was most enthusiastic about the prospect of my Hungarian restaurant.

The Cold War was still very cold, and to work out a deal with Hungarian government officials and the top executives of HungarHotels in Budapest took perhaps more time and effort than opening the food and beverage facilities of the entire Citicorp Market. Finally I was able to import from Budapest three top chefs and two pastry chefs, several of whom had won culinary prizes in Europe. I was even able to bring in the

*Trimming the sausage tree in my own restaurant,
the Hungaria, in 1979*

violinist György Lakatos, who was considered a national treasure, together with his gypsy orchestra. To house all of these people, I had to rent part of a floor of a nearby residential hotel.

Then we started the design with Piroska Savany, an architect-designer on my staff who was, by sheer coincidence, a Hungarian. As guests entered, an eight-foot-high tree greeted them with all kinds of sausages hanging on its limbs so that diners could chop down their own appetizers, help themselves to some of our kitchen-made mustard, and cut a slice from the crisp-crusted ten-pound loaves of bread. The bar area was designed as a transplanted central European town square where local citizens gather. A large selection of Hungarian *eaux de vie* was served, including a green walnut brandy made specially for us in Hungary. Six small rooms—each of which had an open front, to integrate it into the main dining area—were designed as dining rooms in traditional Hungarian homes. One of these, the strudel room—adjacent to a wine-bibber's nook—sat eight people, with a large table at one end, at which the strudel maker practiced her skill right in front of the guests.

Most of the reviews agreed that it was my "love letter to my homeland." One of the magazines noted that it was "a restaurant so brilliantly, thoughtfully, artistically and authentically developed and designed that you are no longer in the Citicorp Market, but in a warm, romantic, and casual dining room of a Magyar patrician family." Unhappily, one of the negative and mean-spirited reviews was from the *New York Times*, which can close any show on 54th Street or on Broadway.

And close we did, after twenty-four months, selling the place to another restaurant group. So it behooves me to offer the usual summation of explanations, excuses, rationalizations, and realities as to why Hungaria and I failed in our mission.

In addition to the insurmountable financial structure, the management company the bank appointed to operate the building was, for reasons that even today I don't quite understand, reluctant to promote the restaurants of the Market as well as the entire Atrium experience, which would have brought in dinner business.

But the real reason we had to sell Hungaria after two years of operation was that when I had accepted the challenge to open a restaurant, I'd felt that I could overcome any obstacle, including the location and the given space, which I knew was utterly wrong for the concept. Or, to put it more bluntly, I was overconfident to the point of feeling infallible—and that is a time bomb for any undertaking.

Porto Carras, La Folie, King Cole Room, Bicentennial Commission, Kuwait, Citicorp Center—the 1970s were filled with a colorful assortment of failures, in addition to a number of triumphs. In this chapter I have mostly concentrated on the failures because they're more interesting—and instructive—than success stories.

CHAPTER 19

36 Girls 36

NOTHING REPRESENTS the spirit of a city better than the way it treats its artists. The Dutch burghers took good care of their artists throughout the centuries in their own country, but when they settled in New York their sole concern was to make more money than their neighbors. By the middle of the nineteenth century, things had changed. Quite a few artists were successful enough to have studios surrounding Washington Square and Gramercy Park.

Then, at the turn of the century, the landscape painter Penrhyn Stanlaws hit upon the idea of creating a building that would have large-scale artists' studios combined with living quarters for the artists' families—essentially re-creating Montmartre in New York. To make the project commercially viable, the studio apartments were to be owned by the artists on a cooperative basis, a novel idea proposed by Walter Russel, a Paris-trained illustrator.

The first of those buildings was built on the north side of 67th street between Columbus Avenue and Central Park West, a block with an inglorious past. The artist James Montgomery Flagg (whose apartment was above ours—Number 33) looking back on 1903 wrote: "There never was such a street in town as West 67th: fine modern apartment houses on the north side, and, on the south, stables; disreputable tenements; a garage that burned up three times; and, on the corner, a notorious saloon, which kept the night raucous with female yells, stabbings, and bums hurtling out onto the icy pavements in wintertime."

All this changed rapidly, between 1903 and 1917. West 67th Street probably had more two-story-high studio/living rooms equipped with large-scale north-light windows than any street in the world. It was in 1917 when the first artist-tenant of the Hotel des Artistes, the painter Henry W. Ranger, moved into this loosely Gothic, Tudor Revival–style building decorated with gargoyles and designed by the noted architect George Mort Pollard. It did offer certain features and services usually found in hotels, but the real reason the builder called this structure a hotel was to get around the zoning law of the neighborhood, which placed severe restrictions on the heights of apartment buildings. The amenities included one of the first indoor swimming pools in New York City, an indoor squash court, a ballroom, and a theater, for the use of the artist-tenants.

The Café des Artistes, located on the street level of the building, was one of the most enticing services offered to the tenants. They could purchase ingredients for their meals and give them to the Café, which then would deliver the prepared dishes via an internal dumbwaiter. A brochure from the early 1920s extolled the system's virtues:

RETIRING THE TYRANT COOKSTOVE

The evening you read this, forty women, including myself, occupants of the building at the above address, will go home, probably tired as active mortals usually are at day's end. With most of us the good man objects to eating out, nor for that matter, do we care for it ourselves. Some of us have good reason to be suspicious of delicatessen ptomaine. If we were in the ordinary position of apartment dwellers we would face summer heat, steaming stoves, fragrant but heavy smells of cooking until—give us credit, anyhow!—a good meal would result, albeit Stewed Wife would probably be one of the chief items of the menu.

But although it will be hot, neither gas stove nor range will raise the temperature of our variously sized duplex apartments. A meal, even a particularly good meal, will be served. It will taste precisely as each family's preferences dictate. Yet no heavy odors of cooking will disturb us. None of us will be dreading the scrubbing of kettles afterward. And the dinner will cost no more than if we had each done all the work ourselves.

Within that period, the famous and the infamous moved into the "des Artistes," as it became known; its residents included Isadora Duncan, Noel Coward, Rudolph Valentino, Zasu Pitts, Alexander Woollcott, Fannie Hurst, Al Jolson, Edna Ferber, Ben Hecht, Maurice Maeterlinck, Childe Hassam, Mayor La Guardia, and Norman Rockwell.

The musicians had to rehearse in their studios, and the artists, who vastly outnumbered them, felt that they made so much noise in the apartments that eventually, when an atelier became available, most of the applicants who were musicians were promptly turned down—including George Gershwin. It is enough to make you cry in your pear champagne.

The tenants were a highly colorful and social group. They even put on the first Miss America pageant at the Chu Chin Chow Ball in the Hotel des Artistes' ballroom in 1919, a year before the one in Atlantic City. Howard Chandler Christy and James Montgomery Flagg (of "Uncle Sam Wants You" fame, and also a resident of this famous block) were the judges. The winner was a Miss Hyde, whose elaborate Arabian harem outfit in ivory satin included see-through pantaloons; it seems very modest by today's standards, but it must have been quite risqué at the time. I have seen this elaborately jeweled and embroidered outfit, which is now in a private collection, insured for $80,000.

After the Depression, the board of the Hotel des Artistes decided that each of the thirty-six resident artists could paint murals for the interior walls of the Café. The artists started bickering about where each one's work would be displayed, so instead the board turned over the entire task to Howard Chandler Christy. His 1932–34 vintage murals depict thirty-six floating nudes in innocently seductive poses, along with one gentleman whose identity has puzzled guests ever since. As Brendan Gill wrote in the foreword of my Café des Artistes cookbook: "The Café is a happier place for the relish with which he carried out the commission of the Board of Directors; his rosy silken hamadryads instruct us by their wanton romps in how far we may have come from those dour Dutch burghers and buttoned-up Britishers of the seventeenth century."

The fifteen delightful panels of perky maids—with slim figures and smiling red lips—disporting against sylvan greenery, managed at the time to *épater les bourgeois,* but today the murals seem more innocent than a Victoria's Secret catalog.

One of our artist neighbors, looking at the "swing girls" in one of the large-scale murals on the terrace level of the restaurant, pointed out to me that Christy must have used real gold for the sizing of the canvas to get the glowing effect. I am convinced, however, that the medium was Cointreau-flavored whipped cream.

Twenty-five years ago, I was fortunate to be able to buy one of the great duplexes on the same block. It belonged to the distinguished art collectors Louise and Walter Arensberg. Unfortunately, Marcel Duchamp's *Nude Descending a Staircase*—which was hanging over the fireplace at the time—did not come with the purchase. I am also sorry that Proust had already written in one of his letters, "When I went to Venice, my dream became my address," because I always wanted to say that about the block we live on.

There are few things more pleasant in the city of New York than strolling by the period façades of its buildings. This unusual block, which resembles a mews more than a street, neatly straddles several worlds— exclusive, democratic, and romantic, all at the same time. And if you are a citizen here, each doorman greets you warmly; you encounter eager autograph seekers in front of the ABC studios (which, until the forties, was a stable for polo ponies belonging to the upper crust of the city); neighbors stop for a bit of local gossip; and you might have a chance to pet the just-washed fur of a friend's dog passing by.

The ever-flowing continuity of life here is most comforting. A young girl whose first howls filled our halls just a few years ago now baby-sits for our children. You can tell the season here without looking at your calendar: our flourishing trees behave appropriately each month, and when it's time to dress up for Christmas, our block greets you with its forty trees wearing the sparkling jewelry of thousands of tiny Tivoli lights. Finally, I must confess why I *really* think this block is the most romantic in the world: it is where I met Jenifer on a fine day in 1979, when she came to my office to interview me.

It was just four years before that, in the spring of 1975, that I received a phone call from David Garth, a political consultant and my 67th Street neighbor.

"George, would you be interested in taking over the Café des Artistes?" he said. "I am on the board of directors of the Hotel des Artistes, and I am calling you on their behalf."

Without missing a beat, I answered him with Lincoln's line purporting to quote a man who has been tarred and feathered, and is being ridden out of town on a rail: "If it weren't for the honor of the thing, I'd rather walk."

Leaving the Washington scene after the five years of intense Bicentennial involvement took some adjustment, even though my consulting business gave me enough work to fill a seven-day week. Also, I did not want to get back into operating a restaurant in an era of steady disintegration of workmanship—especially a dark, dingy little place that was empty most of the time, in spite of the fact that the nearby Lincoln Center was already over a decade old.

A couple of nights after David's phone call, it was raining and, as usual, no taxis were available. Frustrated, I said to my wife, "If I had a successful restaurant on this block, we would always find a taxi." It sounds like one of those middle-European coffeehouse stories, but the next day I called David Garth back and, for the second time in my professional life, bypassing the careful feasibility studies that should precede such a decision, I blithely told him, "Please inform the board that—depending on the conditions—I will take over the restaurant."

To complete the lease with the building was a simple matter. It was signed within a couple of weeks' time; there was not much to concern oneself about regarding a comatose restaurant on its deathbed, except for the murals on its walls. Little did I know what I was getting myself into!

The former lessees of the restaurant claimed that they had originally paid Christy for the murals by exchanging meals for the work over a very long period, and unless they were paid for the paintings, they would not vacate the premises. The building management claimed that the murals belonged to the co-op, citing a number of landmark laws. My lawyers and I were convinced that they were part and parcel of the premises we had leased. As a result of this three-way fight, I was not able to take possession of the restaurant.

In the meantime, the State Supreme Court enjoined the Café's former tenant from removing the canvases, and an endless series of court hearings, negotiations, and accusations and counteraccusations were played out in the newspapers. For instance, the *New York Post* ran the headline, "Café des Artistes Packing Its Paintings to Leave Co-op." The lead sentence continued, "The Café des Artistes at 1 West 67th Street is shutting its doors for the last time on May 31 [1975]."

One day I was sitting at the bar of the Café while the restaurant was still being operated by the previous owners, and I overheard one of the partners, pointing toward a blank wall, say, "We had another mural on this spot, but we sold it to an oilman from Texas." The proverbial light went on inside my head. As I was walking out the door, I turned to him and, forcing myself to sound calm, said, "There are four removable paintings on canvas in the front room. Why don't we make a deal that you take those, and in addition, I will also pay you a sum of money in exchange for signing an agreement and moving out by the end of the week." Before closing the door behind me, I looked back and added, "This proposal stands for only twenty-four hours!"

I immediately called a meeting with key members of the board of the Hotel des Artistes, as well as with my lawyers and theirs. Realizing the tortuous negotiations in which we could get involved, everyone agreed to my proposal, especially since I was the one who had to write the check.

A couple of hours before the deadline, the deal was concluded to everyone's satisfaction: the former tenants received the four paintings plus the money; the building retained the ownership of the murals in the form of a landmark; and I was able to commence my plans to give new life to the then fifty-eight-year-old Café des Artistes. The peace treaty made all the local papers, the *Daily News* winning the prize with the headline, "The Nudes Will Stay on the Café's Walls."

As the very first step I did what I usually do when I have to reckon with the future: I took a look at the past. That view was especially important in this instance, because I knew that none of today's successful restaurant formats would be the right solution for the resuscitation of the Café. It was quite obvious to me that the most important part of the heritage of the Café des Artistes was the fact that the artists who had lived and worked in virtually all of the buildings on our block had used the Café as their dining room.

The dining room I took over had a measure of seedy charm, despite the grimy paintings, filthy red carpets, and surly waiters, and of course there was no such thing as temperature control in any of the seasons. I had to close the restaurant completely in order to rebuild it, but I tried to maintain the essentials of the 1917 character of the place. I attempted to make the grand-scale improvements in such a way that even the guests who had frequented the restaurant for decades would barely notice the drastic alterations. It was not an easy task. Walls and one of the murals had to be moved to enlarge the main dining room by ten feet; seating arrangements, color schemes, lighting, floor levels—just about everything was changed. Heavy drapes that had formerly blocked out the daylight and the connection with the street were removed, and now, when the sun shines through the windows, sneaking in between the banks of flowering plants, the rays dance on the mirrors flanking the cavorting nudes. The murals were liberated from a layer of soot and grime by a curator of the Metropolitan Museum and lit properly for the first time.

I decided to keep the entire staff, and to instruct and motivate them so that they would have the skills of true professionals. At the same time, we started a series of tastings with André Guillou, the Breton-born chef who had been working for the Café for twenty years by that time, and Stephen Gurgely, the director I had hired four months before the reopening.

During my extensive research, I found that the Café was originally fashioned after the English "ordinary," a kind of casual bistro with a limited daily menu based on foods available at the market, that was introduced to New York by a Mr. Thomas Lepper in the mid-eighteenth century. While the bistros of France, the trattorias of Italy, the Beisls of Vienna, and the tavernas of Greece—all more or less variations on the same theme—flourish to this day, the ordinary never developed a following in the United States. So I modified the concept, and it has served the Café well during the last twenty-plus years. The menu is broken up into courses and food categories, and the chef fills in a particular section only if the ingredients are available in prime condition on that particular day or week.

My menu concept excluded foods that were symbols of elegance or of expense-account dining, such as truffles, caviar, and the like, and I was determined to avoid a clever recycling of the past. I made it a point to introduce honest dishes of the *cuisine bourgeoise,* and to pay special attention to "comfort" items—such as bread, butter, coffee, and properly brewed tea. I insisted that we should smoke our own fish and lamb, make our own varieties of charcuterie, and bar all deep-fried foods, which I didn't feel belonged in the Café. In short, I was hoping to eliminate the dividing line between home-cooked and gourmet. I made a point of serving champagne by the carafe and selected wines brought to the table in the traditional basket for the guest to choose—each for eight dollars.

Many of the dishes tested in 1975 still appear on our menu on occasion, including Seafood Gazpacho, Bourride with Aïoli, Swordfish Steak topped with Soft-Shell Crab, Salmon Four Ways, Tripe aux Pruneaux (see page 352 for recipe), Brandade de Morue (the great appetizer of codfish with garlic-mashed potatoes gratinée), Macadamia Nut Tart, and one of our signature desserts: Ilona Torte (recipe on page 360).

I was determined to offer freshly baked desserts; serving Peach Melba and the like seemed to me out of place in the new/old Café. Yet, with the mazelike spaces of the restaurant located on three levels, I was unable, even with the new layout and equipment, to set up a pastry kitchen. One day I hit upon the solution: I would get our neighbors to bake for this neighborhood restaurant.

Soon people, male and female (including several of our waiters), who baked tortes, cakes, and other sweets at home were baking their own specialties for us or using recipes we gave them. Everybody in our office tasted all the sweets that were brought in; they believed my highly scientific observation that if you close your eyes while tasting, the calories can't find you.

Weekend brunch became so popular at the Café that shortly after opening we had to extend Sunday service from ten in the morning until four in the afternoon.

The forerunners of today's brunch were the wedding breakfast and the hunt breakfast. The first perhaps was created to satisfy the impatient bride and groom before they could make their getaway later in the day, and the second developed to offer a sumptuous repast after the hunt. Toward the end of the nineteenth century, brunch was served as a late or second breakfast, a *déjeuner à la fourchette,* but it did not become popular in the United States until the early 1960s. By 1975 it was high time to bring brunches out of the Bloody-Mary-and-omelet syndrome and continue what I had started in 1961 in the Tower Suite. On Saturdays and Sundays, the days when the Café used to be closed, it became the place to drink an Apricot Sour, spread marrow on your thick-crusted toast (scooped from the bone that accompanied your pot-au-feu), indulge in a Smoked Salmon Benedict, read the out-of-town papers, and celebrate the fact that you were spending the weekend in the greatest city in the world.

Shortly after the Café's reopening in 1975, the luminaries of the past were replaced by Lauren Bacall, Alec Baldwin, Kim Basinger, Leonard Bernstein, Robert and Ina Caro, David Halberstam, James Levine, former mayor John Lindsay, Bernard Malamud, Zubin Mehta, Paul Newman, Rudolph Nureyev, Itzhak Perlman, Diane Sawyer, Beverly Sills, Isaac Stern, Kathleen Turner, and Barbara Walters, as well as top editors, financiers, industry captains, and anyone else who was passionate about good conversation, honest wine, and food that satisfies. I like to think that what the *Wall Street Journal* said is true: "At the Café des Artistes you could even fall in love with your IRS agent during an audit."

There have been few days since I reopened the Café when several of its tables were not celebrating birthdays, anniversaries, or—even more often—engagements. I stage-managed a singular event a while ago, working with a young gentleman who was refreshingly nonconformist. When the time came for the dessert, his date refused to order any, saying that she had had a great dinner and just wanted to keep in her mouth the taste of the asparagus spears we served instead of a salad course.

Finally she gave in, and Hiran, our waiter, who has been working at the Café for over three decades, presented a nicely decorated Ilona Torte with the inscription, "*Will you marry me?*"

She burst into tears and embraced the prospective groom.

At that point he nodded imperceptibly to Hiran, who brought in a second little torte with the calligraphic message, "*Thank you, and I love you!*"

The nicest part of the story is that they return every year, on the anniversary of their engagement party. But we serve them only the second torte.

A pub keeper can't afford the luxury of being a partisan of any political party, but when it comes to the president of the United States, my respect for the individual and the office knows no limits. It was about 11:00 A.M. on October 23, 1995, when I received the first of many phone calls from the White House requesting a table for ten for President Clinton.

I was told that the president had decided he would like to return to the Café des Artistes, where he used to have a great time at the corner table in the back room when he was governor of Arkansas. He would be in town to celebrate the fiftieth anniversary of the United Nations, and was expected to attend an official UN function at Lincoln Center that evening. When I told the staff about the impending visit, everyone felt proud that out of the thousands of restaurants in Manhattan, he chose us.

To make the necessary arrangements within ten hours' time, I had to remember the rule I have believed in and practiced since my early Waldorf-Astoria days: The secret of success is to accept the impossible, do without the indispensable, and bear the intolerable.

Before any of the arrangements could be made, we had to figure out how we could make three tables available at 9:00 P.M., even though the restaurant had been fully booked for weeks. We solved this problem by calling people we knew and asking them to come a little earlier or a little later, and by placing extra tables in the room.

Where to seat the president was not up to us, and to make the situation even more difficult, none of his people, or the Secret Service, seemed to agree on the ideal table. Eventually he was seated in the main dining room alongside the windows, but we had to cover the flower-bedecked windows to block any view of the president from the street.

To accommodate the schedule of the president and his guests, we decided to serve family-style first courses, placing them directly on the table so everyone could help him- or herself. The main courses were narrowed down to a carefully balanced quartet, with the thought in mind that the president doesn't like to sprinkle ideological salt on the food he eats. With her honorary degree in avoiding controversy, Jenifer, who has been the managing director of the Café des Artistes since 1990, offered the following main-course choices: Swordfish Paillard Café des Artistes; Long Bone Veal Chop with Prosciutto and Glazed Pearl Onions; Venison Pörkölt, Spätzle and Cucumber Salad; a Brace of Grilled Quail on a Bed of Caramelized Apples and Cranberries macerated in Calvados.

When the president arrived at 9:02 P.M., the air had the heady scent of expectation, and our little son, Simon Lang, greeted Mr. Clinton like a pro as he entered the dining room.

When Mr. Clinton asked Simon how old he was, he replied, "Mr. President, I am eight years old." President Clinton stopped for a second and said quietly, almost to himself, "I guess I was eight years old once, too." This was far from the expected public utterances of a president, and everyone within hearing distance held his breath so as not to break the ensuing silence.

There was lively conversation about the famed Howard Chandler Christy murals, and Mr. Clinton was amused by a story I told him about a young couple who left in the middle of their dinner because the man recognized his mother in one of the Christy nudes, recalling that his mother, as a young girl, had worked as one of Christy's models.

At one point, walking through the dining room, the president said to me, "George, the standard line about New York is that the only thing permanent is change, but I guess the people who keep saying that have not been to the Café des Artistes."

I have only one regret and one wish left regarding our beloved Café. I regret that I will never be able to return the lovely gesture of Madame

Fonaroff, my violin teacher. As I wrote earlier, she lived in the Hotel des Artistes, and after I auditioned for her in 1946, she brought me to the Café for cake and coffee, and the taste will always linger in my memory.

My wish concerns Howard Chandler Christy, whose portrait, done by his friend, James Montgomery Flagg, is hanging on the wall. He was known to be a connoisseur of good food, wine, and beautiful women, and I hope that, gazing around from behind table number 38 at the back of the bar, he is as pleased by it all as I am.

CHAPTER 20

Reflections of a Curious Palate

*E*VER SINCE I took the first long solo trip on my red bicycle at the age of thirteen, riding all the way to a little village eight full miles away from my hometown, and feeling like an explorer, I have always been exhilarated by traveling. It is one of the ways I satisfy my unending curiosity.

In the Kingdom of Lang, the bill of rights includes everyone's right to be curious, but it is coupled with the obligation to do something about it. My lively interest in new sensations has increased over the years. Pursuing enthralling tastes, researching projects, and collecting material for articles has taken me around the world, though on rare occasions I have wished I'd stayed home. Here are a few of my memorable meetings with diverting restaurants and exotic foods.

My mother would surely be surprised to learn that some of the edible exotica in my past have actually become lifetime favorites. For instance, I fell in love with *angulas* (baby river eels) during my first stay in Spain, when I frequented a place in Sevilla called La Dorada. Nobody but a clairvoyant could have guessed that these anemic-looking, three-inch-long, spaghetti-like creatures, fast-fried in a terra-cotta crock with a slightly peppery-tasting olive oil and a chili pod and eaten with a small wooden fork, would make me feel the same way as my mother's crisp goose cracklings. Other little sea creatures that I became rather fond of at this restaurant were *percebes,* barnacles that looked like arthritic fishing worms, but tasted as good as anything from a sushi bar.

Turkish poets have written elegies about the beauty of a roasted and split lamb's head, and of all the riches it contains in its prudently composed shell. So, to those of you who share my view that collecting experiences is essential for growth and that food can entertain and challenge, rather than just simply fill our stomachs, I suggest you book an airline flight to Istanbul for a visit to a type of inexpensive tavern that is called *iskembeci*. It was at one of these, Lale Iskembeci Salonu, where I first had the pleasure of sampling the delicacy of a split lamb's head. These taverns also specialize in tripe dishes (delicious with an avgolemono-type lemon sauce) and roasted or boiled lamb pieces served alongside the spare parts.

My ever-searching palate was challenged during the 1960s in West Berlin at the Ritz Restaurant (which is unrelated to the Ritz hotels). You could start your dinner with a bear-paw soup and continue with armadillos roasted in their armour. The menu included Medallions of Beaver Grand-Veneur, which wore a light perfume of fish (probably because the animal had spent so much of its life underwater) and cognac-marinated roasted seal. The salad, as I recall, was early nouvelle cuisine (or was it early new American?): a combination of Jerusalem artichoke, pineapple, cucumber, and chopped, hard-boiled duck eggs sprinkled with silkworms sautéed in herb butter. The presentation of the dishes was spectacular, using hollowed-out tree trunks, native drums, and twisted snakeskin as vessels, but all in the most elegant manner.

When the maître d'hôtel came over to inquire about my dinner, I, being young and brash at the time, replied offhandedly, "The last time I had ragoût of camel kidneys, the texture seemed better. But my compliments to the chef for the braised eagle—it was just right."

I always wanted to be either the first to get to a place or the last to leave, and in 1976 I was perhaps the first U.S. restaurateur to be able to visit Cuba and write reports for the *New York Times Magazine* and *Esquire*.

There was a serious food shortage, even after eighteen years of the Castro regime, but I did have a remarkable meal in what at that time was probably the one restaurant in the world that served only dishes made of rabbit. Most Cubans had never eaten rabbit until Castro decided in 1966 that rabbits, which are easy to raise, would be one of the answers to the country's never-ending meat shortage. A couple of young chefs in Havana promptly opened a restaurant named El Conejito (The Young Rabbit). Before they opened, the owners set up a rabbit farm where they raised the finest, plumpest animals. The interesting menu featured specialties drawn from Cuban, Spanish, and French cuisines.

Apparently, Castro came almost nightly to El Conejito during its first year, bringing lots of guests with him and celebrating boisterously, which made the place instantly popular. I would be curious to know what has happened to the idea and the restaurant, and if Castro is now telling the headwaiter, "Today, push the rabbit tartare."

On occasion I don't even have to cross an ocean to experience enthralling tastes. A couple of times a year at Café des Artistes, we serve cod cheeks and tongues, which is a great specialty of both New England and Oregon, yet most of the time they are discarded. It takes about three dozen good-sized cod, each weighing about five to ten pounds, to get one pound of the inch-long tongues and elongated oyster-sized pieces of cheek meat. Chef Thomas Ferlesch usually sautés them over high heat with a small amount of finely diced onion and potatoes; the flesh turns snow-white and mellow, and the skin, which is also delicious to eat, becomes as crisp as that of a fat fowl.

Coming back to home base in southern Hungary, I once attended an ox-roasting (actually it was a bull), at which a special several-thousand-pound specimen was turned on a spit to the tunes of rhythmic folk songs. When, hours later, the exterior glowed with the hues of a blushing bride-to-be, I was offered the choice cut, a slice of the very private part of the animal that the French call, with poetic finesse, *amourettes*, and Americans call "prairie oysters."

One year I read in the London *Daily Telegraph* an ad for a children's book titled *Why Do Grownups Have All the Fun?* Because we deserve it, I thought, as any self-respecting parent would. Some of the fun makes us feel like kids again, such as the time when I drove into the Belgian town of Bruges, a miniature Venice with canals, gabled buildings, and carved brick houses, and I felt the joy children must experience on their first trip to Disneyland. My happiness increased as I sampled the pubs of Bruges. Now I knew why everyone in Brueghel's *Rustic Wedding Festivities* looks so happy: They've been drinking lambic, a Flemish-style beer made with a combination of malt and wheat and fermented like wine. In a charming, half-timbered pub called De Garre, I ordered a glass of *gueuze*, which starts its life as a lambic. Because a second fermentation takes place in the bottle, it effervesces almost like champagne. The barkeep told me that the day before, a visitor had asked—after the eighth glass of *gueuze*—where he was. When given the address of De Garre, he had indignantly replied, "Cut the details. Which *town?*"

Often after a ghastly meal on an airline (where there is no lambic to improve our mood), as an antidote, Jenifer and I will play the "Wouldn't It Be Great" game, in which we try to recollect dishes and experiences from our past that each of us particularly enjoyed. Apparently this is a standard exercise for prisoners of war. Following are a couple of my entries from a recent bout.

One is *mulukhiya* (or *miloukia*), the national soup of Egypt that dates back to the pharaohs. This pungent, slightly gelatinous, garlicky brew owes its distinctive flavor and name to a local spinachlike herb. My first taste of it was in the sunny, uncluttered Cairo kitchen of President and Mrs. Anwar al-Sadat. (At the time, Chef Ahmed Miz was preparing lunch for the family.)

Another dish on my list is Chiu Chow braised goose. In this time-consuming preparation, the goose is simmered in a spicy marinade, sliced thin, and served on a bed of dried bean curd with a dip of rice vinegar. The best I ever had was at the Chiu Chow Garden in the relatively elegant China Hotel in Canton, a city that hasn't much else to offer us *fan-kwei*, or "foreign devils." (See recipe on page 354.)

Once I put aside my inbred Hungarian and acquired American food prejudices, I could enjoy all the seductive taste sensations during my travels. On one occasion I dined in a Chinese convent in Hong Kong with a few local friends of mine. The hundreds of temples of this city were about equally divided between Buddhist and Taoist, and many of them served luncheons and dinners. Probably the most modest of these temples was Ching Leung Fat Yuen at Castle Peak in the New Territories, about a forty-five-minute drive from the center of the city.

On our arrival, a diminutive and seemingly ageless woman with a shaved head, dressed in black, led us to a small room with bare walls and an overhead fan. We were seated at a round table. The venerable nun first brought out a large tureen holding a traditional dish, Winter Melon Pond, made with pork, chicken, and seafood. This was followed by the familiar Chinese cold platter with pork chops, slices of sweet ginger, fried shrimp, abalone with mushrooms, and various pickled vegetables. Pagodas and birds made of various foods by chefs with the skill of ivory-carvers decorated the offering.

After a short hiatus, an earthenware pottery dish was placed in the center of our table. Its contents looked disturbingly like a bunch of very young worms—so lifelike that I actually thought they were moving. Taking a taste, I had the sensation of eating vermicelli, spaghettini, and spaghetti, each flavored with different chili peppers. Next came a whole fish, presented as if caught in the motion of swimming against the tide and stuffed with a silver fungus—a food the Chinese treasure for its texture. Bird's-nest soup and shark's-fin soup followed, and we all added the requisite touch of mustard and black vinegar to make them properly piquant. One of the most memorable courses I can recall was ten-ingredients *shokkan* balls with spicy tomato sauce, each stuffed with fried oysters so fresh that we could taste the saline waters they had until very recently been living in.

At the end of the dinner, I asked my hosts, as politely as I could manage, how these nuns could serve pork, chicken, abalone, and shrimp a couple of feet away from a Taoist temple, a religion that forbids the killing of living creatures. Everyone around the table burst into laughter; they were enjoying themselves hugely, obviously at my expense. Finally, one of my Hong Kong friends explained, "We wanted to surprise you. Now I can tell you that you didn't eat pork, shark's fin, fish, or oyster today. This was *chi* cooking, which is based on our belief in not killing animals."

All the dishes I had been eating had been made of various forms of bean curd and other vegetarian foodstuffs. It has taken a few thousand years for Buddhists and Taoists to develop this art form—and it is exquisite. Moreover, many of the foods have a symbolic meaning. The dish served in the earthenware casserole, for instance, called Buddha's Hair, was a visual metaphor: the thicker threads were supposed to resemble worms that live in the ricefields, while the thinner threads on top represented the Buddha's hair.

I'd been raised to think that vegetables were like exercise and abstinence: they're supposed to be good for you because they're so awful. But after this repast, I fell in love with vegetarian cooking—and lost my good standing as a *feinschmecker* (gourmet) from around the Danube.

Recollecting these fascinating but often odd foods, I wonder if it is true that our immune systems rebuild themselves continually, based on what we put into our stomachs. Or—considering their often bizarre character—maybe it is better not to think about it. One should just enjoy such experiences.

Next to searching for exuberant tastes around the world, being a host at a private party is on top of my list of public pleasures. The endless dais at the Waldorf should have turned me off to parties, but it only increased my fondness for them.

My first party memory goes back to our little all-purpose room in my hometown in Hungary. I was listening to our radio, encased in its brown Bakelite box, when the all-star Hungarian soccer team defeated its archrival, the Italian all-stars. Within minutes after this momentous occasion, three couples, friends of my parents who lived nearby (there was *only* nearby in our little town), knew that a celebration would be in order. I must have been about six years old, and the only thing I remember is the weightless meringue kisses served with coffee (hot Ovaltine for me) before I fell asleep.

Since that time I have been a guest or a host at parties all over the world. What follows are a few that are worth recalling.

A party that inspired as many comments from the guests as a Japanese *kaiseki* dinner was an Alice in Wonderland repast I gave in the Tower Suite for a group of friends in the early sixties. The menu appeared to be served backwards, but actually each course was of the right variety. For example, the dinner began with "Café au Lait" served with "Petits Fours," but the café au lait in little cups was really a cream-of-venison soup served with hors d'oeuvre decorated to look like petits fours. The central course was the exception: a stuffed squab baked in pastry sporting two heads, one looking backward and one forward.

There is an ancient tale about a nimble-fingered Hungarian lady who could stretch a fistful of strudel dough so thin that it could cover a Hussar sitting on his horse. Once I performed strudel magic of a different sort. Remembering that a conductor friend of mine preferred a flaky strudel to the most ethereal haute-cuisine dessert, I ordered a six-inch-by-eight-foot piece of pine from the lumberyard to serve as a carving board on top of our long refectory table. We baked loaves of strudel and placed them on top of the board, fitting them so tightly together that they looked like a single eight-foot-long loaf. The guests, seated on both sides of the table, carved their own slices from the section just in front of them. This was one occasion when no one complained about self-service.

It was quite a bit more challenging to offer an all-soup luncheon for soup-loving friends. The first course was a cupful of veal-and-mushroom broth, followed by *solianka,* the flavorful Russian soup made with salmon, pickles, olives, capers, and lemon. Surprisingly, the easy part turned out to be the dessert: *zuppa inglese,* "English soup," which is the Italian adaptation of the English trifle; it was a good dessert and a passable pun.

Acquiring a fine violin is like having a new family member, and it certainly deserves a welcoming party. In the unlikely event that you pick up a Stradivarius in your neighborhood pawnshop, church bells should ring and your mayor should declare a local holiday. The least I could do when this dream came true for me in 1979 was to rejoice and introduce the newly arrived 270-year-old baby to devoted friends. The celebration repast was one that Stradivarius himself could have had as a Sunday meal in his native Cremona, after inserting the sound post into my violin in 1709.

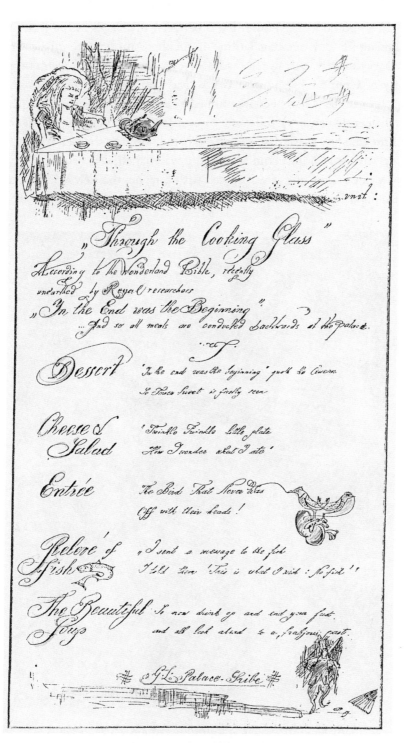

My Alice in Wonderland menu

I composed at my home (I was between marriages at the time) the following midday menu: galantine of duckling stuffed with quail, which itself was stuffed with sweetbreads, served with *mostarda di frutta* (a specialty of Cremona). The next course was tagliatelle with mussel sauce (this type of pasta had been mentioned by a cook from nearby Bologna in the fifteenth century) followed by a salad of arugula and radicchio, accompanied by toasted anise-saffron bread. Tomato sherbet, lightly flavored with lemon juice and served in a wafer shell, was based on an old Florentine recipe, and it was served with torrone, the rich Middle Eastern nougat that, in its present form, also originated in Cremona. I was

In our kitchen before a feast with Renata Scotto, Andrea Ilona Lang, Pavarotti, and Martita Casals, 1977

able to keep each course authentic because the good citizens of Cremona cared as much about their palates as they did about stringed instruments.

Following this eighteenth-century repast, a number of violinist friends tried out the violin, with the assistance of quantities of Freccia-rossa, also of Lombardy origin, and toward the end of the evening, I got into the act as well and played a movement of a Schubert sonatina with Harold C. Schonberg, who at the time was the senior music critic of the *New York Times*.

As a fellow restaurateur was leaving at the end of this party, he remarked to me that he would like to explore all taste sensations from *A* to *Z*. That triggered an idea, and the next day I sent out invitations to him and a few other comrades for the first of twenty-six dinners, each to be based on a letter of the alphabet. My ulterior motive was to create a permanent floating party that would be an oasis of good spirits in the ever-shifting world of divided interests.

The first dinner was devoted to the letter *A*, and included aperitifs (absinthe, aquavit) and appetizers (*amourettes à l'ancienne*, aromatic cream of avocado accompanied by *allumettes* of anise), and as the apotheosis, an Apple Aphrodisiac was served, baked with and accompanied by Ayala champagne.

Melancholy epilogue: After *B*, the project was abandoned. It ended up as an amusing one-line joke and a two-dinner idea.

Two of today's super-tenors have performed in our apartment. Plácido Domingo turned out to be a superb sonata partner, and Luciano Pavarotti cooked pasta in our Manhattan kitchen, after reluctantly agreeing not to sing while preparing the dish. He and his partner, Renata Scotto, who also came to sample Luciano's *Spaghetti Subito*, were allowed to sing the following night at the premiere of the Metropolitan Opera's new production of *La Bohème*.

Luciano brought all the ingredients for the dish in a shopping bag; I guess he didn't trust anyone else with the serious matter of picking the right provisions. In addition to a few other eminent musician friends, the guests included opera lover and frustrated tenor James Beard, who was on a salt-reduced diet at the time, so we served him fettuccine with huge quantities of true Malossol caviar, which, of course is supposed to contain less than 5 percent salt.

*A little Verdi: Pavarotti and Scotto, with Eugene Istomin
at the piano. James Beard reclines at center right*

Texas considers itself the chili capital of the world, but for one night in 1974 the capital moved to 67th Street, when I decided to stage "The Great Chili Confrontation." For years I had been carrying on a feud with a group of chili-head friends of mine. Each of them was dead certain that his or hers was the only authentic chili that would be hailed in the culinary region often called the "Border States."

Ten of us served our chilis from great pots to the sixty-five guests, but nobody danced around the posts and fired shotguns. Our kitchen was "enveloped in a cloud of chili-scented air, guaranteed to intoxicate any chili-lover and drive a chili-hater from the room"—as James Beard wrote in his syndicated column.

One of the guests asked about the menu during the reception, and was gently informed, "If you don't smell it, we ain't got it." Someone called the chili-saturated dishes evidence of the emerging national spirit of masochism. We also served wild duck barbecue, jalapeño cornbread, and pecan brownies. Reckless adults helped themselves to Long Neck Beer in huge tubs, and the frozen-margarita contraption worked overtime. I have always supported wildlife, and this party was a good example of it.

Although my maternal grandmother would say, "George, you are not complaining, you are bragging," I was embarrassed when the results of the scrupulously secret tasting were announced by Calvin Trillin. I came in first with my Chocolate Chili, and Jim Beard was a strong second. (Please find—nay, cook and taste—my chili recipe on page 350.)

CHAPTER 21

The Prince and the Pauper

ONE DAY I was talking to Ferdinand Metz, the president of the Culinary Institute of America, who has made this Hyde Park institution into a kind of culinary Harvard, and I persuaded him to allow me to attend classes as an anonymous student for a week. Reading about George Plimpton's escapades had given me the idea that I could gather some uncommon professional experiences. Decades before, I had had to learn everything from peeling vegetables to ice-carving in professional kitchens without ever going to a cooking school, and I'd always wanted to know how it would feel to learn things from the experts in an organized, academic way.

I cursed my curiosity the morning I woke up in a dorm at the ungodly hour of five-fifteen. By six-thirty, dressed in the traditional garb these students wore (checkered pants, white jacket and apron, and a tall *toque blanche*), and carrying the requisite set of knives fitted in a black carrying case), I walked toward the main building, feeling like a spy in an alien country.

As I waited for my fried eggs in the mess hall, I overheard the chef-instructor tell an eager student cook, "Now, say a short prayer just before flipping them." The prayer seemed to work, and I received my eggs in one piece.

Incognito at the Culinary Institute of America, 1988

After breakfast, each of us entered one of the various professional kitchens. Mine had a fifteen-foot-long table at each end of the room, a battery of ranges in between, and a chef's office in the corner. I was milling around with another dozen or so neophyte students in slow motion. My group had to chop onions, parsley, shallots, tomatoes, and knob celery, then weigh the vegetables before giving them to the group that would brown them. I have always been good at chopping vegetables—perhaps it comes from my bow arm—and the chef commented, "Look, he just joined our class and he knows how to do it clean and fast." I slowed down immediately to blend into the crowd.

The second morning, together with fourteen second-semester students, I entered the charcuterie classroom, where I learned to make head cheese by dumping four pounds of jowl into twenty pounds of cooked pig's head, then adding the seasonings and very cold water. In the next class I learned about making all sorts of sausages in an ominous-looking machine. In the far corner of the room, I noticed how a dainty-looking young female student deftly took the cleaver from a hefty guy and cut through a tough frozen bunch of bones, making it look easy.

In the afternoon I experienced the other end of the culinary spectrum in the airy pastry shop, which contained a bewildering variety of equipment. The chef-instructor's performance was so dramatic that I still remember it almost verbatim: "Making sorbet, this is one of the few occasions where you don't need a recipe. Your tongue will be your recipe. I just mix lemon juice and water, then I drop this uncracked egg into it. [He did.] It sinks. Right? Right.

"Now I put sugar into the liquid—the egg still sinks.

"Now let's add more sugar. [He did.] Now let's see if the egg floats. [It did.] Just a nickel-sized portion of the eggshell should show above the liquid."

He could have been a Shakespearean actor, the way he paused for dramatic effect, then—looking at us—continued, "If the egg sinks, it means the mixture does not have enough sugar, and if too much of the egg sticks up, then it has too much sugar and the sorbet won't freeze, because sugar acts as a natural antifreeze."

During the wine class, the subject was Alsatian wines. After tasting and discussing several types and vintages, we learned about the optimum temperature for serving white wines. Our instructor told us that dry white wines should be served at between forty-three and fifty-five degrees Fahrenheit, but complex wines should be served at close to fifty-five degrees in order to bring out the full range of their flavors and bouquet. Unfortunately, this is a far cry from the arctic temperatures of the wines served in most restaurants, he added. He also explained that a white wine served at the suggested temperature would gain a degree every seven minutes, a piece of information I had not possessed before.

Then on to the cold kitchen, where, in the *garde manger* department, the instructor taught us how to make *pâté en croûte*—pâté baked in crust ("It's like tucking the sheets in under the mattress . . ."), followed by the seafood class, where I participated in the gruesome process of preparing and cooking a live brook trout *en bleu*.

Day after day I attended different classes, and by the end of the week the experience taught me that learning on the job is highly overrated as opposed to the privilege of being a student in a first-rate cooking school.

During my week as a student, I did everything I could to make sure I remained anonymous, and it almost worked. Leaving the staggering activity of the kitchen in their noted Escoffier restaurant (where all of us cooks, during rush hour, displayed conspicuous valor in front of the student waiters), a couple of students stopped me and said, "We were wondering where we know you from. Didn't you work in Poughkeepsie as a short-order cook in a diner?"

One has to pay the price of fame. . . .

The charade which took place in the ring with George Foreman in the early days of 1989 served at the time as a one-minute prank, but quite a different sort of Plimptoniana took place in the spring of same year. When *Travel & Leisure* assigned me a story on London's Savoy, which was celebrating its hundredth anniversary, instead of writing a profile-type article, which had already been done by a competing magazine, I decided I would take different jobs at the hotel to observe the workings of a grand hotel from the viewpoints of a room-service waiter, a cook, and so on. Provided, of course, that the mighty general manager of this conservative hostelry would give me permission to act out such a charade.

With George Foreman in the ring, 1989. I took it easy on him

After months of negotiations, I finally received conditional approval, and I found myself sitting in the comfortably furnished drawing room just off the lobby of the Savoy Hotel. Facing me were Willy Bauer, the renowned general manager of the Savoy, and his very English deputy, Peter Crome. Both were dressed in the traditional morning coats worn by the staffs of European luxury hotels. There were preliminary civilities, and then I asked them about my work schedule. "Now don't get your hopes up," Mr. Bauer said sternly. "You don't have the job yet."

They conducted the mock interview for the job very well, and after a few anxious minutes I was, to my great relief, hired. (Mr. Bauer has since departed the Savoy—but not, I assure you, because of this decision.) I was directed to the laundry room in the basement for a fitting. The next morning I was to report to John Duchi, who was in charge of fifth-floor room service.

Meals on Wheels: At 6:25 a.m., I found the fifth-floor kitchen, which, like the kitchens on all the other floors, was spacious, lined with blue and white tiles, and outfitted with white cupboards with sliding glass doors, a large refrigerator, heaters, broilers, and one gas jet. John (formerly Giovanni) Duchi, who was originally from Milan, had been the *chef d'étage,* or master of this floor, for twenty-one years, and he took a remarkably analytical approach to his work.

"We make changes only when we should," he explained to me. "Take, for instance, this computer. We order our food from the kitchen, and the new triple dumbwaiters deliver it in seconds. But in most things we try to keep our old ways and manners—that's what our guests expect."

We lined up the orders that had come in the night before, and began to set up rolling tables, using the traditional china of the hotel. Duchi looked at the wall clock and said: "It's 6:58—time to serve our first breakfast. And please remember, you speak only if guests ask you a question or you need instructions from them."

A room waiter, I learned in my short career, must possess more discretion than a father confessor. Take, for instance, "Operation Room 536," our first stop of the morning. John knocked on the door and, hearing a faint reply, let us in with a master key.

"May we enter, please?" he asked. Then we pushed the table into the room, where a sleepy young woman in bed was trying to muster a smile. While John arranged the continental breakfast like a window dresser at Harrods, I asked her in my most impersonal voice, "Would you like to sign, Madame?"

She sat up holding the blanket in front of her, and it was pleasantly evident that she was wearing only Chanel No. 5. The scene reminded me of the perennial joke about tact. The professor in a hotel school asks, "What do you do if you enter a room and a nude lady is just coming out of the shower?" The correct answer is, squint a little and say, "Excuse me, sir."

We returned to the room-service kitchen, set up a breakfast of tea, grapefruit juice, and an order of English breakfast sausage (with a cereal filling and very little taste), and at 7:15 A.M.—on the button—entered room 526. A young Japanese gentleman greeted us, fully dressed. The bed was made, the desk was piled high with folders and files, and there were several empty beer bottles, indicating that he must have stayed up all night to prepare for the Big Meeting. Clearly he had no interest in the state of the weather, so we left as quickly as good manners allowed.

We had to work fast to serve all the orders on time and to remove the tables from guests who had finished their breakfasts. After seeing how more than a few rooms looked as though they had been targets of military search-and-destroy missions, I made a secret vow never to bring up the subject of messiness with any member of my family again.

During a short lunch period, we returned to rooms several times to offer guests seconds from gleaming copper pans—in true French service style. Then, when John's partner came to take over the three-o'clock shift, I delivered splendid fruit bowls filled with dwarf pineapples, fresh litchis, passionfruit, and mangosteens to a number of rooms.

All the while, a silver polisher worked diligently in a corner of the kitchen. Upon finishing a platter, he would tilt it at an angle to make sure he could see every tiny blemish, and then, with the care usually given to a newborn baby, place it back on the proper rack. Here, I thought, lay one of the secrets of the Savoy's primacy.

The Doorman as Dormouse: The laundry, with its friendly head, Daphne, and its busy tailors, became part of my daily beat. The second morning, I was outfitted with a dove-gray coat with silver buttons, white gloves, a white silk ascot, and a top hat that could have been used by Oddjob, the ominous Oriental decapitator in the movie *Goldfinger.* Then I joined two doormen on duty, hoping (and dreading) that someone I knew might arrive and discover me in my new career.

Soon those concerns were replaced by others. A London cabbie took the narrow curve in front of the entrance at such a speed that I jumped back in an un-Savoy-like manner, proving to myself that I am more dormouse than doorman.

As a doorman at the Savoy in 1989

When I missed opening the door of a limo, a bespectacled colleague admonished me, "You should always be where you're needed, even if it's impossible to be in five different places at the same time."

Perhaps Thoreau was right when he said, "Beware of all enterprises that require new clothes." As a doorman at the Savoy I was a failure.

Justifying My Salary: When I walked into banqueting manager Julian Small's office at eight o'clock the next morning, he looked at me reproachfully: I was fifteen minutes late. It was time to check out the house, and during our walk I learned that young Julian had started in the banqueting department in 1984, and was now managing the Savoy's function rooms, which brought in six million pounds a year. (When Brian Evans had been offered the position of the banqueting director at the Savoy a couple of decades earlier, the board had required him to change his name to Evangelo Brioni to maintain the tradition of having an Italian in that position. In small ways times do change, even at the Savoy.)

We passed three women rubbing the tendrillike brass and wrought-iron railings with the zeal of boxers working the punching bag. The results were dazzling. We entered the Lancaster Ballroom, where I helped double-check every detail for an important lunch for 240 people, hosted by a private banking firm. Nearby, in a small room that contained a single large table covered with black baize, set for thirty-one diners, I meekly advised the headwaiter to check the corners of the draping.

Then I did a brief stint in the Beaufort Room, where I helped the headwaiter and his staff lay down the pink linen with the care of couturiers and then arrange the heavy silver place plates with geometric precision, leaving no fingerprints. Although the housekeepers had scrubbed every inch of the room a few hours before, a woman with a vacuum cleaner almost sucked us up.

Suddenly a hush fell over the room. When I turned around, I saw the inquisitive face of Giles Shepard, the formidable managing director of the entire Savoy Group, who knew about my arrangement. Within seconds he determined that everything was in order. (Later I wondered if he had just wanted to make sure my activities wouldn't land him in the Tower of London.) I was ushered out of the room at 12:05, just before the guests entered.

I still had to justify my salary (which at that point amounted to three cups of tea, a lovely bowl of fruit in my room, and an invitation to the Centenary Ball), so I sat in on a meeting in Julian Small's office—feeling quite secure for a change with my Waldorf background—and assisted him in arranging a party for a well-known English organization of professional women. For the rest of the day we dealt with assorted functions ranging from modest dinners to a gala event; one of them almost matched the silly extravaganzas of the Edwardian era. At the party celebrating the reaching of the North Pole by Admiral Peary—as I learned from one of the banqueting assistants—the Lancaster Ballroom was turned into a castle of ice and snow, and the waiters were wrapped in furs like Eskimos.

"The Savoy tries to fulfill everyone's fantasies," said Julian Small at the end of a most tiring day and night. "Once we even brought in a designer to deck out a pigpen in the ballroom for a well-to-do farmer and his bride who wanted to share their wedding with their favorite pigs."

The Privy Council: During the following days, I attended several of the general manager's morning meetings in his office, where Willy Bauer sat at his desk surrounded by his department heads. I behaved like a kid in the principal's office, hoping not to be noticed. Like all first-class CEOs, Bauer had the capacity to concentrate on each problem until it was solved—and not a second longer. One after another, the department heads gave their reports on the previous twenty-four hours, then the coming day's events were discussed in detail.

I learned three things in the GM's office: first, even a fine orchestra needs a steady conductor; second, self-criticism is an absolute necessity for improvement; and, third, ideas are like children—your own always seem the most wonderful.

I had brought Arnold Bennett's novel *Imperial Palace* with me, which was based on the Savoy Hotel. Each night, before falling into bed with limbs as rusty as the Tin Man's before an oiling, I read the chapter that took place in the department where I had just worked. To my profound surprise, I found that the descriptions almost paralleled my experiences of that day.

Playing Hotel: Peter Crome, who had the unfortunate task of trying to teach me the job of a duty manager, was a towering, elegant chap, the kind who grow only in certain parts of England. He was the epitome of class, yet he was down-to-earth and decisive during our twelve hours of "working the house," as it is referred to in the hotel trade.

Crome's long day started with a look at the night report, which told everything that had happened in the hotel the previous night—even identifying the person responsible for not turning off a particular light, thus wasting money. Then Crome checked the arrivals list ("seventy arrivals this morning, about average") and the departures report. Meanwhile, I was directing people to the Lancaster Ballroom, where there was a large breakfast meeting with some kind of presentation.

By this time I had begun to sound like a Hungarian whose pregnant mother had been frightened by a visiting Englishman. When an American woman and her two comely young daughters approached the front desk and I inquired about their trip, I overheard them whisper to each other, "So *that's* what a real English accent sounds like."

Then I accompanied Crome to a set of offices on the balcony above the entrance, where I learned how to precheck arrivals, who are color-coded in pink, blue, and yellow to indicate special arrangements or instructions. A famous American movie star was supposed to come in on the Concorde and check into a suite just to shower and change clothes, before she continued in the afternoon to another European location.

"The chief of the French naval staff is going to be the guest of his English equivalent, the First Sea Lord of Britain," Crome said. "George, we must make sure everything goes according to protocol and without a hitch." I was handed a printed booklet with a minute-to-minute schedule and annotations. Whoever set it up was probably the same person who had organized the British end of the Normandy invasion.

Using a computer, Crome went through all reservations, muttering every now and then, "Oh, Mr. and Mrs. ——— are here." Then we ran down to welcome arriving guests, and I found just the right tone of voice located between haughty and hospitable (leaning toward the latter). The fact that we were dressed in tailcoats, vests, and striped trousers intimidated guests used to standing in line at the front desk of a two-thousand-room hotel in Chicago, so a bit of extra civility was in order.

I was gently instructed by one of Crome's assistants on how to take guests up to their rooms and make them feel like stockholders in the Savoy Hotel Corporation. I was to use the lift to go up in style with the guests, but was required to use the steps on the way down. Then I joined Crome on his morning tour, during which he reminded me of a juggler who could keep fifteen balls in the air while playing three different musical instruments and singing "God Save the Queen" at the same time.

Onward, Savoy soldiers, to the lower level, to inspect the staff's changing room, which had been recently redone and was more orderly than a monk's cell. Crome picked up a cushion that didn't belong to a particular sofa, and carried it until he found its rightful place in the Empire Room. Then we took a fast walk through the kitchens, the laundry room, and even the boiler room. We called upstairs to remind one of Crome's assistants about a guest who was supposed to arrive any minute. Crome's cellular phone rang, and he answered, "Duty manager speaking. I understand you want to purchase a shower head, Mr. ———. Please talk to your plumber—I think you will need a one-inch pipe, and also, what is your water pressure at home? Perhaps you will need a pump. Here at the Savoy, we have fifteen pounds per square inch. Yes, it costs fifty pounds, and I shall charge it to your room."

Back at the front desk I saw a couple dressed in black suede getups; the spectacular-looking woman, in her early twenties, wore a pants outfit with thick fringes, and the man had heavy silver bands around his thighs and upper arms. Surrounded by the conservatively dressed people in the dignified lobby, they looked glaringly out of place. But the Savoy's attitude toward eccentrics is affectionately indulgent. "This hotel was always for people with style," Crome remarked. "Wilde, Whistler, and Sarah Bernhardt must have seemed equally strange in their day—and remember, if it wasn't for the theater, the Savoy never would have been built." He was referring to the fact that Richard D'Oyly Carte built the Savoy in 1881 from the money he made by producing Gilbert and Sullivan's operettas.

But the restaurants have always enforced a strict dress code. At 5:00 P.M., a visibly upset young woman from Canada, dressed in a sweatshirt and jeans and accompanied by the headwaiter of the hotel's Thames Foyer, came to the duty manager to complain about not being allowed in for tea in "designer jeans."

"Madame," said Crome, "I am not here to be a fashion arbiter, and the rule of the Savoy unfortunately does not allow denim into any of its restaurants, no matter what way it is tailored."

"You certainly don't keep up with the times," she sputtered.

"No, Madame, we try to keep up with the best part of our past," said my boss.

Cooking for My Supper: Dressed in a white chef's outfit, topped by the traditional *toque blanche,* I entered the kitchen of the Savoy with great trepidation. It wasn't easy to erase the thirty-five-year hiatus since I had last worked in the kitchen of New York's Plaza Hotel. Chef Anton Edelmann proudly showed me the worn copper pots of Escoffier, and I must admit that standing in the spot where the legendary founder of modern cuisine created some of his dishes made me feel what certain generations must experience at Graceland.

First, Edelmann assigned me to assist the breakfast cook. The speed with which you have to perform during the rush hour is quite astonishing. The noise was a bit too much for me, the loudest voice being that of the *annonceur* shouting orders and pickups to roughly thirty cooks working simultaneously in front of the ranges and pantry tables. In the meantime, dishwashers from Bangladesh tried to cope with the incredible number of dishes that accumulated. Everything was served with three or four underliners, and I wouldn't be surprised if, during a meal, at least a dozen pieces of flatware were used per person.

Chef Edelmann, originally from Germany, was a bona fide celebrity in England. He was one of the ablest organizers, as well as a diplomat, an inventor of tastes, and, especially, a teacher of young cooks. No slouch when it came to public relations, he arrived punctually at eight o'clock every morning, shaking hands, greeting everyone by name and kidding around. In a top-notch professional kitchen, it was refreshing. To a butcher who carves meat the way Michelangelo carved marble, he said, "Not bad, you'll learn yet." The butcher had been at the Savoy for twenty-four years.

After breakfast, I toiled with several of the young sauciers and one of the sous-chefs, preparing the bases for the sauces. Edelmann came by and tasted a layered pâté de foie gras: "Aspic needs a little more port," he said. He reminded his steward in charge of ordering fish, "Stop buying from ————. We must punish them for what they did." (Apparently they had been late with a delivery.) He took a sip of consommé from a shallow casserole offered to him by the *potager,* and commented, "The balance is fine, but perhaps it's a little over-reduced.") Finally he headed to the butcher shop, where his ten key staff members were waiting for the daily eight-thirty meeting. I made the eleventh member, just in case they decided to play soccer with the Claridge's team.

After they had dissected the status of the day's parties, I thanked God that I was not responsible for the gala event, the Centenary Ball, even though these days the chef and cooks are not beheaded for less-than-perfect food and service. They just don't get their MBEs after twenty years of service.

Edelmann accompanied me back to my station and watched from the side, while eating a toasted sandwich of fried egg, as I carefully clarified the fish stock. The sprawling kitchen was filled with the motion and sound of perfectly coordinated teamwork. One young cook was slicing fourteen-inch loaves of bread, making about eighty credit-card-thin pieces for melba toast. As the newest member of the kitchen staff, I felt it was not my place to tell him that melba toast, when Escoffier invented it for the diva Nelly Melba, was originally toasted and split, and then the insides were re-toasted, so I kept my mouth shut. Endless trays of elaborately decorated canapés and stuffed miniature vegetables were produced for the reception.

Chef Edelman was watching me with interest. He was one of the few people who knew my identity, but he was going along with the charade.

Later that afternoon I changed roles again when I was summoned to the general manager's staff meeting, at which the main topic was the Centenary Ball. Because the Prince and Princess of Wales would be attending, all preparations had to be completed by 5:30 p.m., when Scotland Yard's security dogs would arrive to sniff for bombs.

Back in the kitchen that afternoon, I worked with a twenty-two-year-old Scot named Gordon Dochard, and my decades-old training on how to make proper bases for sauces came back to me. These essences were dark and glossy, with a jellylike thickness; the contents of a fifty-gallon stockpot ended up as just about one gallon of *glace de viande.* The heat from all the cooking, of course, was tremendous, even in this modern kitchen that had been completely renovated in 1985.

At six o'clock I staggered up to my room, cursing the fate that had diverted me from a glorious career of playing piano in a bordello. I donned my white tie and tails (my collar button broke at the last moment, but was replaced by an unflappable valet), put on my gala-evening smile, and was ready for the big soirée.

I Couldn't Have Danced All Night: As I led my wife, Jenifer (who in her stylish evening gown could have been a princess), down the steps to the River Room, which had received foreign notables such as the Bourbons and Savoys as well as American upstarts like Mark Twain and Consuela Vanderbilt, I wondered whether anyone else had ever worked as a cook on a banquet and then sat down to consume it as a guest. Ladies arrived in elaborate long dresses. Some resembled the costumes in *Les Liaisons Dangereuses;* others looked like slightly altered wedding gowns. At least their hairdos were not arranged as though they'd been caught in the slipstream of a 747, as was the current fashion in America at the time. The men wore tails, starched piqué vests, white ties, and impressive-looking decorations.

At one end of the room, separated by a velvet rope, was the VIP reception. The air was suddenly charged with the kind of electricity that only the Prince and Princess of Wales could generate. I was surprised how dashing Prince Charles was—though quite short for a fairy-tale image—and even tycoons with mega-millions were hypnotized by Princess Diana, whose bony shoulders at that time still seemed to carry the social life of the entire United Kingdom.

A discreet chamber orchestra was playing the "King's Ballet Minuet," and while the superb-looking Lancaster Ballroom was perhaps a bit over-flowered, still, few places on the globe could match its elegance and air of festivity.

The service in the ballroom was so subtle that I was surprised to find my *Terrine de Foie Gras en Gelée au Vieux Porto* in front of me, and I felt exhilarated by the idea that I had tasted it that very morning before any of the illustrious guests. The spectacular fish course was served *sous cloche,* under a glass bell—quite a trick to pull off for three hundred people.

The dessert was Chef Edelmann's witty fantasy variation on Escoffier's Peach Melba, filled with frozen vanilla-strawberry mousse and covered with a transparent dome of spun sugar that looked like a cap of golden threads for a very small angel. This was followed by exquisite little *mignardises*, bits of sweets generally known in our circles as petits-fours, surrounding a candy tower bearing the name: SAVOY.

After the coffee came a child's treat for grownups: a presentation of praline ice cream bonbons on sticks, surrounded by furiously fuming dry ice.

We shared our table with a Canadian couple and their two children, a girl of eight and a boy of twelve. To everyone's amazement, the girl got up and walked boldly over to the royal table, had a chat with the princess, and then asked the prince for a dance. He graciously took her for a spin on the crowded floor.

Then the lights dimmed and the entertainment began. Although at first the Moulin Rouge cancan dancers doing their high kicks seemed an odd choice for this gala occasion, there was a natural connection to the Savoy, for the Moulin Rouge was also celebrating its hundredth anniversary.

A little after midnight, lame of limb, I said a weary farewell to our table, to assorted viscounts and viscountesses and to our headwaiter. Shortly thereafter, we left and I fell into my bed, knowing with an aching heart that although playing hotel had been fun, the next morning I would have to grow up.

As I was leaving for Heathrow Airport, Peter Crome appeared, and said, "George, if you want a summer job, you'd better apply early."

I guess I'd passed muster.

CHAPTER 22

Thank You for Dreaming with Me

EVERY PLAYWRIGHT has a certain number of characters in his or her repertoire, and not wanting to get to the point where I would have to resort to doing variations on my restaurant characters, in 1985 I sold my consulting company to members of my staff. I suddenly felt as if I had a blank sheet on which I could write almost anything; the options were up to me. When I asked myself what I would like to do next, the answers ranged from becoming an industrial designer, an etymologist, or a songwriter, to owning and cultivating a top-notch vineyard, or making violins again. One thing was certain: I would not eat the soup of life with a fork; I would continue to use a big ladle.

I remained a limited partner in the George Lang Corporation for a few more years, and wrote a book, *Lang's Compendium of Culinary Nonsense and Trivia,* as well as articles for a number of publications around the world, appeared on *CBS Sunday Morning* in mini-documentaries as a regular, and steadfastly refused many offers that came my way. Thus I was ready for the telephone call and subsequent breakfast I had with Ronald S. Lauder at the Westbury Hotel in New York in March 1990.

I had read about his Hungarian roots, even such amusing details as that his mother Estée's original name had been Eszti, the Hungarian diminutive of Esther, but I didn't realize his fervent commitment—indeed, his overwhelming desire—to resurrect something of the glory of

Budapest's past. Considering the state of that city, and of Hungary itself at the time, we both realized the improbability and impracticality of any venture there. Two generations in Hungary had grown up just being given work, but not working for a living, and they had gotten used to an extreme form of bureaucracy in which—according to the local wags—an abortion was free, but you had to wait two years for it.

At some point between our grapefruit juice and tea, Ronald asked me if I had ever done anything in Budapest. I started to say no, but then I remembered that in 1976, Hilton International had engaged me to consult on the restaurants in their hotel in Budapest, which had opened the following year.

During our forty-five minutes together (neither of us can suffer long meetings), we also discovered that we both disliked purely commercial ventures, shortcut approaches, and the profit-and-run carpetbagger style of doing business, which began inundating eastern European countries as soon as the walls came down. We didn't set a specific goal, but we fed on each other's enthusiasm, and we decided then and there that we would fly to Budapest together the following week to see if there was a project that would be equally exciting to both of us.

Looking for a reference while writing this chapter, I found the following dedication in a book Ronald bought me in Budapest:

> *Thank you for dreaming with me.*
> *Ronald S. Lauder*
> *13 March 1990*

Several years later, after a bottle of Tokay, he told me that at our first meeting he had sensed a romantic yearning in me to return to the country where I'd grown up, just as he wanted to recapture his roots.

We arrived in Budapest a week after our first breakfast, and because the city had, in effect, changed its face and soul several times since World War II, it was *terra incognita* for me.

Analyzing the country of my birth should have been easy, but unfortunately I found most of the existing reports from foreign observers full of fantasy, and the information by Hungarian experts was strongly influenced by their past and present political standing. It did not make the situation easier that ministers, key government officials, and even the head of the State Property Agency (which held the key to all salable properties) were changing with the unpredictability of a weekly lottery.

I had to remind myself that the generations that had been born at the beginning of or during the war had seen their world sink again in 1956. By then, parents and their Communist-influenced children had used up the quota of beliefs they were born with, and Hungary at the time was a nation living in a kind of limbo. The citizens of Budapest desperately tried to start anew, but their past was their present, and it didn't promise much of a future. Although the original street names, which had been changed during the Communist era, were restored, during the very first days of my search and research in Budapest, I had to face the fact that it would take much more than that to alter the attitudes of people who had never known anything but a life controlled by Big Brothers and Big Stepbrothers.

The Budapest I knew in my youth was comely, full of elegant places and boulevards where nannies in crisp whites pushed fancy baby carriages. It was filled with people who played their parts with style. Following the collapse of the Communist system, there was a struggle to ensure that life continued—that there would be a theater, a restaurant, a bookstore, a record shop, and a café on every block, fresh jokes with the morning coffee, and a tomorrow without a day of judgment.

During the following two weeks it became clear to me that Budapest was a splintered city in a splintered country, and I felt it was a good omen that what the city seemed to need most coincided with Ronald's and my dreams.

Looking for the right project along these lines, within a short time I narrowed down our choices to four final possibilities: the New York Café House (which used to be the most glittering turn-of-the-century establishment of its kind anywhere), Gerbeaud (the Taj Mahal of pastry shops), the spa-hotel Gellért (with its famed artificial-wave indoor swimming pool installed in 1918), and the Restaurant Gundel in the City Park.

My exhaustive study pointed toward Gundel, and included the probable cost and timing of restoration (the place was in a lamentable state), as well as marketing, staffing, finding supplies, and working out the legal snarls, all of which are inherent in most situations. But I realized that this project would be more difficult than any I had tackled before, because my first job would be to motivate the local cast of characters, without whose enthusiastic support my plans would remain nothing more than a theoretical exercise. Ten days later I returned to New York, and by the end of the following week I had finished a sort of "white paper" that became our manifesto as well as our game plan.

After a couple of sessions, during which we maintained a careful balance between our excitement and sober reality, Ronald and I felt that our trophy project had to be the venerable Gundel, and all of our efforts should be concentrated on taking possession as soon as possible.

The reason was quite clear to us: Hospitality is one of the most important signs of civilization. For a century, Gundel had been closely linked to the Hungarian nation, to its ups and downs. Restoring Gundel to its former splendor would send a clear signal that Hungary was on the way to recovery; it would reflect the vitality of Budapest and would be enormously helpful in bringing back a class of tourism that would revitalize many businesses and professions and would supply thousands of desperately needed jobs.

I should point out to non-Hungarian readers that no one there could take lightly the changing of the ownership of such a landmark, especially since the prospective owners would be Americans. Fortunately the authorities and even the Hungarian press realized that Ronald Lauder not only was of Hungarian origin but was committed to long-range developments in eastern Europe, and at the same time he was one of the few people who could support his seemingly unlimited goodwill with in-depth financing. As far as my relationship to Hungary was concerned, in 1986, the Hungarian Chef's and Pastry Chef's Association had given me a special award "for activities on behalf of Hungarian gastronomy."

During negotiations I opened an office in the Grand Hotel Ramada, in the center of Budapest's Margaret Island, and assembled a skeleton team comprising a local attorney, who could navigate in the labyrinth of assorted governmental and city departments; an American-Hungarian lawyer, and a Budapest-based architect. With their collaboration, I began to prepare a letter of intent to the then-head of the State Property Agency.

The result was an album-sized book handsomely bound by one of the few bookbinders left in Budapest, which bore on its cover the gold-embossed title *Gundel, the Next Fifty Years*, a title supplied by Ronald.

The first part of the study dealt with the contemporary state of restaurants in Budapest. I wrote, rather cautiously, that, over the years, Hungarian cooks had lost touch with restaurant developments and colleagues outside of Hungary, and that until a few months before, the borders had been hermetically sealed as far as food ingredients, wines, and, especially, cooking equipment were concerned. To add more weight to my proposal, I quoted John Lukács, one of the most significant historians

301

of the twentieth century: "It was less than one hundred years ago when the French and Viennese influences began to vary and enrich Budapest and its provincial Hungarian cooking. Then the reputation of the Budapest restaurants began to spread as well. A very considerable part of the development is attributable to a *grand bourgeois* Hungarian family of restaurateurs, the Gundels. Their celebrated restaurant still exists but, alas, bearing their name only. That harmony of Gallic refinement with Hungarian solidity is no longer extant."

To remedy the dismal situation, I proposed an ongoing "Gundel college" for the entire staff; the stocking of a library of cookbooks for the chefs; the rebuilding of every inch of the interior by combining Hungarian talent, American technology, and international expertise; a serious effort to restore the good name of Hungarian wines; and the purchase of a Tokay vineyard of our own.

The final chapters projected in detail the possible future of Gundel. What I didn't include in this presentation was an account of two of my previous visits to Gundel.

I must have been a sixteen- or seventeen-year-old student when I got a scholarship to study the violin in Budapest, and one day when my father was there on a business trip, he decided to take me out for lunch at Gundel. We were seated in the garden, intoxicated with the surroundings. I ordered dishes from the menu I had never heard of, feeling like a timid explorer in a magic land. Although at the time I was secretly convinced that one day I was going to succeed Heifetz, still I had a yearning to be part of such a glamorous place. When I discovered, at a nearby table, a young girl of my age—eating with her family—who was so pretty that I had difficulty not staring at her, I also decided that one day I would have a girlfriend like her.

My next and only other previous encounter with Gundel occurred in 1969, when I was making frequent visits to Hungary to do research on my book *The Cuisine of Hungary*. Sadly, the restaurant's socialist-cooperative-designed interior was difficult to swallow, not to mention the food, which would have had to be improved to be called pedestrian. Yet I decided to be photographed with a couple of cooks in Gundel's kitchen for the jacket of my book, mostly because I had devoted quite a few pages to the Gundel dynasty, recalling its glorious history.

After the State Property Agency received our proposal, there was nothing else to do but wait.

Ronald Lauder and I felt the need at that point, however, to give a show-and-tell demonstration to the world—which, for our venture, meant the two million citizens of Budapest. Although I did not have any control over Gundel at that time, the management and staff and I did share a mutual respect, and I knew that I could arrange a party that would demonstrate our intentions.

I still remember an afternoon session with a few of my trusted Hungarian friends in the Hotel Forum's Café Vienna, when I opened the post-coffee discussion (you cannot get anyone's attention in Hungary before this ritual is completed) by talking about the social institution known as *törzsasztal* in Hungary or *Stammtisch* in Vienna, and "regulars' table" in an awkward English translation (it has never been a part of American restaurant culture). Our plan was to invite about 125 writers, artists, businessmen, scientists, musicians, politicians, show-business people, and such to an evening of camaraderie, good food, and wine, combined with fun and games. It turned out to be an all-night job, since each of us had his own idea.

The following excerpt from the invitation I wrote will give you an idea of the flavor of the evening:

ON A CLEAR DAY, WE CAN SEE ALL THE WAY TO 1910

Considering the fact that at this point Hungary desperately needs massive doses of assorted vitamins to stiffen its collective backbone to be able to believe in the future, we decided to invite a group of individuals who would be interested in bringing back the best part of the past and quality to all aspects of life.

Everyone who will join us on Friday, February 8, 1991, should realize that no one deserves a good tomorrow who does not savor and protect the past.

To ensure the proper mood of the assembled worthies, we will take great pains to make available the best of the alcoholic nectars that our national anthem alludes to; by the time the roast is served, it will surely turn everyone into so many Karinthys, Heltais and Molnárs.*

So get ready to tuck in your napkins and enjoy the happy fact that there is life after rebirth.

*Famed wits of pre–World War II Hungary.

When the time came to serve the coffee that evening, we put on each table little square boards made of chocolate that the pastry chef and I concocted with seventeen letters made of bite-sized petit-fours spelling out in Hungarian *Gundel Regulars' Table*. Each table, of course, tried to beat the next one by making new words out of the letters and there were passionate arguments about the relative merits. Toward the end of the party, impromptu performances by leading opera singers, poets, and actors brought back an era when having a good time was not considered an affront to God and country.

At every turn during our efforts to renew the famous restaurant, we kept coming back to the founder of the restaurant, Károly Gundel. Like any small country, Hungary cannot afford the luxury of having too many specialists; perhaps that is why one very often finds a "triple threat" expert. Károly Gundel was such a person, combining the gifts of a Ritz, an Escoffier, and a Prosper Montagné. He was without doubt the greatest restaurateur Hungary ever produced.

During a study trip in 1901 and 1902, Gundel worked for César Ritz, first in his Lucerne hotel and then in Paris, where Ritz eventually took him, trusting him with the arrangement of important parties. Gundel also worked for Louis Adlon in his famed Hotel Adlon in Berlin, and then in Vienna, where he became a friend of the young Sacher. Upon returning to Budapest, Gundel, using Hungarian talent and ingredients, created an experience that—according to contemporary records—was on a par with the best restaurants of Europe.

The word of mouth about our efforts to take over Gundel's restaurant spread fast, and yet we still hadn't dealt with the Gundel family. Ronald and I felt strongly that Gundel's heirs were entitled to reasonable compensation, even though the documents we found, to everyone's surprise, showed that the Gundels had never owned the restaurant buildings, but had simply leased it from the city of Budapest. Surprisingly, the Gundel name was never registered and protected, and the title to the restaurant was not included in Károly Gundel's will.

Károly Gundel and his wife had thirteen children, not to mention a goodly number of grandchildren and great-grandchildren, which added an extra dimension of difficulty to the negotiations, especially since several of the grandchildren were friends of mine. After a period of fruitless

Mixing it up at the new Gundel in 1992

discussion during which their lawyer and the family representative changed, I decided to invite all available members of the Gundel clan to a summer dinner on the graceful marble terrace of the restaurant, over-looking the garden.

The spirit of the dinner was far from homogeneous. A few members of the older generation, understanding their insupportable legal status, were still hoping to receive a modest sum of money; two or three young militants took a tough stand, hoping to strike it rich; and others could not make up their minds which side to follow.

After coffee was served, trying not to show my frustration, I made a straightforward presentation of the facts and probabilities. Then, a few minutes later, one of the grandchildren stood up and made a few less-than-helpful remarks, which amounted to "Let's see what happens in court."

I had been praying for a friendly settlement, but I was also prepared with an alternative. During our research, we had found an invoice from 1911 for a party given a year after Gundel returned from Paris to take over the restaurant, which until then had been called—after the original tenant—Wampetich. The logo, in the elaborate graphic style fashionable in the period, read,

GUNDEL, FORMERLY WAMPETICH

I had copied and enlarged the surprising document, and then held up another one, which I had changed to read,

WAMPETICH, FORMERLY GUNDEL

I then explained to the somewhat shaken guests that I could make an arrangement to use and trademark the Wampetich name. I would follow the eighty-year-old precedent established by their worthy forebear, still legally including the name Gundel without their consent. My case was reinforced by the fact that a popular turn-of-the-century song, still fondly remembered, includes the line, "Let's meet at Wampetich!"

The next day I received by messenger a letter from the attorney who represented the family, agreeing to our proposed sum. We had won an important battle, but the war with the State Property Agency still loomed ahead. But we knew we would prevail—because our hearts were pure and we had ready cash.

At one point I wrote a letter of summation to the account executive at the State Property Agency, which opened as follows:

> *I am beginning to feel like the young suitor who is asking for the hand of the beautiful princess, but the king first puts him through several dozen tests. I fervently hope that this very last one is not going to be impossible to solve.*
>
> *In this instance, of course, Gundel is the princess, who unfortunately has more than one father, mother, and stepmother, each one claiming jurisdiction over the hand.*
>
> *Let me try to sum up our "premarital" situation as briefly as I can, hoping that everyone will try to remember that the most important thing is the welfare of the ninety-seven-year-old princess.*

Our first offer was a formula based on a forty-nine-year lease. Shortly thereafter came our second proposal: a fifty-fifty partnership, hinting that we should have full ownership to ensure the success of the restaurant.

Once evening I went back to the Forum Hotel, exhausted by meeting-fatigue, and fell into the bathtub to get ready for dinner. Even our young children accept the family rule that a closed bathroom door means just that. So I was surprised when Jenifer knocked, asking me to come to the telephone. Her judgment—as always—turned out to be correct, because it was worth standing in front of the night table dripping wet to hear what the executive from the State Property Agency had to say. The conversation went something like this:

"Mr. Lang, we just finished an all-day session in my office, and we agreed on a fifty-fifty ownership. But your arguments about the mutual benefits of full ownership, as it relates to the future of Gundel, persuaded us, the last five minutes of our meeting, to change our position, and we decided to ask you whether you would be interested in full ownership with the following financial formula."

Then he told me the price and conditions, and concluded:

"Mr. Lang, we must have your proposal in our office by 10:00 A.M. tomorrow, since there will be a board meeting at 11:00 A.M., and if it is not presented and approved at that time, anything can happen."

A few minutes before 10:00 A.M. five copies of the agreements based on their formula were delivered to the SPA by fleet-footed messengers, and by the closing of the business day I received the good news, which suddenly reminded me of Bernard Shaw's words about the two greatest misfortunes that can occur in one's life: not getting what one wants, and getting what one wants.

Finally the date was set; we agreed on September 21, 1991, as the day of the signing ceremony in the ballroom of Gundel. Clocks were synchronized, airline and hotel reservations made, and forty-eight hours beforehand, our team was sitting in a private dining room in a Budapest hotel to discuss final details.

I noticed that our Hungarian attorney, usually one of the calmest members of his species, seemed uncommonly agitated. As it turned out, he had good reason to be upset.

"I am sorry and shocked to report to you," he said, "that it is unlikely that we will be able to sign the day after tomorrow as planned. I was officially informed that the city of Budapest and the zoo, which is under their jurisdiction, suddenly claim the ownership of Gundel. The board of directors of the zoo supposedly can prove that the land always belonged to them, and the attorneys for both have assembled records that may or may not prove to be correct."

I immediately demanded a meeting with everyone concerned, and it took place later in the day in the conference room of the deputy mayor of Budapest. The hastily assembled group of a dozen or so participants was sharply divided into three camps: the State of Hungary, the City of Budapest representing the zoo, and us. After another couple of hours of grandstanding and legal bluster, I finally made the following statement in a low-keyed voice:

"We came here from different parts of the world to complete this transaction, and are ready to fulfill every point of our agreement. If the State of Hungary is unable to bring a clear title, ready for signature, by tomorrow at 3:00 P.M. in the Gundel ballroom, I will make a statement to the invited press that will spell out the details of what has happened. The consequences—as I am sure you are aware—will be devastating as far as foreign investors' future attitude toward investment in Hungary is concerned."

We got up and bade a polite farewell to everyone, and went back to our hotel rooms to spend another sleepless night.

With the goodwill of the participants and (I am convinced) the intervention of the spirit of Károly Gundel, the following day, at 3:35 P.M., Gundel was ours for keeps.

A week later I closed the restaurant for twenty-four hours so the entire staff could come to a party in a farmstead restaurant in Lajosmizse, about an hour's drive from Budapest. The four hundred or so guests, including employees, wives, husbands, and children, were all having a ball, watching a horse show, eating the zesty meat of an ox roasted over a giant spit, singing along with gypsy music, and drinking assorted spirits. Clearly they wanted to improve their own spirits, as they were uneasy about the new era to come.

At one point during the party, Susanna Fodor, one of our New York attorneys, a capable woman who had left Hungary at an early age, pulled me aside and reported the following:

"George, while I was waiting in line at the ladies' room, I couldn't help overhearing the conversation of two women who apparently work in the kitchen of Gundel. Of course they could not guess that I understood Hungarian, so they spoke quite freely in front of me. One woman said, 'You know, I did not really believe the letter we all received about how our lives will improve now, the good things that will happen with the new owners, and all that stuff. But I must tell you I am beginning to change my mind now. And if it *really* happens, I will start working as hard as I can. It's only fair.' "

The moment I heard that, I knew that we had a winning hand in this high-stakes game.

For the first time in quite a while, I slept well that night.

Now it was time to put together the complete team. In addition to an array of architects, interior designers, kitchen planners, banquet specialists, wine experts, computer and international accounting specialists, and others, I brought in Dr. Gábor Buday, a leading Hungarian hotelier, and Andrew Young, a senior member of the original George Lang Corporation, who has since become one of our most successful consultants. We even hired the noted Hungarian journalist-author Zoltán Halász to be our in-house historian and researcher. Most of our architectural and interior design plans, as well as the kitchen plans and even many of our permits, were completed before we even closed the restaurant for renovations. Many of our recruits were Hungarians, a few were of Hungarian origin, and others spoke only English or some other language. Interpreters and translators made a pretty good living from us in those days.

After the age of fifty, someone once said, "It's patch, patch, patch." He was referring to the human body, but he might just as easily have meant historic restaurants like Gundel. The difference in this instance was that I could save the "skin" of the building and completely replace interiors.

The project was formidable. Every segment of the restaurant complex had been allowed to run down during the preceding forty-five years, and very little of its original refinement remained. During the Communist era, a massive renovation took place between 1973 and 1981. The comrades had diligently covered up what was left of the original decor with Formica and plywood, and some ceilings were dropped by six feet to approximate—as some said—the look of a Moscow hotel. Many parts of the building were structurally unsound. For instance, we fortunately discovered that the supporting steel beams in the dining room ceiling stopped twelve feet short of the wall; either it was a mistake or some construction foreman had pocketed the difference! The interior had suffered every possible indignity of socialist aesthetics, including dozens of light fixtures on the ceiling that resembled glowing pimples.

We were resolved to bring back the past, but without Disneyspells complete with artificial cobwebs. Members of my team, as well as Ronald, agreed that elegance and style would be key words, and we would have to clarify our interpretation of them. An elegant restaurant is quite easy to design if one sticks to a particular period, but inventing elegance requires an original mind that makes its own rules. I was hoping that the end result would be *haute* style at its best—a kind of revival fantasy supported by superb cuisine and soft music, conjuring up memories of Budapest bon vivants courting beautiful ladies.

Ronald, who since has become the president of the Museum of Modern Art in New York, agreed with me that one cannot live by superb food and heavenly wines alone. (And if you believe that, you will believe anything.) To bring Gundel to the attention of the world at large, we commissioned Milton Glaser to create two posters that we would display on the streets of Budapest and Vienna, heralding the 1992 reopening of the restaurant.

Until Milton came along, we were still groping for a style for the new restaurant. At one time or another we considered the luxurious Jugendstil style, art nouveau, Vienna Secessionist, and late art deco, with a few variations in between. Milton's rendering of a seated lady holding a glass of champagne, with the sinuous logo of Gundel forming her Thonet-like chair, served as a beacon in the forest of styles. Eventually, Madame Gundel's image was built into the paneling of the Colonnade Bar, where we refill her glass every now and then.

Ronald and I wanted to make the work of Hungarian painters a cultural focal point and an organic part of the interior of the restaurant. Happily, the golden age of Hungarian art coincides with that of Gundel, and with the help of an expert, we were able to locate paintings in private hands that were the finest examples of thirteen of the great painters of Hungary. A few of our waiters keep a kind of popularity tally based on how many guests like each painting. We were pleased when a restaurant review mentioned that people who dined at Gundel didn't have to pay an additional museum admission fee.

For the first time in decades, Hungarian craftsmen—architects, artists, wrought-iron workers, glass etchers, stucco artists—were given work that challenged and inspired them. But the project quickly took on a more international scope: carpets were custom-woven in Thailand; fabrics were brought in from France and Belgium; furniture was built in Italy; light fixtures were created in the United States; and a considerable part of the budget was spent on woodwork from Spain, where a small group of craftsmen tried to emulate the great artisans of the past.

In a conversation with one of the Gundel offspring, I learned to my surprise that during the twenties and thirties the Gundel family's apartment had been on the upper floor of the restaurant, and a few of the children were even born there. Trying to invoke the intimacy of the original rooms, I decided that the seven private dining rooms on that level could be designed as if the family were still living there.

A separate, discreet staircase leads to these rooms: the Library, with its comforting environment; the Salon, with its showcase filled with objets d'art collected over a couple of generations; the Winter Garden, which, in spite of its elegant appointments, at night seems like a treetop dining room in the midst of a romantic forest; the understated Crystal Room; the Music Room, which I am especially fond of, with its silhouettes of famous Hungarian composers etched into the window panes to accompany the musical allusions hidden in the furnishings; and the honey-colored Family Room, in which the Biedermeier table seats only a few people, surrounded by faded sepia photos of the remarkable Gundel family.

Quality could be defined as harmony of grace enhanced with sparkling wit; it also could describe Andrea Ilona Lang, my daughter and a prodigiously talented young artist—who had died a few years before in a Santa Barbara forest fire—and whose taste was the inspiration for the delicate yet bold baroque design of the Andrea Room. Whenever I step into this jewellike private dining room, my heart changes its tempo as I look at her portrait, done by master painter György Korga.

Unintentional humor brightened our days on occasion.

We were already halfway through the reconstruction of Gundel when I asked László Somogyi, the supervisor of our entire project and former minister of construction and urban development under the previous administration, to paint the bunker-style office building erected during the Communist era next to Gundel, which came with the property. He informed me that the building was made of stone, and that it was against the law in Hungary to paint stone.

At first I thought he was kidding me. When I found out that this law did exist, I simply told him that we were painting it, and if there was any problem, it would be mine.

He said, "Okay, we paint, but it is against the law!"

Getting madder by the minute, I asked him, "Who made this stupid law?"

"The law was made by me, when I was a minister," he replied.

The entire room burst into laughter.

I too had difficulty composing myself, but finally I said to him: "Okay, you can take a few Valiums and then paint the building."

Whether he took the Valium or not, I do not know, but the building was painted, and three days later the doors of Gundel were opened.

The original estimates from various contractors to complete the project ranged from two years to almost four, but with a military-invasion-like operation, and with double and even triple shifts, along with the gratifying enthusiasm of the workmen and our staff, we actually finished the job in six months and one day.

For a number of reasons, hiring an entirely new crew is considered one of the priceless side benefits of a takeover of an organization, but from the very beginning I felt a kind of a bond with the original Gundel staff. Tradition does not die, even if it is forced into hiding for forty-five years. So I paid full salary to all staff during the reconstruction period, using the time to teach everyone new habits and professional skills.

If you had walked in through the employees' entrance between November 1991 and June 1992, you would have seen all the space that was not torn up by the construction crew filled with small groups of eager adult students. Each instructor was teaching in front of a flip chart or projection camera facing a mixed group of butchers, headwaiters, managers, sauciers, bartenders, waiters, porters, and maintenance people. The subjects included the proper service of food and wine, the history of restaurants, and computer skills. Also, language classes were given in English, French, German, and Italian.

One of our most important tasks was to bring back a sense of urgency, pride in one's work, and a clear understanding that every deed has a consequence of some kind, and that reward is related directly to performance.

But our primary assignment was to serve great food. An opera and a restaurant have surprising similarities in that both combine the talent, skill, and craftsmanship of many professionals, each of whom is convinced

The staff of Gundel and Bagolyvár in 1993

that he or she holds the key to the ultimate success of the endeavor. The truth is that the deciding factor in opera is the singers, and in restaurants it is the cooks.

To develop the menu, we conducted dozens of exciting tasting sessions. Often we invited friends and neighbors—the museum and park directors—and everyone was asked to fill out detailed questionnaires about the dishes they sampled.

Based on the manifold guidelines I set up, our team had agreed to bring back great dishes from the past (one example: sauerkraut baked with catfish and fish sausage, an eighteenth-century recipe), and to feature as well the best of the regional dishes of Hungary; Gundel classics; signature dishes of *chef de cuisine* Kálmán Kalla and his colleagues, such as braided and grilled pork tenderloin, and carp aspic with little *fogas* dumplings; plus a few of my own ideas: rich man's purse stuffed with paprika chicken, strudel tartlet filled with strudel ice cream, espresso parfait served in demitasse with chocolate spoon, etc. I also felt that our menu would be incomplete without an entire section of goose-liver specialties, including hot-smoked to order, which for some reason had never been done before.

I was determined to introduce another first in Budapest—a section on the menu to be called "Lighter Cuisine." I explained to my puzzled team that these dishes would not be heavy-handed health-food offerings for those who get sick worrying about getting sick, but instead an alternative Hungarian cuisine for natives and visitors. On the other hand (in Hungary there is always another hand), we all agreed that we must have a dessert selection that would reduce strong men to indecisive ninnies. After all—as I noted—if God had intended for us to be thin, He would not have invented Hungarian desserts.

I made considerable efforts to bring some relief from the pressure we were all working under. One day, after we had ripped everything out of the kitchen, standing there in the huge, desolate space with the architects, the workmen, and some of the cooks, I suddenly realized it was lunchtime, so I went out to get something for the troops. Soon I was back with fifty hamburgers from McDonald's, which had just opened in Budapest. That was the first meal served in the new Gundel.

The menu that Chef Kalla and I were planning was a bit more complex than McDonald's, and we had to obtain a great number of prime ingredients that were not easily available at the time. So I suggested that we work with small private purveyors—farmers, fishermen, and such—who could produce foods to our exacting specifications with the unusual benefit of receiving payment months in advance. That way we were able to serve natural farm cheeses, unusual fruit brandies from home distilleries, real farm chickens, game birds of all sorts, wild rabbit, and also corn-fed goose and duckling from small Transdanubian farms. When I learned that Hungary supplies France with most of its snails and frogs' legs, I made sure that we would have first pick. And in order to have a constant supply of fresh herbs, our gardeners planted an extensive herb garden surrounding our outdoor seating area. We also sampled an extraordinary collection of natural Hungarian mineral waters, in order to be able to offer the best of them to our guests.

To represent a full spectrum of Hungarian wines from the seventeen wine regions of the country, during the period we were closed, I invited the most ambitious Hungarian vineyard owners to present their wines. They had lengthy discussions with our sommeliers, cellar masters, and dining-room managers, and we eagerly reserved and purchased their worthy vintages. By now the elegant yet rustic vaulted rooms of Gundel's wine cellar encompass many of the good things in life: the leisurely tasting of wines and food with good conversation, accompanied by the soft music of a gypsy *cimbalom* player.

One of the two rooms of the wine cellar is named after the wife of Prince György Rákóczi I of Transylvania—probably the first time that a wine cellar bears the name of a woman. Zsuzsanna Lorántffy was not only a gentlewoman but was responsible for the birth of Tokay Aszú. Fearful of an attack by the Turks in the autumn of 1650, she postponed the harvest of their Oremus Hill vineyard at Tokay. The intense heat of the late-fall sun shriveled up the Tokay grapes as they hung from the vines, and the fungus *Botrytis cinerea* induced the "noble rot," the key to the late-harvest *aszú* wine. The resulting wine has an exceptionally high forty-to-sixty-percent sugar content, counterbalanced by distinct and fine acids.

Paracelsus, the Swiss alchemist, visited Tokay in the sixteenth century to analyze its soil, because it was widely believed that it must contain gold to give the wine its golden color. I couldn't find any record of his findings, but to be able to serve our own vintages at Gundel, Ronald and I bought a prime vineyard together with its eighteenth-century wine cellar in the Tokay-Hegyalja region in the village of Mád, previously owned by Archduke Josef von Habsburg, and another one in the baroque city of Eger, so we could produce the great Merlot, Cabernet, and Bull's Blood of that region.

Generally speaking, I am against music in restaurants. It usually ruins two good things—the food and the music. Yet the discreet sounds of violin, the harpsichordlike *cimbalom,* or the clarinet as it is used in a gypsy band, seem to go with the Hungarian dining experience in the same way as a good Egri Merlot wine goes with cheese. So after months of deliberation, I gave in: the soothing sound of gypsy music would be heard at Gundel.

In the fall of 1992, Walburga von Habsburg, the youngest daughter of Otto von Habsburg and the granddaughter of Charles IV, the last king of Hungary, came to Budapest to discuss her wedding dinner at Gundel; by then the restaurant's transformation was being celebrated throughout the world. I suggested to Princess Walburga and to the groom, Count Archibald Douglas of Sweden, that they have a somewhat abbreviated version of the 1867 coronation dinner of Franz Josef. (The latter illustrious event was orchestrated and prepared by Joseph Marchal, who was the *chef de cuisine* of Napoleon III, and eventually took over the kitchens of the famed National Casino of Budapest.)

After the royal couple were married in King Matthias Church in the Castle district of Buda (where some of the Habsburgs had been crowned), the family and close friends took their places at the large table filling the entire Queen Elizabeth Ballroom of Gundel, named after the wife of Emperor Franz Josef. Empress and Queen Elizabeth was, of course, the bride's great-grandmother, and from her portrait on the wall watched the proceedings with a forebear's critical but loving eyes. The room looked very much like a baronial dining room where the lord of the castle celebrates with his guests.

When the time came for the wedding cake, a magnificent six-tiered tower was brought in by two pageboys in traditional Hungarian ceremonial uniform, wearing so much gold braid that the color of their mantles could barely be seen. Our pastry chef created this torte, which has since become part of our repertoire. Otto von Habsburg, the father of the bride, remarked to me that not only the flavor but also the presentation evoked the days of the imperial household.

Even such festive events can become tiresome in time, but we made certain five years later that the three wedding parties for the marriage of Georg von Habsburg to Princess Eilika von Oldenburg would be quite different from his sister's celebration. During the reception before the first dinner, which was exclusively for the family and for pretenders to the existing and vanished thrones of Europe, Gabriella, one of Georg's sisters, asked me for advice on what might turn out to be a problem.

She told me that she was a cellist and that she hoped to play, together with her three daughters, two movements of a Haydn quartet as soon as the guests were seated.

"How long will it take?" I asked her.

"Oh, about twelve or thirteen minutes."

That gave me pause. I was afraid that the guests would be too hungry to listen to music before dinner, and I suggested instead that we serve the first course and the champagne and then have the music.

She didn't answer for a few seconds and then she surprised me by saying, "But, you see, we are playing the Emperor Quartet, and in the second movement Haydn used the folk tune that later became the German national anthem, 'Deutschland, Deutschland über alles,' and at that point the German guests will probably stop eating and rise from their seats."

I tried to think quickly what would be the right protocol, and came up with this proposal: "Before you start playing, why don't you make a short announcement that the quartet will be offering *Tafelmusik,* and that the tradition is for everyone to go on eating while you are playing— just as it was done in the Emperor's dining room."

When Gabriella von Habsburg and her three lovely teenage daughters, all dressed in evening gowns, came to the familiar melody, a few members of the German contingent looked around anxiously to see if anyone was getting up. But fortunately the players completed the last movement of the quartet just as the Bouquet of "Roses" (composed of marinated salmon and home-smoked Balaton *fogas* á la Eilika) was whisked away.

On May 5, 1993, we had the great honor of arranging the state luncheon for Queen Elizabeth II and the Duke of Edinburgh, in the same ballroom where the wedding had been held. Her visit had no precedent in Hungary's eleven-century history; it was the first time a reigning English monarch had come to my native country.

As the gracious queen and her consort entered the ballroom, I felt there would always be a Gundel.

I came up with the idea of a "four-crown" state luncheon, in which each course would be served in the shape of a crown. I was particularly taken with the Queen when she dunked bits of bread into the rich sour-cream-paprika gravy on her Herend porcelain dinner plate. We served our gold-medal-winning Tokay Hárslevelű wine bearing my handwritten calligraphic labels, and I was surprised when the duke asked the waiter for a bottle of beer. But then, in 1997, Jacques Chirac, the *débonnaire* president of France, toasted the president of Hungary at a state luncheon with a specially requested glass of beer.

Even a nonstop procession of state affairs can become routine, but the luncheon we had on December 5, 1994, for the wives of forty-six heads of state certainly was anything but dull. While the husbands were making speeches littered with clichés, the organizers of this summit arranged a few divertissements for the first ladies, and the lunch at Gundel was a high point, with Zsuzsanna Göncz, the Hungarian president's wife, as the hostess.

*Queen Elizabeth II signing Gundel's guestbook before
entering the ballroom for a state luncheon, 1993*

Mrs. Boris Yeltsin's car came first. Since it is against protocol to arrive before the hostess, her driver circled around the building for a few minutes. Shortly after Mrs. Göncz arrived, Mrs. Yeltsin's car stopped in front of the restaurant, and I greeted her at the foot of the red carpet.

"Welcome to Gundel, we are honored to have you."

She had a very pleasant smile, and the Chanel suit she wore surely didn't come from a Moscow department store. I felt that a bit of levity would be in order to indicate to her that our luncheon would be anything but a typical diplomatic affair.

"Madame Yeltsin," I said, "the next time you arrive early, please don't wait, just come in and perhaps you can help us set the tables."

The young man who haltingly translated the Hungarian to her was clearly discombobulated. I suddenly realized that I was dealing with a different mindset, and that my attempt to be amusing had misfired. For a minute she, too, was taken aback, but then she must have decided that this was a joke, and she made some uneasy cackling noises approximating laughter.

*Ronald S. Lauder and his partner with the Gundel Torte at
the first anniversary of the opening of the restaurant*

Observing the high-caliber gossip among the assembled first ladies
during the reception, our managing director remarked, "Actually, the *real*
decisions are made here and not in the Congress Hall, where their husbands are meeting." At dessert time (individual miniature Christmas
cakes) I brought in the entire kitchen staff, led by Chef Kalla, and the
way the ladies looked at this handsome gentleman sporting a jaunty handlebar moustache, I wasn't so sure about his safety.

After the first dozen successful state affairs, I noticed that all of us
were beginning to feel triumphant as a matter of course, and I had to
remind myself and my staff that the importance of one's achievement is
like contact lenses—it's in the eye of the beholder.

When we bought Gundel, an adjacent 1960s-vintage modernish building had come with the deal. On the third floor we found a laboratory that
had been used to test the restaurant's food for poison, so that it could

then be sent safely to the Communist president and members of Parliament on armed trucks. Ironically, this is where our offices are located today.

I was much more concerned about a third building that was also part of the real-estate package. A few years after Károly Gundel opened his restaurant, he decided that a casual tavern should be built for visitors to the zoo next door, and the city park. The stylized Transylvanian manor house, called Bagolyvár, was opened in 1913, but during the Communist regime it became, to quote the Hungarian magazine *Képes Ujság,* "A place where one can force down monumentally dreadful frozen food in the company of Uzbek tourist groups for outrageous prices."

I closed Bagolyvár the day after we purchased Gundel, and every time I walked past it I was irked that I did not know what to do with it. I kept mulling over a concept that would be right, considering its location and remembering that it was a landmark building that could not be altered. Then one day a telephone call from the chef/owner of a noted restaurant in New York supplied the necessary inspiration. He asked me to suggest a place in Budapest where he could enjoy the home-style cooking of the local middle class. I was searching my memory and looking at a Budapest restaurant guide while we where talking, and I had to admit to him that of the scores of good restaurants that had opened since 1990, none served the kind of food I was brought up on.

The next morning I told this story at our staff meeting, unveiling my idea cautiously.

"I suggest we open up a moderately priced family restaurant where the kind of dishes that act as a bond between members of the family would be served by women. The service would also be home style; for example, the soup would come in tureens so that the guests could help themselves to seconds, and perhaps the cake should even be served in the pan it was baked in."

The world of Hungarian restaurants was, until quite recently, a stronghold of male chauvinism, and there was a shocked silence after I told my mostly male staff—as gently as I could—that I thought the entire staff of Bagolyvár, including the management and the cooks, should be women.

It took me several additional meetings to temper the shock, but as it has turned out, the restaurant's most valuable assets are surely these women, who plan, market, cook, serve the food and beverages, and provide genuine Hungarian hospitality. Crisp linen tablecloths and old-fashioned siphon-type seltzer bottles await the guests. As a starter, a specially baked salt-crusted bread ring is served with the traditional *kőrözött*, a paprika-flavored sheep cheese topped with rings of green peppers.

Arnold Schönberg, the composer, who poured the foundation of atonal music, said, "There is still a lot of good music waiting to be written in C major." Hungarian home cooking is a good example of the fact that there is still a lot of good food to be cooked in a single pot, the C major of cooking. The selection of comfort dishes may change every day, but here are some of my favorites at Bagolyvár (whose name means "Owl's Castle" in English): washday caraway soup with poached eggs and chunky croutons (my mother's easy-to-prepare dish for days when she had very little time to cook; see recipe on page 337); potted goose drumstick with barley and beans; stuffed winter squash (see recipe on page 346); *Túróscsusza* (egg noodles, cottage cheese, sour cream, and bacon cracklings baked together); rhubarb compote; golden dumpling cake (see recipe on page 364); and the popular stack of *csusztatott* ("slid" pancakes). All of these are dishes to offer solace to the weary.

We preserved the original architectural elements of the restaurant, and the interior is decorated in the spirit of the dining room of a Hungarian home circa 1920, although I have added a collection of drawings, etchings, and engravings featuring women at work and at leisure. Customers entering Bagolyvár pass by a small open pantry where jams, fruit compotes, and pickles made by the staff and/or their families are for sale, bearing their homemade labels.

Encouraging guests to express themselves is an important part of keeping any restaurant on its toes. One of our regulars,

My rendering of "Bagolyvár"

an industrialist who could easily eat in the most expensive restaurants of Budapest, said to me when I was greeting him at his usual table a couple of months after we opened Bagolyvár, "George, look at your blackboard! It features crayfish today! Your mother and mine didn't have enough money to put such a fancy dish on the table; they probably only read about it in romantic novels about aristocrats."

As a form of apology, I made sure that his favorite paprika carp with homemade mushroom noodles (see recipe on page 342) would be on the blackboard the very next day.

CHAPTER 23

Appointment in Pannonhalma

PLANNING BANQUETS for several hundred kings, queens, and celebrities, with or without crowns, has spiced the often bland party-ragoût of my life. Arranging a luncheon and dinner for Pope John Paul II served to restore my appetite for new experiences.

It took place on September 6, 1996, in the Benedictine abbey of Pannonhalma, a spiritual and academic center about seventy-five miles west of Budapest. The papal visit was in connection with the thousandth anniversary of the founding of the abbey but, as I learned later, the actual reason was the first meeting in three centuries between the pope and the patriarch of the Russian Orthodox Church. The diplomatic reason why the Russians canceled at the last minute was not disclosed, but the pope kept his promise to visit the Benedictine fathers anyway on this significant occasion.

I stood before the ancient Gothic Romanesque church (which was turned into a mosque during the Turkish occupation of Hungary), overlooking a panorama of green pastures one thousand feet below, as the papal helicopter, like a huge, solemn bird, appeared on the horizon.

The luncheon took place in the dining room of the abbey, where I arranged a U-shaped table for the hundred and forty Benedictine monks, many of whom came from various parts of the world for this event. The sight of the black-clad fathers with the pope in his pure white gown in

323

the center reminded me of a scene from a Zeffirelli production of an opera. The restoration of this Benedictine abbey had begun in the eighteenth century, and this hall, which successfully liberated itself from the purism of the traditional interiors, was converted to an ornate pink candy box, the so-called *Zopf* version of French rococo. The shocking contrast of the plush surroundings and the solemn presence of the monks was far from the monastic images I associated with the Benedictine brotherhood.

The menus were the result of months of dialogue among the fathers of the abbey, Gundel's executive chef, Kálmán Kalla, and our "scribe," the learned journalist and historian Zoltán Halász.

After many changes, the following menus were agreed upon: For the luncheon we served herb-scented wild mushrooms in brioche; filets of *fogas* of Lake Balaton with pearls of root vegetables, Gundel style, accompanied by Zempléni Chardonnay 1994; traditional Hungarian strudel with apple, sour cherry, and cottage-cheese fillings accompanied by ice cream from the abbey's kitchen, served in strudel shells and supported by a pure amber-gold Tokay Aszú wine, vintage 1991.

The dinner menu consisted of roasted trout with fresh dill dressing, accompanied by Gundel's Tokay Furmint 1993; an array of cheeses from the Dóra Farm, with a soft and fruity Egri Merlot 1993 from the Lauder/Lang Vineyards. Three-chocolate mousse with seasonal fruits, accompanied by a sweet version of a Tokay Szamorodni of 1991 vintage, concluded the repast.

Friday's dietary restriction served us well, because we were able to offer the famed *fogas* of Lake Balaton and the delicate filet of roasted trout from Szilvásvárad. Even though each menu had only three courses, we tried to represent the specialties of the different regions of Hungary as a symbolic culinary trip around the country.

The Aszú wine of Tokay carried a special message to our honored guests, since it was the favorite drink of several popes. One story concerns the queen of Hungary and empress of Austria, Maria Theresa, who sent this wine to Pope Benedict XIV, and His Holiness in turn sent the following thanks: "*Benedicta sit terra, quae te germinavit, benedicta sit mulier, quae te misit. Benedictus sum, qui te bibo.*" "Blessed be the land that has produced you, blessed be the woman who has sent you, blessed am I who drink you." A subtle papal wordplay is hidden in the double meaning of the word *benedictus,* which not only means "blessed" but was, of course, also the name of this witty pope.

*The dining room of the abbey of Pannonhalma, set for Pope
John Paul II in 1996*

At the conclusion of the luncheon I lined up the waiters, the manager, and the maîtres d'hotel as well as Chef Kalla's entire kitchen brigade, near the ceremonial entrance of the splendid hall. As the pope passed by, he gave a rosary to each person, then shook their hands and thanked them for their work. One of the waiters with a well-developed sense of humor remarked quietly, "This is the best tip I ever got."

The few of us who had received a security tag from the special security division could wait at the ornamental steps leading to the residence of the chief abbot, Astrid Várszegi, for the 4:30 p.m. arrival of the president of Hungary, who was coming for a private audience with the pope. As the president approached me, we shook hands and I whispered into his ear, "By the way, I am not the pope." President Göncz shot back, "George, there is no danger of mistaking you for the pope."

Later in the afternoon, His Holiness had a press conference in one of the rooms. At the end of the fifteen-minute session he entered the conference room of the abbey, where I was waiting for him. Cardinal Angelo Sodano, the Vatican secretary of state, introduced me, saying a few words about me and Gundel. In retrospect, the conversation was not between His Holiness Pope John Paul II and George Lang, restaurateur, but between the Polish Karol Wojtyla and the Hungarian Láng György.

I wasn't sure what language I should speak with him, so I decided to try my broken-down Italian as I presented him with a handsomely boxed bottle of our Tokay Aszú wine. After he realized that I was struggling with the language, he switched to English as he thanked me for the *fogas* we served, a fish he had heard about but never tasted.

It was one of the few occasions when I had so much to say that I had difficulty starting. I blurted out without thinking, "Meeting you has been one of the most important events of my life!"

With that characteristically gentle smile of his, he asked, "What other experiences do you consider important?"

"When I escaped from labor camp and also, sixty-six days later, when I was liberated."

"Where were you in labor camp, my son?"

"In Komarno," I answered, using the Slovak name of the city, remembering that as a Pole, he might know it that way.

"The Lord is always ready to arrange miracles, when miracles are called for, my son," he answered.

The guest book of Gundel is an enormous leather-bound volume; because it is so difficult to move around, I prepared the scene for the

*Greeting Pope John Paul II; the Gundel guestbook
is in the background*

signing ceremony with great care. I placed the twenty-four-by-twenty-inch book in its special box at the end of the long conference table. To make sure I would be able to find the first blank page for the pope's signature, I placed the silk marker at the proper page and closed the book. This was the time to offer His Holiness a handsome gold-tipped pen. I opened the box, and then the book itself with the help of the marker, without taking my eyes off the pope. But apparently someone was trying to play a practical joke on me: as I glanced at the open book, I realized to my horror that the page featured Madonna's signature; she had been to Gundel a short time before, when she was filming *Evita* in Budapest. It was a good thing that Pope John didn't have twenty-twenty vision, and I had a chance to flip the page as I kept talking to him.

Then I asked him if he was going to give a sermon in Hungarian during his stay, considering his extraordinary talent for languages. At that point, Cardinal Sodano repeated a story I had told him before. Actually, it was a line an English journalist wrote about me, indicating that I spoke five languages—but, unfortunately, simultaneously. The pope laughed heartily. I took the opportunity to show him the pictures of my children in a little silver frame I carry in my pocket. He blessed them and gave me two beautiful medallions as he entered his private residence for a much-needed rest before dinner.

That same night we served a private dinner for the pope and a very small entourage of about fifteen people. Unfortunately, they had to wait fifteen minutes for the roasted trout because the service elevator, filled with our waiters bringing the food, was stuck between floors—which somewhat damaged my belief in the pope's heavenly powers.

Returning to Gundel from the Benedictine abbey of Pannonhalma, I was dizzy with weariness in my mind and bones. After checking out the St. Orbán wine cellar, where an important wine-tasting dinner had been arranged for that night, I made a wrong turn and got completely lost in Gundel's underground labyrinth. I kept searching for the stairs that lead to the ground floor, but I found only places completely unfamiliar to me. Suddenly I felt as if I had stepped into another dimension; the wiring on the walls disappeared, the machines stopped humming, and at that point, I felt someone touch my shoulder. I turned around and an elegant gentleman in an old-fashioned cutaway greeted me. To my great shock I realized that the person standing before me was none other than Károly Gundel himself. I tried to rationalize this encounter with a good measure of Hungarian cynicism and a bit of logic, telling myself that my friends were playing an elaborate practical joke on me, or perhaps it was delirium caused by the nonstop, high pressure life I was leading.

And then Mr. Gundel, who looked very much like the pictures I had seen in books, began to speak:

"I have come back to tell you that decades ago I gave up the hope that my beloved restaurant would ever again offer good tastes and pleasure to its guests and that what I had started would continue in the same manner. But now I am beginning to hope again."

Then he vanished.

It may have been only a specter, but I have remembered every word he said. And I like to think that his hopes have been realized.

CHAPTER 24

Fifty Years and Seven Hours Later

I LIKE TO BELIEVE that everybody is entitled to one miracle in a lifetime. My allotment was the miracle of my survival between February 6, 1944, the first day of my life in the labor camp, and July 15, 1946, when I first saw Lady Liberty. It took another fifty years and seven hours to admire her from a close distance, when Jenifer decided to celebrate the fiftieth anniversary of my arrival.

Everyone who received an invitation was surprised by the location of the party—inside the statue's pedestal. This was the first time the authorities had allowed such an event. I guess it helped that in the early seventies I was engaged by the Hill family, who have been running its restaurant and gift shops for three generations, to reorganize and improve the food and beverage facilities of the Statue of Liberty.

The ferry, which accommodates thousands of people during the day, took the handful of us from Battery Park to Liberty Island, and the ocean that day tried hard to emulate the tempestuous seas we had experienced during our crossing fifty years before. (The party was held during the aftermath of a hurricane, and there were high winds and driving rain.)

I will not forget the warmth of my friends, the superb food, the fireworks, the toasts offered, and the myriad delicious details my brilliant bride arranged.

With Helene and William Safire at the celebration
of the fiftieth anniversary of my arrival
in America, July 15, 1996

Florence Fabricant wrote, in an article in the *New York Times* titled "50-Year Celebration of Seeing Liberty": "In toasting Mr. Lang, who went from being a professional violinist to a career in the food world, Mr. Elie Wiesel said, 'For who else but George could there be a party in a place that says, 'Give me your hungry'?"

Our son, Simon, and Lady Liberty

Then Jenifer read a greeting from my fellow Hungarian, George E. Pataki, the governor of New York State, who remarked, "Just what we needed—another Hungarian. . . . Perhaps someday we might collaborate to open a Gundel in New York—I am sure that Simon could run the place for us!" Mayor Giuliani declared July 15, 1996, "George Lang Day" in the City of New York, and when I received the official decree, I hoped that it would be the first day in the history of New York when only good things happened.

After the witty and heartwarming greetings from Árpád Göncz, the president of the Republic of Hungary, came Bill Clinton's letter, which clearly indicated that the president of the United States was able to keep

The Lang Family—George, Gigi, Jenifer, and Simon—
at the Café des Artistes, 1997

his sense of humor even as the re-election campaign for his second term
had already begun.

> *Dear George:*
>
> *Congratulations on the fiftieth anniversary of your arrival in*
> *America! I would have been waiting at the dock to welcome you on*
> *that historic day, but unfortunately I hadn't been born yet.*
>
> *Word of your culinary exploits did eventually reach me in*
> *Arkansas, however, and my great dream was to eat at one of your*
> *restaurants. I began to make inquiries and was told, "You have to*
> *learn to appreciate good food." And I thought, "I can do that." Then I*
> *was told, "You have to travel around the world—maybe even to New*
> *York." And I thought, "I can do that." Then I was told, "It might help*
> *if you were President of the United States," and I thought . . . well,*
> *you know what I thought.*

Two of my sweet friends, Pamela Fiori and Carina Courtwright, sang old hits with new lyrics about my life, loves, and luck (the three had sort of come together recently), and lots of friends said things I will never forget.

I tried to keep back my tears as I raised a glass filled with my favorite champagne, Billecart Salmon, to offer a toast, concluding with: "I know that my late daughter, Andrea, is watching us and making a brilliant drawing of this gathering, using the blue of the sky; and it's wonderful that Brian, my son, who gives me so much pleasure, is here with us.

"It is said that one must have the exact recipe for blessedness to get through the tollbooth of heaven. My oft-tested recipe goes like this:

'Take one part of Simon-Company and one part of Gigi-Champagne,
and mix it well with sixteen years of Jenifer's love.'

"Whoever is in charge at the entrance of heaven, reading this formula, will surely let me in.

"And now let us drink to those who couldn't make it and to those of us who did."

Having the last word is not necessarily a virtue, but under the circumstances, I guess it's my obligation to the reader.

So here goes:

I had a ball.

(. . . and the ball will continue until further notice.)

Recipes

Since I have lived with, dreamed about, invented, researched, discovered, cooked, and tasted recipes for a good part of my life, choosing only a few of my favorites is like trying to sing a few favorite phrases from all the music I have played or heard in my entire life. So instead I have jotted down recipes that represent different moments of my life. These dishes are for people whose favorite food is "seconds."

BAKED-POTATO SOUP

I do love soups, and this one is adapted from *Through the Kitchen Door* (1938), a now-forgotten American cookbook. I bought it during the 1960s, when Fourth Avenue below Union Square in New York City was still known as "Book Row."

2 pounds baking potatoes (about 5 or 6 large)	2 tablespoons minced chives
4 cups chicken broth	salt and ground white pepper
½ cup heavy cream	sweet Hungarian paprika (see Note)

1. Preheat the oven to 400°F.

2. Wash the potatoes and prick in several places with a fork. Bake for 1 hour.

3. When the potatoes are cool enough to handle, cut them in half lengthwise and scrape the flesh into the bowl of a blender or food processor; discard the skins. Add the chicken broth and process until puréed.

4. Transfer the soup to a saucepan, and stir in the cream and chives. Season with salt and pepper.

5. When ready to serve, gently reheat, stirring occasionally. Sprinkle on a little paprika and serve.

IMPORTANT NOTE ABOUT PAPRIKA: The only kind of paprika to use for any Hungarian recipe is the real thing: fresh (from this year's harvest) sweet paprika (called "Noble Rose") imported from Hungary. By now you may be able to find it in specialty food stores.

Serves 6

CARAWAY-SEED SOUP WITH POACHED EGGS

Without the egg it's called "Poor People's Soup" in Hungary and is usually served with chunks of toasted bread. My happy recollection is that my mother, knowing my father's and my predilection for marrying soup and bread, served it with her economy-sized croutons. The soup becomes a "Rich Man's Soup" when quail eggs are used instead of the regular chicken variety. In either case, you should use a strong meat broth (even though my mother was able to make a satisfying caraway soup using only water).

2 tablespoons vegetable oil	3 cups water
1 tablespoon caraway seeds	2 cups beef or chicken broth
2 tablespoons flour	Salt
½ teaspoon sweet Hungarian paprika	4 eggs

1. Heat the oil in a medium soup pot over medium heat. Sprinkle the caraway seeds into the oil, stir, and sauté until the seeds begin to jump around. Sprinkle on the flour and stir continually until it turns light golden brown. Off the heat, stir in the paprika (if you add it over the heat, you'll burn out its sugar content).

2. Add the water and broth, and season with salt to taste. Bring to a boil, then lower the heat immediately to a simmer, and cook, uncovered, 25 minutes.

4. Strain the soup through a cheesecloth (if you use a regular strainer, you will end up with caraway seeds in the soup and eventually in your teeth).

4. Just before serving, bring the soup to a simmer and very carefully break in the eggs one by one, making sure that they remain whole and separate. Simmer 2 minutes, so that the yolks remain soft.

6. To serve, carefully spoon an egg into a warm soup plate and ladle the soup around it.

Serves 4

TOMATO SOUP WITH
LITTLE STUFFED PEPPERS

Over the years I have written a number of articles about soup. This recipe, from my column "Table for One" in *Travel and Leisure,* received a lot of responses from contented readers. Use the smallest peppers you can find.

FOR THE SOUP:

2 slices bacon, chopped, or
   1 tablespoon olive oil
1 cup diced celery root
1½ cups diced celery
1 cup chopped onion
2 tablespoons flour
2 quarts water

1 pound fresh tomatoes (about
   3 medium), quartered
29-ounce can (3½ cups)
   tomato purée
¼ cup sugar
Salt and ground black pepper
   to taste

FOR THE PEPPERS:

12 small Italian green frying
   peppers
⅓ cup finely chopped onion
2 tablespoons olive oil

1 pound lean ground pork
½ cup cooked rice
1 egg
Salt and ground black pepper

1. *To make the soup:* Cook the bacon in a large, heavy pot over medium heat 5 minutes, stirring occasionally, or heat the olive oil.

2. Add the celery root, celery, and onion, and cook over medium heat, stirring frequently, until the vegetables are soft, about 20 minutes. Stir in the flour and cook 3 minutes, stirring. Pour in 2 quarts water, and stir until the ingredients are blended. Stir in the tomatoes and tomato purée. Bring to a boil, reduce the heat, and simmer, partially covered, 1 hour, stirring occasionally.

3. Add the sugar, and season with salt and pepper. Purée the soup by putting it through a vegetable mill, or use a food processor.

Taste for consistency and seasoning. If the soup seems too thick, thin it by whisking in a little water.

4. *To make the stuffed peppers:* Cut off the stem end of each pepper, and remove the seeds and the thick part of the core.

5. Sauté the onion in the olive oil until light golden brown. When cool, mix the sautéed onion with the pork, rice, and egg, and season with salt and pepper.

6. Lightly stuff the peppers and place them in a single layer in a large skillet or soup pot. Cover with the tomato soup and simmer, uncovered, 30 minutes.

7. *To serve:* Place two stuffed peppers in each of 6 soup plates and ladle the soup over them.

Serves 6

APPLE AND GOOSE-LIVER "SANDWICH"

These little "sandwiches" (which are served at Gundel) bring back memories of the Brobdingnagian goose-liver snacks of the first eighteen years of my life.

I have known all along that one day I would have to confess: I prefer a light red Bordeaux, or perhaps a cool Beaujolais, to the traditional Sauternes or Tokay Aszú as the ideal complement to foie gras.

3 medium-size firm apples (about 1⅓ pounds)
4 tablespoons unsalted butter
7 ounces fresh (raw) duck or goose liver (foie gras),* cut into thin slices

Salt and freshly ground white pepper

1. Core and peel the apples; cut each one into three horizontal slices.

2. Divide the butter between two medium frying pans (preferably nonstick) and melt it over medium heat. Sauté the apple slices until golden brown on both sides, about 4 minutes per side. Remove the apples and keep warm.

3. Season the liver slices with salt and pepper and sauté them in the butter remaining in the frying pans until light golden brown on both sides, about 3 minutes per side.

4. To assemble the dish, layer the apples and liver slices alternately, starting and finishing with apple, to make 4 three-layered foie gras "sandwiches." Serve immediately.

Serves 4 as a first course

*Note: The best American foie gras can be ordered from D'Artagnan, 399–419 St. Paul Ave., Jersey City, NJ 07306; (201) 792-0748.

BEEF MARROW ON TOAST

I have described my father's ritual of eating the Austro-Hungarian version of pot-au-feu, which always began with the marrow bone on a toasted Kaiser roll sprinkled with paprika and salt. I think he would have liked the following version as well, even though he wouldn't have been able to show off his technique of removing the marrow from the bone in one motion. This recipe is based on preparations that date from the beginning of the century, combined with a recollected version from my days in the kitchen of the Plaza Hotel.

1 good-sized piece of beef
    marrow bone, cracked,
    approximately 2½″ × 2½″
1 hard-boiled egg yolk, finely
    chopped
2 tablespoons minced chives

Pinch cayenne
2 slices rye bread
2 tablespoons fresh bread
    crumbs
Coarse salt

1. In a small pan of boiling salted water, cook the marrow bone for 1 minute. Rinse under cold water. Remove the marrow, pat dry with paper towels, and chop fine.

2. Mix the marrow with the egg yolk, chives, and cayenne.

3. Toast both sides of the rye bread, and spread one side of each piece with equal amounts of the marrow mixture. Place under a preheated broiler for about 30 seconds, sprinkle with coarse salt, and serve.

Serves 2 as an hors d'oeuvre

PAPRIKA CARP WITH MUSHROOM NOODLES DOROZSMAI-STYLE

This regional specialty is a satisfying combination of what in the Lang household are considered three of the basics of the good life: noodles, mushrooms, and paprika. It can be made with any rich fish, such as catfish. Make the Paprika-Mushroom Sauce first.

5 pieces uncooked lasagne (about 5 ounces), broken into rough pieces
Paprika-Mushroom Sauce (recipe follows)
¼ cup flour
1 teaspoon sweet Hungarian paprika

½ teaspoon salt
1½ pounds carp fillets
3 tablespoons vegetable oil
⅓ cup sour cream
2 tablespoons milk
½ cup minced yellow, orange, or red sweet peppers (or a combination)

1. Bring a large pot of salted water to a boil and drop in the broken lasagne. Cook until tender. Drain the noodles and mix them with the Paprika-Mushroom Sauce. Cover and keep warm until you are ready to assemble the dish.

2. Toss together the flour, paprika, and salt in a large plastic bag. Dredge the fish in the flour mixture by shaking them in the bag until well coated. Remove and shake to remove excess flour coating.

3. Heat the oil in a large, heavy frying pan until very hot. Sauté the fish until brown and crisp on both sides and cooked through; time will depend on the thickness of the fillets, about 5 minutes per side. You may need to do this in 2 batches.

4. Divide the sauced noodles among four plates and top with a piece of fish. Stir together the sour cream and milk, and drizzle over the fish. Garnish each plate by sprinkling the colorful minced peppers over the top. Serve immediately.

Serves 4

PAPRIKA-MUSHROOM SAUCE

This is a delicious sauce for meat, poultry, fish—even pasta (if you can get dispensation from the Italians). The savory reduction delivers the essence of fresh paprika. Use chicken, beef, or fish broth, depending on how the sauce will be used.

4 cups chicken, beef, or fish broth	3 slices bacon, finely chopped
⅓ cup chopped ripe tomato	¼ cup finely chopped onion
⅓ cup sliced onion	2 cups sliced mushrooms (about 6 ounces)
⅓ cup chopped green pepper	½ cup sour cream
1-inch piece jalapeño pepper, chopped (optional)	½ cup light cream
2 teaspoons sweet Hungarian paprika	1 teaspoon flour
	Salt and pepper to taste

1. Put the broth, tomato, sliced onion, green pepper, jalapeño pepper, and 1 teaspoon of the paprika in a medium saucepan. Bring to a boil, then simmer, stirring occasionally, until reduced to 1½ cups, about 20 minutes. Strain, discarding the vegetables and reserving the liquid.

2. Cook the bacon in a heavy medium saucepan over medium heat until it is brown and rendered, about 4 minutes. Add the chopped onion and sauté until it begins to color, about 6 minutes. Remove the pan from the heat and stir in the remaining 1 teaspoon paprika. Whisk in the reserved liquid. Add the mushrooms and cook over medium-low heat about 10 minutes, stirring occasionally.

3. Whisk together the sour cream, light cream, and flour. Stir into the sauce and cook 3 more minutes, until the flavors are blended. Taste for seasoning and add salt and pepper if needed.

Yield: 2¼ cups

WALNUT-CRUSTED SOLE

Some fish need all the help they can get, and supermarket sole belongs to this category. At the Festival Restaurant at the 1964 New York World's Fair we came to its rescue, and with the almost soufléed crust created by chef Albert Stöckli it became a seductive dish on our menu.

½ cup flour
¼ cup fine cracker crumbs
2 cups finely chopped walnuts
4 egg whites
3 tablespoons chopped parsley
¼ pound (1 stick) unsalted butter

4 fillets grey or lemon sole (about 2 pounds)
Salt and freshly ground black pepper
Lemon wedges and watercress for garnish

1. Sprinkle the flour evenly on a large sheet of wax paper.
2. Mix the cracker crumbs and chopped walnuts together and spread them on a second large sheet of wax paper.
3. Beat the egg whites in a large bowl until stiff but not dry. Gently fold in the parsley with a rubber spatula.
4. Melt the butter in 2 large skillets over medium-low heat.
5. Season the sole fillets with salt and pepper. Dredge the fish in the flour, shaking off any excess. Dip each fillet into the egg white, then into the cracker-walnut mixture, coating them heavily and patting on any extra with your hands.
6. Sauté the coated fillets in the two skillets over low heat until golden brown, 5 to 8 minutes per side, turning once. Garnish with lemon wedges and watercress, and serve.

Serves 4

POTATO DUMPLINGS IN BREAD CRUMBS

Dumplings came to Hungary at the end of the fifteenth century, courtesy of the wife of King Matthias, the Italian princess Beatrice, whose cooks brought to Hungary (among other dishes) gnocchi. While in Italy maybe half a dozen gnocchi variations exist, my mother could have prepared a different type of dumpling every day of the month without repeating herself.

4 medium potatoes (about 1½ pounds)	2 eggs, beaten
	Salt
¼ pound (1 stick) plus 2 table- spoons unsalted butter	2 cups fresh bread crumbs
	Applesauce or sour cream
2 cups flour	

1. Cook the potatoes in plenty of boiling salted water until soft, 15 to 20 minutes. Drain and peel the potatoes. While they are still warm, press them through a sieve or ricer into a large mixing bowl and stir in 2 tablespoons of the butter, the flour, and the eggs, and season with salt to taste.

3. Turn the mixture out onto a pastry board or put it in the bowl of a standing mixer with the paddle attachment. Knead the dough until it is no longer sticky.

4. Bring a large pot of salted water to a boil.

5. With floured hands, form pieces of dough the size of golf balls, then roll them on a floured surface to make 1-inch logs.

6. Drop dumplings gently into the boiling water (you do not want to crowd the pan), and cook them until they float to the surface, about 5 minutes. Remove the cooked dumplings with a slotted spoon to a large baking sheet and repeat with the remaining dumplings.

7. Melt 4 tablespoons butter in each of 2 large frying pans, add 1 cup bread crumbs to each pan and cook over low heat until lightly browned. Divide the dumplings among the 2 pans and cook until golden brown, about 10 minutes, turning once or twice.

8. Serve with homemade applesauce and/or sour cream.

Serves 6

STUFFED WINTER SQUASH

There are people, places, and dishes that become more popular than they have any right to, yet others don't achieve the acclaim they deserve. I am so fond of stuffed vegetables—which belong to the second category—that I dedicated an entire chapter to them in *The Cuisine of Hungary*. The two places where this Stuffed Winter Squash and the Stuffed Savoy Cabbage that follows can be tasted are at our Owl's Castle (Bagolyvár) restaurant in Budapest and at our own family table (my wife, Jenifer, prepares them frequently).

2 acorn squash, about
   1 pound each
1 roll or 1 piece of white
   bread, soaked in cold
   water (about 1 cup loosely
   packed)
1 pound ground pork
1 egg, beaten
3 tablespoons finely chopped
   fresh dill

2 tablespoons finely chopped
   fresh Italian parsley
salt and freshly ground black
   pepper
6 tablespoons unsalted butter
¼ cup flour
1 cup milk
2 teaspoons freshly squeezed
   lemon juice

1. Preheat the oven to 350°F. Grease a large roasting pan.

2. Cut a 1-inch piece from the top of each squash and discard. With a spoon, scoop out and discard the seeds. Cut the squash into 1-inch-thick rings and place them side by side in the roasting pan.

3. Squeeze the water out of the roll or bread and break it into small pieces. Put the bread, pork, egg, half the dill, and half the parsley in a mixing bowl, season with salt and pepper, and mix well.

4. Melt 2 tablespoons of the butter. Fill the centers of the squash rings with the pork mixture and brush with melted butter. Pour 1½ cups hot water into the pan, cover with foil, and bake 45 to 50 minutes, removing the foil for the last 10 minutes.

5. To make the sauce, melt the remaining 4 tablespoons butter in a medium saucepan over moderate heat. Whisk in the flour and

cook 1 minute. Add the milk, whisking constantly, bring to a boil, and cook, stirring, until thickened, 3 to 4 minutes. Stir in the remaining dill and parsley and the lemon juice, and season with salt and pepper to taste.

  6. Serve the stuffed squash with the sauce.

Serves 4

STUFFED SAVOY CABBAGE

2 savoy cabbages
  (about 4 pounds)
3 slices white bread, crusts
  removed
1 cup milk
½ pound bacon, diced
2 medium onions, finely
  chopped
½ pound baked ham, diced
1¼ pounds ground pork
3 eggs, beaten
3½ tablespoons sweet
  Hungarian paprika

1¼ teaspoons dried
  marjoram
1½ teaspoons chopped garlic
2 teaspoons salt
1 teaspoon freshly ground
  black pepper
1 egg yolk
4 cups sour cream
2 cups tomato juice
2 tablespoons lemon juice

1. Bring a large pot of salted water to a boil. Remove the core and any tough outer leaves from the cabbages. Simmer the whole cabbages, covered, 10 minutes. Drain.

2. In the meantime, soak the white bread in a small bowl with the milk.

3. Cook the bacon in a frying pan over medium heat for about 5 minutes, or until it begins to render some of its fat. Add the onion and cook 2 minutes. Add the ham and cook 2 minutes, stirring occasionally. Pour off and discard the fat, and allow the mixture to cool.

4. Squeeze the bread dry and tear it into small pieces. Put the bread, pork, egg, paprika, marjoram, garlic, salt, and pepper and mix well. Stir the cooled bacon mixture into the pork.

5. Beat the egg yolk into 3 cups of the sour cream.

6. Preheat the oven to 400°F. To form the cabbage parcels, gently tear off 4 cabbage leaves and place 2 of them, one on top of the other, on your work surface. Spoon 2 tablespoons of the sour-cream mixture into the middle of the leaves and top with ½ cup of the stuffing. Spoon 2 more tablespoons of the sour-cream mixture over the stuffing and top with the remaining 2 cabbage leaves. Fold

the leaves firmly around the filling on all sides to make a small par‐
cel, and place it, seam side down, in a 9 × 12-inch baking dish.
Repeat with the remaining filling and cabbage leaves.

7. Mix together the tomato juice and lemon juice, and pour
into the baking dish. Bake 1 hour, or until the cabbage parcels are
golden brown.

8. Serve the stuffed cabbage with the remaining 1 cup sour
cream.

Serves 10

LANG'S CHOCOLATE CHILI

To make the best of all possible chilis can become an obsession. I've tasted a chili with oysters (horrifying) and another made with alligator meat and finished with crème fraiche. As for the most potent chili, Irish chili wins the prize (naturally Irish whiskey replaces all the liquids in this version).

For the "Great Chili Confrontation" (see page 282) I got my inspiration from the Mexican mole sauce, which contains both chilis and unsweetened chocolate. While the origin of mole is disputed by food historians with too much time on their hands, I am glad I was able to supply a footnote to the birth of chocolate chili.

3 red bell peppers
2 tablespoons bacon drippings
1 pound lean pork, cut into ½-inch cubes
5 pounds lean beef brisket, cut into ½-inch cubes
1½ tablespoons salt
½ cup beer
½ cup water
½ teaspoon hot pepper flakes (or more if you can take the heat)
4½ teaspoons crushed cumin seed
1 tablespoon tomato paste

4½ teaspoons paprika
1 cup chopped onion
1 tablespoon freshly squeezed lime juice
½ teaspoon grated lemon zest
1 clove garlic, peeled and crushed
½ teaspoon sugar
1 small bay leaf
2 ounces unsweetened chocolate, chopped into large pieces
¼ cup masa harina (Mexican corn flour)

1. Preheat the oven to 400°F.
2. Cut the peppers into quarters, and discard the seeds and membranes. Grill or broil the peppers until charred on all sides. Put the peppers in a bowl and cover tightly with plastic wrap. When cool, remove the skin and chop the peppers coarsely.

3. Heat the bacon drippings in a Dutch oven over high heat. Add the pork and brown, stirring occasionally, 5 minutes. Add the beef a little at a time, cooking until browned on all sides. Add the salt, beer, and water, cover, reduce the heat, and simmer 30 minutes.

4. Put the pepper flakes and cumin in a frying pan over moderate heat for about 1 minute, shaking the pan constantly. Stir the spices into the meat mixture, along with the chopped peppers, tomato paste, paprika, chopped onion, lime juice, lemon zest, garlic, sugar, and bay leaf. Simmer, uncovered, 1 hour, stirring occasionally. If the meat seems dry, add more water and beer.

5. Add the chocolate and stir until melted.

6. Mix the masa harina with ½ cup warm water and some liquid from the chili. Stir this slurry into the chili and simmer 10 minutes. Adjust the seasonings and serve.

Serves 8 to 10

TRIPE AUX PRUNEAUX

There is a secret brotherhood of tripe lovers, and they are just as misunderstood as the Rosicrucians were in the seventeenth century. The surprising combination of ingredients in this recipe yields a silky fusion of flavors and lip-smacking texture. If you leave leftovers in the refrigerator overnight, a pleasant surprise awaits you: a firm, easily sliced headcheese-like delicacy, which can be a great first course for dinner, with or without a traditional vinaigrette.

I learned this recipe from André Guillou, who was the chef of the Café des Artistes for three decades, and it has often been on our menu over the last twenty years. This dish gets better each time you reheat it; we always cook twice as much at home as we serve for our family dinner.

A rather large quantity is suggested because this recipe takes a long time to prepare and it is nice to have those leftovers; it also freezes very well.

5 pounds calf's feet	dried thyme, wrapped in
3 pounds honeycomb tripe	a double thickness of
4½ quarts unsalted beef	cheesecloth and tied
stock	with butcher's twine
2 cups dry white wine	½ cup chopped carrots
3 large carrots, peeled	½ pound pitted prunes
1 large onion, peeled	2 tablespoons Calvados or
2 tablespoons tomato puree	applejack
1 spice bag: 5 bay leaves,	Salt and freshly ground black
4 black peppercorns,	pepper to taste
3 parsley sprigs, 3 whole	12 medium potatoes, boiled
cloves, 1 clove garlic, quar-	and peeled
tered, and 1 teaspoon	

1. Soak the calf's feet and tripe separately in water to cover overnight in the refrigerator. Drain.

2. In two separate large saucepans, blanch the calf's feet and tripe separately in boiling salted water 15 minutes. Drain.

3. Put the calf's feet, stock, wine, whole carrots, onion, tomato puree, and spice bag in a stockpot and bring to a rolling boil. Reduce the heat and simmer, covered, 2 hours, stirring occasionally.

4. Add the tripe to the stockpot and simmer 2 more hours.

5. Remove the calf's feet from the stockpot and let cool. Remove and discard the carrots, onion, and spice bag. Add the chopped carrots to the pot and cook 30 minutes.

6. When the calf's feet are cool enough to handle, remove and discard the bones. Cut the tender skin and usable meat into ½-inch chunks.

7. Using a slotted spoon, remove the chopped carrots and reserve. Remove the tripe and when cool enough to handle, cut it into 1½-inch triangles.

8. Divide the stock between two shallow pans and cook over high heat until reduced to a total of 4 cups, about 30 minutes. Return the reduced stock to the stockpot and add the calf's feet, tripe, chopped carrots, prunes, and Calvados, and cook 10 minutes. Taste, and season with salt and pepper.

9. Serve in shallow soup bowls with a boiled potato.

Serves 12

CHIU CHOW BRAISED DUCK

The cunningly sophisticated cooking of the Chiu Chow people—from an area some 200 miles east of Canton—is virtually unknown in the U.S. We discovered this zesty dish on a trip to Hong Kong in search of Chiu Chow food. Traditionally the recipe is prepared with goose, but I have substituted duck, since goose is difficult to get in the U.S. Fortunately, the recipe works just as splendidly with duck.

P.S. You'll probably need to make a trip to a Chinese grocery store before you start cooking.

1 fresh duck, about 4–5 pounds, excess fat removed

8 cups chicken or beef broth

2 cups Chinese dark soy sauce

1 cup shaoxing wine (Chinese rice wine) or dry Fino sherry

¼ cup Chinese dried orange peel

2 pieces Chinese cinnamon bark, each approximately 4 inches long

2-inch piece fresh ginger, peeled and cut into ¼-inch-thick slices

7 star anise

1 tablespoon whole cloves

1 tablespoon salt

1 teaspoon Szechwan peppercorns

1 small dried hot pepper or 1 teaspoon hot pepper flakes

5 medium cloves garlic, peeled and crushed

1 teaspoon black peppercorns

¾ cup Chinese black vinegar

4 medium cloves garlic, minced

1. The day before you plan to serve the duck, put it in a large pot with the broth, soy sauce, and wine. Make a bouquet garni of the orange peel, cinnamon, ginger, star anise, cloves, salt, Szechwan pepper, hot pepper, garlic cloves, and black pepper, and add it to the pot. Bring to a boil, reduce the heat, and simmer, uncovered, 15 minutes.

2. Remove and discard the bouquet garni. Refrigerate the duck in the braising liquid at least 10 hours but not more than 24 hours. Remove and discard any visible fat from the duck and the braising liquid. Let the duck sit at room temperature in the braising liquid 4 to 5 hours.

3. A few hours before you plan to serve the duck, remove it from the braising liquid. With a sharp knife cut away the excess fat from the neck.

4. Bring the braising liquid to a boil in a roasting pan and lower the duck into it. Add water to bring the level of the liquid to within one inch of the top of the pan. Cover the exposed portion of the duck with a piece of cheesecloth. Adjust the heat so that the liquid simmers, cover the pan with foil, and simmer 30 minutes, basting two or three times. Turn the duck and cover the exposed portion with cheesecloth. Cover the pan and simmer 30 minutes more, basting two or three times. Remove the duck from the braising liquid and let stand 15 minutes.

5. Meanwhile, mix together the minced garlic and the vinegar, and divide this sauce among 4 small dishes, one for each diner.

6. Carve the duck. Remove the legs and wings and arrange them on a serving platter. Remove the breasts and thighs and cut them into small horizontal slices about the size of a quarter; each slice should contain a piece of skin and a thin layer of the fat underneath the skin, as well as some of the meat. Arrange the pieces on the serving platter and ladle ½ cup of the warm braising liquid over the duck.

7. To serve, place the platter in the center of the table. Each diner takes a portion from the communal platter and dips each bite-size piece, skin-side down, into the vinegar-garlic dip.

Serves 4 as a main course, 6 as part of a Chinese banquet

CHICKEN AND KOHLRABI FRICASSEE
WITH DUMPLINGS

Alice B. Toklas described kohlrabi as having "the pungency of a high-born radish bred with a low-born cucumber." Maybe it is so popular in Hungary because it is rumored that it came to Europe courtesy of Attila the Hun. Heaven knows, it is not because the natives would care about its supposedly therapeutic properties.

My cousin Évi simply hated cooked kohlrabi. Once when she was asked to go to the kitchen and bring the prepared dish to the dinner table, little Évi, probably then about twelve years old, "accidentally" slipped, and the tureen filled with Kohlrabi Fricassee smashed to the floor. She didn't have to eat it, but was in the doghouse the rest of the week.

FOR THE DUMPLINGS:

½ pound skinless, boneless chicken breasts
1 tablespoon minced dill
½ teaspoon salt

Freshly ground black pepper, to taste
1 egg white
1 cup heavy cream
1½ quarts chicken broth

FOR THE CHICKEN FRICASSEE:

4 tablespoons (½ stick) unsalted butter
⅓ cup flour
2 cups chicken broth
1 cup dry white wine
Salt and freshly ground black pepper, to taste
2 young kohlrabi (about ½ pound), peeled and sliced ½-inch thick*

½ pound baby carrots or large carrots, peeled and cut into ½-inch diagonal slices
1 chicken (about 3 pounds), well rinsed, patted dry, and cut into 8 pieces

*If young and freshly picked, kohlrabi leaves can be cooked just like spinach.

TO FINISH:

3 tablespoons sugar   Freshly squeezed juice of
                                                1 lemon

1. *To make the dumplings:* Cut up the chicken breasts and put them along with the dill, salt, and pepper in the bowl of a food processor. Process until finely minced, about 30 seconds. Add the egg white and process again. With the motor running, slowly pour the cream through the feed tube. As soon as the cream is incorporated, turn off the machine. Transfer the mixture to a bowl, cover, and refrigerate at least 4 hours, preferably overnight.

2. *To make the fricassee:* Melt the butter in a large, heavy, non-reactive pot over medium heat. Stir in the flour and cook, stirring constantly with a wooden spoon, until pale golden, about 5 minutes.

3. Pour in the 1½ cups chicken broth and the wine, and bring to a boil, whisking constantly. Season generously with salt and pepper. Reduce the heat and simmer, stirring occasionally, 10 minutes.

4. Meanwhile, parboil the kohlrabi and carrots together in a large pot of boiling salted water 6 minutes. Drain, then rinse under cold water to stop the cooking.

5. Add the vegetables and chicken pieces to the sauce, cover with a tight-fitting lid, and simmer 45 minutes.

6. Meanwhile, remove the dumpling mixture from the refrigerator. Bring the 1½ quarts chicken broth to a boil, then reduce the heat to a simmer.

7. Using two large soup spoons, make egg-shaped dumplings and drop them into the simmering broth, lowering the heat if necessary to prevent the broth from boiling. Cook the dumplings 8 to 10 minutes, or until cooked through. Remove the dumplings with a slotted spoon and drain them for a few seconds on a clean cloth towel or napkin. Reserve the broth for another use.

8. Remove the fricassee from the heat. Add the dumplings and replace the cover.

9. *To finish the dish:* In a heavy skillet, heat the sugar until it melts and then caramelizes. As soon as it turns a golden brown, remove the pan from the heat and stir in the lemon juice. Remove about 1 cup of

sauce from the stew and add it to the skillet. Stir over medium heat until well blended, about 30 seconds.

10. Skim off any excess fat from the stew. Drizzle the caramel sauce over the fricassee, stir, reheat just to a simmer, and serve.

Serves 5 to 6

DOCE DE LEITE

There are foods I tolerate, others I like, and a few I love. Beyond these categories, there are a small number of dishes to which I am addicted, and one of them is the creamy, caramel-sweet doce de leite. It is popular in most countries in Central and South America, with slight differences in name and taste. It can be eaten as a dip with salty pretzels as a foil, or perhaps spread on a slice of fresh pineapple, or accompanied by a bland cheese, or used as a layer in cakes, or even as a filler in sandwich cookies. Usually it takes a great deal of time and care to prepare, but this version is so simple that you are likely to feel guilty for getting so much reward for so little work.

**14-ounce can sweetened
condensed milk**

Remove the label from the can and immerse it, unopened, in boiling water. Boil 2½ hours, replacing the water as it evaporates. When cool, open the can. Serve cold or at room temperature.

ILONA TORTE

I tried to re-create my mother's flourless chocolate torte during the late sixties for my *Cuisine of Hungary,* and I have to thank a number of friends who helped me recapture the flavor of my childhood birthdays. I named this richest of all chocolate tortes after my mother and my late daughter, Andrea Ilona. A few years ago, my wife and I discovered this same torte, with the same name, on the menu of a popular Seattle restaurant, and we asked the chef-proprietor about its provenance. He told us proudly how his grand-mother used to bake this chocolate cake, and that he named it after her. Funny to have a Neapolitan grandmother with the name Ilona. . . . This is one of the two dishes that appear on the menus of both Gundel in Budapest and the Café des Artistes in New York. Use a high-quality imported chocolate, such as Lindt, Valrhôna, or Callebaut.

FOR THE TORTE:

5 ounces semisweet choco-late, chopped

1 cup sugar

¼ teaspoon salt

¼ cup water

6 tablespoons unsalted but-ter, softened

8 eggs, separated

½ teaspoon cream of tartar

2 cups plus 1 heaping table-spoon coarsely ground walnuts (make sure the walnuts are not stale)

2 tablespoons fresh white bread crumbs

10 walnut halves for decora-tion

FOR THE BUTTERCREAM:

8 ounces semisweet choco-late, cut into small pieces

2½ teaspoons instant espresso powder

⅓ cup water

½ pound plus 6 tablespoons unsalted butter, softened

4 egg yolks (see Step 7)

1 cup confectioners' sugar

1. Preheat the oven to 375°F.

2. Grease a 9-inch springform pan. Sprinkle flour into the pan, then knock out any excess. Line the bottom of the pan with parchment paper and grease the paper.

3. Put the chocolate, sugar, salt, and water in the top of a double boiler over low heat. Stir occasionally until the mixture is smooth. Let cool 15 minutes.

4. Beat the butter in a medium mixing bowl until light and fluffy. Add the 8 egg yolks one at a time, beating well after each addition. Slowly add the melted chocolate and beat until well blended.

5. Whip the 8 egg whites with the cream of tartar in a large mixing bowl until peaks form. Beat ⅓ of the whites into the chocolate mixture. Gently fold in the remaining egg whites, along with the ground walnuts and bread crumbs. Pour the batter into the prepared pan and bake 35 to 40 minutes, or until the center springs back when lightly pressed. Let the cake cool on a rack 15 minutes. Run a knife around the edge of the cake and let sit 10 more minutes. Invert the torte onto the rack and let cool completely.

6. Meanwhile, make the buttercream. Put the chocolate, espresso powder, and water in a double boiler or small, heavy saucepan over low heat and stir occasionally until the mixture is smooth. Transfer to a bowl and let cool.

7. Beat the butter in an electric mixer until light and fluffy. Add the egg yolks, one at a time (if you are concerned about eating raw eggs, leave them out). Beat well after each addition. Gradually beat in the confectioners' sugar. Stir in the chocolate mixture and blend thoroughly. Set aside ½ cup of the buttercream for decoration.

8. To assemble, cut the cooled torte into two layers using a serrated knife. Remove the top layer. Frost the bottom layer with about 1 cup of the buttercream. Place the second layer on top, cut side up. Cover the top and sides of the cake with the remaining buttercream. Put the reserved buttercream into a pastry bag fitted with a small star tip and decorate the top edges and base of the cake with little rosettes. Garnish the top of the cake with the walnut halves.

APPLE CLOUDS

The Sheraton Carlton Hotel in Washington, D.C., two blocks from the White House, has served presidents, public figures, and Washington society since its opening in 1926. When the owners asked me in 1977 if I would be interested in creating a new restaurant there, I enthusiastically accepted the assignment. The opening menu featured Apple Clouds for dessert; it's difficult to believe that a few basic ingredients could produce such a luscious complexity of taste.

FOR THE PASTRY:

2 cups flour	½ teaspoon vanilla extract
⅓ cup confectioners' sugar	3 egg yolks, lightly beaten
¾ teaspoon salt	3–4 tablespoons ice water
¼ pound (1 stick) plus 4 tablespoons cold unsalted butter, cut into bits	

FOR THE FILLING:

1½ pounds (3 to 4) apples, preferably Granny Smith	¼ cup sugar
½ teaspoon grated lemon rind	¼ cup water

FOR THE MERINGUE:

3 egg whites	½ teaspoon vanilla extract
¼ teaspoon cream of tartar	3 tablespoons sugar

1. *To make the crust:* Put the flour, confectioners' sugar, salt, and butter in the bowl of a food processor and pulse until the mixture resembles bread crumbs. Add the vanilla and egg yolks and process briefly. With the motor running, add the ice water, 1 tablespoon at a time, through the feed tube, and process just until the dough holds together (do not process more than 30 seconds). After adding the

third tablespoon of water, test the dough by squeezing a small amount between your fingers; if it does not hold together, add another tablespoon of ice water and process briefly.

2. Form the dough into a ball, press into a disc, and wrap in plastic wrap. Refrigerate at least 30 minutes.

3. Meanwhile, peel, core, and chop the apples. Put them in a frying pan over low heat with the lemon rind, sugar, and water, and cook, stirring occasionally, until the apples are soft, about 15 minutes, adding more water if needed. Raise the heat to high and boil hard until all of the water evaporates, being careful not to allow the mixture to burn. Remove the pan from the heat and mash or purée the apples until smooth. Set aside.

4. Preheat the oven to 375°F. Roll out the dough on a lightly floured surface to ⅛-inch thickness and line a tart pan or individual tartlet molds with it. Prick the base of the tart or tartlets with a fork and line with aluminum foil filled with beans, rice, or ceramic weights. Partially bake, 12 minutes, and place on a rack to cool, leaving the oven on.

5. *To make the meringue:* Beat the egg whites, cream of tartar, and vanilla with an electric mixer until soft peaks form. Add the sugar, a tablespoon at a time, beating well after each addition. Continue beating until stiff, glossy peaks form.

6. Fill the cooled tart or tartlet crusts with the applesauce. Spoon meringue on top and spread it evenly so that it touches the edges of the crust. Bake just until the meringue turns golden brown (10 to 15 minutes for the tart; 5 minutes for tartlets).

Makes one 9-inch tart or 12 3-inch tartlets

GOLDEN DUMPLING CAKE

My mother limited tortes and other fancy desserts to birthdays, name days, and other vitally important events. Lunch often consisted of yeast-dough-based sweet dumplings, usually preceded by a bowl of soup, but here we serve the dumplings as a cake for dessert.

1 envelope active dry yeast (not "rapid rise")	2 tablespoons fresh cake or bread crumbs
1 cup lukewarm milk	1 cup ground walnuts
2 tablespoons sugar	1 tablespoon grated lemon zest
3 ½ cups flour	
6 egg yolks	½ cup apricot jam
Pinch salt	½ lemon
¼ pound (1 stick) plus 2 tablespoons unsalted butter, melted	¼ cup vanilla sugar (see Note)

Note: Vanilla sugar is simply sugar in which a vanilla bean has been buried for at least a week to impart a vanilla flavor. Plan ahead so you will have it on hand. It keeps indefinitely.

1. Put the yeast, ¼ cup of the milk, 1½ teaspoons of the sugar, and 3 tablespoons of the flour in the bowl of an electric mixer fitted with the paddle attachment, and stir to mix. Let stand 10 minutes.

2. Mix into the dissolved yeast the egg yolks and salt, and the remaining milk, sugar, and flour. Slowly add 4 tablespoons of the melted butter, mixing well to incorporate it, until the dough becomes blistered and separates easily from the paddle. Brush the dough with a little of the melted butter, cover the bowl with plastic wrap, and let rise in a warm place 1 hour.

3. Preheat the oven to 375°F. Butter a 7 × 3-inch springform pan, line the base with a piece of parchment paper, butter the paper, and sprinkle it with the cake or bread crumbs.

4. Put the dough on a floured pastry board and stretch it with your hands until it is ½-inch thick. The dough will shrink back, but just keep stretching it again and again. Using a 1-inch round cookie cutter, cut little rounds of dough.

5. Mix together the walnuts and lemon zest. Dip some dough rounds in the remaining melted butter and fit a layer of them tightly into the bottom of the pan. Sprinkle with half the walnut mixture. Make a second layer of buttered dough rounds, melting additional butter if necessary.

6. Warm the jam in a microwave and purée it in a blender, squeezing in a couple drops of fresh juice from the cut lemon. Spread some of the jam over the second cookie layer. Repeat the layers, alternating the walnut mixture with the jam, until the pan is filled. Pour any remaining melted butter over the surface. Bake 50 to 55 minutes, covering the top with foil if it is browning too much.

6. Remove pan from the oven and let cool on a rack 10 minutes. Run a thin knife around the edge and remove the cake from the pan.

7. Sprinkle with the vanilla sugar and serve with fresh whipped cream, if you like.

Yield: 7-inch cake

JENNY'S WALNUT COOKIES

This is not an easy dough to handle, but it is worth the effort, because these are the best cookies in the presently known universe. I named them after the late Jenny Szemere, from whom I learned a lot about the unbendable rules of baking.

FOR THE COOKIES:

1½ cups flour, plus more as
     necessary
½ pound (2 sticks) cold
     unsalted butter, cut into
     bits

½ cup confectioners' sugar
½ cup ground walnuts
¼ teaspoon salt

FOR THE FILLING:

¼ cup milk
¼ cup sugar
1-inch piece vanilla bean
¾ cup ground walnuts

2 tablespoons lemon juice
5 tablespoons plus 1 teaspoon
     unsalted butter, softened

1. *To prepare the cookies:* Put the flour and butter in the bowl of a food processor and pulse until the mixture resembles bread crumbs. Add the confectioners' sugar, walnuts, and salt, and process to mix. If the dough feels too sticky, add more flour, a tablespoon at a time.

2. Flatten the dough into a disk, wrap in plastic wrap, and refrigerate at least 30 minutes, or overnight.

3. Preheat the oven to 375°F. Roll out half the dough between two sheets of waxed paper to ¼-inch thick. With a 1½-inch round cookie cutter, cut out rounds of dough. If the dough becomes too soft to remove the rounds, refrigerate it until it is firmer. Transfer the rounds to an ungreased baking sheet and bake 8 to 12 minutes, or until lightly browned around the edges.

4. Cool the cookies on a rack, preferably overnight, so that they will harden slightly.

5. *To make the filling:* Put the milk, sugar, and vanilla bean in a small saucepan and bring to a boil (do not let the mixture boil over). Reduce the heat, stir in the walnuts and lemon juice, and simmer until thickened. Allow to cool completely. Discard the vanilla bean.

7. When the filling is completely cooled, beat the butter until softened, then stir in the cooled walnut mixture.

8. *To assemble:* Spread about 2 teaspoons of the filling on one cookie and top with another. Repeat with the remaining cookies and filling.

Yield: 2 dozen cookies

PEAR CHAMPAGNE

During one of our luncheons in the Waldorf's Men's Bar in the late 1950s, Lucius Beebe, the late, great journalist, recalled the glamour of drinking champagne concoctions in the twenties, when the smart set first discovered them. The following champagne cocktail made its debut at the Café des Artistes in the fall of 1977, when I served it to a pear-loving friend.

1 Bartlett, Anjou, or Comice pear, peeled and cored
½ cup water
¼ cup sugar
1 slice fresh ginger, about the size of a quarter

2 tablespoons Williams pear brandy
1 bottle dry Champagne, chilled

1. Place the pear upright in a saucepan and add the water, sugar, and ginger. Bring to a boil, then reduce the heat, cover, and simmer until the pear is almost cooked but still slightly crunchy. Quarter the pear and refrigerate until you are ready to serve the pear champagne.

2. To serve, place a pear segment in each of 4 champagne glasses, add ½ tablespoon of the pear brandy, and fill with champagne. Serve immediately.

Yield: 4 cocktails

RECEIPT FOR ORDERLY
DOMESTIC MANAGEMENT

Let the mistress of the house take 2 lbs. of the very best self-control, 1½ lbs. of justice, 1 lb. of consideration, 5 lbs. of patience, and 1 lb. of discipline. Let this be sweetened with charity; let it simmer well, and let it be taken daily—in extreme cases in hourly doses—and be kept always on hand; then the domestic wheels will run quite smoothly.

Rare Old Receipts
Philadelphia, 1906

[Sorry, no matter how hard I tried, I couldn't find a "receipt" concerning the master of the house.]

Page references to illustrations are in *italics*.

Jennersdorf (Austria), 100
Jenny's Walnut Cookies, recipe for, 366–7
Jewish underground in Hungary, 53, 66–7
John Paul II, Pope, luncheon and dinner
　for, 323–8, *325, 327*
Johnson, Lyndon, 186
Johnson, Philip, 211
Johnson, Samuel, 21, 228, 229
Jolson, Al, 263
Jones, Evan, 157
Josef, Archduke, 315
Justin, Brother, 212

kakavia, 238
Kális, Jenö, 53–4
Kalla, Kálmán, 313, 314, 319, 324, 326
Kallir, Lilian, 120
Kapell, William, 120
Kaunitzer, Vera, 61–4, 88, *95*
Keilt, Bob, 180–1
Keller, Dale, 233–4
Keller, Pat, 233–4
Kellner, Annuska (aunt), 10
Kellner, Évi (cousin), 9–10, 19, 95, 97, 102,
　350
　in concentration camp, 46
　trip to U.S. by, 103–5
Kellner, Györgyi (Georgina; cousin), 95
Kelly, Grace, 153, 163–5, *164*
Kennedy Airport, *see* Idlewild Airport
Kent State University, 1970 killings at, 250
Kentucky Derby, 246
Kentucky Fried Chicken, 174
Kenyon & Eckhart advertising agency, 180
kepiting isi, 197
Khalkidhiki peninsula (Greece), 234, 235
Khrushchev, Nikita, 204
Kilgallen, Dorothy, 162
King, Alexander, 160
Kiss sisters, 87
Kistarcsa internment camp, 46
kohlrabi, 350
Komárom (Komarno, Hungary)
　Ágnes's letter from, 96
　labor camp at, 37, 41–9, 181, 326, 329
Korga, György, 311
Körösi, Imre, 88–9
kőrözött, 321
Koussevitzky, Serge, 120
Kovács (violin-maker), 28
Kovi, Paul, 181, 203
Krisher, Bonnie, 194
Krishna Menon, V. K., 155
Kumaraswami (driver), 193
Kumin, Albert, 209
Kún, Béla, 32
Kuwait, 251–2

labor camps, in Hungary, 37, 41–9, 181, 326,
　329
La Dorada (Seville restaurant), 272
La Folie (New York City restaurant),
　245–9, 260
La Guardia, Fiorello, 263
Lajosmizse (Hungary), 308
Lakatos, George, 259
Lake Iskembeci Salonu (Istanbul restau-
　rant), 273
Lakewood (N.J.), 229
Lalla Amina (princess), 156
lambanog, 254
lambic (beer), 275
lamb's head, split, 273
Lang, Andrea Ilona (daughter), 156, 218,
　257, *280*, 311, 333
Lang, Brian (son), 5, 218, 333
Lang, Dorothy Caplow (wife), 122–3, 124,
　149, 218
　in Italy, 125–30
Lang, Eugene (Jenő; uncle), 106–8, 110
Lang, George
　and Arrowcross Militia, *see* the subentry
　　in World War II and aftermath
　asparagus and, 223, *224*
　Austrian escape of, 98–101
　on Bicentennial Commission, 250, 260,
　　265
　birth of, 5, 80
　books by, 298, 302, 346
　boyhood of, 5–16, *7*, 23–7, *24*, 277; athlet-
　　ics, 21, 22; bar mitzvah, 26, 85; early
　　cooking, 26; high school, *29*, 64
　CARE packages sent from America by,
　　95
　on Carnegie Hall Board of Directors,
　　113
　cat of, *224*
　change of name by, 95
　as consultant: Citicorp project, 256–8;
　　company sold to staff, 298; disaster
　　encountered, 232; Essex House office,
　　225; for Greek resort and cruise line,
　　233–45; on Hilton hotel in Budapest,
　　299; King Cole Room, 250; La Folie
　　restaurant, 245–9; Loews Hotels, 219,
　　221, 222, 230–2; Manila Hotel renova-
　　tion, 252–6; Marriott Corporation,
　　219–22, 225, 227–9; name and logo of
　　company, 222–3; Saudi Arabian–
　　Kuwaiti projects, 251–2; Statue of Lib-
　　erty facilities, 329; working principles,
　　225–7
　culinary career: banquet management
　　course, 162; at Brass Rail, 168–75, 214;
　　Café des Artistes, 264–71, 274;

Index

The photographs and illustrations reproduced in this book were provided with the permission and courtesy of the following:

American Way magazine: 305
David Gamble/*Travel & Leisure* magazine: 290
Al Hirschfeld: 167
Tim Kantor: 205
L'Osservatore Romano: 325, 327
George Lange: 285, 313
LIFE magazine: 154
Rhoda Nathans: 124
Marvin E. Newman: 332
Joseph Standart: 259
United States Holocaust Memorial Museum: 104
Dann Wynn: 280, 282

All other photographs and illustrations are from the author's personal collection.

A NOTE ON THE TYPE

This book was set in a modern adaptation of a type designed by the first William Caslon (1692–1766). The Caslon face, an artistic, easily read type, has enjoyed over two centuries of popularity in our own country. It is of interest to note that the first copies of the Declaration of Independence and the first paper currency distributed to the citizens of the new-born nation were printed in this typeface.

Composed by North Market Street Graphics,
Lancaster, Pennsylvania
Designed by Barbara Balch
Calligraphy by George Lang